After Physicalism

After Physicalism

edited by

BENEDIKT PAUL GÖCKE

University of Notre Dame Press

Notre Dame, Indiana

Manufactured in the United States of America

Chapter 4 by Alvin Plantinga, "Against Materialism," is reproduced by permission of its author and the editor of *Faith and Philosophy* and originally appeared in *Faith and Philosophy* 23, no. 1 (2006): 3–32.

Chapter 5 by Richard Swinburne, "From Mental/Physical Identity to Substance Dualism," is reproduced by permission of Oxford University Press and originally appeared in *Persons: Human and Divine*, edited by Peter van Inwagen and Dean Zimmerman (Oxford: Oxford University Press, 2007), 142–65.

Library of Congress Cataloging-in-Publication Data
After physicalism / edited by Benedikt Paul Göcke.
p.   cm.
Includes bibliographical references and index.
ISBN-13: 978-0-268-03000-1 (pbk. : alk. paper)
ISBN-10: 0-268-03000-6 (pbk. : alk. paper)
E-ISBN: 978-0-268-08068-6
1. Dualism. 2. Materialism. I. Göcke, Benedikt Paul, 1981–
B812.A38 2012
147'.4—dc23

2012014926

In memory of

John Foster

(1941–2009)

Contents

Acknowledgments

All but two essays in this book are new essays on dualism and physicalism. Richard Swinburne's essay "From Mental/Physical Identity to Substance Dualism" appeared in *Persons: Human and Divine*, edited by Peter van Inwagen and Dean Zimmerman (Oxford: Oxford University Press, 2007), 142–65. Alvin Plantinga's essay "Against Materialism" appeared in *Faith and Philosophy* 23, no. 1 (2006): 3–32. I am grateful to Oxford University Press and the editor of *Faith and Philosophy* for granting me permission to reprint the essays. I am also grateful to the University of Notre Dame Press, and to Andre Banning, Justyna Göcke, Andreas Hüttemann, Klaus Müller, Alexander Norman, Michael Olenick, and Stephen Priest. Finally, I would like to thank Blackfriars Hall, Oxford, and the *Seminar für philosophische Grundfragen der Theologie*, Westfälische Wilhelms-Universität Münster, for providing room for excellent philosophical discussions.

Introduction

After Physicalism

BENEDIKT PAUL GÖCKE

What am I? Who, if those questions are supposed to be different, am I? Understanding these questions is understanding what philosophy of mind, or rational psychology, as it used to be called, is about. Philosophy of mind is concerned with the one asking the question, not with objects surrounding the one asking the question. It is concerned primarily with subjectivity, not with objectivity.

1. THE VAIN AGENDA OF PHYSICALISM—A PROGRAMMATIC ACCOUNT

Since the middle of the last century, the default answer to the questions of what and who we are has been the physicalist's objectivist answer: because everything is physical—so it went—we, too, have to be physical.[1]

Assuming that particulars and properties are the relevant ontological categories, we can state the thesis that everything is physical more precisely in terms of particulars and properties. In terms of particulars, that everything is physical means that every particular is a physical particular, and in terms of properties it means that every exemplified property is physical. Combining the respective claims about particulars and properties, we can say that physicalism is either the thesis that every particular and every property is physical or the thesis that although every particular is physical, not every property is.[2] The first thesis is known as reductive physicalism; the second one is the thesis of nonreductive physicalism.[3]

For reasons well known, reductive physicalism failed. There could not be a coherent account identifying all nonphysical properties with physical properties because, as Lowe rightly points out, "a physical state is, by its very nature, one whose possession by a thing makes some real difference to at least part of the space which that thing occupies . . . , but my consciously thinking of Paris has no spatial connotations of this sort whatsoever . . . consequently the thesis that mental states 'just are' (identical with) physical states is simply unintelligible" (Lowe 2008: 23).[4]

Nonreductive physicalism is the only other *prima facie* plausible version of physicalism, but it also failed. The physicalists' attempts to identify ourselves with our bodies, or parts of our bodies, could not be successful for the (often ignored) dualist reason that what it is to be a *body* or a *brain* is not what it is to be *you*—even if there are relations of dependency or emergence between you and your body.[5]

The failure of both reductive and nonreductive physicalism, however, does not entail that we should leave physicalism behind forever. There might be overwhelming arguments for physicalism which commit us to its truth, even if that truth were to be beyond understanding.[6] But there is no such argument as yet. That there are such arguments is an article of faith held by the physicalist.

A recent argument for physicalism is the argument from causal closure, the "canonical argument for physicalism" (Papineau 2002: 17). The fundamental assumption is that physical effects are not systematically causally overdetermined by ontologically distinct causes, and that the physical realm is causally complete (i.e., physical effects have purely physical causal histories). For those who assume the reality of mental causation, these assumptions entail that mental states have to be physical states in order to be able to be causally efficacious at all.

The argument is unconvincing because its crucial premise, the completeness of physics, is either consistent with dualist accounts of causation or else an arbitrary assumption only physicalists are likely to adopt.[7]

The completeness of physics is consistent with dualist accounts of mental causation since the dualist can argue that mental causation works in quite a different way from physical causation, and that therefore even if the physical realm were causally closed, there would be room for genuine mental causes. As Lowe suggests, "it could conceivably be the case that, even though [every physical event contains only other physical events in its transitive causal closure], sometimes a non-physical mental event *M* causes it to be the case that certain physical events, *P1, P2, . . . Pn*, have a certain physical effect, *P*" (Lowe 2008: 54). But even on the assumption that the causal closure of the physical realm is not consistent with dualist accounts of causation, the argument does not succeed since, as I have argued elsewhere (Göcke 2008), the causal closure of the physical realm is neither an entailment of science nor a matter of metaphysical necessity. Our world could be one where at least sometimes mental events are genuine causes of physical events. The only option for the physicalist is to assume that as a matter of metaphysical contingency the actual world is in fact causally closed. To adopt this assumption is attractive only for those who already assume that there is no room for genuine mental causation, which is to say that it is convincing for those who already accept the conclusion of the argument.

Papineau argues that the completeness of physics is the cornerstone of almost any argument for physicalism:

> It is true that these founding fathers of modern materialism offered a number of variant arguments for materialism, and that not all of these arguments feature the completeness of physics as prominently as does the causal argument. . . . Even so, it is not hard to see that nearly all these other arguments presuppose the completeness of physics in one way or another, and would not stand up without it. . . . Thus, for example, consider J. J. Smart's (1959) thought that we should identify mental states with brain states, for otherwise those mental states would be 'nomological danglers' which play no

role in the explanation of behaviour. Similarly, reflect on David Lewis's (1966) and David Armstrong's (1968) argument that, since mental states are picked out by their a priori causal roles, including their roles as causes of behaviour, and since we know that physical states play these roles, mental states must be identical with those physical states. Or again, consider Donald Davidson's (1970) argument that, since the only laws governing behaviour are those connecting behaviour with physical antecedents, mental events can only be causes of behaviour if they are identical with those physical antecedents. Now, these are all rather different arguments, and they give rise to rather different versions of materialism. But the point I want to make here is not sensitive to these differences. It is simply that none of these arguments would seem even slightly plausible without the completeness of physics. (Papineau 2002: 233–34)

Papineau is right that without the completeness of physics almost none of the arguments for physicalism is remotely plausible. Since the completeness of physics is either consistent with dualism or else question begging, almost none of the arguments for physicalism is remotely plausible. Because I am not aware of any recent argument for physicalism which is remotely plausible and independent of the causal closure of the physical realm, I take it that physicalism has in fact no argumentative support.

Although both reductive and nonreductive physicalism cannot hope to achieve their goal, and although there are no remotely plausible arguments for physicalism, there is a considerable number of philosophers who still pledge allegiance to physicalism and prefer to deny the existence of what they cannot account for. The trend is this: instead of arguing that because everything is physical we and our conscious life have to be physical, physicalists now argue the other way around: if something is not physical, then it simply can't exist! This thesis is, to put it very mildly, question begging. Take as an example Kim on the qualitative feature of experience. As a first step, Kim recognizes that physicalism is false:

So qualia . . . are physically irreducible. Qualia, therefore, are the 'mental residue' that cannot be accommodated within the physical domain. This means that global physicalism is untenable. It is not the case that all phenomena of the world are physical phenomena; nor is it the case that physical facts imply all the facts. There is a possible world that is like this world in all respects except for the fact that in that world qualia are distributed differently. I don't think we can show otherwise. (Kim 2005: 170)

That not all facts are physical facts, and that physical facts do not entail all facts, *is what the dualist said all along.* Instead of taking this seriously, however, by accepting that the realm of consciousness has its own being independently of the physical, Kim just denies that qualitative aspects of our experiences exist. Here is the quotation which leaves me, again, to put it mildly, perplexed:

Are mental properties physically reducible? Yes and no: intentional/cognitive properties are reducible, but qualitative properties of consciousness, or "qualia," are not. In saving the causal efficacy of the former, we are saving cognition and agency. Moreover, we are not losing sensory experiences altogether: Qualia similarities and differences can be saved. *What we cannot save are their intrinsic qualities—the fact that yellow looks like that, and so on. But I say, this isn't losing much, and when we think about it, we should have expected it all along.* (Kim 2005: 174; my italics)

No more yellow in my life! Alas, we cannot save the intrinsic qualities of our experiences—they are gone! They just do not exist.

Kim is one of the most reasonable and clear-cut of physicalists, but what he is saying here is straightforwardly false. There is no such choice between "saving" the causal efficacy of mentality and "saving" the intrinsic qualities of our conscious life. Any account of ourselves which denies *either* the causal efficacy of our mental states *or* the intrinsic qualities of our experiences (what it is like to have them) is plainly to be rejected since it ignores the explanandum and thus is doomed to go astray—even if nowadays a lot of people *say* something like that for, as Aristotle might have said, want of education.[8] Be that as it may, the general physicalist strategy should be clear: since within the physicalist paradigm Kim cannot account for the obviously given intrinsic qualities of our experiences, he denies the existence of what he cannot account for. If you want to be a physicalist, you have to deny the obvious.

2. A MINIMAL ACCOUNT OF CONSCIOUS BEINGS

Let us now turn to beings like ourselves, conscious beings. Quite independently of the ontological theses of dualism and physicalism—that is, independently of the question whether a conscious being, from an ontological point of view, is a physical or a nonphysical particular—a conscious being is at least at some point of time in at least one possible world the subject of a *stream of consciousness*. This is a minimal part of what we mean when we say that something is a conscious being: on the one hand, we do not demand that a conscious being is the subject of a stream of consciousness at every point of time of its existence, as perhaps it is not in a narcotic sleep (therefore, it is *possible* that a conscious being is not the subject of a stream of consciousness). On the other hand, we have difficulty in imagining a conscious being that is never the subject of a stream of consciousness. Therefore, it is *necessary* that there is at least some possible world where a conscious being is the subject of a stream of consciousness.

Because there are different senses of the term 'consciousness,' we have to find a sense in which a conscious being can properly be said to be the subject of consciousness. Husserl distinguishes three different notions:

1. Consciousness as the entire phenomenological being of the spiritual ego. (Consciousness = the phenomenological ego, as "bundle" or interweaving of psychic experiences.)
2. Consciousness as the inner becoming aware of one's own psychic experiences.
3. Consciousness as a comprehensive designation for "psychic acts" or "intentional experiences" of any sort. (Husserl 1984: 356)[9]

The notion of consciousness as the entire phenomenological being of what Husserl calls the spiritual ego is the appropriate notion of consciousness: a stream of consciousness *is* an entirety of phenomenological being. The second and third notions of consciousness suggested by Husserl both presuppose the existence of consciousness as an entirety of phenomenological being. If there were no "bundle of interweaving psychic experiences," then one could not be aware of one's own psychic experiences and there could not be any intentional experiences.[10]

The notion of phenomenological being is synonymous with the notion of *experiences* or *qualia*. The existence of the one is necessary and sufficient for the existence of the other. In fact, there is no difference between being the subject of an experience or qualia and being the subject of phenomenological being.[11] A stream of consciousness therefore can be addressed as an entirety of experiences or qualia; it is, in other words, what each of us takes to be his conscious life with all its experiential diversity, and precisely in this sense it is an entirety.

There is a sense according to which consciousness is always self-consciousness because consciousness is always consciousness of a conscious being and therefore *eo ipso* is consciousness for a *self*.[12] The existence of phenomenological being, experiences, or qualia is not possible without there being *someone*, that is, a self in a minimal sense of the term, which is the subject of the phenomenological being (or, equivalently, of the experiences or qualia) in question.[13] This is not to say that to be conscious entails being *aware* of one's own consciousness.[14]

From an epistemological point of view, I can speak only for myself about being the subject of a stream of consciousness, as I am the only instance of that kind of being to which I can *epistemologically*, immediately and with certainty, apply the term 'stream of consciousness' and thus apply the term 'conscious being.' The reason is that I am the only conscious being which for me is *directly* epistemologically accessible. Reflection on my consciousness provides me with knowledge that I am a conscious being; that is, I can be aware of myself as a conscious being by taking my consciousness as an object of my consciousness.[15] I can say that you are, or the frog over there is, a conscious being only based on *hints* given in observable physical manifestations. You do, or the frog does, certain things which I understand as consequences of your or the frog's being conscious shortly prior to these physical manifestations because I *already* understand those reactions as consequences of someone who is a conscious being and in this sense is *one like me.*[16]

This seems to prejudge the nature of consciousness. One may be philosophically tempted to demand that in order to qualify as a subject of a stream of consciousness an entity has to be in an epistemologically identical situation to the one I am in or can be in, such that subjects of streams of consciousness are those and only those beings which can know that they are. But it is doubtful that the application of the term 'being which is or can be aware that it is a conscious being' really is a *conditio sine qua non* for the correct application of the term 'conscious being.' One may argue this way if one does not keep the *epistemological* and the *ontological* aspect of the matter separated; and it is tempting not to do so because the claim that "I know that I am a conscious being because I can be aware that I am conscious" supports a strong epistemological connection between consciousness and awareness of, or reflection on, one's consciousness. Without question, such awareness is sufficient for being a conscious being. But although there are cases like mine in which consciousness is *de facto* sometimes aware of itself, I do not know a convincing argument to show that it should be a necessary condition for some entity's being a conscious being that it must be able to be aware of its own consciousness in order for the term 'conscious being' to be truly applied to it.[17] There are no inconsistencies in the view that a conscious being cannot be aware of its consciousness. As Husserl says: "That a . . . train of sensations or images is *experienced* and in this sense is conscious does not and cannot mean that it is the *object* of consciousness, in the sense that a perception, a presentation or judgement is directed upon it" (Husserl 1984: 165).[18]

Two consequences follow immediately: firstly, there might be conscious beings such that we have no way to determine with epistemological certainty whether they are conscious beings or not. But that is not too high a price to pay, as I do not have epistemological *certainty* that you are a conscious being without taking that as a reason to be uncertain about whether you are conscious. Although I have no epistemological certainty that you are a conscious being, I also have no reason to doubt it, and this is the sense in which I am certain that you are a conscious being.[19] Secondly, there are conscious beings which will never know that they are conscious beings because they cannot be aware of their consciousness. Consciousness can remain unknown to itself, although it is necessarily acquainted with itself in the sense of its being self-consciousness as specified above. In this way, a frog may be conscious of the world without being ever aware of its consciousness.[20]

The subject of a stream of consciousness is that particular which has an immediate though not necessarily reflected acquaintance with a self-consciously given set of experiences, and a conscious being is at least at some point of time in some possible world the subject of a stream of consciousness. Dualism entails that such a particular, a conscious being, exists in the actual world but that, from an ontological point of view, this entity is not a physical particular.

3. AN ARGUMENT FOR DUALISM

On the assumption that there are physical particulars, the general structure of arguments for dualism is this: firstly, specify the identity conditions for conscious beings like ourselves (we did so above), secondly, show that a conscious being can exist without exemplifying any physical property or that there is no physical particular with which a conscious being could be identified. To show that a conscious being can exist without exemplifying any physical property is a positive way to establish dualism; to show that there is no physical particular a conscious being could be identified with is a negative way to establish the truth of dualism.[21]

I present a negative way to establish the truth of dualism, where it is assumed that an experience is *complex* if and only if it is not simple, and that an experience is *simple* if and only if it cannot be analysed as the simultaneous existence of experiences of in principle independent types of experiences. The idea is that experiences such as my *seeing* something are simple experiences because they cannot be analysed as the simultaneous existence of experiences of in principle independent types of experiences. In contrast, if we *hear and feel* at the same time, or taste and hear at the same time, then we are a subject of a complex experience because this experience can be analysed as the simultaneous existence of experiences of in principle independent types of experiences:[22] instead of hearing and seeing something I could only see something *or* hear something.

I focus paradigmatically on the complex experience of someone feeling, seeing, and hearing something simultaneously. I call this complex experience *c* and I let *a*, *b*, and *d* refer, respectively, to the simple experiences of this someone of feeling something, seeing something, and hearing something such that $c = \{a, b, d\}$. The symbols *a*, *b*, and *d* stand for experiences which are in principle independent of each other because it is not necessarily the case that a subject always feels, sees, and hears something at the same time: Just feel, hear, and see something and then close your eyes—you will not stop hearing and feeling. As things actually are, however, this someone is the one and only subject of *a*, of *b*, and of *d* because the simultaneous existence of *a*, *b*, and *d* is the existence of *c*—*a*, *b*, and *d* are phenomenally unified as *c*—and by assumption this someone is the one and only subject experiencing *c*.

However, neither the existence of *b* nor that of *b* nor that of *d* considered as such entails that there is one and only one conscious being experiencing *c even if* the existence of *a* entails that there is a conscious being experiencing *a*, the existence of *b* entails that there is a conscious being experiencing *b*, and the existence of *d* entails that there is a conscious being experiencing *d*: because *a*, *b*, and *d* are different experiences, they exist in principle independently of each other, even if they actually exist simultaneously. To see this, assume that *a* is exemplified but not *b* and not *d*. If the exemplification of *a* entails that there is one and only one conscious being experiencing *c*, it would entail that *b* and *d* exist because *b* and *d* together with *a* are just *c*. The exemplification of *a* would not be possible without *b* and *d* being exemplified. By assumption, however, *a* is exemplified but *b* and *d* are not. This assumption is coherent, and therefore, neither the existence of *a* nor that of *b* nor that of *d* entails the fact that there is one and only one conscious being experiencing *c*. It is therefore a primitive fact about a conscious being which cannot be accounted for in terms of the simple experiences constituting the complex experience, and it is only the conscious being itself which can inform us about the experiences it is simultaneously the subject of.

Now could it be a fact about a physical particular that it is the one and only subject of *c*? No, the fact that there exists a particular which is the one and only conscious being experiencing *c* is metaphysically independent of the physical facts concerning your body or some parts of it (like your brain). There is no contradiction involved in assuming that there is a possible world which is a physical duplicate simpliciter of the actual world in which the relevant experiences are part of different streams of consciousness. That is to say, while in fact there is one and only one conscious being experiencing the seeing, hearing, and feeling together, there might be a world in which there is one stream of consciousness in which the hearing and seeing takes place and another stream of consciousness in which there is only the feeling. Therefore, there might be two distinct conscious beings. Nothing we could ever know about body and brain, even assuming that experiences supervene on physical properties of the brain, allows us to infer that there is one and only one conscious being experiencing *c*. Because this is a primitive fact about a conscious being but not a fact about a physical particular, and since it is a fact about a particular—that is, a certain conscious being—it is a fact about a nonphysical particular. Conscious beings therefore are nonphysical particulars.

Here is a possible rejoinder. It is assumed that a functional physical entity is a physical object composed of physical particulars which stand in certain functional relations that are physically realized. A conscious being, the physicalist might object, is a physically realized function. On this assumption the fact that there is one and only one conscious being experiencing *c*, the physicalist could argue, is entailed by the fact that *a*, *b*, and *d* are part of the same function. This objection rests on the assumption that it is possible that a conscious being is a physically realized functioning. Could this be true?

Suppose that you are a physical functioning and that the government of some country had a spy following you for some time such that the spy recorded the functioning of your brain during a certain interval of time. With this information the government decides to realize this function in a robot brain. Assume that you are still alive when this happens: *Where are you?* Do you suddenly exist twice such that both of your existents are independent of each other? The one doing whatever you are doing right now, and the other having the experiences which you had while the spy was recording the function realized in your brain? This is absurd. But even worse: suppose you are dead. Would you be back alive whenever the function is realized? If we allow for such absurdities, which all point to a problem of subjectivity, then we could as well count on the possibility that somewhere in the universe by chance a function is realized which is a conscious being. A conscious being cannot be a physical functioning.

4. After Physicalism: Dualism

The recent revival of dualism is not only due to the failure of physicalism but is also due to the revival of *a priori* metaphysics. A priori metaphysics and dualism go hand in hand because the former is the method to establish the claims of the latter, which is why often the physicalist rejects the possibility of the former and adopts the method of the empirical sciences as a method of philosophy instead. The essays in the present collection all firmly engage in a priori metaphysics. The essays by Meixner, Lowe, Foster, Plantinga, and Swinburne are concerned with ways to establish the truth of dualism; the essays by Hasker, Smith, and Robinson deal with the relation between physicalism and dualism. Göcke argues that the I is not a particular. Priest says that, fundamentally, I have to understand myself not as a thing but as *no-thing-ness*. In both essays, there is a strong connection between metaphysics and spirituality. In the last essay, Schärtl argues that there are limits to dualism which we can see when looking at resurrection.

In more detail, in the first essay, Uwe Meixner argues for the naturalness of dualism. He clarifies that against common physicalist opinion, physicalism is not a consequence of science, since then the negation of physicalism would be incompatible with science itself—

which, as Meixner argues, is not the case. The philosophical support in favor of physicalism rather consists in the alleged difficulties of the dualist's thesis. The dualist, it is often argued, cannot account either for the causal relation between physical and mental items or for the intentional relation between mental states and the objects they are about. Now, even if those problems were insurmountable, it would not follow that materialism is true, because the choice is not between dualism and materialism alone, but between materialism, dualism, and idealism. Therefore, if dualism is false, it only follows that either materialism or idealism has to be true. The dualist problems concerning causation and intentionality, however, are not insurmountable. Meixner provides the outlines of a solution to each problem, and ends by suggesting an account of three different respects in which dualism is a natural position: dualism is culturally, philosophically, and most importantly, also biologically natural.

In the second essay, "Non-Cartesian Substance Dualism," E. J. Lowe argues for a dualism according to which a human person is not identical with its body, but nevertheless is not a Cartesian ego. Rather, human persons belong to the ontological category of psychological substances, which are able to possess physical states. Lowe rejects Cartesian dualism because of the problem it has accounting for the relationship between an essentially immaterial and an essentially material substance. Given that the human person itself possesses certain physical characteristics, he argues that its connection to a particular body rests on perception and will since it is only one particular body through the eyes of which we perceive and act in the world. Lowe ends by way of arguing that although the self is not an essentially immaterial substance, it is nevertheless a simple substance without substantial parts.

In "Subjects of Mentality," John Foster distinguishes between items of mentality and subjects of mentality. He argues that on a realist understanding of the physical world human subjects of mentality turn out to be wholly nonphysical in nature. According to Foster, this is to say that human subjects of mentality are devoid of corporal properties, location in physical space, and also devoid of any components that have such properties or location. One kind of argument for this dualism consists in the fact that the physicalist cannot successfully determine a corporal subject of mentality, and that the dualist's proposal is the only available option. The deeper problem, according to Foster, however, is the fundamental issue of whether it makes sense to think of any type of corporal object as a mental subject, as in the case of reductive physicalism, or whether it makes sense to suppose that a physical particular has a nonphysical side to its nature, as in the case of nonreductive physicalism. Foster argues against both proposals and ends with considerations pertaining to the nature of animal subjects of mentality and the relationship between the subjects of mentality and their bodies, both of which, according to Foster, are intelligible on theistic assumptions.

Alvin Plantinga's essay is directed against materialism. He presents two arguments for dualism on the assumption that human beings can consider or envisage a proposition or state of affairs such that at least sometimes they can determine its modal status, that is, whether the proposition or state of affairs is necessary, contingent, or impossible. His first argument is from possibility to actuality: he can exist while neither his body nor any part of it exists because it is metaphysically possible that in an infinitely small time his body could be removed, destroyed, and replaced by a new body without him ceasing to exist. The second argument is from impossibility to actuality. Recurring to Leibniz, Plantinga argues that it is impossible for a material thing to think because a material state of, say, the nervous system cannot be an intentional conscious state. Since our mental states very often are intentional states, they cannot be material states. Plantinga ends by showing that none of the most common arguments for physicalism is sound.

In his "From Mental/Physical Identity to Substance Dualism," Richard Swinburne clarifies the basic notions 'substance,' 'property,' 'event,' 'mental,' and 'physical.' A mental property, according to Swinburne, is a property to which the bearer has privileged access on all occasions of its instantiation, whereas a *pure* mental property is one which does not entail that physical properties are exemplified at all. Swinburne then argues against reductive physicalism that a fully informative description of the world in purely physical terms does not entail that mental properties are exemplified. If, however, mental properties were identical with or supervened on physical ones, such a description would have to entail their existence. Therefore, mental properties are not identical with physical properties. Swinburne continues to argue that conscious beings like ourselves are pure mental substances which possess only pure mental properties as their essential properties. The idea behind the argument is that pure mental substances can be distributed independently of the distribution of physical substances because a full description of a possible world does not entail that pure mental substances are connected to the bodies they are in fact connected to.

The next essay, by William Hasker, deals with the question of whether materialism is equivalent to dualism. Although materialism and dualism, considered as a family of views about the place of conscious beings in the world, are far from being equivalent, Hasker argues that the most plausible versions of each, materialism and dualism, are nearly equivalent. Hasker considers emergent materialism and emergent dualism. According to emergent dualism, the human person is a new substance emerging from its physical body. Although the human person is not identical with its body, it is generated and sustained by its body. According to emergent materialism, however, the human person is an emergent substance in the following sense: although the human person is entirely constituted by physical matter and nothing else, it possesses a thisness which is distinct from the thisness possessed by its constituents. The emerging substance thus is the human person as a whole. Hasker ends by considering arguments against and in favor of each position, and concludes that although prima facie some differences remain, the most promising theses of dualism and materialism are nearly equivalent.

In "Benign Physicalism," A. D. Smith argues that after all there might be a physicalist thesis which is not demonstrably false. He suggests that because ultimately our concepts of fundamental physical properties are only functional concepts which give us no clue as regards the intrinsic nature of physical entities, it might be our own conscious experiences which are the intrinsic natures or 'realizers' of causally and functionally specified physical items. According to this account, we grasp the intrinsic natures of physical entities by way of being aware of the irreducible qualitative character of our own experiences, where our experiences themselves are *autonomously* physical. Although experiences are not to be identified with, for instance, brain states, they might thus fulfill yet unknown causal, and therefore physical, roles. Since, however, the causal role of experiences thus understood might be only contingent, and since experiences also might have failed to be the realizers of certain causal roles, Smith ends by arguing that although such a thesis of physicalism is the most plausible one, it is philosophically rather uninteresting because it depends on the contingent causal structure of the world.

In "Qualia, Qualitites, and our Conception of the Physical World," Howard Robinson presents a strengthened version of the argument from knowledge against physicalism. Although commonly the argument is taken to show that the physicalist cannot account for qualitatives features of mental states, Robinson argues that in fact the argument shows that the physicalist himself is unable to provide an intelligible notion of the physical realm which goes beyond the purely abstract and mathematical. Since experiential qualities are an essential feature of any adequate conception of the physical which goes beyond the purely abstract, it follows that the physicalist cannot account for an adequate notion of the physical which goes beyond the purely abstract. Robinson ends by showing that the physicalist cannot escape this conclusion in a monistic way by extending the notion of matter in such a way as to ascribe proto-mental or full-fledged mental properties to physical matter.

In his "Groundwork for a Dualism of Indistinction," Benedikt Paul Göcke firstly provides a framework of possible worlds according to which possible worlds are constituted by individual essences which at once are the objects of our conceivings. He then goes on to argue that physicalism as a thesis about particulars existing in the actual world is simply irrelevant because the I is no particular at all. Rather, insofar as the I is connected to a particular human being, it is indistinguishable from that human being, that is, is neither identical to nor distinct from it. He ends by providing the resources for how to unite theories of the I thus understood, according to which it is the Absolute, with those theories of the I according to which the I does not exist at all.

In "The Unconditioned Soul" Stephen Priest draws, in an exploratory way, a distinction between conditioned and unconditioned philosophy. He argues that materialist and physicalist solutions to problems in the philosophy of mind are guaranteed to fail because they do not do justice to the reality of one's own existence. By "deconditioning," it is disclosed that I am an unbounded and unchanging inner space in which the time is always now. Priest claims that this inner space is a substance and is to be correctly identified with the immaterial soul. The existence of this deconditioned self is one of the hidden root causes of problems in the philosophy of mind, including the problem of personal identity, the mind-body problem, the problem of difference between the past and the future, and the problem of free will and determinism. Any plausible solution to those problems has to take account of the existence of the deconditioned self, or "unconditioned soul."

In the last essay, "Beyond Dualism," Thomas Schärtl argues that although contemporary materialists offer an understanding of resurrection as bodily fission, some dualistic intuitions seem to be unavoidable in order to spell out an appropriate understanding of the doctrine. The essay proposes a model of resurrection which goes beyond a materialistic understanding of the person on the one side and substance dualism on the other side. Based on phenomenological insights, the essay tries to avoid the burdens of Cartesian substance dualism, but it seeks an understanding of realization and embodiment which goes beyond a purely materialistic metaphysics.

NOTES

1. Consider the following: "The world is as physics says it is, and there's no more to say" (Lewis 1983: 361); "Physicalism: Being the claim that everything there is in the world—including human minds—is either itself a basic physical entity or else constituted by basic physical entities" (Walter 2003: v); "The doctrine of physicalism . . . is generally taken to hold that everything in the world is physical, or that there is nothing over and above the physical, or that the physical facts in a certain sense exhaust all the facts about the world" (Chalmers 1996: 41); "Physicalism is the thesis—call it ontological physicalism—that whatever exists or occurs is ultimately

constituted out of physical entities" (Shoemaker 2001: 706). For further clarification of the thesis of physicalism see Göcke 2009.

2. That not every particular is physical and every property is physical is an incoherent claim: if there is a nonphysical particular, then the property of being a nonphysical particular is exemplified. But then it is not the case that every property is physical.

3. Francescotti (1998: 51) states the following: "Non-reductionism has become a dominant position in the philosophy of mind. In its standard formulations, this position implies that mental properties are not identical with physical properties. Most non-reductionists, however, still pledge their allegiance to physicalism by insisting that mental properties supervene on, and are realized by, purely physical phenomena."

4. Smith is more explicit on the matter: "It is, I believe, sufficient for any sensible person simply to read the [thesis of reductive physicalism] in order to see [its] inadequacy" (Smith 1993: 225).

5. This, of course, does not entail *eo ipso* that Cartesian Dualism is true. See Lowe's essay in this volume for an argument in favor of non-Cartesian substance dualism.

6. McGinn (2000) is essentially arguing that physicalism is true but that we lack the right cognitive constitution to understand its truth.

7. Cf. Lowe (2008: 41–78) and Göcke (2008).

8. To deny the existence of intrinsic qualities of our experiences is philosophically on the same level as to assert that it is possible for the same thing to be and not to be: "But we have now posited that it is impossible for anything at the same time to be and not to be, and by this means have shown that this is the most indisputable of all principles.—Some indeed demand that even this shall be demonstrated, but this they do through want of education, for not to know of what things one may demand demonstration, and of what one may not, argues simply want of education. For it is impossible that there should be demonstration of absolutely everything" (Aristotle 1995: 1588).

9. Here is the German original: "1. Bewusstsein als der gesamte (reelle) phänomenologische Bestand des * empirischen Ich, als Verwebung der psychischen Erlebnisse in der Einheit des Erlebnisstroms*. (A: * geistigen Ich. (Bewusstsein = das phänomenologische Ich, als 'Bündel' oder Verwebung der psychischen Erlebnisse.)*). 2. Bewusstsein als inneres Gewahrwerden von eigenen psychischen Erlebnisse. 3. Bewusstsein als zusammenfassende Bezeichnung für jederlei 'psychische Akte' oder 'intentionale Erlebnisse.'" For a thoughtful study on Husserl's notion of the transcendental ego and Sartre's critique, cf. Priest (2000).

10. Phenomenological being thus is a *conditio sine qua non* for intentional acts and inner awareness of oneself. Even if one were to distinguish

more senses of the word 'consciousness,' that consciousness is a totality of phenomenological being is the most fundamental sense in which we can use the term 'consciousness.' Pope and Singer (1978: 1) provide a rough circumscription of what belongs to an instance of consciousness thus understood: "The stream of consciousness—that flow of perceptions, purposeful thoughts, fragmentary images, distant recollections, bodily sensations, emotions, plans, wishes, and impossible fantasies—is our experience of life, our own personal life, from its beginning to its end."

11. The synonymy of those terms is also argued for by Chalmers. He is right in stating that 'experience' is a term in line with the notions of "'qualia,' 'phenomenology,' phenomenal,' 'subjective experience,' and 'what it is like.' Apart from grammatical differences, the differences among these terms are mostly subtle matters of connotation. 'To be conscious' in this sense is roughly synonymous with 'to have qualia,' 'to have subjective experience,' and so on. Any differences in the class of phenomena picked out are insignificant" (Chalmers 1996: 6).

12. Heidegger states it thus: "Der Mensch hat Bewusstsein von Objekten und hat dabei auch ein Bewusstsein von sich, Selbstbewusstsein. *Jedes Bewusstsein ist auch Selbstbewusstsein*" (Heidegger 2001: 135; my italics). This fact is seen not only in the tradition of phenomenology, but also in recent analytic philosophy. Chalmers essentially states the same feature of experiences in Russelian terms of acquaintance: "My experiences are part of my epistemic situation and simply having them gives me evidence for some of my beliefs. All this is to say that there is something intrinsically epistemic about experience. To have an experience is automatically to stand in some sort of intimate epistemic relation to the experience—a relation that we might call 'acquaintance'" (Chalmers 1996: 196–97).

13. If an experience exists, then there is someone this experience is the experience of. As Foster states: "If P is a pain-sensation occurring at a certain time *t* . . . we should ultimately represent the occurrence of P as the event of a certain subject's being in pain at *t*. And if D is a decision occurring at *t*, . . . we should ultimately represent the occurrence of D as the event of a certain subject's taking a decision at *t*. Quite generally, . . . we must represent each episode of mentality as the event of a subject's being in a certain mental state at a certain time, or performing a certain act at a certain time, or engaging in a certain mental activity over a certain period of time" (Foster 1991: 205).

14. In Heideggerian terms, not all forms of conscious life are *Dasein*, whereby Dasein is understood to be "this entity . . . which includes inquiring as one of the possibilities of its Being" (Heidegger 1962: 27) and which "does not just occur among other entities. Rather it is ontologically distinguished by the fact that, in its very Being, that Being is an issue for it" (Heidegger

1962: 32). If awareness of one's consciousness is a *conditio sine qua non* for the possibility that one's being becomes an issue for a conscious Being, then not for all conscious beings their Being is an issue for them.

15. I ignore Wittgensteinian worries about the function of the concept of knowledge in reference to self-ascriptions. Wittgenstein expressed these worries in his *On Certainty:* "'I know where I am feeling pain,' 'I know that I feel it here' is as wrong as 'I know that I am in pain.' But 'I know where you touched my arm' is right" (Wittgenstein 2006: 41).

16. Because it is in the nature of hints that they are not knowledge-entailing, my understanding, of course, does not preclude the possibility of me making mistakes in my ascriptions of consciousness to certain entities.

17. Let us consider an argument by Carruthers which could be taken to support views like the one that (the potential of) self-awareness is a necessary condition for being a conscious being. The first step of Carruthers's argument is as follows: "In order to think about your own thoughts, or your own experiences, you have to possess the concepts of thought and experience. And these get their life and significance from being embedded in a folk-psychological theory of the structure and functioning of the mind. So in the case of any creature to whom it is implausible to attribute a theory of mind—and I assume that this includes most animals and young children—it will be equally implausible to suppose that they engage in conscious thinking" (Carruthers 1996: 221). Carruthers argues that in order to think about your own thoughts you need to have the concepts of thought and experience. Let's agree on this for the sake of argument. In order to reflect on your consciousness you need some concepts to grasp your consciousness as your consciousness. Carruthers goes on to deny conscious thinking of entities which do not possess such concepts, whereby, in order for the argument to be plausible, he has to understand "conscious thinking" as synonymous with "thinking about your own thoughts"—otherwise the first and the last point lack internal coherence. Let's also agree on this. However, Carruthers goes on: "If animals (or most animals) lack higher-order thoughts, then by the same token they will lack conscious *experiences*. For there will be just as little reason to believe that they are capable of thinking about their own experiences, as such" (Carruthers 1996: 221; my italics). This is baffling. As in the case of conscious thinking, which turned out to mean thinking about your own thoughts, he has to take the notion "conscious experiences" to mean "thinking about your own experiences." Otherwise the premises won't support the conclusion. If, however, this were an appropriate demand on some entity's being a conscious being, then, I'm afraid, most of the time I would be unconscious for the reason that, from a phenomenological point of view, the cases in which I think about my experiences or even experience them as experiences are desperately few compared with those of my experiences

which I never think about or otherwise reflect on. It does not follow therefore that in order to have conscious experiences I must be able to take my consciousness as an object of my consciousness.

18. Here is the German original: "Daß der zugehörige Belauf an Empfindungen oder Phantasmen *erlebt* und in diesem Sinne bewußt ist, besagt nicht und kann nicht besagen, daß er *Gegenstand* eines Bewußtseins in dem Sinne eines darauf gerichteten Wahrnehmens, Vorstellens, Urteilens ist." Sartre circumscribes the pre-reflective consciousness, which he calls pre-reflective cogito, in the following quotation, which is worth quoting at length, thus: "Every positional consciousness of an object is at the same time a non-positional consciousness of itself. If I count the cigarettes which are in that case, I have the impression of disclosing an objective property of this collection of cigarettes: they are a dozen. This property appears to my consciousness as a property existing in the world. *It is very possible that I have no positional consciousness of counting them. Then I do not know myself as counting.* Proof of this is that children who are capable of making an addition spontaneously can not explain subsequently how they set about it. . . . Yet at the moment when these cigarettes are revealed to me as a dozen, *I have a non-thetic consciousness of my adding activity.* If anyone questioned me, indeed, if anyone should ask, 'What are you doing there?' I should reply at once, 'I am counting.' *This reply aims not only at the instantaneous consciousness which I can achieve by reflection but at those fleeting consciousnesses which have passed without being reflected-on, those which are forever not reflected-on in my immediate past.* It is not reflection which reveals the consciousness reflected-on to itself. Quite the contrary, it is the non-reflective consciousness which renders the reflection possible; there is a pre-reflective cogito which is the condition of the Cartesian cogito" (Sartre 1956: liii; my italics).

19. Here I agree with Wittgenstein: "From its seeming to me—or to everyone—to be so, it doesn't follow that it is so. What we can ask is whether it can make sense to doubt it" (Wittgenstein 2006: 1).

20. Baker introduces the notions "weak first person" and "strong first person": "A conscious being becomes self-conscious on acquiring a first-person perspective—a perspective from which one thinks of oneself as an individual facing a world, as a subject distinct from everything else— *All sentient beings are subjects of experience, but not all sentient beings have first person concepts of themselves.* Only those who do—those with first-person perspectives—are fully self-conscious. Beginning with nonhuman sentient beings, I shall distinguish two grades of first-person phenomena: weak and strong" (Baker 2000: 60; my italics). Baker's weak first person comes close to what I dub the pre-reflective subject of a stream of consciousness, and her strong first person comes close to what is my self-reflective subject. However, whereas on my conception a conscious being can be both—sometimes

a weak first person and only in reflection a strong first person—Baker's account seems to be an either-or classification.

21. Because every particular is essentially a physical particular or a nonphysical one, questions concerning the identity of conscious beings are modal questions. Arguments for dualism reflect this by presupposing that we are able to get in contact with the modal realm itself. In other words, arguments for dualism presuppose that conceivability broadly understood is a reliable guide to possibility. There would be no point in arguing that a conscious being can exist without exemplifying physical properties, or that there is no physical particular a conscious being could be identified with, if that did not entail that a conscious being in fact cannot be a physical particular. Because conceivability is an a priori affair, arguments of dualism are a priori arguments, which, if sound, cannot be refuted by any kind of empirical observation. For some, however, it is doubtful whether conceivability entails possibility. They argue that there are counterexamples concerning a posteriori necessities. They argue that, for instance, water turns out to be H_2O, and that since identities are necessary, it is impossible for water not to be H_2O. Because, however, we needed experience to identify water with H_2O, there is no a priori contradiction involved in assuming that water is not H_2O. It is conceivable, but not possible, that water is not H_2O. Therefore, it seems doubtful that conceivability is a reliable guide to possibility, which means on this view that arguments for dualism are as doubtful as the relation between conceivability and possibility is. The question who and what we are, in this Kripkean discussion, is not primarily concerned with the question whether we are physical or nonphysical particulars, but with the question of whether we are beings of such a kind that their conceivings entail possibility. If we are, then it is hard to escape the truth of dualism, and if we are not, then it is doubtful whether philosophy as a whole is possible at all.

22. That a subject is subject of a complex experience does not mean that the experience appears as a complex experience to its subject: complex experiences appear as one in the same way in which a simple experience appears as one; this is why one can refer to them directly as *this* complex experience.

REFERENCES

Aristotle. 1995. *The Complete Works of Aristotle: The Revised Oxford Translation.* Edited by Jonathan Barnes. Vol. 2. Princeton: Princeton University Press.

Armstrong, David. 1968. *A Materialist Theory of the Mind.* London: Routledge & Kegan Paul.

Baker, L. R. 2000. *Persons and Bodies.* Cambridge: Cambridge University Press.

Carruthers, P. 1996. *Language, Thoughts, and Consciousness: An Essay in Philosophical Psychology.* Cambridge: Cambridge University Press.

Chalmers, D. 1996. *The Conscious Mind: In Search of a Fundamental Theory.* Oxford: Oxford University Press.

Davidson, Donald. 1970. "Mental Events." In *Experience and Theory*, edited by L. Foster and J. Swanson, 79–101. London: Duckworth.

Foster, J. 1991. *The Immaterial Self: A Defence of the Cartesian Dualist Conception of the Mind.* London: Routledge.

Francescotti, R. M. 1998. "Defining 'Physicalism.'" *Journal of Mind and Behaviour* 19:51–64.

Göcke, B. P. 2008. "Physicalism Quaerens Intellectum." *The Philosophical Forum* 49 (4): 463–68.

———. 2009. "What Is Physicalism?" *Ratio* 22:291–307.

Heidegger, M. 1962. *Being and Time.* Translated by John Macquarrie and Edward Robinson. New York: Harper & Row.

———. 2001. *Einleitung in die Philosophie.* Gesamtausgabe Band 27. Frankfurt am Main: Vittorio Klostermann.

Husserl, E. 1984. *Husserliana 19: Logische Untersuchungen. Zweiter Band. Untersuchungen zur Phänomenologie und Theorie der Erkenntnis.* Den Haag: Martinus Nijhoff.

Kim, J. 1993. *Supervenience and Mind: Selected Philosophical Essays.* Cambridge: Cambridge University Press.

———. 2005. *Physicalism or Something Near Enough.* Princeton: Princeton University Press.

Lewis, D. 1966. "An Argument for the Identity Theory." *Journal of Philosophy* 63:17–25.

———. 1983. "New Work for a Theory of Universals." *Australasian Journal of Philosophy* 61:343–77.

Lowe, E. J. 2008. *Personal Agency: The Metaphysics of Mind and Action.* Oxford: Oxford University Press.

McGinn, C. 2000. *The Mysterious Flame: Conscious Minds in a Material World.* New York: Basic Books.

Papineau, D. 2002. *Thinking about Consciousness.* Oxford: Oxford University Press.

Pope, K., and J. L. Singer. 1978. *The Stream of Consciousness: Scientific Investigations into the Flow of Human Experience.* Chichester: Wiley.

Priest, S. 2000. *The Subject in Question: Sartre's Critique of Husserl in "The Transcendence of the Ego."* London and New York: Routledge.

Sartre, J.-P. 1956. *Being and Nothingness: A Phenomenological Essay on Ontology.* New York: Kensington.

Shoemaker, S. 2001. "Physicalism." In *The Cambridge Dictionary of Philosophy*, edited by R. Audi. Cambridge: Cambridge University Press.

Smart, J. J. 1959. "Sensations and Brain Processes." *Philosophical Review* 68:141–56.

Smith, A. D. 1993. "Non-Reductive Physicalism?" In *Objections to Physicalism*, edited by Howard Robinson, 225–50. Oxford: Oxford University Press.

Walter, S., and H.-D. Heckmann, eds. 2003. *Physicalism and Mental Causation: The Metaphysics of Mind and Action*. Exeter: Imprint Academic.

Wittgenstein, L. 2006. *On Certainty*. Oxford: Blackwell.

1

The Naturalness of Dualism

UWE MEIXNER

In his famous biography of Samuel Johnson, James Boswell recounts the following anecdote (see, for example, Boswell 1986: 122):

> After we came out of the church, we stood talking for some time to-gether of Bishop Berkeley's ingenious sophistry to prove the non-existence of matter, and that every thing in the universe is merely ideal. I observed, that though we are satisfied his doctrine is not true, it is impossible to refute it. I shall never forget the alacrity with which Johnson answered, striking his foot with mighty force against a large stone, till he rebounded from it, 'I refute it *thus.*'

This anecdote can serve as a catalyst for various insights. In particu-lar, it enables one to see the doctrine of psychophysical dualism in a new light. I hope that this will become apparent in this essay as it progresses.

1. THE NATURE OF PHILOSOPHICAL OPINION

Boswell's text takes us back to a time (precisely speaking, it is the year 1763) when ontological idealism seemed irrefutable—though it was perceived to be false—and even first-rate intellectuals did not manage to argue against it without helping themselves to wordless means of argument, exhibiting in doing so a certain amount of exasperation. Johnson's eighteenth-century kick argument (it can be strengthened by any amount of knock, push, and pull arguments) against ontological idealism (and for the existence of an external and material world) is strikingly similar to G. E. Moore's twentieth-century "proof" for the existence of an external and material world (and against ontological idealism): Moore's holding up his two hands and concluding that there are at least two external (and material) objects in the world.[1] Both Moore's argument and Johnson's argument are of the same type: they both *enact*—by *bodily* activity—a commonsensical objection against ontological idealism. Both Moore's argument and Johnson's are, however, not entirely successful—for Bishop Berkeley (or any other reasonable ontological idealist, for that matter) was of course far from denying that there are hands in the world (which one can lift) or large stones (against which one can strike one's foot). Berkeley merely denied that there are such things as *mind-independent* (or external) material objects; according to Berkeley, hands and stones, properly conceived, exist all right, but are not mind-independent material objects.[2] Much later in the history of ideas, Edmund Husserl—perhaps the most sophisticated ontological idealist of all time—held that hands, stones, and other cases of material objects are *according to their essence* the (intentional) correlates of (intentional) conscious states, that (therefore) the idea of these things existing independently of (or: external to) conscious states cannot be rationally defended and is indeed substantially ("sachlich") absurd.[3]

Ontological idealism is still very much worthy of philosophical attention, though most philosophers nowadays are satisfied merely to consider some popular caricature of it. Deplorably, they take the caricature to be properly representative of the doctrine. The caricature indeed—not the doctrine—can be easily dismissed, whether it be by lifting hands or by striking stones, or by emphasizing (usually somewhat indignantly) that we cannot normally make the world be so-and-so simply by thinking it to be so-and-so.

But the pervasive substituting of popular caricature for the real thing is symptomatic of the fact that the time of a philosophical doctrine is over. The time of (the widespread belief of the philosophers in) ontological idealism is over (which does not mean that ontological idealism might not have a comeback someday). By and large, the doctrine is no longer taken seriously. Today, quite a different philosophical opinion rules among the philosophers: materialism, the very opposite of ontological idealism. It is illuminating to consider the similarities and dissimilarities between the hegemony of ontological idealism in the eighteenth and nineteenth centuries and the hegemony of materialism in the latter part of the twentieth and at the beginning of the twenty-first century.

Two Hegemonies

Ontological idealism once was felt to be a tyrant who usurped the throne of truth. But it was also felt that this tyrant doctrine was quite unassailable in its act of usurpation, because of its philosophical reasonableness, the quality of philosophical argument in favor of it. See the above quotation from Johnson's biography, where Boswell observes that "though we are satisfied [this] doctrine is not true, it is impossible to refute it." I take it that many knowledgeable people of the eighteenth and nineteenth centuries would have made a similar comment, if given the opportunity.

Materialism, in contrast, is not felt these days to be a tyrant who usurps the throne of truth; at least, most of today's (Western) philosophers do not consider it in that light. The simple reason for this is that most of today's philosophers are firmly convinced of the truth of materialism.

As a consequence of the firmness of their commitment to materialism, the doctrine turns out to be irrefutable for *extrinsic* reasons. Every attempt to refute materialism must—qua attempted refutation—address those who believe in materialism and must consist in an argument; but every argument has premises; no argument can succeed in the eyes of those it addresses if they believe in the negation of its conclusion invariably—one is tempted to say: automatically—more firmly than in the conjunction of the argument's premises. This is the present situation. Unsurprisingly, it creates in the adherents of materialism the idea that the doctrine is irrefutable for *intrinsic* reasons, that is, because of its philosophical reasonableness.

But one wonders what could have lodged the doctrine of materialism so firmly with so many reasonable people in the first place. In this regard, a comparison with that other at-one-time-hegemonic monistic doctrine—ontological idealism—does afford interesting perspectives. Ontological idealism grew out of a philosophical atmosphere which was, in the main, created by Descartes. Descartes discovered that his realm of consciousness could be regarded as a closed world all by itself—a world, he perceived, which in principle might also exist all by itself. It was not some dogmatic belief—above all, no religious interests of any kind—that led him to this view, which he put forward in his immensely influential *Meditations*.[4] The driving force behind Descartes's discovery was radical skepticism, a skepticism which, as far as Descartes was concerned, is indeed in (optimistic) search of absolute certainty, but which is radical nonetheless. Note that radical skepticism is an attitude that is at home solely among the philosophers—and therefore, a philosophical doctrine that grows out of radical skepticism has perhaps more right to be called philosophical than a doctrine whose inspiration is common sense, science, religion, or some combination of these three non-philosophical sources of ideas.

To Descartes's discovery Berkeley added—and I present what seems to me the best way to reconstruct the essence of his thought—that because one cannot help being located in one's closed, perspectival realm of consciousness and cannot ever leave it,[5] one has no reason whatsoever to suppose that there exists anything that could exist even if no realm of consciousness existed, in other words, that there exists anything which is mind-independent. Considerations of parsimony and non-arbitrariness, therefore, dictate that there does not exist anything mind-independent.

It should be noted that the above Berkeleyan argumentation for ontological idealism (which thesis is, in fact, not identical to but entailed by the thesis that there does not exist anything mind-independent; see below) is strictly philosophical—just as is Descartes's argumentation for the in-principle possibility that his realm of consciousness is all there is. It is true that Berkeley had ulterior motives—religious motives—for his position. But this does nothing to alter the essential fact: Berkeley—whether in ideal reconstruction (as above) or without such treatment, in his raw arguments—was arguing for ontological idealism exclusively on philosophical grounds.

How strikingly different is the picture if we now turn to the monism that is diametrically opposite to ontological idealism: to the currently hegemonic monism, materialism! If a proponent of materialism is asked on what grounds he accepts this doctrine, the very likely first answer is this: it is the only global metaphysical doctrine that is compatible with science. If this were true, then materialism would have to be a consequence of science: if materialism is the only global metaphysical doctrine that is compatible with science, then the negation of materialism—which is also a global metaphysical doctrine—is not compatible with science, and therefore materialism is a consequence of science; that is, it is either a logical consequence of science alone or at least a logical consequence of science *plus* some uncontroversial philosophical principles of reason (methodological or otherwise) that "go without saying." But materialism does not seem to be a consequence of science—neither a straight consequence of it (following logically from science alone) nor a philosophically uncontroversially supported consequence of it (following logically from science *plus* some uncontroversial philosophical principles of reason).

It does not seem to be a consequence of science that every concrete (i.e., nonabstract) entity is physical (which is the thesis of materialism, or physicalism),[6] though perhaps at some time in the future it will be a consequence of science that every concrete entity is one-to-one correlated with a physical entity. But there do not seem to be uncontroversial philosophical principles of reason that would allow one to conclude from *this* that every concrete entity is identical with a physical one. Therefore, that some concrete entity is nonphysical (the negation of the thesis of materialism) does not seem to be incompatible with science, and therefore materialism does not seem to be the only global metaphysical doctrine that is compatible with science.

However, the position of the proponents of materialism does not appear as untenable as it would have to appear if they had to rely solely on the incompatibility of every other global metaphysical doctrine with science. For materialism, there is a "hidden" source of philosophical strength. What is that hidden source of strength?

The Strength of Materialism

That source provides strength to materialism *ex negativo,* for it simply consists in the difficulties (the wounds, so to speak) of dualism—dualism being the global metaphysical doctrine that some concrete entities are physical, and some nonphysical. Dualism, materialists say (when they become philosophically thoughtful and stop harping on an alleged preference of science for materialism), is untenable because of certain difficulties connected with it. There are indeed such difficulties; they have to do with two salient relations between physical concrete entities and nonphysical ones. These two relations between what is physical and what is nonphysical but concrete do pose difficulties—which, indeed, are frequently believed to be insurmountable. As a matter of fact, the discussion has focused on only one of the two relations: the *causal relation.* But we shall see in the next section that the *intentional relation* poses a difficulty for dualism that is even greater than the difficulty posed by the causal one.

Dualism has its difficulties—it is quite another question whether they make dualism untenable. But suppose, for the sake of the argument, that those difficulties are indeed insurmountable, and that dualism is, therefore, untenable. Does it follow that materialism is correct, or at least that materialism is the position which one ought to believe in? It does not follow. The following disjunction is logically true, and its degree of rational credence is 1:

> All concrete entities[7] are physical[8] (materialism), or
> some concrete entities are physical, and some nonphysical
>   (dualism), or
> all concrete entities are nonphysical (ontological idealism).

Therefore, in terms of truth, if dualism is not true, then it follows that the disjunction of materialism and ontological idealism is true; it does not follow that materialism is true. And in terms of rational credence, if the degree of rational credence for dualism becomes 0, then it follows that the degree of rational credence for the disjunction of materialism and ontological idealism is 1; it does not follow that the degree of rational credence for materialism is 1.

The difficulties of dualism are not insurmountable—and indeed the situation is such that if they were insurmountable, then this would be far from pointing us towards materialism more strongly than towards ontological idealism. (For the justification of this assertion, which goes beyond what was established in the previous paragraph, see the next section.) What does this suggest about the nature of belief in materialism—given that materialism is, as we have seen, not the only global metaphysical doctrine that is compatible with science? That belief in materialism is not as well-founded—scientifically or philosophically—as materialist believers usually think it is. In fact, it is less well-founded than, say, Husserl's belief in ontological idealism. Nevertheless, the hegemony of ontological idealism, which once seemed unshakable (see Boswell's anecdote), is over. The current hegemony of materialism, which seems just as unshakable, will be over, too. It is to be hoped that the passing of the hegemony of materialism will not happen for reasons that are foreign to reason.

2. The Difficulties of Dualism

Johnson and Boswell were dualists. This tickles the imagination. How would Johnson have refuted *materialism* if materialism had been the ruling global metaphysical doctrine of his days—that is, how would he have refuted materialism in a way that is *of one kind* with his "refutation" of ontological idealism? Consider the following variant of Boswell's anecdote:

> After we came from the beach, we stood talking for some time together of Daniel Dennett's—the famous atheist's—ingenious sophistry to prove the non-existence of consciousness,[9] and that every thing in the universe is merely material. I observed, that though we are satisfied his doctrine is not true, it is impossible to refute it. I shall never forget the alacrity with which Johnson answered, striking his naked foot with mighty force against a large stone, till he rebounded from it, 'I refute it *thus*.'

Imagine Johnson's pain! Surely Johnson has demonstrated (in this counterfactual situation) that there is pain in the world (just as in the historical situation that Boswell recounts Johnson has certainly demonstrated that there is at least one large stone in the world). But does this refute materialism? Has he shown that at least one concrete entity is nonphysical, that is, not mind-independently physical* (for elucidation, see the—admittedly rather important—note 8)?

In Boswell's anecdote, Johnson does not succeed in demonstrating that there is at least one concrete *mind-independently physical**, that is, *physical*, entity (cf. note 8), namely, the large stone against which he strikes his foot. Though it is obvious that that stone is an entity that is concrete and *physical** (in a neutral root-sense; see note 8), Johnson has not shown that it is also a *mind-independent entity* (which shortcoming, one may be sure, Berkeley would have pointed out against Johnson).[10] In the (obviously fictitious) variant of Boswell's anecdote, however, it does indeed seem that Johnson has succeeded in demonstrating that there is at least one concrete *not* mind-independently physical*, that is, *nonphysical*, entity, namely, the pain he feels in his naked foot when he strikes this foot against the large stone. This pain is certainly a concrete entity. Now suppose—for *reductio*—that it is also a physical entity. Hence it is a mind-independently physical* entity, and therefore a mind-independent entity. Hence that pain could exist even if no realm of consciousness existed—which, however, is plainly absurd.

The merits of this argument seem considerable to me. It hinges on two things: (1) on the conception of physicalness employed, namely, mind-independent physicalness*, and (2) on the conception of mind-independence employed, namely, being able to exist even if no realm of consciousness existed. However, the use of both conceptions seems entirely appropriate in formulating the thesis of materialism/physicalism. If materialists speak of physical entities, they mean mind-independently physical* entities,[11] and by this, in turn, they mean entities that are physical* and could exist even if no realm of consciousness existed.[12]

Thus, materialism stands refuted. And it has become clear why I remarked in the previous section that the situation regarding the difficulties of dualism is such that if those difficulties were insurmountable (disqualifying dualism), then this would be far from pointing us towards materialism more strongly than towards ontological idealism: this is trivially so, because, as we have just seen, ontological idealism is the only viable alternative to dualism (since materialism stands refuted).

But it is time to look at the difficulties of dualism. They are the following two, of which the first one gets practically all of the attention:

(1) Dualism assumes that some concrete entities are physical, and some nonphysical. This means that according to dualism some concrete entities are mind-independently physical*, and some are not. But if this is true, how can any of the concrete entities that are not mind-independently physical*—for example, certain mental events—causally interact with any of the entities that *are* mind-independently physical*—for example, certain brain states? This is a problem, for it seems that we cannot do without such causal interactions.

(2) According to dualism some concrete entities are mind-independently physical* and some are not. But if this is true, how can any of the concrete objects that are mind-independently physical*—for example, stones and trees—be the intentional objects of experiences—for example, of the visual experiences of Samuel Johnson, which, qua (dualistically conceived) experiences, are not mind-independently physical* objects? This is a problem, for it seems that we cannot do without physical (i.e., mind-independently physical*) objects being the intentional objects of experiences.

If one considers the kind of opposition to dualism that these two difficulties, each in its turn, appear to favor, then one finds that the first difficulty primarily suggests materialism (as *the* way to escape from it), whereas the second difficulty primarily suggests ontological idealism. Since ontological idealism is not much *en vogue* these days, the second difficulty, as far as I know, lies idle and makes no converts from dualism to ontological idealism (but I am not sure of this and cannot be); I submit, however, that the second difficulty played a considerable role in making Husserl an ontological idealist. The first difficulty, in contrast, is cited these days ad nauseam as the main motivation for (accepting) materialism—in spite of the fact that if a monistic position were indeed the key to healthy causal relationships between the mental and the physical*, then ontological idealism would seem to fit this role just as well as materialism.

Both difficulties have solutions that leave dualism intact. But the second difficulty—despite its current state of neglect—is considerably more difficult than the first one.

3. The Difficulties of Dualism Overcome

The solution to difficulty 1 consists in conceiving of causation in such a manner that entities which are mind-independently physical*— that is, which are physical* and could exist even if no realm of consciousness existed—can still causally interact with entities that are not mind-independently physical*, for example, with pain experiences. Such a conception of causation is possible, and an adequate theory of causation had better not rule it out. From the fact that A could exist without C existing (i.e., from the fact that A is in a certain manner ontologically independent of C),[13] whereas B could not exist without C existing, it simply does not in general follow that B cannot be a cause of A.[14] From the fact that moonshine could exist without the sun existing, whereas sunshine could not exist without the sun existing, it simply does not follow that sunshine cannot be a cause of moonshine (on the contrary: sunshine *is* a cause of moonshine). There is nothing to be balked at in the preceding statement. And there is as little to be balked at in the following statement: from the fact that a certain avoidance action of an animal could exist without (any realm of) consciousness existing, whereas the attendant pain experience of the animal could not exist without consciousness existing, it simply does not follow that the animal's pain experience is not *a* cause of the animal's avoidance action (especially if that action is prolonged).

The existence of nonphysical causation of physical events—that is, that there are mind-independently physical* events which are caused by entities that are not mind-independently physical*—is often denied on the basis of some principle or other of the causal closure of the physical world. There would be reason to be impressed by closure principles if they were consequences of science (in the sense explained in the section "Two Hegemonies" above). But they are not consequences of science; they are just plain metaphysical postulates, which are motivated to a large part by—materialism. This bias in favor of materialism disqualifies them from being legitimately made use of in arguing against nonphysical causation of physical events if the ultimate purpose in doing so is to attack dualism. And attacking dualism usually *is* the ultimate purpose of using closure principles against the nonphysical causation of physical events, in view of the fact that the nonphysical causation of physical events is indeed something that dualism can hardly do without: the general causal impotence of the nonphysical (even of the nonphysical and concrete) with regard to physical events is not really an attractive option for dualists.[15]

A solution to difficulty 2 is much harder to find (and, in fact, I am not at all sure that I have found one). The point of the difficulty has been very well expressed by Kant in his *Prolegomena*, §9:

> For what is contained in the object [Gegenstand; Kant is speaking about nonabstract objects] as it is in itself, I can know only if the object is present to me and given to me. But even then it is incomprehensible how the intuiting [die Anschauung] of a present thing should make it known to me as it is in itself, since its properties cannot transmigrate into my power of presentation [meine Vorstellungskraft]. (Kant 1968: 144; my translation)

Kant's proposed solution to the difficulty is to *dissolve* it by maintaining that, contrary to the assumption that gives rise to the difficulty, mind-independent concrete objects (Dinge an sich) cannot, in fact, ever be present and given (as intentional objects) to anyone, and that therefore what is contained in a concrete object as it is in itself—what properties it has in itself, that is, as a mind-independent object—cannot ever be known. In particular, mind-independent physical* objects are not (intentional) objects of experience; all we ever deal with in experience are *representations* (Erscheinungen) *of* mind-independent concrete objects (in the existence of which Kant, however, continued to believe)—representations that invariably are not mind-independently physical* objects.

Kant was a *representationalist.* But in contrast to so many others who think that all that we ever deal with are representations and not the represented objects themselves, Kant was not epistemologically naïve: if representations are *all* that we ever deal with, then, indeed, the reality which they represent must remain unknown to us; after all, we cannot then take a look at what is behind the scenes and make comparisons between the representations on the one hand and what they represent on the other (since, according to supposition, representations are all that we ever deal with). Kant resolutely bit this bullet. Other philosophers, however, found the skeptical consequences of Kantianism regarding our knowledge of *reality in itself* unpalatable.

Our epistemic grip on reality in itself can, however, be vindicated in a surprising way if one adopts ontological idealism—and, of course, is correct in doing so. Then there is nothing behind Kant's "Erscheinungen"; then they—the appearances (that is, appearances qua objects of appearance, not appearances qua vehicles of appearance)—do not represent anything; rather, they themselves *are* the reality in itself, and that reality is given, present to us, and therefore can be known by us. The price for this is that there are no physical objects:

Suppose there were some physical object. Hence some concrete object would be physical—this follows because 'physical' entails 'concrete' (since 'physical*' entails 'concrete'). But that some concrete object is physical contradicts the thesis of ontological idealism (see the section "The Strength of Materialism" above), according to which every concrete entity—hence also every concrete object[16]—is nonphysical.

The consequence that there are no physical objects is not as bad as it sounds. It is not as bad as it sounds because ontological idealists can combine their denial of physical objects—that is, their denial of mind-independently physical* objects—with accepting as many mind-*dependently* physical* objects as are needed as intentional objects of our experiences and thoughts of the physical*. Berkeley left the mind-dependence of mind-dependently physical* objects unanalyzed (and, notoriously, he often confused appearances qua objects of appearance with appearances qua vehicles of appearance),[17] whereas Husserl set himself the tremendous task of exploring and exhibiting the essential structure of their constitution—of the constitution of their reality and of their so-being, including their peculiar "mind-transcendence"—as an achievement in consciousness.[18]

But the advantages of ontological idealism are not for dualists, who, after all, normally find the thesis that there are no physical objects simply preposterous (just as materialists find that thesis preposterous; note that the thesis is incompatible not only with normal dualism, but also with materialism, since there certainly are some concrete objects). But how can dualists, in struggling with difficulty 2, sail through between the Scylla of representationalism and the Charybdis of ontological idealism?

Consider, for further clarification, a difficulty which is similar to difficulty 2: consider the proposition that the moon orbits around the earth (*not* the statement "The moon orbits around the earth"). Somehow this proposition—which is not a physical* entity, not even a concrete entity—manages to be about the moon, which is a paradigmatic mind-independently physical* object. But how can this be? Neither can the moon be plausibly considered an abstract entity (if this *could* be done, it would put the moon *into* the proposition—and, indeed, solve the problem), nor can it be plausibly maintained that the proposition is not directly about the moon: that it is about the moon only via some abstract representation of it, *the moon-in-the-proposition*, so to speak. I will not try so solve this conundrum.

Consider instead your experience of seeing the moon. Somehow also this experience—which, again, is not a physical* entity, although this time it is a concrete entity—manages to be about the moon. How can this be—without the moon being taken, so to speak, into the experience and losing its mind-independence, and without the experience being not really (i.e., not immediately) about the moon, but about a mind-dependent representation of it? This is the problem.

Its solution (or rather: the direction for its solution) is this: there's *one* concrete and homogeneous reality, which is nevertheless divided into (A) the mind-independently physical* (= the physical) and (B) the concrete but not mind-independently physical* (= the concrete and nonphysical, in other words: the mental *broadly conceived*), part

(B) being divided in its turn into (B1) the concrete but nonphysical* (= the mental *narrowly conceived*) and (B2) the mind-dependently
physical*. Thus, the one concrete and homogeneous reality is divided, and the means of dividing it is negation. But this in no way
compromises the essential oneness and homogeneity of the one concrete and homogeneous reality—no more so than the essential one-
ness and homogeneity of the realm of natural numbers is in any way
compromised by dividing that realm into various disjunctive classes
of numbers (say, [B2] uneven primes, [B1] uneven nonprimes, and
[A] even numbers). The difficulty in envisaging mind-independently
physical* objects as intentional objects of experiences (experiences
being—for dualists—concrete, nonphysical*, and trivially mind-
dependent events) is, therefore, largely illusory. It is a product of fal-
laciously interpreting *division* and *exclusion* as *unrelatedness* or even as
repugnance. Though a mind-independently physical* object can exist
without any realm of consciousness existing, it can nevertheless fit
into a mind-dependently nonphysical* experience—not, of course, as
a part of it, but as that which the experience *grasps*. The oneness and
homogeneity of the one concrete reality enables this sui generis relation, just as it enables causal interaction between experiences and
mind-independently physical* objects.

4. The Threefold Naturalness of Dualism

Dualism is natural in a threefold manner. For one thing, dualism is
philosophically natural—in striking contrast to the two monistic positions of materialism and ontological idealism.[19] A position is philosophically natural if, and only if, that position seems correct to most
people who have not steeped themselves in philosophical reflection,
in short, to most of the philosophically innocent. It does seem correct
to most of the philosophically innocent—to common sense, in other
words—that there is a mind-independently physical* (therefore—
ipso facto—concrete) world; this disqualifies ontological idealism
from being philosophically natural. And it does seem correct to most
of the philosophically innocent—to common sense—that there is a
concrete world which is not mind-independently physical*, but, in
part, even mind-dependently nonphysical* (i.e., the realm of con-

sciousness); this disqualifies materialism from being philosophically natural. Dualism is the remaining, philosophically natural, position.

Philosophical innocence is not cultural innocence. In fact, for us human beings, there is no such thing as cultural innocence. Cultural naturalness, therefore, has nothing to do with cultural innocence. Nevertheless, dualism is also *culturally* natural—in the sense that the overwhelming number of cultures in the course of human history was, by and large, based on dualism, with materialism and ontological idealism occurring in some of the most highly developed cultures as elitist positions, parasitic on dualism (i.e., living mainly by opposition to dualism).

What is philosophically or culturally natural need not be true. But neither need it be false. We have seen that dualism does not fare badly on philosophical reflection, either. Dualism's philosophically reflected standing is certainly not as bad as it is proclaimed to be by dualism's many enemies in the Western world. Indeed, much of the criticism that is leveled against dualism is neither fair nor free of a peculiar bigotry. (For a spirited response to such criticism, see Meixner 2004.) Dualism can hold its own against materialism, and it can also hold its own against ontological idealism (though it will not have escaped notice that the position of dualism is much harder to maintain against ontological idealism than against materialism). This gives the philosophical and cultural naturalness of dualism a rational sanction. It also should be noted that already the philosophical naturalness of dualism—and the cultural naturalness of dualism—provide, in themselves, some rational support to dualism (I am not, of course, saying that this support is rationally decisive).

Finally, but most importantly, dualism is also *biologically* natural. The fact of dualism is an outcome of biological evolution. I have defended this position at length in several of my publications.[20] Here I will be content to point out the central ideas. Much of an animal's life can be taken care of by a deterministic automaton—and this is what animals (including human beings) to a large part are: deterministic automata. But, as a matter of fact, the world is also in such a way that the property of being provided with a causally powerful (hence nonepiphenomenal), nonpredetermined subject of experience—in other words, with a free consciousness-guided *decision maker*[21]—is an evolutionary asset for an animal (in the familiar sense: having such a subject of experience is advantageous to the animal's survival and well-being). Therefore, the continual emergence and sophistication of the *mind property* (i.e., the property of having an active and free subject of experience)—the existence of which is a natural possibility (that is, is allowed by the laws of nature)—was favored by evolution, once that property had made its appearance on the stage of the world. Its appearance was brought about by the confluence of the right causes, under the right circumstances (whether that confluence was entirely fortuitous or at least in part the effect of design—it does not here matter),[22] and by variation and selection the mind property has finally developed to its present (known) height in human beings. But subjects of experience, and experiences themselves, are nonphysical* and (trivially) mind-dependent entities, not only in human beings but in all conscious animals. Hence dualism is a product of natural evolution, and therefore dualism is not only philosophically and culturally natural; it is biologically natural as well. The former two kinds of dualism's naturalness can in fact be said to find their natural explanation in this latter naturalness of dualism.

APPENDIX: MOORE'S PROOF OF AN EXTERNAL WORLD

Moore argues as follows:

> Obviously, then, there are thousands of different things such that, if, at any time, I can prove any one of them, I shall have proved the existence of things outside of us. . . . I can prove now, for instance, that two human hands exist. How? By holding up my two hands, and saying, as I make a certain gesture with the right hand, 'Here is one hand,' and adding, as I make a certain gesture with the left, 'and here is another.' (Moore 1959: 145–46)

This argument was first presented to the public in 1939. But already in a lecture of 1928/1929 Moore had spelled out a main reason for being dissatisfied with his argument—if intended as a refutation of ontological idealism (but only with this intention can his argument be considered interesting):

B. [Berkeley] is commonly held to have denied the reality of matter; and so, in a sense, he does. But if you read him carefully you will find he does *not* deny the reality of human bodies, & clouds, & mountains & loaves of bread. On the contrary he insists he holds such things are real. He is careful to say that what he denies is only *matter in the philosophical sense*. . . . And in trying to define what the sense [the philosophical sense] is, he mentions one characteristic which is, I think, often included—that of being independent of perception. . . . It may *possibly* be true, as B. would have said, that this desk is not independent of perception. (Moore 1966: 15–16; emphasis original)

Thus, Berkeley would surely have pointed out against Moore's argument for the existence of an external world that Moore has failed to show that the hands he holds up are independent of perception, indeed, that he has failed to show that they are mind-independent, and that, therefore, Moore has failed to present us (and himself) with things that are outside of us (and himself)—in the sense of 'outside of' (or 'external to') that is relevant for refuting ontological idealism. And it seems indeed that by making this objection, Berkeley would have rendered Moore's argument ineffectual against ontological idealism. (Moore does have a response to the Berkeleyan objection. But although Moore is entirely within his rights to give that response, against the ontological idealists it simply amounts to a begging of the question. The nature of the response will become apparent at the end of this appendix.)

Curiously, Moore does not seem to remember in 1939 what once was already clear enough to him, when he lectured on the question whether material things are real back in the twenties of the twentieth century. Compare the last quotation from Moore with the following:

There is, therefore, according to him [Kant], *a* sense of 'external,' a sense in which the word has been commonly used by philosophers—such that, if 'external' be used in that sense, then from the proposition 'Two dogs exist' it will *not* follow that there are some external things. What this supposed sense is I do not think that Kant himself ever succeeded in explaining clearly; nor do I know of any reason for supposing that philosophers ever have used 'external' in a sense, such that in *that* sense things that are met with in space are *not* external. (Moore 1959: 139; emphasis original)

Apparently it has escaped Moore's attention that in the sense of 'external' that Kant has in mind the word designates the very characteristic which turns 'matter' into Berkeley's "matter in the philosophical sense," namely, the characteristic of being mind-independent (or independent of perception). And, contrary to what Moore thinks to be the case, there is good reason for supposing that Kant is right in believing that the word 'external' in this sense—namely, the sense of 'mind-independent'—has been commonly used by philosophers. Moreover, Kant is surely right in supposing that, if 'external' be used in that sense, then from the proposition 'Two dogs exist' it will *not* follow that there are some external things; nor will this follow from the proposition 'Two hands exist'—because neither two existing dogs nor two existing hands are ipso facto mind-independent things, as Berkeley and Kant would have objected against Moore's "proof of an external world" if it had come to their attention. Finally, not a few philosophers have used 'external' in a sense—namely, in the sense of 'mind-independent'—such that, according to them, things that are met with in space are *not* external. Indeed, neither Kant nor Berkeley would have been averse to seeing his own view expressed in that way, *provided* it was clear that the word 'external' was, in the relevant context, just a synonym for 'mind-independent.'

It should not go without mention that Moore does, after all, hit on this philosophical sense of the word 'external,' the sense in which it means as much as 'mind-independent': "To say of anything that it is external to our minds . . . [means] . . . that from a proposition to the effect that it existed at a specified time, it in no case follows that any of *us* were having experiences at the time in question" (Moore 1959: 143; emphasis original). This is near enough to "it could exist without any realm of consciousness existing" and can, in fact, be made equivalent to it (for this, one just needs to give the "us" the greatest possible extension and replace the "at the time in question" by "at any time"—modifications, I believe, Moore could not have had any reason to be averse to if they had been proposed to him). Moore does decide to use the word 'external' in the sense of 'mind-independent,' and he therefore does intend his "proof of an external world" as a proof of a mind-independent world. With his hand action, Moore is indeed attacking ontological idealism, just like Dr. Johnson—176 years earlier—was attacking ontological idealism with his foot action.

How, exactly, does he do so? Moore believes that dogs and hands and, for that matter, soap-bubbles are *ipso facto* (qua dogs, hands, soap-bubbles) mind-independent objects: "I think . . . that from any proposition of the form 'There's a soap-bubble!' there does really *follow* the proposition 'There's an external object!' 'There's an object external to *all* our minds!'" (Moore 1959: 145; emphasis original). Here Moore is asserting what Berkeley (and Husserl, and every reasonable ontological idealist) firmly denies: that the proposition 'X is a mind-independent object' (or 'X could exist without any realm of consciousness existing') is a logical consequence of 'X is a common-sense object (a dog, hand, soap-bubble, etc.).'

Who is right in this controversy regarding a question of *logic* (broadly conceived)? Moore or Berkeley? To be precise, the question is whether Berkeley or *Moore in 1939* is right. For, as a matter of fact, Moore can be said to have believed in 1928/1929 that Berkeley is right. See the last sentence of the above quotation from Moore's 1928/1929 lecture: "It may *possibly* be true, as B. would have said, that this desk is not independent of perception."[23] But in 1939, Moore had changed his mind. Did Moore in 1939 have a better grasp of the logical grammar of English than Berkeley had in the eighteenth century? Or *vice versa?*—I rather doubt it. What we really have before us in this controversy is an utterly fundamental conceptual question that has no preformed answer whatsoever; it marks the great divide between two philosophical worlds.

NOTES

1. See Moore 1959: 145–46, and the appendix to this essay for a brief discussion of Moore's argument, with Berkeley and Kant in the vicinity.

2. See Berkeley 1965: §22–§24, §34.

3. See, for example, Husserl 1950: §47, §48, §135.

4. See the first and second of Descartes's *Meditations*. The in-principle possibility of the world of consciousness existing all by itself can be used as a premise for establishing substance dualism; see my neo-Cartesian argument in Meixner 2004.

5. The attempt to do so leads to absurdity, because it seeks to obtain a perspective for the acquisition of knowledge that is not a perspective for a conscious subject: the view from nowhere, as Thomas Nagel was to call this impossible perspective.

6. The terms 'physicalism' and 'materialism' are used as synonyms in this essay. Aside from this special, stipulated usage, the first designation is accurate in describing the modern content of the doctrine (whereas the second designation is not); the second designation is continuous with the long history of the doctrine (whereas the first designation is not).

7. In this essay, the words 'entity,' 'exist(s),' and 'existent' are taken to express, with different grammatical functions, the same content. Moreover, 'entity,' 'exist(s),' and 'existent' are stipulated to be synonymous with 'actual (or real) entity,' 'actually exist(s),' and 'actually existent.' (Note that 'actually' adds content here, and is not a mere device of emphasis.) "There exists a P," "there is an existent P," "some P exists," "some entity is (a) P," "some existent entity is (a) P"—all these sentences are taken to mean the same thing. But "something is (a) P" and "there is a P" do not necessarily prolong the list; to see this, replace "P" by the adjectival expression "merely possible" or by the corresponding substantive expression "mere *possibile*" (just as the grammar of the context of replacement requires).

8. The word 'physical'—this ambiguous word—is in this essay taken to be synonymous with 'mind-independently physical*' (where 'physical*' expresses a neutral root-sense). Accordingly, something is nonphysical if, and only if, it is not mind-independently physical*. Only in the described sense of 'physical' and 'nonphysical' can the thesis that all concrete entities are nonphysical be regarded as an adequate formulation of ontological idealism (since an ontological idealist will not hesitate to assert that a chair is a 'physical object'—meaning by this: mind-dependently physical* object).

9. Dennett 1991 can certainly be read in this way.

10. I note in passing that Berkeley corresponded with *a* Samuel Johnson, but *not* with the famous Doctor. See Berkeley 1965.

11. Not all physical* entities are physical* in the same neutral root-sense. For example, an existent *property* which is physical* is not physical* in the same sense in which an existent physical* *individual* is physical*. The large stone against which Johnson strikes his foot is an existent *individual*, and it is shown to be physical* by the fact that Johnson strikes his foot against it. Being a large stone is an existent *property*, and it is, indeed, physical*; but this property is certainly not shown to be physical* by Johnson's

striking his foot against it (one cannot strike a property). Rather, that property is existent and physical* (i.e., a physical* entity) because it is exemplified by individuals which are physical*, and exemplified solely by such individuals. (Note that exemplification is taken to require that the exemplifier is existent.)

12. Here the words 'mind' and 'consciousness' must of course be taken in their normal—mentalistic—sense. There are also specifically materialistic ways of understanding the words 'mind' and 'consciousness,' which, however, are useless for formulating the materialistic doctrine in such a way that it stands in contrast to dualism. A materialist can understand 'mind' in such a way that she can agree to the assertion "Some concrete entities are *not* mind-independently physical*." Why? "Because my current brain states, though physical* entities, do not exist in a way that is independent of every waking brain." And she can understand 'consciousness' in such a way that she can agree to the assertion "Some concrete entities are *not* such that they are physical* and could exist even if no realm of consciousness existed." Why? "Because my current brain states, though physical* entities, do not exist in such a way that they could exist even if no waking brain existed."

13. The other manner of ontological independence of *A* from *C* is this: with *C* existing, *A* might still not exist.

14. Nor does it follow that *A* cannot be a cause of *B*. But I will concentrate on the other alleged impossibility of causation, the already mentioned converse one.

15. For a closer scrutiny of principles of causal closure, see Meixner 2008 and Meixner 2009.

16. Every object is per se an entity; the converse of this per-se inclusion, however, I consider to be false. Just like the word 'entity' (cf. note 7), the word 'object' has existential import, as in fact follows (on the basis of note 7) from 'entity' being entailed by 'object.' Note that the word 'object' has a different, entirely relative sense in the expression 'intentional object (of).' Properties, for example, which are not objects, can yet be intentional objects, and so can nonentities.

17. This is rather evident in the following passage: "[Try] whether you can conceive it possible for a sound, or figure, or motion, or colour to exist without the mind or unperceived. This easy trial may perhaps make you see that what you contend for is a downright contradiction" (Berkeley 1965: 69 [§22]).

18. See Husserl 1952: §§1–18; Husserl 1950: §135. Husserl never fell into the (just-mentioned) confusion that Berkeley—and so many other ontological idealists—did not manage to stay clear of.

19. Above (in the section "The Strength of Materialism"), materialism, dualism, and ontological idealism have been formulated in such a way that

they form a complete disjunction. Hence, according to that way of formulation, there is no place for a third monism, *neutral monism*, as it is usually called. Yet the end of the previous section suggests that there is a place for neutral monism *in a manner of speaking*—not *besides* materialism, dualism, and ontological idealism, but *underlying* dualism.

20. See Meixner 2004, Meixner 2006, Meixner 2008.

21. Decision makers are distinguished from mere generators of (genuine) chance events by their (at least rudimentary) rationality.

22. If the confluence of the right causes, under the right circumstances, came about by design, it is still correct to say that the appearance of the mind property is an outcome of natural evolution, that it is, in short, natural; for only its *first*, remote cause is supernatural; its *second*, nearer causes are natural.

23. The desk is a commonsense object. Therefore, according to Moore in 1939, it follows that the desk is a mind-independent object; in other words, according to Moore in 1939, relative to the desk being a commonsense object, it is *necessary* that it be a mind-independent object. But according to Moore in 1928/1929, relative to the desk being a commonsense object, it is *possible* that it be *not* a mind-independent object.

REFERENCES

Berkeley, G. 1965. *The Principles of Human Knowledge*. In *Berkeley's Philosophical Writings*, edited by D. M. Armstrong, 41–128. New York: Collier Books.

Boswell, J. 1986. *The Life of Samuel Johnson*, edited and abridged by C. Hibbert. Harmondsworth: Penguin.

Dennett, D. C. 1991. *Consciousness Explained*. Boston: Little, Brown.

Husserl, E. 1950. *Ideen zu einer reinen Phänomenologie und phänomenologischen Philosophie [Ideas Pertaining to Pure Phenomenology . . .]*. Erstes Buch [book 1]. edited by W. Biemel. The Hague: Martinus Nijhoff.

Husserl, E. 1952. *Ideen zu einer reinen Phänomenologie und phänomenologischen Philosophie [Ideas Pertaining to Pure Phenomenology . . .]*. Zweites Buch [book 2]. edited by M. Biemel. The Hague: Martinus Nijhoff.

Kant, I. 1968. *Prolegomena zu einer jeden künftigen Metaphysik, die als Wissenschaft wird auftreten können [Prolegomena to Any Future Metaphysics . . .]*. In vol. 5 of *Werkausgabe*, edited by W. Weischedel, 109–264. Frankfurt am Main: Suhrkamp.

Meixner, U. 2004. *The Two Sides of Being: A Reassessment of Psycho-Physical Dualism*. Paderborn: Mentis.

————. 2006. "Consciousness and Freedom." In *Analytic Philosophy without Naturalism*, edited by A. Corradini, S. Galvan, and E. J. Lowe, 183–96. London: Routledge.

————. 2008. "New Perspectives for a Dualistic Conception of Mental Causation." *Journal of Consciousness Studies* 15:17–38.

————. 2009. "Three Indications for the Existence of God in Causal Metaphysics." *International Journal for Philosophy of Religion* 66:33–46.

Moore, G. E. 1959. "Proof of an External World." In Moore, *Philosophical Papers*, 127–50. London: Allen & Unwin.

————. 1966. "Are Material Things Real?" In Moore, *Lectures in Philosophy*, edited by C. Lewy, 12–19. London: Allen & Unwin.

Nagel, T. 1986. *The View from Nowhere*. New York: Oxford University Press.

2

Non-Cartesian Substance Dualism

E. J. LOWE

Non-Cartesian substance dualism is a position in the philosophy of mind concerning the nature of the mind-body relation—or, more exactly, the *person*-body relation. It maintains that this is a relationship between two distinct, but not necessary separable, individual substances, in the sense of 'individual substance' according to which this term denotes a persisting, concrete object or bearer of properties, capable of undergoing change in respect of at least some of those properties as time passes. When such an object undergoes such a change, it undergoes a change of state, for a state of an object consists in its possession of some property at a time, or during a period of time. Using a more traditional terminology, we may speak of these states as modes of the object or individual substance in question.[1] As we shall see, non-Cartesian substance dualism differs from its more familiar cousin, Cartesian substance dualism, with regard to the class of modes that it considers persons—as opposed to their bodies—to be capable of possessing. Therefore, it takes a different view concerning what kind of individual substance a person—or, more generally, a subject of experience—should be taken to be. More precisely, whereas Cartesian substance dualism takes subjects of experience to be necessarily immaterial and indeed nonphysical substances, non-Cartesian substance dualism does not insist on this. As we shall also see, this distinctive feature of non-Cartesian substance dualism gives it certain advantages over Cartesian dualism, without compelling it to forfeit any of the intuitive appeal that attaches to its more traditional rival.

1. The Self as a Psychological Substance

The view that I wish to defend in this essay is that a human person, conceived as a subject of mental states, must be regarded as a substance of which those states are modes—and yet not as a *biological* substance: not, that is, as a living organism of any kind, even though a human person's body is clearly just such an organism. What sort of substance, then? Quite simply, a psychological substance. More specifically, a person, in my view, is a substantial individual belonging to a natural kind which is governed by distinctively psychological laws, with the consequence that individuals of this kind possess persistence conditions which are likewise distinctively psychological in character. However, saying just this about persons is consistent with regarding a person as being something like a Cartesian ego or soul—and this is a position from which I expressly wish to distance myself. The distinctive feature of the Cartesian conception of a psychological substance is that such a substance is regarded as possessing *only* mental characteristics, not physical ones. And this is largely why it is vulnerable to certain skeptical arguments to be found in the writings of numerous philosophers during the past three hundred years, including Locke and Kant. The burden of those arguments is that if psychological substances—by which the proponents of the arguments mean immaterial 'souls' or 'spirits'—are the real subjects of mental states, then for all I know the substance having 'my' thoughts today is not numerically identical with the substance that had 'my' thoughts yesterday. The lesson of this is taken to be that—on pain of having to countenance the possibility that my existence is very much more ephemeral than I care to believe—I had better not identify *myself* with the psychological substance, if any, that is currently having 'my' thoughts, or currently 'doing the thinking in me.' But if *I* am

not a psychological substance, then it seems gratuitous even to suppose that such substances exist. Certainly, their existence cannot be
established by the Cartesian cogito.

But why should we suppose, with Descartes, that psychological
substances must be essentially immaterial? Descartes believed this
because he held a conception of substance according to which each
distinct kind of substance has only one principal 'attribute,' which is
peculiar to substances of that kind, such that all of the states of any
individual substance of this kind are modes of this unique and exclusive attribute.[2] In the case of psychological or mental substances, the
attribute is supposed to be thought, whereas in the case of physical or
material substances, the attribute is supposed to be extension. On
this view, no psychological substance can possess a mode of extension, nor any physical substance a mode of thought. However, I am
aware of no good argument, advanced either by Descartes himself or
by anyone else, in support of his doctrine of unique and exclusive attributes. Accordingly, I am perfectly ready to allow that psychological substances should possess material characteristics—that is, that
they should include physical states among their modes. It may be
that there is no material characteristic which an individual psychological substance possesses essentially, in the sense that its persistence conditions preclude its surviving the loss of this characteristic.
But this does not, of course, imply that an individual psychological
substance essentially possesses *no* material characteristics: indeed, to
suppose that it did imply this would be to commit a 'quantifier shift
fallacy' of such a blatant kind that I am loath to accuse Descartes
himself of falling prey to it.

How, though, does this repudiation of the Cartesian conception of a psychological substance help against the skeptical arguments mentioned a moment ago? Well, the main reason why those
arguments seem to get any purchase is, I think, that in presupposing that psychological substances would have to be wholly nonphysical, they are able to take it for granted that such substances are not
possible objects of ordinary sense perception. Such arguments represent psychological substances as being invisible and intangible
and, as such, perceptible, at best, only by some mysterious faculty of
introspection—and hence only by each such substance in respect of
itself. But once it is allowed that psychological substances have quite

familiar physical characteristics and can thus be seen and touched at least as 'directly' as any ordinary physical thing, the suggestion that we might be unable to detect a rapid exchange of these substances becomes as fanciful as the skeptical suggestion that the table on which I am now writing might 'in reality' be a succession of different but very short-lived tables successively replacing one another undetectably. Whether one can conclusively refute such skepticism may be an open question, but I see no reason to take it seriously or to allow it to influence our choice of ontological categories.

I believe, then, that a perfectly tenable conception of psychological substance may be developed which permits us to regard such substances as being the subjects of mental states: which is just to say that nothing stands in the way of our regarding persons precisely as being psychological substances. The detailed development of such a conception is the topic of the remaining sections of this essay, and for the time being it must suffice to say that I conceive of psychological substances as being the proper subject-matter of the science of psychology, which in turn I conceive to be an autonomous science whose laws are not reducible to those of biology or chemistry or physics. However, it will be appropriate to close the present section with some remarks on the relationship between psychological and biological substances, that is, between persons and their bodies. I restrict myself here, thus, to the case of persons who—like human persons—have animal bodies.

With regard to this issue I am, as I indicated at the outset, a *substantial dualist*. Persons are substances, as are their bodies. But the two are not identical substances, for persons and bodies have different persistence conditions, just as do persons' bodies and the masses of matter constituting those bodies at different times. I should perhaps emphasize here that where a person's body is a biological substance, as in the case of human persons, the body is to be conceived of as a living organism, not as a mere mass of matter or assemblage of physical particles. Clearly, though, my version of substance dualism is quite different from Descartes's. Descartes, it seems, conceived a human being to be the product of a 'substantial union' of two distinct substances: a mental but immaterial substance and a material but nonmental substance. How such a union was possible perplexed him and every subsequent philosopher who endeavored to understand it. The chief stumbling block was, once again, Descartes's doctrine of unique and exclusive attributes. How could something essentially immaterial be 'united' with something essentially material? But psychological substances as I conceive of them are *not* essentially immaterial. Moreover, on my view, human persons are themselves just such psychological substances, rather than being a queer hybrid of two radically alien substances. I should perhaps stress, though, that my criticism of Descartes here pertains solely to his doctrine of 'substantial union' and not to his conception of psychophysical causation, which I consider to be far more defensible.[3]

So, as far as the relationship between a person and his body is concerned, I do not see that this need be considered more mysterious in principle than any of the other intersubstantial relationships with which the natural sciences are faced: for instance, the relationship between a biological entity, such as a tree, and the assemblage of physical particles that constitutes it at any given time. Most decidedly, I do not wish to minimize the scientific and metaphysical difficulties involved here. I do not, for example, think that it would be correct to say that a person is 'constituted' by her body in anything like the sense in which a tree is 'constituted' by an assemblage of physical particles.[4] Nonetheless, it is my hope that by adopting a broadly Aristotelian conception of substance and by emphasizing not only the autonomy but also the continuity of the special sciences, including psychology and biology, we may see a coherent picture begin to emerge of persons as a wholly distinctive kind of being fully integrated into the natural world: a picture which simultaneously preserves the 'Lockean' insight that the concept of a person is fundamentally a psychological as opposed to a biological one, the 'Cartesian' insight that persons are a distinctive kind of substantial particulars in their own right, and the 'Aristotelian' insight that persons are not essentially immaterial beings.

2. The Self as a Bearer of Physical Characteristics

Let us recall that we are not required to deny that a person or self has physical characteristics and recall that, although we have to regard it as being *distinct* from its body, we are not required to think of the two as separable—except, perhaps, purely conceptually, or purely in imagination. But what physical characteristics can we allow the embodied self to possess? All of those physical characteristics that are also ascribable to its body? Or only some of these? Or some or all of these plus others that are not ascribable to its body? What we need at this point, above all, is a principled way of distinguishing between those statements of the form 'I am *F*'—where '*F*' is a physical predicate—which are more properly analyzed as 'I have a body which is *F*,' and those which can be accepted at their face value as being literally true. And here it may help us to consider whether or not the self is a *simple* substance—that is, whether or not it has parts. For if it does not, then no statement of the form 'I am *F*' can be taken at face value if being *F* implies having parts. My own view is that the self is indeed a simple substance, and I shall argue for this later.

But does not *every* physical predicate imply divisibility into parts, as Descartes held—this being the basis of one of his main arguments for the immateriality of the self? No, it does not. For instance, 'has a mass of seventy kilograms' does not imply having parts. A self could, thus, strictly and literally have a mass of seventy kilograms without it following logically that it possessed various parts with masses of less than that amount. After all, an electron has a finite rest mass, but it does not, according to current physical theory, have parts possessing fractions of that rest mass. Again, 'is six feet tall' does not, I consider, imply having parts, in the relevant sense of 'part.' The relevant sense of 'part' is this: something is to be accounted a 'part' of a substance in this sense only if that thing is itself a substance. We may call such a part a 'substantial part.' Simple substances have no substantial parts. We must, then, distinguish between a substantial part of a thing and a merely spatial part of it. A spatial part of an extended object is simply some geometrically defined 'section' of it—not literally a section, in the sense of something cut out from it, but merely a region of it defined by certain purely geometrical boundaries. Thus, for example, the left-hand third of my desk as it faces me is a spatial part of it. It is doubtless the case that there is also a substantial part of my desk which at present coincides exactly with that spatial part—namely, the mass of wood contained within that region. But it would be a category mistake to identify that mass of wood with the left-hand third of my desk.[5] Now, 'is six feet tall' certainly implies having spatial parts, but it does not imply having substantial parts. Extended things—the claims of Descartes and Leibniz notwithstanding—*can* be simple substances.

So far, then, I can allow that physical statements such as 'I weigh seventy kilograms' and 'I am six feet tall' may be taken at their face value. But a statement like 'I am composed of organic molecules' *cannot* be so taken, but must be analysed rather as 'I have a body which is composed of organic molecules.' Even so, it is surely evident that if 'I weigh seventy kilograms' is literally true of me, it will be so only in virtue of the fact that I have a body which weighs seventy kilograms. And, indeed, it seems clear that all of the purely physical characteristics which are literally ascribable to the self will be thus ascribable in virtue of their being ascribable to the self's body—so that we can say that the self's purely physical characteristics 'supervene' upon those of its body.

But what, now, *is* it for the self to 'have' a certain body as 'its' body? Partly, it *is* just a matter of that self having certain physical characteristics which supervene upon those of *that* body rather than any other—although it is clear that this fact must be derivative from some more fundamental relationship. More than that, then, it must clearly also be a matter of the self's perceiving and acting 'through' that body: and this indeed must be the crucial factor which determines *which* body's physical characteristics belong also to a given self. But what *is* it to perceive and act 'through' a certain body rather than any other? As far as agency is concerned, this is a matter of certain parts of that body being directly subject to the agent's—that is, the self's—will: I can, of necessity, move certain parts of *my* body 'at will' and cannot move 'at will' any part of any body that is not part of mine.[6] Here it may be conceded that someone who is completely paralyzed may still possess a certain body, although only because he *could* once move parts of it 'at will' and still perceives through it. But someone who was completely paralyzed from birth—if such a condition is even possible—could only in a more attenuated sense be said to 'have' a body. So much for agency. As far as perception is concerned, apart from the obvious point that one perceives the world from the position at which one's body is located—except under abnormal circumstances, as when one looks through a periscope—it may be remarked that a person perceives her own body in a different manner from how she perceives others' bodies in that her sensations of it are phenomenologically localized in the parts perceived. For example, when one feels one's foot, one locates that feeling in the foot, whereas when one feels a wall, one does not locate that feeling in the wall.

Now it is true that in a less interesting sense all action and perception is 'through' a certain body, namely, in the sense that as an empirically ascertainable matter of fact I need my limbs to move and my eyes to see. But *these* facts do not as such serve to qualify my limbs and eyes as especially *mine*, that is, as parts of *my* body. For, of course, I can be fitted with various prosthetic devices for locomotion and vision, and yet these do not *thereby* become parts of my body, although they *may* do so if they enter into the more intimate relationships discussed a moment ago. What makes my body peculiarly mine, then, is not determined merely by the empirically ascertainable dependencies that obtain between its proper functioning and my ability to engage in perception and agency. Thus, for example, even though it turns out that I need a brain in order to be able to think, it does not follow that this relationship suffices to make that brain peculiarly mine. In fact, I should say that a certain brain qualifies as mine only derivatively, in virtue of being the brain belonging to *my* body, where the latter qualifies as mine in virtue of having parts related to me in the more intimate ways mentioned earlier. As far as these more intimate relationships are concerned, however, my brain is as alien to me as a stone or a chair.

My thoughts, feelings, intentions, desires, and so forth all belong properly to *me*, not to my body, and are to be associated with my body only in virtue of those intimate relationships which make it peculiarly mine. It is impossible to associate such mental states with a body non-derivatively, that is, without relying upon their ascription to the self or person whose body it is—or so I would claim. No mere examination of brain function or physical movement can warrant such an association, without a detour through a recognition of the

. existence of a self or person to whom the body belongs. This recognition, in interpersonal cases, will naturally have to issue from empirical evidence—but it will be evidence of *embodied selfhood* in the first instance, not directly and independently of particular mental goings-on.

3. THE SELF AS A SIMPLE SUBSTANCE

But what now of my crucial claim that the self is simple, or lacks substantial parts? Well, what substantial parts *could* it have, given that the self is not to be identified with the body? Parts of the body cannot be parts of the self. If the self and the body had exactly the same parts, then they would apparently have to be identical substances after all. Certainly, standard mereological theory would imply this.[7] Similarly, if it were urged that all and only parts of the brain, say, are parts of the self, this would imply that self and brain are identical. So I conclude that the self can have none of the body's parts as parts of itself, unless perhaps the self could have other substantial entities in addition to bodily parts as parts of itself.

However, no other substantial entity does appear to be a tenable candidate for being a substantial part of the self, whether or not in addition to bodily parts. For instance, the self patently does not consist of a plurality of lesser 'selves' acting cooperatively, despite the picturesque 'homuncular' descriptions of mental functioning advanced by some philosophers.[8] Such descriptions are not intelligible if taken literally. Similarly, we should not take literally talk of 'corporate persons,' that is, the idea that institutions like clubs and firms are genuinely persons in their own right.[9] At neither level—neither the subpersonal nor the suprapersonal—does the concept of a person find anything other than merely metaphorical application. Nor should we regard the mind's various 'faculties'—will, intellect, and appetite, or modern variants of these, such as linguistic or visual information-processing 'modules'—as being 'parts' of the self. For, in the first place, it is a mistake to reify such mental faculties or modules, and, in any case, they certainly could not qualify as *substantial* parts, which are what are now at issue. Mental faculties or modules, unlike sub-

stances, enjoy no possibility of an independent existence, and talk of
them should be interpreted as referring to nothing more than certain
abstractions from the overall psychology of a person. Thus, for instance, the notion of a will without an intellect, or of a language
module in the absence of belief and desire, is just plain nonsense.
Finally, it will not do to speak of the self's psychological states and
processes themselves—its beliefs, intentions, experiences, and so
forth—as being 'parts,' much less as being substantial parts, of it. For
this would at best be at all appropriate only on a Humean construc-
tivist view of the self—the so-called bundle theory—which I reject
entirely as incoherent. I conclude, therefore, that if the self is a substance, then it must indeed be a simple substance, entirely lacking
substantial parts.[10]

The simplicity of the self goes some way towards explaining its
unity, including the unity of consciousness that characterizes its normal condition. Where this unity threatens to break down—as in
various clinical conditions such as those of so-called multiple personality, schizophrenia, brain bisection, and so on—we are indeed inclined to speak of a plurality of selves, or of divided selves. But I
think, in fact, that such talk should again not be taken literally, and
that the psychological unity that most fundamentally characterizes
the self is not merely to be located at the level of consciousness. A
divided consciousness is, I think, in principle consistent with self-
identity: what is not consistent with this is a radical disunity of
beliefs and values, manifested in a radical inconsistency of thought
and action. Of course, we all display mild inconsistencies, but no one
person could intelligibly be interpreted as possessing the incompati-
bilities of belief and value that typically characterize two different
persons. Now, a *complex* entity can act in disunified ways because the
various incompatible or conflicting activities can be referred to different parts of that entity. Thus a corporate entity such as a firm or a
club can act inconsistently because its members may act in conflicting ways. But the actions of the self—those that are truly predicable
of *it*, because they are genuinely intentional, and not merely of *the
body*, such as so-called reflex actions—cannot in this way be ascribed
to different elements or parts within the self. So we see that the simplicity and the unity of the self are indeed intimately related, even

though there must clearly be much more to the matter than these brief remarks reveal.[11]

Another consequence of the simplicity of the self is this. If the self is a simple substance, then it appears that there can be no diachronic criterion of identity which grounds its persistence through time.[12] This is not to say that there may not be some *cause* of its persistence. It may well be, thus, that the continued normal functioning of the brain is a causally necessary condition of the persistence of the self, at least in the case of embodied, human persons. But it would not follow from this that the identity of the self over time is *grounded* in continuity of brain function, or indeed anything else. Nor should we think it contrary to the self's status as a substance that its existence may be thus causally dependent upon the functioning of another, distinct substance—the brain or, more generally, the body. No tenable account of substance can insist that a true substance must be causally independent of all other substances. For instance, a tree provides as clear an example of a substantial entity as anyone could wish for— and yet, of course, a tree's continuing existence depends upon the maintenance of a delicate balance of forces in nature, both within it and between it and its environment. However, a tree is a *complex* substance, and accordingly its persistence can be understood as being grounded in the preservation of certain relationships between its substantial parts, despite the gradual replacement of those parts through natural processes of metabolism and growth. Not so with a self, any more than with, say, an electron or other 'fundamental' particle. Thus the reason why the self—or indeed any simple substance— cannot be provided with a criterion of diachronic identity is that such a criterion, in the case of a substance or 'continuant,' always makes reference to the substance's constituent parts, of which simple substances have none.[13]

That the diachronic identity of simple substances, including the self, is primitive or ungrounded should not be seen as making their persistence over time somehow mysterious or inscrutable. For, in the first place, as I have already remarked, it does not preclude us from recognizing the involvement of various causal factors in their persistence. Secondly, we can still concede—or indeed, better, insist—that there are certain necessary constraints on the possible history of a simple substance of any given kind: that is to say, limits on the sorts of changes that it can intelligibly be said to undergo, or limits arising from empirically discoverable natural laws governing substances of this kind. Thus in the case of the self, a possible history must have a certain internal coherence to be intelligible, not least because perception and action are possible only within a temporal framework that includes both forward- and backward-looking mental states—intention and memory. Finally, the persistence of at least some simple substances is, I consider, presumed at the very heart of our understanding of time and change in general, so that we should not expect to be able to give an exhaustive or reductive account of all such persistence.[14] Indeed, since the only simple substances *directly* known to us, without benefit of scientific speculation and experimentation, are precisely ourselves, I would urge that the pretheoretical intelligibility of time and change that is presupposed by all scientific theorizing actually rests upon our acquaintance with ourselves as simple persisting substances. So, although in the *ontological* order of nature it may well be the primitive persistence of fundamental physical particles which underpins objective time-order—in other words, which makes the world *one* world in time—still, in the *conceptual* order of thought it is the persistence of the self that underpins our very grasp of the notion of objective time-order. If this is indeed so, then it would clearly be futile to expect the concept of the self to reveal upon analysis an account of the self's identity over time which did not implicitly presume the very thing in question.

A consequence of the ungroundedness of the self's identity over time is that there is, and can be, no definitive condition that necessarily determines the ceasing-to-be or, indeed, the coming-to-be of a self. In the case of complex substances, which are governed by clearly specifiable criteria of identity, the conditions for substantial change—that is, for their coming- or ceasing-to-be—can be stated fairly exactly, even though these conditions may in some cases be infected by some degree of vagueness. But not so with simple substances. And this is not, with them, a matter of vagueness at all—not, at least, in the sense in which 'vagueness' implies the existence of 'fuzzy' boundaries, whose 'fuzziness' may be measured in degrees. This observation certainly seems to apply in the realm of fundamental particle physics, as far as I can judge. Thus if, in a particle interaction, an electron collides with an atomic nucleus and various fission products arise, including a number of electrons, it would seem that there may be no determinate 'fact of the matter' as to whether the original electron is, or is not, identical with a given one of the electrons emerging from the impact event. There is here, it would seem, a genuine indeterminateness—I prefer not to say *vagueness*—of identity.[15] But this should not lead us to view with suspicion the idea that electrons do genuinely persist identically through time. Note, too, that known constraints on the possible history of an electron *may* enable us to rule out *some* re-identifications as impossible in a case such as that described—so that the indeterminacy is not totally unconstrained, which would be bizarre indeed. However, the point is that, even when all such constraints are taken into account, there may still be a residual indeterminacy in a given case.

Returning to the self, we see, thus, that while we may well think that we have good scientific grounds for believing that the functioning of the brain is *causally* necessary for the continued existence of the self, nonetheless, in the nature of the case, such evidence as we possess for this is bound to be inconclusive—and not just for the reason that all empirical evidence is defeasible—since we lack any reductive analysis of what would constitute the ceasing-to-be of a self. Lacking such an analysis, we cannot really say what empirical evidence would or would not support a claim that a self had definitely ceased to be. This is why the prospects for life after bodily death must inevitably remain imponderable and unamenable to decisive empirical determination.

Against this it may be urged that, since I have insisted that perception and agency are essential to selfhood, I must allow that the cessation of these *would* constitute a decisive terminus for the self's existence. However, it is the *capacity* for perception and agency that is essential, not its perpetual *exercise*. Very well, so can we not say that the demise of this capacity—and certainly its *permanent* demise—would constitute the demise of the self? But the trouble is that saying this is not really informative. For what would *constitute* the permanent demise of this capacity? Only, as far as I can see, the very demise of the self—in other words, no genuinely *noncircular* answer to the question can be provided. It will not do to say that the permanent cessation of brain function would constitute the demise of the capacity for perception and agency. For the most that we can really say is that there seems to be an empirical correlation between mental activity and brain function, at least in the case of human persons. But the capacity for perception and agency does not by its very nature reside in any sort of cerebral condition. Indeed, there is nothing whatever unintelligible about supposing the existence of a capacity for perception and agency in a being entirely lacking a brain.

4. PHYSICALISM, NATURALISM, AND THE SELF

Here it may be asked: is physiological psychology, or neuropsychology, simply a contradiction in terms, then—because psychology has, in essence, nothing to do with the brain as such? Not at all, so long as this branch of science is simply seen as telling us various empirical facts about the condition of embodied human persons or selves—that is, as telling us what sorts of processes, as a matter of fact, go on in their brains and nervous systems when they think or feel or act. This is not, however, and cannot be, an account of what *constitutes* thought or feeling or agency in a human person. Thought can no more *be*, or be constituted by, a brain process than a chair can *be*, or be constituted by, a set of prime numbers.[16] Nor should we be tempted into saying such things as that brain processes may 'realize' episodes of thinking, as more cautious modern physicalists sometimes put it—for what, really, is this supposed to mean?

In answer to this last question, it will perhaps be said that what it means to say that brain processes 'realize' thought episodes is that thought episodes *supervene* upon brain processes, at least in the case of human persons. But saying this sheds no real illumination either, for the notion of supervenience—however useful it may be in some contexts—is entirely out of its depth here. Suppose we ask what it means to say that thought episodes supervene upon brain processes. We shall be told, perhaps, that what this means is that if A and B are two human persons who share type-identical brain states at any given time—that is, whose brain structures are atom-for-atom, neuron-for-neuron, indistinguishable at that time, with all of these neurons in identical states of excitation—then A and B must be enjoying type-identical thought episodes at that time. Perhaps it will be conceded that A's and B's thought episodes need not be identical in content—if Putnam and Burge's verdicts regarding so-called Twin-Earth cases are accepted[17]—but it may nonetheless be insisted that their thought episodes must be subjectively indistinguishable, whatever that may be exactly taken to mean. However, the empirical status of this sort of claim—and, presumably, it cannot be advertised as being anything more than a merely empirical claim, since it can have no a priori justification—is highly problematic, as I shall now try to explain.

Let us, first of all, be clear that the thesis being advanced must be that thought episodes supervene globally or holistically—rather than just piecemeal—upon brain processes. For it is evident that, to the extent that thought is dependent on the brain, it can be so only in a holistic way which will not permit us to make any empirically confirmable claims about individual dependencies between particular or 'token' thought episodes and particular or 'token' brain events and processes.[18] So the thesis must be that a person with a brain *exactly replicating mine* at a level of neuronal organization and excitation will enjoy a mental life—feelings, beliefs, memories, and so on—indistinguishable from mine, but *not* that any partial replication would necessarily engender any corresponding partial similarity in mental life. Nothing short of whole-brain replication will do. But what we now need to ask is this: what causal constraints would there be upon the process of bringing two distinct brains into such a state of exact neural replication? It is irrelevant to point out that one might, in some sense, be able to imagine this being done, perhaps instantaneously, by means of a machine that we rather question-beggingly call a 'brain replicator.' In this imaginary scenario, I walk in through one door of the machine, the operator throws the switch, and then I and my doppelgänger walk out through another door. One might as well say that the trick could be performed by magic. So too might pigs fly. But in fact it seems clear that there is simply no non-miraculous way in which this feat could be achieved. It would not even suffice, for instance, to take identical twins from the moment of

conception and attempt to submit them to exactly similar environmental and social stimuli. For, first of all, the growth of nerve cells
involves a good deal of randomness,[19] and secondly, it seems likely
that brains, at the relevant level of organization, constitute a class of
so-called chaotic systems.[20] Thus, it could be that because the twins
are subjected to minutely different influences for brief periods during
their early development—as is effectively unavoidable—neural connections end up getting laid down in quite different ways in the two
brains. The more that one reflects on the matter, I suggest, the more
evident it should become that the whole idea of bringing two different human brains into identical neural states is so completely fanciful that it merits no place in serious philosophical inquiry.[21]

It will not do for the physicalist to protest here that all that he is
interested in or committed to is the bare conceptual possibility of
such whole-brain replication: for even if one can really make sense of
this notion, what is one supposed to do with it? Precisely because the
notion of such replication is the stuff of pure fantasy, utterly beyond
the realm of scientific possibility, it cannot be conjoined with any
genuine scientific findings from neuropsychology in order to yield a
verdict on the truth or falsehood of the supervenience thesis. Nor can
we justify such a verdict by consulting our 'intuitions' regarding the
upshot of the imagined replication experiment—for we are simply
not entitled to any 'intuitions' about the matter, and any that we do
have we probably owe simply to our own prejudices. So my conclusion is that even if the supervenience thesis is coherently statable—
and even this may be in question—we can have no possible basis,
either empirical or a priori, for judging it to be true.

Now, however, it may be objected that this rejection of physicalism even in the comparatively weak form of the supervenience thesis
is unacceptably at odds with a 'naturalistic' view of human beings
and their minds. The emergence of the human mind, it may be said,
must be recognized as being a result of evolutionary processes working upon the genetic makeup of animal life-forms, through wholly
biochemical means. Hence, it may be concluded, a biological account
of human mentality is inescapable if one has any pretense to being
'scientific.' There cannot—so it will be said—be anything more to
thought than can be exhaustively explained in biochemical terms, for

otherwise the emergence of mind seems to be an inexplicable freak or accident. But, again, this is an objection which just reflects a dogmatic prejudice. Indeed, it is thoroughly question-begging and circular. It is just assumed from the outset that any wholly adequate explanation of the *emergence* of mind must be purely biological in character, because it is already presupposed that mind or mentality is a wholly biological characteristic of biological entities—animal life-forms. But the whole burden of my position is precisely that the mind is *not* a biological phenomenon and that mentality is *not* a property of the biological entities which constitute human bodies. That such entities should be apt to embody selves or persons can, indeed, be no accident—but why presume that the evolution of such bodies or organisms is to be explained in exclusively biochemical terms? It is the *environment* of organisms that determines the evolutionary pressures on them to adapt and change: but the 'environment,' in the present instance, cannot necessarily be specified in wholly physical and biochemical terms. All that can be said is that the *proximate* causes of genetic mutation are biochemical, as are the *proximate* causal factors favoring selection. But these causal factors are themselves effects of other causes—and the chain of causation can easily take us beyond the biochemical sphere. After all, we know that minds can affect the evolution of organisms, for the intelligent activities of human beings have done so within historical time. So there is nothing miraculous or non-naturalistic in the idea that the evolution of mind and that of body are mutually interactive, just as, on my view, individual minds and bodies are themselves mutually interactive. Thus, my answer to the 'evolutionary' objection is that, unless it is presumed, quite unwarrantably, that the mental must be biologically based in order to contribute to the environmental selective pressures on organisms, it cannot be held that a nonbiological view of the mental such as mine is in any way in conflict with evolutionary theory.

But we need not take a purely defensive stance on this issue. It is worth remarking that archaeological evidence points to the occurrence of a fundamental intellectual transition in the human race some 35,000 or so years ago, not apparently connected with any very radical biological or neurological development in the human organism.[22] This was a rather sudden transition from a markedly primitive sociocultural condition—which had endured virtually unaltered for many millennia and in which human creativity was limited to the production of the most rudimentary and severely practical tools—to a condition recognizably akin to our own, with the flourishing of visual and plastic arts reflective of a sophisticated aesthetic sensibility. The development of this condition, we may reasonably suppose, went hand in hand with that of true language, systems of religious thought, and the beginnings of political structures. At the root of these developments, it seems, was the emergence of genuine systems of representation, without which the sophisticated level of thought, communication, and social structure essential for personal existence as we know it would be impossible. Now, as I say, it seems likely that these developments were not the upshot of any radical change in human brain structure or neural processing capacity, but arose rather through concomitant changes in patterns of social interaction and organization.[23] And, indeed, we can observe essentially the same phenomenon in microcosm today in the education and socialization of human infants—who, unless they are subjected to appropriate social, cultural, and linguistic stimuli at an early age, are doomed never to develop a truly human personality and character. The implication of all this, I suggest, is that selves or persons are not, in essence, created through *biological* processes but rather by means of sociocultural forces, that is, through the cooperative efforts of other selves or persons. Quite literally, *persons* create other persons.

The picture that I am sketching of self-creation and the evolution of human personality is, I believe, not at all fanciful or 'unscientific.' On the contrary, what seems utterly fanciful and facile is the biological reductionism that we see so forcefully promoted by many philosophers today.[24] When we reflect on how much we depend for our human condition upon the artificial and social environment that we ourselves have created, it seems quite incredible to suppose that one could hope to explain the human condition as having a basis solely in the organization of the human brain. Indeed, where human brain development and structure do differ significantly from those of the higher primates, such as chimpanzees—for instance, in connection with our respective linguistic capacities—it seems proper to regard the difference as being at least as much a product as a cause of the different lifestyles of human beings and primates. For, of course, the neural structures in these distinctive parts of the human brain develop in human infants only in response to the right sorts of educative and social influences. It is true that a chimpanzee cannot, by being treated from birth like a human child, be made to develop in the way that the latter does, and this seems to indicate some innate biological difference between them. But we cannot assume that what we possess and the chimpanzees lack is some innate propensity specifically to develop human personality, language use, aesthetic appreciation, mathematical abilities, and so forth. For it may be that what prevents the chimpanzees from benefiting by our human processes of socialization and personality-creation is not an innate incapacity to acquire the abilities which these processes confer upon us, but rather just an incapacity to engage appropriately with these particular processes, geared as they are to specifically human needs and characteristics. After all, a human being could probably never learn to swim if it had to take lessons from dolphins! But this doesn't show, of course, that it is impossible for human beings to acquire a capacity to swim—only that the acquisition process must be one that is geared to distinctively human limitations. Similarly, then, it is not altogether inconceivable that chimpanzees could be successfully subjected to processes of personality-creation analogous to our own, if processes appropriately tailored to their particular limitations could be discovered and exploited for that purpose.[25] In partial confirmation of this, it is worth noting that, whatever one makes of the various attempts to teach chimpanzees the genuine use of language, it is clear that those attempts began to look successful only when they took into account the fact that chimpanzees have severely restricted capacities for vocalization, and substituted sign language for speech.[26]

Perhaps the following analogy will help to convey the general sense of my proposal. A potter takes a lump of clay—which has, as such, no special propensity to be formed into any particular type of artifact, such as a statue or a vase, even though it is *suitable* material for such a purpose, in a way that a bunch of feathers, for example, would not be—and he forms it, let us suppose, into a vase. In creating the vase, he has created a new substantial individual which is distinct from, although at the same time embodied in, the lump of clay. In a

somewhat similar manner, I suggest, human persons acting cooperatively take the biological 'clay' of their children and 'shape' it into
new persons. And this 'clay'—although, of course, it has to be *suited*
to the 'shaping' processes applied to it—need not be thought of as
having any special propensity to receive just such a 'shape.' Finally—
to complete the analogy—the human person emerging from this
'shaping' process is a new substantial individual which is distinct
from, although embodied in, the biological entity that is the 'clay.' It
is no accident, surely, that it is precisely this metaphor for the creation of persons that we find so often in religious and mythic literature.

Notice, furthermore, one other aspect of the analogy that is particularly apt: what constitutes 'suitable' material for formation into
an artifact of any given type is not purely a function of the inherent
properties of that material together with the nature of the type of artifact in question, but also a function of the sorts of creative processes
that the artificer is equipped to apply to the material. Clay is a suitable material to make into vases as far as *human* artificers are concerned, but only because human beings have hands with which they
can shape the clay. However, it should also be remarked that many
processes of artifact creation can be facilitated through—and, indeed,
are sometimes made possible only by—the use of previously created
artifacts, such as, for example, the potter's wheel. In an analogous
manner, then, what makes *human* biological material 'suitable' for the
creation of persons is not just a function of the inherent biological
characteristics of that material together with the nature of the psychological capacities which need to be conferred, but also a function
of the creative processes available to us given our own particular
limitations—although, indeed, some of these limitations may be pro-
gressively transcended through the exploitation of previous products of our own creativity, that is, through the exploitation of our
growing sociocultural, linguistic, and technological heritage.

I should perhaps stress, in conclusion, that what I have just been
developing is only an analogy: I do not want to suggest that persons
literally *are* artifacts, other than in the very liberal sense that they are
products of personal creativity. Above all, unlike material artifacts,
persons or selves are *simple* substances: parts of their bodies are not

parts of *them*, as bits of clay are parts of a vase. Moreover, whereas it is plausible to hold that all of a vase's intrinsic properties supervene upon certain properties of its constituent clay, it is not, as we have seen, reasonable to regard the self's psychological properties as supervening upon any properties of its body, such as neurophysiological properties of its brain. As Joseph Butler, the famous Bishop of Durham, might have said, *the self is what it is, and not another thing.*

NOTES

1. For more on the ontology of substance and mode, see Lowe 2006.

2. See Descartes, *Principles*, part 1, §53.

3. See further Lowe 1992 (repr. 2003).

4. For criticism of this suggestion, see Lowe 1989a: 119–20. The view in question is, notably, advanced by Baker (2000).

5. For further discussion of these issues, see Lowe 1998, chs. 5 and 7.

6. In another terminology, we may say that movements of certain parts of its own body can necessarily be executed as 'basic' actions by the self. The locus classicus for the notion of a 'basic' action is Danto 1965.

7. See, e.g., Goodman 1977: 33–40. Standard mereological theory is possibly wrong on this score, if it is correct, as I myself believe, to differentiate between a tree, for example, and the mass of wood which temporarily composes it—for these may seem to have the same parts, at least during the period in which the one composes the other. However, while the tree and the wood arguably have the same *spatial* parts, it is much more debatable whether they have the same *substantial* parts. For instance, a certain root will be a substantial part of the *tree*, but hardly of the wood composing the tree. By contrast, a substantial part of the wood composing the tree arguably *is* also a substantial part of the tree. The issue is a complex one, which I cannot go into in further depth here. But, in any case, I think it independently reasonable to deny that substantial parts of the body are literally parts of the self—and I do not think of the body as in any sense *composing* the self.

8. See, e.g., Dennett 1979: 122–24.

9. See, e.g., Scruton 1989.

10. For a much fuller exposition and defense of this view, see Lowe 2001.

11. I say much more about such matters in Lowe 2005a.

12. For more general discussion of persistence and criteria of identity, see Lowe 1998: ch. 5 and also Lowe 1989b.

13. See further Lowe 1998: chs. 5 and 7.

14. Ibid.

15. A sizable literature related to this issue has grown out of Evans 1978, although this is no place for me to attempt to engage with it. I discuss the electron case more fully and challenge Evans's argument against indeterminate identity in Lowe 1994. See also Lowe 1998: 63–69 and Lowe 2005b.

16. Compare Geach 1979: 134.

17. See, especially, Burge 1979.

18. This appears to be an inescapable implication of Donald Davidson's well-known thesis of the 'holism of the mental,' for which see Davidson 1980: 217. I do not, however, accept Davidson's own view of the relations between mental and physical events, which is a 'token-token' identity theory. See further Lowe 1989a: 113–14, 132–33.

19. See further Edelman 1989: 33–37.

20. See, e.g., Crutchfield et al. 1986: 38–49 and Goldberger et al. 1990: 34–41.

21. It has also been pointed out that if quantum states of the brain have to be taken into account (as they will be if mental states are at all dependent on them), then exact duplication at the relevant level of organization will be ruled out by quantum mechanical principles. See Penrose 1989: 270.

22. See White 1989 and 1982. See also the essays by White and others in Mellars and Stringer 1989, especially section 2.

23. This would be consistent with much of the recent work of psychologists, anthropologists, and ethologists presented in Byrne and Whiten 1988.

24. My opposition extends even to the most sophisticated modern proponents of the biological approach, such as Ruth G. Millikan: see Millikan 1984. However, a detailed critique must await another occasion.

25. I should remark, incidentally, that I by no means wish to deny mentality to chimpanzees and other higher primates, although I very much doubt whether any such animal may be said to possess or embody a 'self,' as I would define that term—for, as I understand it, a 'self' is a being capable of rational thought and conscious self-reflection. Thus, inasmuch as mental states necessarily attach to psychological subjects which are not to be identified with their biological bodies, I am committed to the view that persons or selves are not the only species of psychological substance, and that—in an older terminology—there are 'animal souls' which find a place 'below' ourselves in a hierarchy of psychological substances. I hope to discuss this issue more fully elsewhere.

26. See, e.g., Linden 1976.

REFERENCES

Baker, Lynne Rudder. 2000. *Persons and Bodies: A Constitution View.* Cambridge: Cambridge University Press.

Burge, Tyler. 1979. "Individualism and the Mental." *Midwest Studies in Philosophy* 4:73–121.

Byrne, Richard, and Andrew Whiten, eds. 1988. *Machiavellian Intelligence: Social Expertise and the Evolution of Intellect in Monkeys, Apes, and Humans.* Oxford: Clarendon.

Crutchfield, James P., et al. 1986. "Chaos." *Scientific American* 255:38–49.

Danto, Arthur C. 1965. "Basic Actions." *American Philosophical Quarterly* 2:141–48.

Davidson, Donald. 1980. *Essays on Actions and Events.* Oxford: Clarendon.

Dennett, Daniel C. 1979. *Brainstorms: Philosophical Essays on Mind and Psychology.* Hassocks: Harvester Press.

Descartes, René. 1984. *Principles of Philosophy.* In *The Philosophical Writings of Descartes*, translated by John Cottingham, Robert Stoothoff, and Dugald Murdoch. Cambridge: Cambridge University Press.

Edelman, Gerald M. 1989. *Neural Darwinism: The Theory of Neuronal Group Selection.* Oxford: Oxford University Press.

Evans, Gareth. 1978. "Can There Be Vague Objects?" *Analysis* 38:208.

Geach, P. T. 1979. *Truth, Love and Immortality: An Introduction to McTaggart's Philosophy.* London: Hutchinson.

Goldberger, Ary L., et al. 1990. "Chaos and Fractals in Human Physiology." *Scientific American* 262:42–49.

Goodman, Nelson. 1977. *The Structure of Appearance*, 3rd ed. Dordrecht: D. Reidel.

Linden, Eugene. 1976. *Apes, Men and Language.* Harmondsworth: Penguin.

Lowe, E. J. 1989a. *Kinds of Being: A Study of Individuation, Identity and the Logic of Sortal Terms.* Oxford: Blackwell.

———. 1989b. "What Is a Criterion of Identity?" *Philosophical Quarterly* 39:1–21.

———. 1992. "The Problem of Psychophysical Causation." *Australasian Journal of Philosophy* 70:263–76. Reprinted, 2003, in *Philosophy of Mind: Contemporary Readings*, edited by Timothy O'Connor and David Robb. London & New York: Routledge.

———. 1994. "Vague Identity and Quantum Indeterminacy." *Analysis* 54:110–14.

———. 1998. *The Possibility of Metaphysics: Substance, Identity, and Time.* Oxford: Clarendon.

————. 2001. "Identity, Composition, and the Simplicity of the Self." In *Soul, Body, and Survival: Essays on the Metaphysics of Human Persons*, edited by Kevin J. Corcoran. Ithaca: Cornell University Press.

————. 2005a. "Can the Self Disintegrate? Personal Identity, Psychopathology, and Disunities of Consciousness." In *Dementia: Mind, Meaning, and the Person*, edited by J. Hughes, S. Louw, and S. Sabat, 89–103. Oxford: Oxford University Press.

————. 2005b. "Identity, Vagueness, and Modality." In *Thought, Reference, and Experience: Themes from the Philosophy of Gareth Evans*, edited by J. L. Bermúdez, 290–310. Oxford: Clarendon.

————. 2006. *The Four-Category Ontology: A Metaphysical Foundation for Natural Science.* Oxford: Clarendon.

Mellars, Paul, and Chris Stringer, eds. 1989. *The Human Revolution: Behavioural and Biological Perspectives on the Origins of Modern Humans.* Edinburgh: Edinburgh University Press.

Millikan, Ruth G. 1984. *Language, Thought, and Other Biological Categories.* Cambridge, MA: MIT Press.

Penrose, Roger. 1989. *The Emperor's New Mind: Concerning Computers, Minds, and the Laws of Physics.* Oxford: Oxford University Press.

Scruton, Roger. 1989. "Corporate Persons." *Proceedings of the Aristotelian Society,* Supp. Vol. 63:239–66.

White, Randall. 1982. "Rethinking the Middle/Upper Paleolithic Transition." *Current Anthropology* 23:169–92.

————. 1989. "Visual Thinking in the Ice Age." *Scientific American* 261:74–81.

3

Subjects of Mentality

JOHN FOSTER

1.

There are two kinds of entity that feature in the mental realm. On the one hand, there are *items* of mentality (mental items). These are such things as sense experiences, beliefs, emotions, and decisions, which form the concrete ingredients of the mind. On the other hand, there are *subjects* of mentality (mental subjects). These are the persisting entities that have mental lives and in whose mental lives mental items occur; they are the things that *have* experiences, *hold* beliefs, *feel* emotions, and *make* decisions. Mental items can occur only as elements in the lives of mental subjects. This is because our very concept of any type of mental item just is the concept of a subject's being in a certain mental state, or performing a certain kind of mental act, or engaging in a certain kind of mental activity. It is fundamental to our understanding of the forms of mentality in question that for an experience to occur is for a subject to experience something, for a belief to occur is for a subject to believe something, for a decision to occur is for a subject to decide something, and so on for each type of mental item. To suppose that an item of mentality could occur without a subject of mentality would be as absurd as supposing that there could be an instance of motion without something that moves, or an instance of smiling without something that smiles.

Some philosophers of a radically empiricist persuasion have rejected an ontology of mental subjects on the grounds that the attachment of mental items to subjects is not introspectively detectable.[1] They have insisted that what we ordinarily think of as the mental life of a persisting subject is really only an organized collection of ontologically autonomous mental items that stand to one another in certain psychological and causal relations, and are typically causally associated with the same biological organism. There is a double confusion here.

In the first place, even if these philosophers were right in supposing that the attachment of mental items to subjects is not introspectively detectable, there is no getting around the point that our very concept of any type of mental item is the concept of a certain form of 'mentalizing' by a subject. Whatever the introspective situation, it simply makes no sense to envisage the occurrence of an experience without someone who has it, or the occurrence of a belief without someone who holds it, or the occurrence of a decision without someone who makes it. If the recognition of an ontology of subjects fails to pass some empiricist test of respectability, this serves to show only that the test is misconceived.

Secondly, those philosophers who have denied that the attachment of mental items to subjects is introspectively detectable have approached the issue of such detection in the wrong way. They have wrongly supposed that the introspective awareness of a mental item is similar in character to the perceptual awareness of a physical item, except that it is directed onto objects that exist in the inner arena of the mind rather than in the outer arena of the physical world. And because they have employed this perceptual model of the introspective awareness of mental items, they have further assumed, again wrongly, that if the attachment of a mental item to a subject is to be introspectively detected, this detection will have to take the form of the presentation of an additional object alongside the mental item in the inner arena, the two objects being presented in a form which displays the one as the subject of the other. It is hardly surprising that, on this basis, they have concluded that the attachment of mental items to subjects is not introspectively detectable. But it is the model of introspection that is at fault. When someone is introspectively aware of a mental item, he is not aware of it as an object presented to him. He is aware of it, more intimately, from the inside, as an instance of his own mentalizing—as an instance of his being in a certain mental state, or performing a certain kind of mental act, or engaging in a certain kind of mental activity. The subject's awareness of himself, and of his role as mental subject, is an essential element of his awareness of the item itself.[2]

There should be no issue, then, over the need for an ontology of mental subjects. One has only to focus on the nature of any type of mental item as our concept of that type reveals it—be it pain, visual experience, belief, decision making, desire, anger, or whatever—to be able to see quite plainly that that sort of thing can be realized only as an instance of mentalizing by a subject. And one has only to think about introspective awareness in the right way to see quite plainly that someone's introspective awareness of a mental item includes the awareness of himself as its subject. Where there remains an important issue is over the nature of the entities that form the subjects of mentality, and, in particular, over how these entities stand in relation to the physical world. It is this issue that I want to discuss. Specifically, I want to address the issue of the nature of *human* mental subjects, though I shall briefly consider the case of nonhuman animals at the end.

When I say that I want to discuss the issue of the nature of those entities that form the subjects of mentality, I should, to be precise, say that I want to discuss the issue of the nature of the *fundamental* subjects. Let us say that a fact F is *constituted by* a fact F', or set of facts A, if and only if the obtaining of F is logically due to, and nothing over and above, the obtaining of F' (the members of A).[3] And let us say that S is a derivative subject of mentality if and only if S is a subject of mentality and, for every fact F about S's mentality, there is some other subject S', or set of subjects G, such that F is constituted by facts about the mentality of S' (the members of G), together with certain further facts. Then something qualifies as a fundamental subject of mentality if and only if it is a subject of mentality and is not a derivative subject in that sense. One way in which derivative mental subjects feature in our ordinary thinking is in our ascription of forms of mentality to certain kinds of unified groups of people. For example, we may speak of a crowd as angry, or of a committee as making a decision. Obviously, we have to think of these putative subjects as merely derivative: any psychological facts about them are wholly constituted by psychological facts about the individual subjects that compose them, together with certain further facts (in part, at least, facts about how the individual subjects combine to form a unified collective).

My concern in this discussion will be exclusively with the nature of those entities that form the fundamental subjects of mentality. For ease of style, I shall normally in what follows omit the qualifying term 'fundamental' and simply speak of subjects *tout court*. But it must be understood that, apart from those occasions when I explicitly indicate that I have a broader domain of subjects in mind, it is always the situation of the fundamental subjects that is under discussion.

2.

We ordinarily think of human subjects as—whatever else they may be—corporeal objects, with shape, size, and material composition. My neighbor, Mr. Smith, is a mental subject—a human individual who persists through time and is the subject of various forms of mental state, act, and activity. He would normally be thought of as someone of average height and build, with dark hair, ruddy complexion, and rounded shoulders—properties which can be possessed only by a material occupant of physical space. His wife, too, is a human subject, and she would normally be thought of as short and thin, with auburn hair and a pale complexion—again, properties which can characterize only a material occupant of space. There are, admittedly, aspects of our ordinary thinking, or at least the ordinary thinking of a great many people, that seem to be in conflict with this corporealist conception of human subjects. In particular, many people believe that such subjects survive their physical death in some nonembodied form, and even more accept that such survival is a possibility. These views are hard to reconcile with the view that, prior to death, the subjects in question are entities with spatial location and material composition. Nonetheless, it cannot be denied that, whatever our views about life after death, we ordinarily take it for granted that, in the contexts in which we standardly encounter them, human subjects are, whatever else, corporeal objects, with the full range of properties of spatial structure and physical content that such objects have to possess. Specifically, we take it for granted that they are, whatever else, biological organisms belonging to a certain animal species, Homo sapiens, and so, in that respect, are of the same general kind as monkeys, badgers, and cats.

The fact that we ordinarily take human subjects to be corporeal objects does not, of course, ensure that that view of them is correct. It is a commonplace of philosophy that views whose truth we take for granted in the course of everyday life are sometimes shown to be untenable by deeper or more adequately informed reflection. Back in the seventeenth century, René Descartes thought that it required only a small amount of properly focused reflection to reveal the untenability of the corporealist view. He thought that, by attending to what is revealed by introspection, he could form a clear conception of himself as a subject of mentality (as a *res cogitans*); and because this introspective conception did not in itself represent him as an object in space, and indeed, at least as he supposed, allowed him to coherently think of himself as something without spatial extension or spatial location, he concluded that spatiality was not an ingredient of his essential nature. Since spatiality is clearly an ingredient of the essential nature of any corporeal object (as indeed of anything existing in space), he was able to conclude that he was not something corporeal.[4]

It is now universally acknowledged that Descartes's reasoning was flawed, and doubly so. In the first place, even if Descartes was right to suppose that, relying on his introspective conception alone, he could coherently think of himself as wholly nonspatial, he was not entitled to conclude that spatiality was not an ingredient of his essential nature. For he was not entitled to assume that this introspective conception, however clear in its own terms, included all the information needed to settle the issue. For all he has shown, it might be that he (and indeed any human mental subject) is, in reality, a corporeal object, and hence essentially spatial, but that this is not something which introspection is equipped to reveal. Secondly, even Descartes's supposition that his introspective conception allows for the coherent envisaging of himself as something nonspatial is controversial. Many philosophers, particularly in the modern era, would insist that we cannot ultimately make sense of a noncorporeal mental subject. And since Descartes's conception of himself is a conception of himself as a mental subject, they would say that it implicitly commits him to accepting the corporeality, and hence spatiality, of his nature. Prior to further investigation of the issue, the most that Descartes is entitled to claim is that his introspective conception does not explicitly represent him as an object in space, and so allows him *provisionally* to entertain the hypothesis of his nonspatial, and hence noncorporeal, nature.

Although Descartes's reasoning was flawed, I think that he was right in the conclusion to which it led him, and it is this Cartesian view of the situation that I want here to defend. Thus, in opposition to what we ordinarily suppose, and what almost all current philosophy of mind takes for granted, I shall argue that human subjects are wholly nonphysical in nature—that they are devoid of corporeal properties and location in physical space, and devoid of components that have such properties or location. This endorsement of a nonphysicalist view of human subjects obviously commits me to a similarly nonphysicalist view of their mentality. It commits me, in other words, to a full-blooded dualist account of the human mind, which takes both the relevant mental subjects and the items that feature in their mental lives to be ontologically separate from all that exists or occurs in the physical world. This full-blooded ontological dualism was again, of course, Descartes's own position, and it is a position which I have elaborated and defended in much greater detail elsewhere (see Foster 1991). It stands in opposition not only to a thoroughgoing materialist view of the mind, but also to the compromise position of property dualism, which combines a materialist account of human subjects with a nonphysicalist account of their mentality.

In embracing this Cartesian—radically dualist—view of the human mind, I am not wanting to deny that the relevant nonphysical subjects are intimately associated with certain corporeal objects. I accept that, at least standardly, each human subject is functionally linked with a unique biological organism (a human organism) in a way that makes provision for a complex system of causal interaction between them. And I accept that the nature of this functional link— in particular, the fact that it enables the subject to have perceptual access to the organism's environment through sensory experiences controlled by input to the organism's receptors, and to act on this environment through volitional control of the organism's behavior— makes it appropriate to think of the subject as embodied by the organism with which it is linked, and to think of this organism as the representative of the subject in third-person perspective. I am even prepared to treat human organisms as *derivative* mental subjects, whose possession of mentality constitutively reduces to the mentality of the nonphysical subjects they embody and the fact of this embodiment. I have already made it clear that it is only the nature of the *fundamental* subjects of mentality that here concerns me, and that, except where there is an explicit indication to the contrary, anything I say about subjects should be understood as restricted to the case of subjects of this sort.

As I have conceded, I cannot establish that human subjects are nonphysical by merely appealing to the fact that the introspective conception of a subject is not explicitly spatial: the fact that this conception is not *explicitly* spatial does not ensure that to envisage ourselves as nonspatial (so nonphysical) in nature is ultimately coherent; and even if it did, this would not ensure that a nonspatial (nonphysical) account of our natures was in fact correct. The argument I shall offer in support of my position will be on very different lines. Put at its simplest, my claim will be that we cannot ultimately make sense of any alternative to the Cartesian view and preserve an acceptable account of human mentality. In presenting this argument, I shall assume—what I take to be uncontroversial—that the only non-Cartesian positions we need to consider are ones which represent human subjects as corporeal objects—as things which, whatever else may pertain to their natures, are endowed with properties of three-dimensional extension and material composition. In practice, of course, the range of corporealist options that have any chance of acceptability, and so merit serious discussion, is much more narrowly circumscribed.

The view of the subject that I am defending is one that Descartes held in the framework of a realist conception of the physical world— a conception that represents the world as something whose existence is both logically independent of the human mind and metaphysically fundamental. And it is only when it is held within this framework that the view can properly be described as dualist. But the view itself is neutral between (physically realist) dualism and idealism: it is as much the position of George Berkeley as of René Descartes, and, indeed, for someone with an idealist view of the physical world, any other view of the human subject would be automatically excluded.[5] As it happens, my own theory of the world is an idealist one, a theory in key respects akin to that of Berkeley.[6] But in the present discussion (as in Foster 1991), I shall retain allegiance to the commonsense realist framework, in which there are rival views of the subject to be considered. I want to show that the corporealist view can be discredited even when the conception of the world which it presupposes is accepted.

3.

The corporealist view of the subject admits of a weaker and a stronger form. The stronger form of the view is that, leaving aside their mental states, acts, and activities, human subjects are not only corporeal objects, but ones whose natures are purely physical—restricted to properties which the objects possess as material occupants of space. This would commit the corporealist to thinking that the relevant corporeal objects are equipped to be mental subjects by their physical properties alone. The alternative and weaker form of the view is that, in addition to their physical properties, the corporeal subjects have a nonphysical side to their natures—a side which, though not consisting in aspects of the subjects' mentality, is what logically enables them to be mental subjects. This weaker form of the view is, I think, the one which we implicitly accept in our ordinary thinking. We ordinarily take it for granted that human subjects are corporeal objects, with shape, size, and material composition. But we also recognize a fundamental distinction between what pertains to the mental life of a subject and what pertains to his physical character and physical life, and I think that, at least implicitly, we see the distinctive nonphysical character of the subject's mentality as involving a corresponding nonphysical aspect to his underlying nature, sustaining his capacity to be a mental subject and to have this kind of mentality.

As well as having to decide between the weak and the strong forms of his view, the corporealist has to decide on the corporeal character of the objects that are to play the subject role, and I shall look at this issue first. At first sight, it might seem that there is no real issue here at all. If human subjects are corporeal objects, they must surely be human biological organisms, members of the animal species Homo sapiens; certainly, as already noted, this is what we ordinarily take for granted. But, on closer scrutiny, it becomes clear that the situation is not straightforward, and, indeed, not easy for the corporealist to satisfactorily deal with in any way at all.

What creates the complications is that while human organisms (human animals) are what we ordinarily take to be the corporeal subjects of human mentality, and are the corporeal objects through whose behavior such mentality is publicly exhibited, the corporeal objects whose states and processes are immediately involved in the causal production and sustainment of the relevant forms of mentality are the organisms' brains; at least, this is the most natural way of interpreting the empirical evidence. The way in which this complicates the issue becomes clear when we focus on a hypothetical situation in which a human brain continues to perform its normal functions outside the context of the organism to which it originally belonged.

Suppose, for example, that human organisms Tom and Dick are identical twins and that, by a double transplant operation, their brains are exchanged.[7] Suppose also that the operation is a complete success, so that neither of the brains is damaged or altered by its transplantation, and each is able to function normally in its new bodily setting; in particular, each brain continues to perform its normal functions in relation to mentality. Let us give the name

'Tom*' to the organism formed from Tom's body and Dick's brain, 'Dick*' to the organism formed from Dick's body and Tom's brain, 'T' and 'D' to the subjects of the mentality respectively associated with Tom and Dick prior to the brain exchange, and 'T*' and 'D*' to the subjects of the mentality respectively associated with Tom* and Dick*. Now, given that the transplanted brains preserve their original character and continue to perform their normal psychological functions, we know that $T*$'s memories, beliefs, intellectual capacities, and personality will, immediately after the transplant, coincide with those of D immediately before it, and that $D*$'s memories, beliefs, intellectual capacities, and personality will, immediately after the transplant, coincide with those of T immediately before it. This makes it intuitively plausible to identify $T*$ with D, and $D*$ with T. On the other hand, with the brain as the only common physical component, it is very hard to identify the organism Tom* with the organism Dick, and the organism Dick* with the organism Tom. So, if he accepts the identity of $T*$ with D and of $D*$ with T, it seems that the corporealist is obliged to think of the relevant subjects as human brains rather than whole human organisms, with T ($= D*$) as the brain that moves from Tom to Dick*, and D ($= T*$) as the brain that moves from Dick to Tom*. And if this is how he understands the situation in the hypothetical case envisaged, he presumably has to identify human subjects with human brains quite generally.

So should the corporealist opt for the cerebral version of his view in preference to the standard version? Well, the trouble with the cerebral version is that the notion of a brain as a mental subject does not seem to make sense. I see no conceptual problem over thinking of the brain as intimately involved in the production and sustainment of mentality—for example, envisaging a brain process as inducing a sensory experience, or recognizing a brain state as causally underlying the holding of a belief. But to suppose that the brain is what forms the subject of mentality—what *has* experiences, *holds* beliefs, *makes* decisions, *feels* emotions—seems to be a clear-cut instance of a category mistake, comparable with supposing that it is an organism's mouth that speaks, or its hands that steal. It seems that the whole organism is the only corporeal entity that we could begin to think of as a genuine subject of mental states, acts, and activities.

If the corporealist decides to retain the standard version of his view, which identifies human subjects with whole human organisms, his best way of handling the transplant case would be to say that what results from the exchange of brains are two new organisms, forming two new mental subjects. This would involve saying that although T^* and D^* preserve the memories, beliefs, intellectual capacities, and personalities of, respectively, D and T, and although, in a sense, their mental lives are continuations of the mental lives of D and T, $T^*(= \text{Tom}^*)$ and $D^*(= \text{Dick}^*)$ come into existence only as a result of the brain exchange and so are not the same subjects as $D (= \text{Dick})$ and $T (= \text{Tom})$. There may be a certain degree of awkwardness in having to recognize a change in the identities of the relevant subjects within the histories of what amount to the same continuing mental lives. But, arguably, this awkwardness is not intolerable, and, on the face of it, it is easier to accept than an identification of the subjects with brains.

Unfortunately for the corporealist, the complications over this issue do not stop there. Suppose that, instead of transplanting Tom's brain to a new body, we had simply removed it intact and kept it alive and physiologically healthy by means of some elaborate artificial support system. It seems at least conceivable, and arguably even plausible, that, even in this physiologically impoverished context, the brain would continue to sustain some form of mental life—a life which was a continuation of the one it had sustained when it was located within Tom's body. After all, the situation envisaged does not appear to differ in psychologically relevant respects from what would have obtained if the brain had remained within the body, but, as a result of some degenerative disease, its afferent and efferent neural extensions had been destroyed. But assuming that the corporeally isolated brain would continue to sustain a mental life, what can the corporealist take to be the corporeal subject of this life other than the brain itself?—and let us, for the sake of argument, assume that the rest of Tom's body has been incinerated. Well, one alternative would be to say that the subject is the whole organism, Tom, but surviving in a corporeally depleted form. In other words, it would be to view the situation that results from the isolation of the brain as simply an extreme version of the case in which an organism survives the loss of some bodily part, such as an eye or an arm—a version in which the whole original organism continues in existence, but with its brain now forming the whole of its body. But this would not be a comfortable position for the corporealist to adopt. It is far from clear that we can intelligibly think of the survival of the functioning brain as sufficing for the survival of the whole organism. And even if we can, the proposal creates problems for the interpretation of the transplant case. It is very hard to think that the whole organism we are left with when Tom's brain is inserted into Dick's body is the same organism as Tom. But if we decide that Tom manages to survive when his brain is preserved and functioning in the artificial context, we can hardly say that he would fail to survive when his brain is transferred to a new body.

Notwithstanding these further complications, I do not think that the corporealist can afford to give up the identification of human subjects with human organisms. But, to retain it, he will have to say that when the brain is separated from anything that qualifies as a human organism (a human animal) in the ordinary sense, it loses its capacity to produce or sustain mentality. The prima facie drawback of this is that we can plausibly envisage the continuation of a mental life in the case where the brain remains physically located in the body, but (with the degeneration of the afferent and efferent nerves) in a neurally isolated form; and, as we noted, this case does not at first sight seem to differ in psychologically relevant respects from the case of the corporeally isolated brain on which we were focusing. But the corporealist could say that what makes the two cases crucially different is that in the one case there is a continuation of the organism that would form the subject of any mentality that was cerebrally produced or sustained, and in the other case there is not. In other words, he could say that the reason why the physically isolated brain loses the capacity to produce or sustain mentality is simply that any mentality would require a subject, and, with the loss of the organism, there is no longer any subject to which such mentality could belong. Whether this reply would be entirely adequate is still, I think, unclear. One thing which suggests that it might not be is that there seems to be no objective answer to the question of how much of an organism's body can be destroyed before the organism itself ceases to exist. And, on the face of it, it is not plausible to conclude that, in circumstances of bodily depletion, there is sometimes no objective answer to the question of whether there is still a capacity for a mental life.

4.

Whatever difficulties the corporealist encounters over deciding on the type of corporeal object that is to play the subject role, the main problem he faces is over the more fundamental issue of whether it makes sense to think of any type of corporeal object as a mental subject. In elaborating this problem, I shall assume that the corporealist takes human subjects to have the physical character of whole human organisms, rather than of their brains, since I regard this as his best (or least bad) option. But the problem itself is one that arises whatever type of corporeal subject is envisaged.

I have already indicated that the corporealist view can assume a weaker and a stronger form. In its stronger form, it claims that, leaving aside the ingredients of their mental lives, human subjects are corporeal objects whose whole natures are physical—natures entirely composed of properties which the objects possess as material occupants of space. If we say that the 'core' nature of an object covers all that that object is like in itself apart from the ingredients of its mental life, if it has one, we can express this stronger position, more succinctly, as the claim that human subjects are corporeal objects whose core natures are purely physical. In its weaker form, the view claims that human subjects are corporeal objects whose core natures are partly nonphysical, and that the nonphysical component of their natures is what logically enables them to be mental subjects—what makes them the sorts of thing that can be in mental states, perform mental acts, and engage in mental activities. The problem over the coherence of the corporealist view comes in correspondingly different forms, according to the form of the view which is at issue, and so I shall need to take its elaboration in two stages. I shall begin by considering the view in its stronger form, which is the theoretically simplest corporealist position. I shall speak of this as the *pure corpo-*

realist view, or simply the *pure view*. With human organisms as the relevant corporeal objects, the claim of the pure view is that human subjects are human organisms and that such organisms are purely physical in their core natures. In effect, the claim is that, leaving aside the nature of what takes place in their minds, human subjects are simply biological organisms and nothing more.

When the corporealist view assumes this strong form, it is not difficult to see how a prima facie problem arises. As I have already noted, although we ordinarily think of human subjects as corporeal objects, we also ordinarily recognize a fundamental distinction between what pertains to a subject's mental life and what pertains to his physical character and physical life. This is why we speak of the influence of 'mind over matter' (for example, when we suppose that someone's positive attitude has directly contributed to his recovery from a physical illness), and why we sometimes wonder whether a certain pathological symptom has a physical or a psychological cause. But if a subject's mentality is something fundamentally different from all that pertains to his physical character and physical life, it seems impossible to understand how something whose core nature is wholly physical could be equipped, by its nature, to be a mental subject. How could something which—leaving aside the nature of any mentality we may want to ascribe to it—is nothing more than a physical organism be capable of being in states or performing acts or engaging in activities that are extraneous to its character and life as a physical thing? Once we accept that a subject's mentality is something sui generis, and radically different in nature from all that pertains to his character and life as a physical thing, it seems to make no more sense to ascribe mentality to a biological organism whose core nature is purely physical than to ascribe it to a stone or a pen. Of course, unlike these latter objects, human organisms behave in ways which we take to indicate the presence of mentality, and we can plausibly think of their brains as directly causally involved in the production and sustainment of mentality. But these facts would not help us to understand how, without some further aspect to their natures, the organisms could be what *possessed* the mentality behaviorally exhibited or cerebrally caused—how they could be what *have* experiences, *hold* beliefs, *make* decisions, and *feel* emotions. The physical nature of an organism seems no better equipped than the physical nature of a pen or a stone to give the thing that instantiates it the capacity to have a nonphysical mental life.

It is important that we do not confuse this problem with something else. Philosophers who accept what I have termed the pure corporealist view often suppose that the main problem they face is over understanding how a purely material system can *give rise to* mentality, and, in particular, to mentality in its conscious (experiential) forms. Colin McGinn, for example, identifies the "hard nut of the mind–body problem" as that of understanding how it is "possible for conscious states to depend on brain states"—possible for "technicolour phenomenology" to "arise from soggy grey matter," and for the "aggregation of millions of neurons" to "generate subjective awareness."[8] In similar vein, David Chalmers identifies the "hard problem" of consciousness as the difficulty of envisaging an explanation of how "experience arises from a physical basis."[9] The problem I have in mind is more fundamental. It is not the difficulty of understanding how something purely physical could be equipped to *generate* mentality, or conscious mentality, but the difficulty of understanding how something purely physical, or purely physical in its core nature, could be a *subject of* mentality, as mentality is ordinarily conceived—and the fact that the brain of an organism generated mentality would not in itself render the organism (or its brain) a subject of mentality (an entity which comes into mental states, performs mental acts, or engages in mental activities). In their different ways, both McGinn and Chalmers think that they can satisfactorily deal with the problem they identify—in Chalmers's case, by providing the outline of an account of how conscious states get physically generated, in McGinn's case, by arguing that we should not expect to be able to understand how the physical generation of conscious states might work.[10] But neither of them faces up to, or even seems to notice, the more basic problem for the pure corporealist of how, in whatever way mentality is generated, there could be something equipped to play the role of its subject.

This problem for the pure view is, it seems to me, insuperable so long as we continue to accept the radical difference between the mental and the physical that we ordinarily recognize. The only way in which the pure corporealist can try to render his position intelligible is by rejecting that supposed difference and claiming that when the nature of mentality is properly understood, the problem of ascribing it to something whose core nature is purely physical disappears. The reason why we ordinarily think of a subject's mentality as radically different in nature from all that pertains to his physical character and physical life is that we ordinarily conceive of mentality in its own mentalistic terms (conceiving of pain *as pain*, belief *as belief*, and so on), and, conceived of in its own terms, mentality conceptually presents itself as something of its own distinctive and nonphysical kind. What the pure corporealist must try to show is that while this way of conceiving of mentality has to be the *initial* way of conceiving of it—the way in which we first identify the types of state, act, and activity that our mental terms signify—it is not what provides the *philosophically fundamental* understanding of its nature, and that once this fundamental understanding is in place, the way in which a purely physical organism can be the subject of mentality becomes clear. In effect, what he must try to show is that, in line with the subjects that possess it, mentality has to be ultimately understood in purely physical terms.

There are three main ways in which the pure corporealist could pursue this physicalistic strategy.

The first would be to endorse a behaviorist account of mentality. It would be to claim that any aspect of a subject's mental condition at a time should be ultimately understood as an aspect of his behavioral condition at that time—an aspect of how, at that time, the subject is behaving or is disposed to behave. This behaviorist position hardly features in the current philosophical debate, but it was quite fashionable in the first half of twentieth century, when its advocates offered it as an account of how the factual content of psychological statements should be represented on conceptual analysis.[11] The underlying idea, reflecting the acceptance of a verificationist theory of meaning, was that it is only when psychological statements are construed as claims about the subject's behavior and behavioral dispositions that they become amenable to empirical verification, and that only if they are amenable to empirical verification can they have factual content at all.

The second way in which the corporealist could pursue the physicalistic strategy would be to offer a functionalist account of mentality.[12] This would be to claim that any aspect of a subject's mental condition at a time should be taken to be an aspect of his functional condition at that time. More precisely, it would be to claim that, for any type M of mental item, there is a certain functional role or cluster of roles R such that, for any subject S and time t, if M is realized in S at t, its being so consists in the fact that there is some type C of concrete internal item occurring in S at t such that R is the role or role cluster which the intrinsic makeup of S, together with the laws of nature, equips C items standardly to play in S's system—play in relation to physical sensory input, behavioral output, and other internal states. Like the behaviorist understanding of mentality, this functionalist position is normally offered as a theory of conceptual analysis—a theory of how, on analysis, the content of psychological concepts and psychological statements is to be ultimately represented. Although it is not essential to the functionalist position as such, in practice (and not surprisingly) functionalists take the internal items that play the relevant functional roles to be purely physical. More specifically, and in the light of what is known about the internal workings of the human organism, functionalists take them to be neural items in the brain. In the present context, I shall assume that functionalism is developed in this physicalistic way, since this is what pursuing the relevant strategy requires.

The third option for the corporealist would be to endorse the type–type version of the mind–brain identity theory.[13] This would be to claim that, at least when relativized to the life of a particular subject, each type of mental item is the same as a certain type of cerebral item. In other words, it would be to claim that, for any type M of mental item and any subject S, there is a type C of cerebral item such that, for any time t, if M is realized in S at t, the state of affairs of its being thus realized is the same as the state of affairs of C's being realized in S at t. Advocates of this form of identity theory often combine it with something which comes close to the functionalist account. For they often claim that, for each type of mental item, our ordinary mentalistic concept of that type is to be analyzed in functional terms, as the concept of that type of concrete internal item (whatever it happens to be) which is equipped to play a certain functional role or cluster of roles; and they then claim that the way to discover which cerebral type is to be equated with that mental type (or to be equated with it in the case of a given subject) is to discover which cerebral type (which cerebral type in respect of that subject) is functionally equipped in the relevant way. But even when it comes with this kind of functionalist underpinning, the identity theory does not count as a form of functionalism in the sense defined. Functionalism itself takes mental types to be functional types which are physically realized, while the functionalist form of the identity theory takes them to be physical types which satisfy certain functional conditions.[14]

On all three of these accounts of mentality, it is clear that there would be no difficulty in thinking of human subjects as objects whose core natures, indeed whose *whole* natures, are purely physical. For each of them is offering an ultimate understanding of human mentality in purely physical terms, whether in terms of the subject's behavior and behavioral dispositions, or in terms of the functional roles of his internal physical states and processes, or in terms of the character of these internal states and processes themselves. And if we understand human mentality in purely physical terms, there is no reason to think of the subjects of this mentality as having any nonphysical side to their natures. Indeed, it would be irrational even to entertain such an idea. But the problem now for the corporealist, at least as I see it, is that each of these physicalistic accounts can be shown to be unacceptable. There is a long and complex story to be told here—examining each of the accounts in turn, identifying the ways in which it is open to objection, considering how a defender of the account might try to answer these objections, and showing how each such line of defense fails. It is a story that I have told in detail elsewhere (see Foster 1991).[15] In the present context, I can offer only a brief summary of a few of the main points.

One of the things which make functionalism hopelessly implausible is that if we take the mentality of human organisms to be purely a matter of their functional organization and the specific functional states that characterize them on particular occasions, we would be obliged to ascribe mentality to a hypothetical robot that had the appropriate functional organization and repertoire of functional states. This would be so even if the robot's central information-processing components worked in a crudely mechanical way—by means of such things as cogs, levers, pulleys, and springs, rather than the silicon chips and electronic circuitry of the modern computer. Behaviorism is hopelessly implausible for the same reason, and it is vulnerable to the further objection that even if we wanted to pursue it, we could at best represent any specific form of mentality as having logical consequences for behavior and behavioral dispositions when it is set in the context of (and of what is specified to be) the subject's total psychological condition at the relevant time—something that makes it impossible to offer an account of the relevant form of mentality in purely behavioral terms. One of the ways in which the type identity theory fails is that the association of a given type of mental item with a given type of cerebral item does not have the modal status required for identity. Thus, even if, within the life of a single subject, each mental type is uniformly correlated with a particular cerebral type (so that any realization of the mental type is accompanied by a realization of the cerebral type, and vice versa), this correlation is only contingent, and, as Kripke has shown, numerical identity, whether between particulars or between universals, is always logically necessary.[16]

In addition to their individual failings, all three physicalistic accounts are vulnerable to the objection that they do not do justice to the nature of conscious experience, as introspection reveals it, and as our experiential concepts require it to be. The basic problem is that the specifications they offer of the nature of any form of mentality do not cover the way in which the realization of that form subjectively presents itself to the one in whom it occurs. And in the case of a form of mentality that is experiential, how its realization subjectively presents itself is an essential aspect of its psychological character: unless we know what it is subjectively like to have an experience of this kind—what the occurrence of such an experience feels like from the inside—we do not know what, as a form of mentality, this kind of experience is. Take, for instance, the case of pain. There is no denying that there is much to be said about pain in behavioral, functional, and cerebral terms: someone who suffers a sharp pain is liable to wince or cry out; certain types of pain tend to be induced by certain kinds of physical stimuli; certain areas of the brain are standardly involved in the occurrence of pain. These are just a few examples. But pain is a form of experience, and to grasp its psychological nature—to know what, as a form of experiential mentality, pain is—involves knowing what it is subjectively like to have an experience of that kind; it involves knowing what it feels like, from the inside, to be in pain. No amount of behavioral, functional, or cerebral information about pain can provide that knowledge—can cover how pain presents itself to the subject who has it. The same is true of all forms of experiential mentality. So, as in the case of pain, we cannot grasp the psychological character of the experience of color, or of sound, or of sweetness, without knowing what having an experience of such a kind is like subjectively, and such knowledge cannot be supplied in behavioral, functional, or cerebral terms.[17]

None of the three physicalistic accounts of mentality we have considered does justice to the nature of conscious experience, as we know it to be. And it is clear that the same inadequacy would characterize any attempt to understand mentality in purely physical terms—any account that represented psychological facts about a human subject as physical facts, or as facts whose obtaining is ultimately nothing over and above the obtaining of physical facts. This means that the initial problem for the pure corporealist view remains. If mentality has to be ultimately understood in its own mentalistic terms—resisting identification with, or reduction to, something physical—we still have no way of making sense of its being realized in subjects whose core natures are wholly physical. We still have no way of understanding how something which, in its core nature, is simply a corporeal object and nothing more could be equipped to undergo mental states, perform mental acts, or engage in mental activities.

5.

If the corporealist view of the human subject is to have any chance of acceptability, it will have to be in its weaker form, where the putative corporeal subjects are assigned core natures that include a nonphysical component. So, assuming that the putative subjects are human organisms, the view will have to be that, along with the physical properties that he has as a biological organism, each human subject possesses, in his core nature, an additional nonphysical character, which is what gives him the capacity to be a mental subject. And the rationale for this view would be that, given that mentality itself is something sui generis and physically irreducible—something whose nature can be properly understood only in its own terms, and whose obtaining involves something genuinely additional to all that obtains in the physical realm—we can make sense of a corporeal object's being a mental subject only if we suppose that there is a nonphysical aspect to its nature which equips it to play this role. Let us speak of this as the *moderate* corporealist view, or simply the *moderate view*. As I have indicated, I take this moderate view to be the position which we implicitly accept in our ordinary thinking.

There is no denying that the moderate corporealist view avoids the specific problem of the pure view; it is expressly designed to do so. But it also seems to me that, like trying to remove the proverbial bubble in the carpet, trying to avoid the specific problem in that way serves only to generate an analogous problem at another point. For just as we have no way of understanding how something whose core nature is purely physical could be the subject of nonphysical mentality, so, I would claim, we have no way of understanding how a corporeal object could be anything other than physical in nature through and through. Suppose we begin by considering the situation of some material object that we have no temptation to think of as anything other than purely physical. My pen, for example. The pen does not behave in ways that suggest that it possesses any mentality, and so there is nothing about it that might lead us to doubt that it is purely physical in nature. And let us assume that it *is* purely physical in nature. But now the question is, would it be logically possible for there to be something that had the physical character of the pen but had a nonphysical side to its nature as well? It is surely clear that it would not. It is surely clear that any instantiation of this physical character would form something ontologically and qualitatively complete, whose nature would not leave room for the presence of a further ingredient. It is not just that there is nothing to suggest that there is anything with the physical character of a pen that has a nature which is partly nonphysical. It is that we cannot even understand what it would be for such a situation to obtain—that the idea of a pen whose nature is not purely physical is one that we cannot make sense of. But if we cannot make sense of something with the physical character of a pen having an additional nonphysical side to its nature, I do not see how we can make sense of this in the case of *any* kind of material object. In particular, I do not see how we can make sense of this in the case of a human organism.

Of course, because human organisms behave in ways that suggest their possession of mentality, and because mentality cannot be equated with, or reduced to, anything physical, the suggestion that such organisms are partly nonphysical in nature has a rationale. But it is not a rationale that helps us to understand how such a thing would be possible. Within the bounds of what we can make sense of, the closest we can come to envisaging a human organism with a non-physical side to its nature is by envisaging it as functionally combining with a nonphysical subject to form a complex functional whole. And this would be to envisage the mind–body setup of Cartesian dualism, not of the moderate corporealist view. The only way of turning it into something that might look like a version of moderate corporealism would be by thinking of the functional union of the organism and the subject as logically creating a new form of mental subject—a subject whose existence is constituted by the existence of the nonphysical subject, the existence of the organism, and the functional relationship between them—and then taking this new subject to combine the contrasting natures of the two ontological items that feature in its creation. But even if we could make sense of such an idea, it would not yield a version of the corporealist view in the relevant sense, since it would not offer a corporealist account of the *fundamental* subjects of mentality. In the case of each such created corporeal subject, all the facts about its mentality would be ultimately constituted by facts about the mentality of the nonphysical subject involved and its functional union with the relevant organism.

6.

I have argued that we cannot make sense of the corporealist view of the human subject in either its pure or its moderate form. We cannot make sense of the pure version of the view because we cannot understand how it would be possible for something whose core nature is purely physical to be a subject of mentality; at least, we cannot do so without a gross misrepresentation of the nature of mentality. We cannot make sense of the moderate view because we cannot understand how it would be possible for a corporeal object to have an additional nonphysical side to its nature.

But assuming that these claims are correct, what conclusion should we draw from them? The conclusion that I, as a Cartesian, would like to be able to draw is that the corporealist view is incoherent and needs to be rejected. But this conclusion does not strictly follow from the claims themselves. For the fact that we are unable to make sense of a certain suggestion, or that we cannot understand how a certain sort of situation would be possible, does not entail that the relevant suggestion does not in itself make sense, or that the sort of thing in question is in fact impossible. Our inability to see sense in something, or to understand how something would be possible, could just reflect some limitation on our own powers of comprehension. This gives the corporealist an opportunity to dig his heels in. He could say that it makes perfectly good sense in the abstract to suppose that a corporeal object has a mental life (perhaps in the form envisaged by the pure view, perhaps in the form envisaged by the moderate view), but that our minds are not equipped to see how this makes sense.[18]

There are two things I want to say in response to this. The first is that when I claim that we cannot make sense of the corporealist view, or that we cannot understand how what this view envisages would be possible, I do not intend to be making a claim which is neutral between the conclusion that there is a problem with the view and the conclusion that there is a deficiency in us. I intend to be claiming that, on proper reflection, and with a proper understanding of the nature of mentality, it positively seems to us that the view does not make sense and that what it envisages could not obtain. Now, of course, there is still a logical gap between something's positively seeming to be the case and its actually being the case. So, there is still an opportunity for the corporealist to insist that it is not his own position, but our reflective intuitions, that are at fault. But this response would not, on its own, give him an effective defense: one cannot avoid the force of an argument by merely pointing out that although it seems cogent, this might be because we are intellectually unequipped to discern its defects. To secure an effective defense, the corporealist needs to provide some positive reason for doubting the veridicality of the reflective intuitions in question. Until we are given such a reason, it must be rational for us to treat the intuitions as trustworthy and accept the conclusion they deliver.

The second thing I want to say takes up the issue at this point, and it will involve my accepting a certain limitation on the scope of what I can hope to achieve in the present discussion.

If the corporealist is to provide a positive reason for doubting the veridicality of the relevant intuitions, this will have to come by providing an argument against the Cartesian alternative—an argument which shows that it is even more difficult to accept this alternative than to accept the corporealist view itself. And let me at once acknowledge that a number of anti-Cartesian arguments have been developed. To mention some of the more familiar, it has been argued that the Cartesian view cannot accommodate the fact that we have a mental language; that it cannot provide an adequate positive account of the nonphysical subjects it postulates; that it does not allow us to understand how mind and body are able to interact; and that, barring epiphenomenalism (which is itself unacceptable), it cannot be reconciled with what we know from physical science about the workings of the world. For all I have here shown, it could turn out that, properly developed, some of these lines of argument, or others that I have not mentioned, would suffice to reveal the Cartesian view as untenable, and make it reasonable to conclude that our inability to make sense of the corporealist view stems from a deficiency in ourselves, rather than a defect in the view.

What this means is that even if my argument against the corporealist view is successful in its own terms, it is not in its present form conclusive. To make it so, I would have to show that the various arguments against the Cartesian alternative are unsuccessful. This is where I have to accept a limitation on the scope of what I can hope to achieve in the present discussion. For although I am in no doubt that these various anti-Cartesian arguments all fail, it would require a further and large-scale work to consider them all in adequate detail and identify their faults. To a large extent, I have already attempted to do this in the later chapters of *The Immaterial Self*—a book whose arguments and conclusions I would still endorse. But, in the present context, I must be content with presenting the positive case in favor of the Cartesian view, and leave its defense against objections on one side.

This said, there is one apparent difficulty for the Cartesian that I did not discuss in the book, and which I want briefly to take account of now.

I think I succeeded, in that earlier discussion, in showing that the Cartesian can provide an adequate account of the nature of the functional attachment of human subjects to human organisms and of the way in which this attachment makes provision for mind–body interaction.[19] But where he may still seem to face a problem is over providing a plausible account of how the nonphysical subjects come into existence and get functionally attached to the organisms in the relevant way. The organisms come into existence at biological conception, as a result of the fusion of an ovum and a sperm. It would be very difficult to think of this physical process of fusion, or the subsequent physical development of the embryo, as having the capacity to create a nonphysical subject as well; and, indeed, it is hard to see how the creation of such an entity and its attachment to the relevant organism could be accounted for in natural terms at all. Although I cannot discuss the issue in any detail, I think that the right solution for the Cartesian is to appeal to the creative role of God. He should say that it is God who brings the nonphysical subjects into being at the appropriate times and attaches them to the relevant organisms in the appropriate way. This, it seems to me, provides a fully adequate explanation of what needs to be explained, and I cannot think of any remotely plausible alternative.[20]

I am aware that most current philosophers would not regard this appeal to the role of God as a serious option. They would say that if the Cartesian has to rely on a theistic solution, this serves only to underline the bankruptcy of his position. I see the situation the other way round. Quite apart from the present issue, I think that there are a number of things about the world and ourselves which can be adequately accounted for only by appeal to the existence and role of God.[21] The fact that we cannot make sense of the corporealist view of the subject, and that we can achieve a satisfactory version of the Cartesian alternative only if we accept the existence of God, is simply a further indication of the bankruptcy of atheism.

7.

In discussing the issue of the nature of the subjects of mentality, and the rival Cartesian and corporealist approaches, I have focused exclusively on the case of *human* subjects. This is hardly surprising, since the human case is the most important one from our standpoint, as well as the main focus of the traditional philosophical debate. But I want to conclude by saying something about the situation of nonhuman animals, and, in particular, looking at their situation in the light of our findings with respect to human subjects. In doing so, I shall assume that we now know that the Cartesian view of the human subject is correct and that our inability to make sense of the corporealist alternatives reflects the objective incoherence of those alternatives rather than some deficiency in ourselves.

In the course of everyday life, we take it for granted that animals of a sufficient degree of behavioral sophistication have some form of mental life, however limited in comparison to our own. Thus, if we come across an injured dog that is howling, we assume that it is in pain, and if we see a cat stalking (going through the behavioral motions of stalking) a bird, we assume that it sees the bird and pursues it with a purpose. To suggest that perhaps animals are devoid of mentality seems, on the face of it, almost as absurd as the suggestion, made in first-person perspective, that perhaps other human beings do not have minds. At the same time, it is undeniable that animals are corporeal objects: they are biological organisms, with shape, size, and material composition. Whatever our ultimate theory about animal mentality and the nature of animal subjects, a nonphysicalist account of the animals themselves is not an option.

So what account of animal mentality and its subjects should we accept? Well, given our previous discussion, there are two further options that we can immediately dismiss. The first would be to say that the mentality in question does not belong to subjects at all. I have already stressed that our very concept of any form of mentality is the concept of how things are mentally with a subject—the concept of a subject's being in a certain mental state, or performing a certain kind of mental act, or engaging in a certain kind of mental activity—and this applies whether the mentality is in the domain of human beings or in that of animals. So, if we are prepared to recognize animal mentality, we must also recognize the existence of animal subjects who possess it. The second dismissible option would be to say that animals themselves—the biological organisms—are the subjects of the relevant mentality. This is excluded by exactly the same considerations as excluded the corporealist view in the case of human subjects. If we take animals to be purely physical in their core natures, there is no way of making sense of their being subjects of mentality without a gross misrepresentation of the nature of the mentality involved. But nor can we suppose that animals are equipped to be mental subjects by some nonphysical side to their natures, since we cannot make sense of something corporeal being anything other than physical in nature through and through.

With these options excluded, there are only two options that remain. One would be to deny the existence of animal mentality altogether. As I said, such a denial seems, on the face of it, almost as absurd as someone's refusing to accept the existence of mentality in other human beings. But, on closer scrutiny, I think we can see that the situation is not so clear-cut. When we are in conversation with other human beings, it seems quite clear to us that we are directly aware of other mental subjects and can non-inferentially register aspects of their mentality in the things they say, and even in our reflective thinking we cannot detach ourselves from the perspective of that seeming. It is true that philosophers can go through the motions of a skeptical challenge: they can demand that we provide independent grounds for supposing that the way things seem to us is correct. But, whether or not we can satisfy that demand, the suggestion that the other subjects with whom we seem to be in communicative contact may be illusory is not one that, even on philosophical reflection, we can seriously entertain. No amount of immersion in the so-called

problem of other minds can bring me to seriously entertain the possibility that the contact I have with other humans is not contact with
other mentally endowed beings of the same kind as myself. In contrast, in the case of animals there is a genuine issue over whether the
ascription of mentality is ultimately successful. Certainly, we find it
natural to ascribe pain to a howling dog, and seeing and purposive-
ness to a stalking cat. But because we cannot converse with animals,
and because there is nothing at all in our experience of animals that
we could reasonably think of as giving us direct access to animal
minds, we can try to gauge their mentality only by inference from
other factors—factors such as their behavior and physical circumstances. And for this reason we are able to stand back from our ordinary ascriptive practice and seriously wonder whether the evidence
justifies it, or justifies a recognition of animal mentality at all.

The other remaining option would be to treat the case of animals
in the same way as I have treated the case of humans. It would be to
recognize animal mentality, but insist that, just as in the case of
human mentality, the entities that form its subjects are devoid of corporeal properties and spatial location. It would be to insist that in the
situation of the howling dog or the stalking cat, what is in pain and
what sees the bird are not the animals themselves, but nonphysical
entities that are functionally attached to them—attached in the same
kind of way as human subjects are attached to human organisms. I
am speaking here, of course, of the *fundamental* subjects of animal
mentality. The option would still allow us to think of animals as *derivative* mental subjects. Thus, we could continue to think of the dog
as in pain and of the cat as seeing the bird so long as we recognized
that any facts about the mentality of these animals were ultimately
constituted by corresponding facts about the mentality of the nonphysical subjects attached to them, together with the relevant facts
about the nature of this attachment. I have already acknowledged the
analogous point in the case of human beings.

The issue between these two options is one that I shall leave
open. Before I could endorse either of them, I would need to reach a
conclusion about something else, namely whether there was any aspect of the behavior or internal functioning of the kinds of animal
in question which, with full knowledge of all the physical factors

involved, could be adequately explained only by supposing the presence and influence of animal minds. If I could be confident that there was no such aspect, and that, with sufficient knowledge, animal behavior and functioning could be adequately explained in purely physical terms, I would apply Ockham's razor and avoid postulating anything beyond what a physical understanding of the situation requires. This would oblige me to deny animal mentality. On the other hand, if I could be confident that there was such an aspect, I would accept the existence of animal mentality and the nonphysical subjects that this would require. As it is, I do not feel I am in a position to pass judgment on the issue. Perhaps I would be in a better position if I were fully apprised of the existing behavioral and physiological evidence; certainly, this is not an area where I can claim any expertise. But, given the enormous complexity of what is involved, as well as the practical difficulties of monitoring the fine detail of animal brain functioning without disturbing it, I suspect that the evidence needed to reach a rational conclusion is not yet available. Perhaps it never will be.

NOTES

1. See in particular Hume 1978, bk. 1, pt. 4, §6; Russell 1921: 17–18; and Ayer 1946: ch. 7.

2. I discuss these issues more fully in Foster 1991: 212–19.

3. For a fuller account of how I understand the relation of constitution, see Foster 2008: 1–6.

4. This, at least, is what I take to be the gist of his reasoning. See in particular meditation 6 of his *Meditations on First Philosophy*, Descartes 1984a, and the relevant parts of the associated *Objections and Replies*, Descartes 1984b.

5. Berkeley expounds his idealist view in his *Principles of Human Knowledge*. See Berkeley 1975.

6. See in particular Foster 2008, which contains the most recent version of my idealist position. Earlier versions can be found in Foster 1982 and Foster 1993.

7. This is a variant of the example devised and discussed by Sydney Shoemaker in his *Self-Knowledge and Self-Identity* (1963).

8. McGinn 1989. The passage cited occurs in McGinn's opening remarks.

9. Chalmers 1995: §2.

10. In addition to the articles already cited, see Chalmers 1996 and McGinn 1999.

11. Thus see Carnap 1959, Hempel 1949, and Ryle 1949.

12. Advocates of such an account include Hilary Putnam (see for example Putnam 1975) and Sydney Shoemaker (see for example Shoemaker 1984: chs. 9, 12, and 14).

13. Defenders of this form of identity theory include J. J. C. Smart (see for example Smart 1959), David Lewis (see for example Lewis 1983), and David Armstrong (see for example Armstrong 1968).

14. For a fuller discussion of this distinction, see Foster 1991: 98–108.

15. Cf. Foster 1991: chs. 2–5.

16. See Kripke 1980. The various passages that concern the logical necessity of identity relationships can be located by looking up the topic of identity in the index.

17. In elaborating this point, philosophers sometimes focus on the situation of someone who, while having all the relevant behavioral, functional, and physical information about a certain kind of experience, lacks a knowledge of its subjective character because he has never had experiences of that kind himself. See, for example, Jackson 1982 and Robinson 1993. But this focus is not essential to the point itself. It can even have the effect of obscuring it, as Michael Lockwood pointed out (Lockwood 1989: 131–32).

18. There is an echo here of Colin McGinn's 'mysterian' position, to which I briefly referred in section 4. But what McGinn takes to be beyond our powers of comprehension is how it is possible for the brain to *give rise to* conscious mentality, while, as I have stressed, the issue on which I am focusing is whether corporeal objects could be equipped to be *subjects* of mentality.

19. See Foster 1991: 156–201, 261–66.

20. I endorsed this solution in the final section of my subsequent essay (Foster 2001), though, again, without discussing the issue in any detail.

21. I elaborated two of these in Foster 2004 and Foster 2008, respectively, though in the latter case the need for an explanatory appeal to theism arises in the context of an idealist account of the physical world.

REFERENCES

Armstrong, D. 1968. *A Materialist Theory of the Mind.* London: Routledge & Kegan Paul.

Ayer, A. J. 1946. *Language, Truth, and Logic,* 2nd ed. London: Gollancz.

Berkeley, G. 1975. *A Treatise concerning the Principles of Human Knowledge.* In Berkeley, *Philosophical Works,* edited by M. Ayers, 61–127. London: Dent.

Carnap, R. 1959. "Psychology in Physical Language." In *Logical Positivism,* edited by A. J. Ayer, 165–98. Glencoe, IL: Free Press.

Chalmers, D. 1995. "Facing Up to the Problem of Consciousness." *Journal of Consciousness Studies* 2:200–219.

———. 1996. *The Conscious Mind.* Oxford: Oxford University Press.

Descartes, R. 1984a. *Meditations on First Philosophy.* In vol. 2 of *The Philosophical Writings of Descartes,* translated by J. Cottingham, R. Stoothoff, and D. Murdoch, 1–62. Cambridge: Cambridge University Press.

——— 1984b. *Objections and Replies.* In vol. 2 of *The Philosophical Writings of Descartes,* translated by J. Cottingham, R. Stoothoff, and D. Murdoch, 63–398. Cambridge: Cambridge University Press.

Foster, J. 1982. *The Case for Idealism.* London: Routledge & Kegan Paul.

———. 1985. "Berkeley on the Physical World." In *Essays on Berkeley,* edited by J. Foster and H. Robinson, 83–108. Oxford: Oxford University Press.

———. 1991. *The Immaterial Self.* London: Routledge.

———. 1993. "The Succinct Case for Idealism." In *Objections to Physicalism,* edited by H. Robinson, 293–313. Oxford: Oxford University Press.

———. 2001. "A Brief Defence of the Cartesian View." In *Soul, Body, and Survival,* edited by K. Corcoran, 15–29. Ithaca: Cornell University Press.

———. 2004. *The Divine Lawmaker.* Oxford: Oxford University Press.

———. 2008. *A World for Us.* Oxford: Oxford University Press.

Hempel, C. 1949. "The Logical Analysis of Psychology." In *Readings in Philosophical Analysis,* edited by H. Feigl and W. Sellars, 373–84. New York: Appleton-Century-Crofts.

Hume, D. 1978. *A Treatise of Human Nature.* Edited by L. Selby-Bigge. Revised by P. Nidditch. 2nd ed. Oxford: Oxford University Press.

Jackson, F. 1982. "Epiphenomenal Qualia." *Philosophical Quarterly* 32: 127–36.

Kripke, S. 1980. *Naming and Necessity.* Oxford: Blackwell.

Lewis, D. 1983. "An Argument for the Identity Theory." In vol. 1 of *Philosophical Papers,* 99–107. Oxford: Oxford University Press.

Lockwood, M. 1989. *Mind, Brain, and the Quantum.* Oxford: Blackwell.

McGinn, C. 1989. "Can We Solve the Mind–Body Problem?" *Mind* 98: 349–66.

———. 1999. *The Mysterious Flame.* New York: Basic Books.

Putnam, H. 1975. "The Nature of Mental States." In *Mind, Language, and Reality,* 429–40. Cambridge: Cambridge University Press.

Robinson, H. 1993. "The Anti-materialist Strategy and the 'Knowledge Argument.'" In *Objections to Physicalism,* edited by H. Robinson, 159–83. Oxford: Oxford University Press.

Russell, B. 1921. *The Analysis of Mind.* London: Allen & Unwin.

Ryle, G. 1949. *The Concept of Mind.* London: Hutchinson.

Shoemaker, S. 1963. *Self-Knowledge and Self-Identity.* Ithaca: Cornell University Press.

———. 1984. *Identity, Cause, and Mind.* Cambridge: Cambridge University Press.

Smart, J. 1959. "Sensations and Brain Processes." *Philosophical Review* 68:141–56.

4

Against Materialism

ALVIN PLANTINGA

I propose to give two arguments against materialism—or, if you
think that's too negative, two arguments for substantial dualism.
'Substantial' is to be taken in two senses: first, the dualism in question, the dualism for which I mean to argue, is substantial as opposed
to trivial; some versions of property dualism seem to me to be at best
wholly insubstantial. Second, according to the most popular form of
dualism—one embraced by Plato, Augustine, Descartes, and a thousand others—a human person is an immaterial substance: a thing, an
object, a substance, a suppositum (as my Thomist colleagues would
put it), and a thing that isn't material, although, of course, it is intimately connected with a material body. But there is also the view the
name 'dualism' suggests: the view according to which a human person is somehow a sort of composite substance S composed of a material substance S^* and an immaterial substance S^{**}.[1] We can sensibly
include this view under 'dualism'—provided, that is, that having S^*
as a part is not essential to S. (I add this proviso because my first argument is for the conclusion that possibly, I exist when my body
does not.)

Perhaps a better name for the view I mean to defend is 'immaterialism,' the view that a human person is not a material object. Of course it's far from easy to say just what a material object is.[2] For present purposes let's put it recursively: a material object is either an atom, or is composed of atoms. Thus atoms, molecules, cells, hearts, brains and human bodies are all material objects; we'll leave open the question whether such things as electrons, quarks, protons, fields, and superstrings (if indeed there are such things) are material objects. What I'll argue for, accordingly, is the view that human persons are not material objects. They *are* objects (substances), however; therefore they are immaterial objects. My conclusion, of course, is hardly original (going back at least to Plato); my general style of argument also lacks originality (going back at least to Descartes and possibly Augustine). But the method of true philosophy, unlike that of liberal theology and contemporary French thought, aims less at novelty than at truth.

Three more initial comments: (i) When I speak of possibility and necessity, I mean possibility and necessity in the broadly logical sense—metaphysical possibility and necessity, as it is also called. (ii) I won't be arguing that it is possible that I (or others) can exist disembodied, with no body at all.[3] (iii) I will make no claims about what is or isn't conceivable or imaginable. That is because imaginability isn't strictly relevant to possibility at all; conceivability, on the other hand, is relevant only if 'it's conceivable that *p*' is to be understood as implying or offering evidence for 'it's possible that *p*.' (Similarly for 'it's inconceivable that *p*.') It is therefore simpler and much less conducive to confusion to speak just of possibility. I take it we human beings have the following epistemic capacity: we can consider or envisage a proposition or state of affairs and, at least sometimes, determine its modal status—whether it is necessary, contingent, or impossible—just by thinking, just by an exercise of thought.[4]

1. THE REPLACEMENT ARGUMENT: AN ARGUMENT FROM POSSIBILITY

I begin by assuming that there really is such a thing, substance, or suppositum as I, I myself. Of course I'm not unique in that respect;

you too are such that there really is such a thing as you, and the same goes for everybody else. We are substances. Now suppose I were a material substance: which material substance would I be? The answer, I should think, is that I would be my body, or some part of my body, such as my brain or part of my brain. Or perhaps I would be something more exotic: an object distinct from my body that is constituted from the same matter as my body and is colocated with it.[5] What I propose to argue is that I am none of those things: I am not my body, or some part of it such as my brain or a hemisphere or other part of the latter, or an object composed of the same matter as my body (or some part of it) and colocated with it. (I'll call these 'eligible' material objects.) For simplicity (and nothing I say will depend on this simplification) I shall talk for the most part just about my body, which I'll name 'B.' (I was thinking of naming it 'Hercules' or maybe 'Arnold,' but people insisted that would be unduly self-congratulatory.)

The general strategy of this first argument is as follows. It seems possible that I continue to exist when B, my body, does not. I therefore have the property *possibly exists when B does not. B*, however, clearly lacks that property. By Leibniz's Law, therefore (more specifically, the Diversity of Discernibles), I am not identical with B. But why think it possible that I exist when my body does not? Strictly speaking, the replacement argument is an argument for this premise. Again, I conduct the argument in the first person, but naturally enough the same goes for you (although of course you will have to speak for yourself).

So first, at a macroscopic level. A familiar fact of modern medicine is the possibility and actuality of limb and organ transplants and prostheses. You can get a new heart, liver, lungs; you can also get knee, hip, and ankle replacements; you can get prostheses for hands and feet, arms and legs, and so on. Now it seems possible—possible in that broadly logical sense—that medical science should advance to the point where I remain fully dressed and in my right mind (perhaps reading the *South Bend Tribune*) throughout a process during which each of the macroscopic parts of my body is replaced by other such parts, the original parts being vaporized in a nuclear explosion—or better, annihilated by God. But if this process occurs rapidly—during a period of 1 microsecond, let's say—B will no longer exist. I, however, will continue to exist, having been reading the comic page during the entire process.

But what about my brain, you ask—is it possible that my brain be replaced by another, the brain I now have being destroyed, and I continue to exist? It certainly seems so. Think of it like this. It seems possible (in the broadly logical sense) that one hemisphere of my brain be dormant at any given time, the other hemisphere doing all that a brain ordinarily does. At midnight, we can suppose, all the relevant 'data' and 'information' is 'transferred' via the corpus callosum from one hemisphere—call it 'H_1' —to the other hemisphere—H_2—whereupon H_2 takes over operation of the body and H_1 goes dormant. This seems possible; if it were actual, it would also be possible that the original dormant half, H_2, be replaced by a different dormant half (in the same computational or functional state, if you like) just before that midnight transfer; then the transfer occurs, control switches to the new H_2, and H_1 goes dormant—at which time it is replaced by another hemisphere in the same computational or functional condition. In a period of time as brief as you like, therefore, both hemispheres will have been replaced by others, the original hemispheres and all of their parts annihilated by God. Throughout the whole process I serenely continue to read the comics.

This suffices, I think, to show that it's possible that I exist when neither my body nor any part of it exists. What about material objects distinct from my body and its parts, but colocated with it (or one of them) and constituted by the same matter as they? I doubt very much that there could be any such things. If objects of this kind are possible, however, the above argument also shows or at least suggests that possibly, I exist when none of them does. For example, if there is such a thing as *the matter of which B is composed*—if that phrase denotes a thing or object[6]—it too would be destroyed by God's annihilating all the parts of my body.

Of course very many different sorts of an object of this kind—an object constituted by the matter of my body and colocated with it—have been suggested, and I don't have the space here to deal with them all. However, we can offer a version of the replacement argument that will be relevant to many of them. Turn from macroscopic replacement to microscopic replacement. This could go on at several levels: the levels of atoms, molecules, or cells, for example. Let's think about it at the cellular level. It seems entirely possible that the cells of which my body is composed be rapidly—within a microsecond or two—replaced by other cells of the same kind, the original cells being instantly destroyed. It also seems entirely possible that this process of replacement take place while I remain conscious, thinking about dualism and marveling at some of the appalling arguments against it produced by certain materialists.[7] Then I would exist at a time at which *B* did not exist.

But is it really true that this process of replacement would result in the destruction of *B?* After all, according to current science, all the matter in our bodies is replaced over a period of years, without any obvious compromise of bodily integrity or identity. As a matter of fact, so they say, the matter in our brains is completely replaced in a much shorter time.[8] Why should merely accelerating this process make a difference?[9]

Well, as they say, speed kills. When a cell is removed from an organism and replaced by another cell, the new cell doesn't become part of the organism instantaneously; it must be integrated into the organism and assimilated by it.[10] What does this assimilation consist in? A cell in a (properly functioning) body is involved in a network of causal relations; a neuron, for example, emits and responds to electrical signals. A cell receives nourishment from the blood, and cooperates with other cells in various causal activities. All these things take time—maybe not much time, but still a certain period of time. At the instant the new part[11] is inserted into the organism, and until it has begun to play this causal role (both as cause and effect), the new part is not yet a part of the organism, but a foreign body occupying space within the spatial boundaries of the organism. (Clearly not everything, nor even everything organic, within the spatial boundaries of your body is *part* of your body: think of the goldfish you just swallowed, or a tapeworm.) Let's use the phrase 'assimilation time' to denote the time required for the cell to start playing this causal role. The assimilation time is the time required for the cell to become assimilated into the body; before that time has elapsed the cell is not yet part of the body. To be rigorous, we should index this to the part (or kind of part) and the organism in question; different parts may require different periods of time for their assimilation by different organisms. For simplicity, though, let's assume all parts and organisms have the same assimilation time; this simplification won't make any difference to the argument.

That a given part and organism are such that the time of assimilation for the former with respect to the latter is *dt*, for some specific period of time *dt*, is, I take it, a contingent fact. One thinks the velocity of light imposes a lower limit here, but the time of assimilation could be much greater. (For example, it could depend on the rate of blood flow, the rate of intracellular transport, and the rate at which information is transmitted through neuron or nerve.) God could presumably slow down this process, or speed it up.

There is also what we might call 'the replacement time': the period of time from the beginning of the replacement of the first part by a new part to the end of the time of the replacement of the last part (the last to be replaced) by a different part. The time of replacement is also, of course, contingent; a replacement can occur rapidly or slowly. Presumably there is no nonzero lower limit here; no matter how rapidly the parts are replaced, it is possible in the broadly logical sense that they be replaced still more rapidly.

What's required by the Replacement Argument, therefore (or at any rate what's sufficient for it), is

> (Replacement) It is possible that: the cells in *B* are replaced by other cells and the originals instantly annihilated while I continue to exist; and the replacement time for *B* and those cells is shorter than the assimilation time.

Objections and Replies

(1) Doesn't a Star Trek scenario seem possible, one in which you are beamed up from the surface of a planet to an orbiting spacecraft, both you and, in this context more importantly, your body surviving the process? This objection is relevant to the Replacement Argument, however, only if in this scenario your body survives a process in which its matter is replaced by other matter, the original matter being annihilated. But that's not how the Star Trek scenario works: what happens instead is that the matter of which your body is composed is beamed up (perhaps after having been converted to energy),

not annihilated. You might think of this case as one of disassembly (and perhaps conversion into energy) and then reassembly. Perhaps your body could survive this sort of treatment; what I claim it can't survive is the rapid replacement of the matter in question by other matter, the original matter being annihilated.

(2) I've been assuming that you and I are objects, substances; but that assumption may not be as innocent as it looks. Might I not be an *event*[12]—perhaps an event like a computer's running a certain program? We ordinarily think of an event as one or more objects $O_1, \ldots O_n$, exemplifying a property P or relation R (where P or R may be complex in various ways and may of course entail extension over time). Perhaps what I am is an event involving (consisting in) many material objects (organs, limbs, cells, etc.) standing in a complex relation. Then, although I wouldn't be a material object, I *would* be an event involving nothing but material objects—a material event, as we might call it; and why wouldn't that be enough to satisfy the materialist?

Further, suppose I were a material event: why couldn't that event persist through arbitrarily rapid replacement of the objects involved in it? Think of an event such as a battle; clearly there could be a battle in which the combatants were removed and replaced by other combatants with extremely great rapidity. Let's suppose the commanding officer has an unlimited number of troops at his command. He needs 1000 combatants at any given time: eager to spread the risk, he decrees that each combatant will fight for just 30 seconds and then be instantly replaced by another combatant. (Imagine that technology has advanced to the point where the obvious technical problems can be dealt with.) The battle, we may suppose, begins on Monday morning and ends Tuesday night; this one event, although no doubt including many subevents, lasts from Monday morning to Tuesday night—and this despite the constant and rapid replacement of the combatants. Although there are never more than 1000 troops in the field at any one time, several million are involved in the event, by virtue of those rapid replacements. Of course the replacement could be much faster; indeed, there is no logical limit on the rapidity of replacement of the combatants, the same event (i.e., the battle) persisting throughout. More generally:

(a) For any duration d and event E and substances $S_1, S_2 \ldots, S_n$ involved in E, if $S_1, S_2 \ldots, S_n$ are replaced by substances $S_{n+1}, S_{n+2} \ldots S_{n+n}$ during d, then there is an event E^* that persists through d and is such that at the beginning of d, E^* involves $S_1, S_2 \ldots S_n$, and at the end of d does not involve $S_1, S_2 \ldots S_n$, but does involve $S_{n+1}, S_{n+2} \ldots S_{n+n}$.

So events have a certain modal flexibility along this dimension.[13] Now suppose I were an event. Why couldn't the event which I am persist through arbitrarily rapid replacement of the material objects involved in it? Is there any reason, intuitive or otherwise, to suppose not? Perhaps a material *substance* can't survive the arbitrarily rapid replacement of its parts; is there any reason to think a material *event* suffers from the same limitation?

(3) We can conveniently deal with objection (2) by considering it together with another. According to Peter van Inwagen, human beings are material objects; a material object, furthermore, is either an elementary particle or a living being. Living beings comprise the usual suspects: organisms such as horses, flies, and oak trees, but also cells (neurons, for example), which may not rise to the lofty heights of being organisms, but are nonetheless living beings. It is *living* horses, flies, etc., that are objects or substances. Indeed, 'living horse' is a pleonasm. On van Inwagen's view, there aren't any dead horses; a 'dead horse,' strictly speaking, is not really a thing at all and a fortiori not a horse; it is instead a mere heap or pile of organic matter. Once that horse has died, its remains (as we say in the case of human beings) are a mere assemblage of elementary particles related in a certain way; there is no entity or being there in addition to the particles. A living horse, on the other hand, is a thing, a substance, in its own right and has as parts only other living beings (cells, e.g.) and elementary particles. Strictly speaking, therefore, there isn't any such thing as a hand, or arm or leg or head; rather, in the place we think of as where the hand is, there are elementary particles and other living things (cells, e.g.) related in a certain way.

But by virtue of what is this horse a thing or a substance: under what conditions does an assemblage of elementary particles constitute a thing, i.e., become *parts* of a *substance?* When those particles are involved in a certain complex event: a *life*. Elementary particles can stand in many relations and be involved in many kinds of events; among these many kinds of events are lives; and when elementary particles are involved in that sort of event, then they become parts of a substance. Further, the object, that living thing, exists when and only when the event which is its life exists or occurs. Still further (and here we may be taking leave of van Inwagen), the survival and identity conditions of the organism are determined by the survival and identity conditions of that event, that life. Consider an organism *O* and its life *L(O)*. The idea is that *O* exists in just those possible worlds in which *L(O)* occurs; more precisely, *O* and *L(O)* are such that for any world *W* and time *t*, *O* exists in *W* at *t* if and only if *L(O)* exists at *t* in *W*. Hence

> (b) Given an organism *O* and the event *L(O)* that constitutes its life, necessarily, *O* exists at a time *t* just if *L(O)* occurs at *t*. (We can think of 'exists' as short for 'exists, did exist, or will exist'; similarly for 'occurs.')

This elegant position certainly has its attractions. It's not wholly clear, of course, that there *are* any elementary particles (perhaps all particles are composed of other particles so that it's composition all the way down, or perhaps what there really is, is 'atomless gunk' con-figured in various ways);[14] perhaps electrons, and so on, aren't par-ticles at all, but perturbances of fields; and it's a bit harsh to be told that there really aren't any such things as tables and chairs, automo-biles and television sets. Nevertheless van Inwagen's view is attrac-tive. Now suppose we add (b) to van Inwagen's view; the resulting position suggests an objection to the Replacement Argument (an ob-jection that doesn't have van Inwagen's blessing). For (again) why couldn't the event which is my life persist through arbitrarily rapid replacement of the objects it involves? Is there any intuitive support for the thought that there is a lower limit on the rapidity of replace-ment through which this event could persist? If not, then even if I couldn't be a material substance, I could be a material event; no doubt the materialist would find this materialism enough.

We can respond to these two objections together. According to objection (2), I can sensibly think of myself as an event: presumably the event that constitutes my life. Now perhaps the objector's (a) is true: for any replacement, no matter how rapid, there will be an event of the sort (a) suggests. But of course nothing follows about the modal properties of any particular event. So suppose I am an event: nothing about my modal properties follows from or is even suggested by (a); and it is my modal properties that are at issue here. In particular, it doesn't follow that if I were my life, then I could have continued to exist (or occur) through the sort of rapid replacement envisaged in the Replacement Argument. Now turn to (3). Suppose for the moment we concede (b): we still have no reason to think my life, that particular event, the event which is in fact my life, could have survived those rapid replacements of the objects involved in it. No doubt for any such replacement event, there is an event of the sort suggested by (a); nothing follows with respect to the modal properties of the event which is my life. In particular it doesn't follow that it could have persisted through the sort of rapid replacements we've been thinking about.

So (a) is really a red herring. But there is a more decisive response here. Objection (3) endorses (b), the claim that there is an event—my life—such that, necessarily, I exist just when it does. Objection (2) also (and trivially) entails (b); if I just *am* my life then, naturally enough, (b) is true. Fortunately, however, (b) is false. For (b) entails

(c) I and my life are such that necessarily, I exist just when it occurs,

and (as I'll now argue) (c) is false.

Why think (c) is false? First, it's far from clear just which properties events have essentially. Some think it essential to any event that it include just those objects that it does in fact include, and also that these objects exemplify just the properties and relations they do in fact exemplify. If that were true, an event involving an object O's having a certain property could not have occurred if O had not had that property. But that seems a bit strong; surely the Civil War, for example (that very event), could have taken place even if a particular

Confederate soldier had not trodden on a blade of grass he did in fact step on. Still, there are serious limits here. Perhaps the Civil War (the event which is the Civil War) would have existed even if that soldier hadn't trampled that blade of grass; but the Civil War (that event) could not have lasted only ten minutes. There is a possible world in which there is a very short war between the states (and it could even be called 'The Civil War'); but there is no possible world in which the war that did in fact take place occurs, and lasts for only ten minutes. Similarly for my life (call it 'L'): if (b) is true, then of course L has existed exactly as long as I have. L, therefore, has by now existed for more than seventy years. Clearly enough, however, I could have existed for a much shorter time: for example, I could have been run over by a Mack truck at the age of six months (and not been subsequently sustained in existence by God). L, however, could not have existed or occurred for only those first few months, just as the Civil War could not have existed or occurred for only ten minutes. There is a possible world in which I exist for just those first few months, or even for just a few minutes; there is no possible world in which L exists for that period of time. Of course, if I had existed for, say, just ten minutes, there w*ould have been* an event which would have been my life, and which would have existed for just ten minutes; that event, however, would not have been L. We can put it like this: in any world in which I exist, there is an event which is my life; but it is not the case that there is an event which is my life, and which is my life in every world in which I exist.

Proposition (c), therefore, is false; it is not the case that I and the life of my body are such that necessarily, we exist at all the same times—that is, it is not the case that I and the life of my body are such that I have essentially the property of existing when and only when it does. But if (c) is false, the same goes for (b); since objections (2) and (3) both entail (b), both objections fail.

(4) If, as I say is possible, the replacement time for B and those parts is shorter than the assimilation time, there will be a brief period during which I don't have a body at all.[15] I will no longer have B, because all of B's parts have been replaced (and destroyed) during a time too brief for the new parts to be assimilated into B. I won't have any other body either, however; I won't have a body distinct from B, because there hasn't been time for these new parts to coalesce into a

body. I therefore have no body at all during this time; there is no body that is *my* body at this time. How, then, can I continue to be conscious during this time, serenely reading the comics? Isn't it necessary that there be neurological activity supporting my consciousness during this time, if I am to be conscious then?

But is it *logically* necessary that there be neurological or other physical activity supporting my consciousness at any time at which I am conscious? That's a whopping assumption. The most I need for my argument is that it is *logically possible* that I remain conscious during a brief period in which no neurological activity is supporting my consciousness; that's compatible with its being causally required that there be neurological activity when I am conscious. My entire argument has to do with what *could* happen; not with what *would* as a matter of fact happen, if this sort of replacement were to occur.[16] So the most that argument needs is that possibly, I exist and am conscious when no neurological activity is supporting my consciousness.[17] But the fact is it doesn't require even that. For consider a time *t* after the end of the replacement time but before the assimilation time has ended; let *t* be as close as you please to the end of the replacement time. At *t*, the replacing elements, the new parts, haven't yet had time to coalesce into a body. Nonetheless, any one of the new elements could be performing one of the several functions it will be performing when it has been integrated into a functioning human body. It could be playing part of the whole causal role it will be playing when the assimilation time has elapsed. In particular, therefore, the new neurons, before they have become part of a body, could be doing whatever it is they have to do in order to support consciousness. Accordingly, my argument requires that possibly I am conscious when I do not have a body; it does not require that possibly I am conscious when no neuronal or neurological activity is occurring.

2. CAN A MATERIAL THING THINK? AN ARGUMENT FROM IMPOSSIBILITY

The Replacement Argument is an argument from possibility; as such, it proceeds from an intuition, the intuition that it is possible that my bodily parts, macroscopic or microscopic, be replaced while

I remain conscious. But some people distrust modal intuitions. Of course it's impossible to do philosophy (or for that matter physics) without invoking modal intuitions of one sort or another or at any rate making modal declarations of one sort or another.[18] Still, it must be conceded that intuition can sometimes be a bit of a frail reed. True, there is no way to conduct philosophy that isn't a frail reed, but intuition is certainly fallible. Further, some might think modal intuitions particularly fallible—although almost all of the intuitions involved in philosophy have important modal connections. Still further, one might think further that intuitions of *possibility* are especially suspect. That is because it seems easy to confuse *seeing the possibility of p* with *failing to see the impossibility of p*. You can't see why numbers couldn't be sets; it doesn't follow that what you see is that they *could* be sets. Maybe I can't see why water couldn't be composed of something other than H_2O; it doesn't follow that what I see is that water could be something other than H_2O. And perhaps, so the claim might go, one who finds the replacement argument attractive is really confusing seeing the possibility of the replacements in question with failing to see their impossibility. Granted: I can't see that these replacements are impossible; it doesn't follow that what I see is that they are indeed possible.

To be aware of this possible source of error, however, is to be forewarned and thus forearmed. But for those who aren't mollified and continue to distrust possibility intuitions, I have another argument for dualism—one that depends on an intuition, not, this time, of possibility, but of impossibility. One who distrusts possibility intuitions may think more kindly of intuitions of impossibility—perhaps because she thinks that for the latter there isn't any obvious analogue of the possible confusion between failing to see that something is impossible and seeing that it is possible. Or rather, while there *is* an analogue—it would be confusing failure to see the possibility of *p* with seeing the impossibility of *p*—falling into that confusion seems less likely. In any event, the argument I'll now propose is for the conclusion that no material objects can think—i.e., reason and believe, entertain propositions, draw inferences, and the like. But of course I can think; therefore I am not a material object.

Leibniz's Problem

I (and the same goes for you) am a certain kind of thing: a thing that can think. I believe many things; I also hope, fear, expect, anticipate many things. I desire certain states of affairs (desire that certain states of affairs be actual). I am capable of making decisions. I am capable of acting, and capable of acting on the basis of my beliefs and desires. I am conscious, and conscious of a rich, kaleidoscopic constellation of feelings, mental images, beliefs, and ways of being appeared to, some of which I enjoy and some of which I dislike. Naturally enough, therefore, I am not identical with any object that lacks any or all of these properties. What I propose to argue next is that some of these properties are such that no material object can have them. Again, others have offered similar arguments. In particular, many have seen a real problem for materialism in *consciousness:* it is extremely difficult to see how a material object could be conscious, could enjoy that vivid and varied constellation of feelings, mental images, and ways of being appeared to. Others have argued that a material object can't make a decision (although of course we properly speak, in the loose and popular sense, of the chess-playing computer as deciding which move to make next). These arguments seem to me to be cogent.[19] Here, however, I want to develop another argument of the same sort, another problem for materialism, a problem I believe is equally debilitating, and in fact fatal to materialism. Again, this problem is not a recent invention; you can find it or something like it in Plato. Leibniz, however, offers a famous and particularly forceful statement of it:

> 17. It must be confessed, moreover, that perception, and that which depends on it, are inexplicable by mechanical causes, that is by figures and motions. And supposing there were a machine so constructed as to think, feel and have perception, we could conceive of it as enlarged and yet preserving the same proportions, so that we might enter it as into a mill. And this granted, we should only find on visiting it, pieces which push one against another, but never anything by which to explain a perception. This must be sought for,

therefore, in the simple substance and not in the composite or in the machine. (Leibniz 1951: 536 [*Monadology* 17])

Now Leibniz uses the word 'perception' here; he's really thinking of mental life generally. His point, in this passage, is that mental life—perception, thought, decision—cannot arise by way of the mechanical interaction of parts. Consider a bicycle; like Leibniz's mill, it does what it does by virtue of the mechanical interaction of its parts. Stepping down on the pedals causes the front sprocket to turn, which causes the chain to move, which causes the rear sprocket to turn, which causes the back wheel to rotate. By virtue of these mechanical interactions, the bicycle does what it does, i.e., transports someone from one place to another. And of course machines generally—jet aircraft, refrigerators, computers, centrifuges—do their things and accomplish their functions in the same way. So Leibniz's claim, here, is that thinking can't arise in this way. A thing can't think by virtue of the mechanical interaction of its parts.

Leibniz is thinking of *mechanical* interactions—interactions involving pushes and pulls, gears and pulleys, chains and sprockets. But I think he would say the same of other interactions studied in physics, for example those involving gravity, electromagnetism, and the strong and weak nuclear forces. Call these 'physical interactions.' Leibniz's claim is that thinking can't arise by virtue of physical interaction among objects or parts of objects. According to current science, electrons and quarks are simple, without parts.[20] Presumably neither can think—neither can adopt propositional attitudes; neither can believe, doubt, hope, want, or fear. But then a proton composed of quarks won't be able to think either, at least by way of physical relations between its component quarks, and the same will go for an atom composed of protons and electrons, a molecule composed of atoms, a cell composed of molecules, and an organ (e.g., a brain), composed of cells. If electrons and quarks can't think, we won't find anything composed of them that can think by way of the physical interaction of its parts.

Leibniz is talking about thinking generally; suppose we narrow our focus to belief (although the same considerations apply to other propositional attitudes). What, first of all, would a belief be, from a materialist perspective? Suppose you are a materialist, and also think, as we ordinarily do, that there are such things as beliefs. For example, you hold the belief that Marcel Proust is more subtle than Louis L'Amour. What kind of a thing is this belief? Well, from a materialist perspective, it looks as if it would have to be something like a long-standing event or structure in your brain or nervous system. Presumably this event will involve many neurons related to each other in subtle and complex ways. There are plenty of neurons to go around: a normal human brain contains some 100 billion. These neurons, furthermore, are connected with other neurons at synapses; a single neuron can be involved in several thousand synapses, and there are some 10^{15} synaptic connections. The total number of possible brain states, then, is absolutely enormous, vastly greater than the 10^{80} electrons they say the universe contains. And the total number of possible neuronal events, while no doubt vastly smaller, is still enormous. Under certain conditions, groups of neurons involved in such an event fire, producing electrical impulses that can be transmitted (with appropriate modification and input from other structures) down the cables of neurons that constitute effector nerves to muscles or glands, causing, e.g., muscular contraction and thus behavior.

From the materialist's point of view, therefore, a belief will be a neuronal event or structure of this sort. But if this is what beliefs are, they will have two very different sorts of properties. On the one hand there will be *electrochemical* or *neurophysiological* properties ('NP properties,' for short). Among these would be such properties as that of involving *n* neurons and *n** connections between neurons, properties that specify which neurons are connected with which others, what the rates of fire in the various parts of the event are, how these rates of fire change in response to changes in input, and so on. But if the event in question is really a *belief*, then in addition to those NP properties it will have another property as well: it will have to have a *content*. It will have to be the belief that *p*, for some proposition *p*. If this event is the belief that Proust is a more subtle writer than Louis L'Amour, then its content is the proposition *Proust is more subtle than Louis L'Amour*. My belief that naturalism is all the rage these days has as content the proposition *Naturalism is all the rage these days*.

(That same proposition is the content of the German speaker's belief that naturalism is all the rage these days, even though she expresses this belief by uttering the German sentence 'Der Naturalismus ist dieser Tage ganz groß in Mode'; beliefs, unlike sentences, do not come in different languages.) It is in virtue of having a content, of course, that a belief is true or false: it is true if the proposition which is its content is true, and false otherwise. My belief that all men are mortal is true because the proposition which constitutes its content is true, but Hitler's belief that the Third Reich would last a thousand years was false, because the proposition that constituted its content was false.[21]

And now the difficulty for materialism is this: how does it happen, how can it be, that an assemblage of neurons, a group of material objects firing away *has a content?* How can that happen? More poignantly, *what is it* for such an event to have a content? What is it for this structured group of neurons, or the event of which they are a part, to be related, for example, to the proposition *Cleveland is a beautiful city* in such a way that the latter is its content? A single neuron (or quark, electron, atom, or whatever) presumably isn't a belief and doesn't have content; but how can belief, content, arise from physical interaction among such material entities as neurons? As Leibniz suggests, we can examine this neuronal event as carefully as we please; we can measure the number of neurons it contains, their connections, their rates of fire, the strength of the electrical impulses involved, the potential across the synapses—we can measure all this with as much precision as you could possibly desire; we can consider its electrochemical, neurophysiological properties in the most exquisite detail; but nowhere, here, will we find so much as a hint of content. Indeed, none of this seems even vaguely *relevant* to its having content. None of this so much as slyly suggests that this bunch of neurons firing away is the belief that Proust is more subtle than Louis L'Amour, as opposed, e.g., to the belief that Louis L'Amour is the most widely published author from Jamestown, North Dakota. Indeed, nothing we find here will so much as slyly suggest that it has a content of *any* sort. Nothing here will so much as slyly suggest that it is *about* something, in the way a belief about horses is about horses.

The fact is, we can't see how it *could* have a content. It's not just that we don't know or can't see how it's done. When light strikes photoreceptor cells in the retina, there is an enormously complex cascade of electrical activity, resulting in an electrical signal to the brain. I have no idea how all that works; but of course I know it happens all the time. But the case under consideration is different. Here it's not merely that I don't know how physical interaction among neurons brings it about that an assemblage of them has content and is a belief. No, in this case, it seems upon reflection that such an event could *not* have content. It's a little like trying to understand what it would be for the number 7, e.g., to weigh five pounds, or for an elephant (or the unit set of an elephant) to be a proposition. (Pace the late—and great—David Lewis, according to whom the unit set of an elephant *could* be a proposition; in fact, on his view, there are uncountably many elephants the unit sets of which *are* propositions.) We can't see how that could happen; more exactly, what we can see is that it *couldn't* happen. A number just isn't the sort of thing that can have weight; there is no way in which that number or any other number could weigh anything at all. The unit set of an elephant, let alone the elephant itself, can't be a proposition; it's not the right sort of thing. Similarly, we can see, I think, that physical activity among neurons can't constitute content. There they are, those neurons, clicking away, sending electrical impulses hither and yon. But what has this to do with content? How is content or aboutness supposed to arise from this neuronal activity? How can such a thing possibly be a belief? But then no neuronal event can as such have a content, can be *about* something, in the way in which my belief that the number seven is prime is about the number seven, or my belief that the oak tree in my backyard is without leaves is about that oak tree.

Here we must be very clear about an important distinction. Clearly there is such a thing as *indication* or *indicator meaning*.[22] Deer tracks in my backyard indicate that deer have run through it; smoke indicates fire; the height of the mercury column indicates the ambient temperature; buds on the trees indicate the coming of spring. We could speak here of 'natural signs': smoke is a natural sign of fire, and the height of the mercury column is a natural sign of the temperature. When one event indicates or is a natural sign of another, there is ordinarily some sort of causal or nomic connection, or at least regular association, between them by virtue of which the first is reliably correlated with the second. Smoke is caused by fire, which is why it indicates fire; measles cause red spots on your face, which is why red spots on your face indicate measles; there is a causal connection between the height of the mercury column and the temperature, so that the former indicates the latter.

The nervous systems of organisms contain such indicators. A widely discussed example: when a frog sees a fly zooming by, the frog's brain (so it is thought) displays a certain pattern of neural firing; we could call such patterns 'fly detectors.' Another famous example: some anaerobic marine bacteria have magnetosomes, tiny internal magnets. These function like compass needles, indicating magnetic north. The direction to magnetic north is downward; hence these bacteria, which can't flourish in the oxygen-rich surface water, move towards the more oxygen-free water at the bottom of the ocean.[23] Of course there are also indicators in human bodies. There are structures that respond in a regular way to blood temperature; they are part of a complex feedback system that maintains a more or less constant blood temperature by inducing (e.g.) shivering if the temperature is too low and sweating if it is too high. There are structures that monitor the amount of sugar in the blood and its sodium content. There are structures that respond in a regular way to light of a certain pattern striking the retina, to the amount of food in your stomach, to its progress through your digestive system, and so on. Presumably there are structures in the brain that are correlated with features of the environment; it is widely assumed that when you see a tree, there is a distinctive pattern of neural firing (or some other kind of structure) in your brain that is correlated with and caused by it.

Now we can, if we like, speak of 'content' here; it's a free country. We can say that the mercury column, on a given occasion, has a certain content: the state of affairs correlated with its having the height it has on that occasion. We could say, if we like, that those structures in the body that indicate blood pressure or temperature or saline content have a content on a given occasion: whatever it is that the structure indicates on that occasion. We could say, if we like, that the neural structure that is correlated with my looking at a tree has a content: its content, we could say, is what it indicates on that occasion. We can also, if we like, speak of information in these cases: the structure that registers my blood temperature, we can say, carries the information that my blood temperature is thus and so.

What is crucially important to see, however, is that this sort of content or information has nothing as such to do with *belief*, or belief content. There are those who—no doubt in the pursuit of greater generality—gloss over this distinction. Donald T. Campbell, for example, in arguing for the relevance of natural selection to epistemology, claims that "evolution—even in its biological aspects—is a knowledge process. . . ." (Campbell 1974: 413). Commenting on Campbell's claim, Franz Wuketits explains that

> the claim is based on the idea that any living system is a "knowledge-gaining system." This means that organisms accumulate information about certain properties of their environment. Hence life generally may be described as an information process, or, to put it more precisely, an information-increasing process. (Wuketits 1986: 193)

At any rate Wuketits has the grace to put 'knowledge' in scare quotes here. Knowledge requires belief; correlation, causal or otherwise, is not belief; information and content of this sort do not require belief. Neither the thermostat nor any of its components believes that the room temperature is thus and so. When the saline content of my blood is too low, neither I nor the structure correlated with that state of affairs (nor my blood) believes the saline content is less than it should be—or, indeed, anything else about the saline content. Indication, carrying information, is not belief; indicator content is not belief content, and these structures don't have belief content just by virtue of having indicator content. And now the point here: I am not, of course, claiming that material structures can't have indicator content; obviously they can. What I am claiming is that they can't have belief content: no material structure can be a belief.

Here someone might object as follows. "You say we can't see how a neural event can have content; but in fact we understand this perfectly well, and something similar happens all the time. For there is, after all, the computer analogy. A computer, of course, is a material object, an assemblage of wires, switches, relays, and the like. Now suppose I am typing in a document. Take any particular sentence in the document: say the sentence 'Naturalism is all the rage these days.' That sentence is represented and stored on the computer's hard disk. We don't have to know in exactly what *way* it's stored (it's plusses and minuses, or a magnetic configuration, or something else; it doesn't matter). Now the sentence 'Naturalism is all the rage these days' expresses the proposition *Naturalism is all the rage these days.* That sentence, therefore, has the proposition *Naturalism is all the rage these days* as its content. But then consider the analogue of that sentence on the computer disk: doesn't it, too, express the same proposition as the sentence it represents? That bit of the computer disk with its plusses and minuses, therefore, has propositional content. But of course that bit of the computer disk is also (part of) a material object (as is any inscription of the sentence in question). Contrary to your claim, therefore, a material object can perfectly well have propositional content; indeed, it happens all the time. But if a computer disk or an inscription of a sentence can have a proposition as content, why can't an assemblage of neurons? Just as a magnetic pattern has as content the proposition *Naturalism is all the rage these days*, so too a pattern of neuronal firing can have that proposition as content. Your claim to the contrary is completely bogus and you should be ashamed of yourself." Thus far the objector.

If the sentence or the computer disk really *did* have content, then I guess the assemblage of neurons could too. But the fact is neither does—or rather, neither has the right kind of content: neither has *original* content; each has, at most, *derived* content. For how does it happen that the sentence has content? It's simply by virtue of the fact that we human beings *treat* that sentence in a certain way, *use* the sentence in a certain way, a way such that if a sentence is used in that way, then it expresses the proposition in question. Upon hearing that sentence, I think of, grasp, apprehend the proposition *Naturalism is all the rage these days.* You can get me to grasp, entertain, and perhaps believe that proposition by uttering that sentence. How exactly all this works is complicated and not at all well understood; but the point is that the sentence has content only because of something *we,* we who are *already* thinkers, do with it. We could put this by saying that the sentence has *secondary* or *derived* content; it has content only because we, we creatures whose thoughts and beliefs already have content, treat it in a certain way. The same goes for the magnetic pattern on the computer disk; it represents or expresses that proposition because we assign that proposition to that configuration. But of course that isn't how it goes (given materialism) with that pattern of neural firing. That pattern doesn't get its content by way of being used in a certain way by some other creatures whose thoughts and beliefs already have content. If that pattern has content at all, then, according to materialism, it must have *original* or *primary* content. And what it is hard or impossible to see is how it could be that an assemblage of neurons (or a sentence, or a computer disk) could have original or primary content. To repeat: it isn't just that we can't see how it's done, in the way in which we can't see how the sleight of hand artist gets the pea to wind up under the middle shell. It is rather that we can see, to at least some degree, that it can't be done, just as we can see that an elephant can't be a proposition, and that the number 7 can't weigh seven pounds.

Parity?

Peter van Inwagen agrees that it is hard indeed to see how physical interaction among material entities can produce thought: "It seems to me that the notion of a physical thing that thinks is a mysterious notion, and that Leibniz's thought-experiment brings out this mystery very effectively" (van Inwagen 2002: 176).

Now I am taking this fact as a reason to reject materialism and hence as an argument for dualism. But of course it is a successful argument only if there is no similar difficulty for substance dualism itself. Van Inwagen believes there *is* a similar difficulty for dualism:

> For it is thinking itself that is the source of the mystery of a thinking physical thing. The notion of a non-physical thing that thinks is, I would argue, equally mysterious. How any sort of thing could think is a mystery. It is just that it is a bit easier to see that thinking is a mystery when we suppose that the thing that does the thinking

is physical, for we can form mental images of the operations of a physical thing and we can see that the physical interactions represented in these images—the only interactions that can be represented in these images—have no connection with thought or sensation, or none we are able to imagine, conceive or articulate. The only reason we do not readily find the notion of a non-physical thing that thinks equally mysterious is that we have no clear procedure for forming mental images of non-physical things. (van Inwagen 2002: 176)

So dualism is no better off than materialism; they both have the same problem. But what precisely *is* this problem, according to van Inwagen? "We can form mental images of the operations of a physical thing and we can see that the physical interactions represented in these images—the only interactions that can be represented in these images—have no connection with thought or sensation or none we are able to imagine, conceive or articulate." As I understand van Inwagen here, he is saying that we can imagine physical interactions or changes in a physical thing; but we can see that the physical interactions represented in those images have no connection with thought. We can imagine neurons in the brain firing; we can imagine electrical impulses or perhaps clouds of electrons moving through parts of neurons, or whole chains of neurons; we can imagine neural structures with rates of fire in certain parts of the structure changing in response to rates of fire elsewhere in or out of that structure: but we can see that these interactions have no connection with thought. Now I'm not quite sure whether or not I can imagine electrons, or their movements, or electrical impulses; but it does seem to me that I can see that electrical impulses and the motions of electrons, if indeed there are any such things, have nothing to do with thought.

Another way to put van Inwagen's point: no change we can imagine in a physical thing could be a mental change, i.e., could constitute thought or sensation, or a change in thought or sensation. But then we can't imagine a physical thing's thinking: i.e., we can't form a mental image of a physical thing thinking. And this suggests that the problem for materialism is that we can't form a mental image of a material thing thinking. But the same goes, says van Inwagen, for an immaterial thing: we also can't imagine or form a mental image of an immaterial thing thinking. Indeed, we can't form a mental image of any kind of thinking thing: "My point," he says, "is that nothing could possibly count as a mental image of a thinking thing" (van Inwagen 2002: 177). Materialism and dualism, therefore, are so far on a par; there is nothing here to incline us to the latter rather than the former.

Thus far van Inwagen. The thought of a physical thing's thinking, he concedes, is mysterious; that is because we can't form a mental image of a physical thing's thinking. But the thought of an immaterial thing's thinking is equally mysterious; for we can't form a mental image of that either. This, however, seems to me to mislocate the problem for materialism. What inclines us to reject the idea of a physical thing's thinking is not just the fact that we can't form a mental image of a physical thing's thinking. There are plenty of things of which we can't form a mental image, where we're not in the least inclined to reject them as impossible. As Descartes pointed out, I can't form a mental image of a chiliagon, a 1000-sided rectilinear plane figure (or at least an image that distinguishes it from a 100-sided rectilinear plane figure); that doesn't even suggest that there can't be any such thing. I can't form a mental image of the number 79's being prime: that doesn't incline me to believe that the number 79 could not be prime; as a matter of fact I know how to prove that it is prime. The fact is I can't form a mental image of the number 79 at all—or for that matter of any number; this doesn't incline me to think there aren't any numbers.

Or is all that a mistake? Is it really true that I can't form a mental image of the number 7, for example? Maybe I *can* form an image of the number 7; when I think of the number 7, sometimes there is a mental image present; it's as if one catches a quick glimpse of a sort of partial and fragmented numeral 7; we could say that I'm appeared to numeral-7ly. When I think of the actual world, I am sometimes presented with an image of the Greek letter alpha; when I think of the proposition *All men are mortal*, I am sometimes presented with a sort of fleeting, fragmentary, partial image of the corresponding English sentence. Sets are nonphysical, but maybe I can imagine the pair set of Mic and Martha; when I try, it's like I catch a fleeting glimpse of curly brackets, enclosing indistinct images that don't look a whole lot like Mic and Martha. But is that really imagining the number 7, or the actual world, or the pair set of Mic and Martha? Here I'm of two minds. On the one hand, I'm inclined to think that this isn't imagining the number 7 at all, but instead imagining something connected with it, namely the numeral 7 (and the same for the actual world and the set of Mic and Martha). On the other hand I'm a bit favorably disposed to the idea that that's just how you imagine something like the number 7; you do it by imagining the numeral 7. (Just as you state a proposition by uttering a sentence or uttering certain sounds.) So I don't really know what to say. Can I or can't I imagine nonphysical things like numbers, propositions, possible worlds, angels, God? I'm not sure.

What is clear, here, is this: if imagining the numeral 7 is sufficient for imagining the number 7, then imagining, forming mental images of, has nothing to do with possibility. For in this same way I can easily imagine impossibilities. I can imagine the proposition *all men are mortal* being red: first I just imagine the proposition, e.g., by forming a mental image of the sentence 'All men are mortal,' and then I imagine this sentence as red. I think I can even imagine that elephant's being a proposition. David Kaplan once claimed he could imagine his refuting Gödel's Incompleteness Theorem: he imagined the *Los Angeles Times* carrying huge headlines: "UCLA PROF REFUTES GÖDEL; ALL REPUTABLE EXPERTS AGREE." In this loose sense, most anything can be imagined; but then the loose sense has little to do with what is or isn't possible. So really neither the loose nor the strong sense of 'imagining' (neither the weak nor the strong version of imagination) has much to do with possibility. There are many clearly possible things one can't imagine in the strong sense; in the weak sense, one can imagine many things that are clearly impossible.

What is it, then, that inclines me to think a proposition can't be red, or a horse, or an even number? The answer, I think, is that one can just see upon reflection that these things are impossible. I can't form a mental image of a proposition's having members; but that's not why I think no proposition has members; I also can't form a mental image of a set's having members. It's rather that one sees that a set is the sort of thing that (null set aside) has members, and a proposition is the sort of thing that cannot have members. It is the same with a physical thing's thinking. True, one can't imagine it. The reason for rejecting the idea, thinking it impossible, however, is not that one can't imagine it. It's rather that on reflection one can see that a physical object just can't do that sort of thing. I grant that this isn't as clear and obvious, perhaps, as that a proposition can't be red; some impossibilities (necessities) are more clearly impossible (necessary) than others. But one can see it to at least a significant degree. Indeed, van Inwagen might be inclined to endorse this thought; elsewhere he says: "Leibniz's thought experiment shows that when we carefully examine the idea of a material thing having sensuous properties, it seems to be an impossible idea" (van Inwagen 1995: 478).[24] But (and here is the important point) the same clearly doesn't go for an immaterial thing's thinking; we certainly can't see that no immaterial thing can think. (If we could, we'd have a quick and easy argument against the existence of God: no immaterial thing can think; if there were such a person as God, he would be both immaterial and a thinker; therefore . . .)

Van Inwagen has a second suggestion:

> In general, to attempt to explain how an underlying reality generates some phenomenon is to construct a representation of the working of that underlying reality, a representation that in some sense "shows how" the underlying reality generates the phenomenon. Essentially the same considerations as those that show that we are unable to form a mental image that displays the generation of thought and sensation by the workings of some underlying reality (whether the underlying reality involves one thing or many, and whether the things it involves are physical or non-physical) show that we are unable to form any sort of representation that displays the generation of thought and sensation by the workings of an underlying reality. (van Inwagen 2002: 177–78)

The suggestion is that we can't form an image or any other representation displaying the generation of thought by way of the workings of an underlying reality; hence we can't see how it can be generated by physical interaction among material objects such as neurons. This much seems right—at any rate we certainly can't see how thought could be generated in that way. Van Inwagen goes on to say, however, that this doesn't favor dualism over materialism, because we also can't see how thought can be generated by the workings of an underlying *non*physical reality. And perhaps this last is also right. But here there is an important dissimilarity between dualism and materialism. The materialist thinks of thought as generated by the workings of an underlying reality—i.e., by the physical interaction of such physical things as neurons; the dualist, however, typically thinks of an immaterial self, a soul, a thing that thinks, as *simple*. An immaterial self doesn't have any parts; hence, of course, thought isn't generated by the interaction of its parts. Say that a property *P* is basic to a thing *x* if *x* has *P*, but *x*'s having *P* is not generated by the interaction of its parts. Thought is then a basic property of selves, or better, a basic activity of selves. It's not that (for example) there are various underlying immaterial parts of a self whose interaction produces thought. Of course a self stands in causal relation to its body: retinal stimulation causes a certain sort of brain activity which (so we think) in turn somehow causes a certain kind of experience in the self. But there isn't any *way* in which the self produces a thought; it does so immediately. To ask "How does a self produce thought?" is to ask an improper question. There isn't any how about it.

By way of analogy: consider the lowly electron. According to current science, electrons are simple, not composed of other things. Now an electron has basic properties, such as having a negative charge. But the question 'How does an electron manage to have a charge?' is an improper question. There's no how to it; it doesn't do something else that results in its having such a charge, and it doesn't have parts by virtue of whose interaction it has such a charge. Its having a negative charge is rather a basic and immediate property of the thing (if thing it is). The same is true of a self and thinking: it's not done by underlying activity or workings; it's a basic and immediate activity of the self. But then the important difference, here, between materialism and immaterialism is that if a material thing managed to think, it would have to be by way of the activity of its parts: and it seems upon reflection that this can't happen.[25] Not so for an immaterial self. Its activity of thinking is basic and immediate. And it's not the case that we are inclined upon reflection to think this can't happen—there's nothing at all against it, just as there is nothing against an electron's having a negative charge, not by virtue of the interaction of parts, but in that basic and immediate way. The fact of the matter then is that we can't see how a material object can think—that is, upon reflection it seems that a material object can't think. Again, not so for an immaterial self.

True, as van Inwagen says, thought can sometimes seem mysterious and wonderful, something at which to marvel. (Although from another point of view it is more familiar than hands and feet.) But there is nothing here to suggest that it can't be done. I find myself perceiving my computer; there is nothing at all, here, to suggest impossibility or paradox. Part of the mystery of thought is that it is wholly unlike what material objects can do: but of course that's not to suggest that it can't be done at all. Propositions are also mysterious and have wonderful properties: they manage to be about things; they are true or false; they can be believed; they stand in logical relations to each other. How do they manage to do those things? Well, certainly not by way of interaction among material parts. Sets manage, somehow, to have members—how do they do a thing like that? And why is it that a given set has just the members it has? How does the unit set of Lance Armstrong manage to have just *him* as a member? What mysterious force, or fence, keeps Leopold out of that set? Well, it's just the nature of sets to be like this. These properties can't be explained by way of physical interactions among material parts, but that's nothing at all against sets. Indeed, these properties can't be explained at all. Of course if you began with the idea that everything has to be a material object, then thought (and propositions and sets) would indeed be mysterious and paradoxical. But why begin with that idea? Thought is seriously mysterious, I think, only when we assume that it would have to be generated in some physical way, by physical interaction among physical objects. That is certainly mysterious; indeed it goes far beyond mystery, all the way to apparent impossibility. But that's not a problem for thought; it's a problem for materialism.

3. Arguments for Materialism

The above arguments for dualism and others like them are powerful. Like philosophical arguments generally, however, they are not of that wholly apodictic and irrefragable character Kant liked to claim for his arguments; they are defeasible. It is possible to disregard or downgrade the intuitions of possibility and impossibility to which they appeal. Further, if there were really powerful arguments for materialism—stronger than these arguments against it—then perhaps the appropriate course would be to embrace materialism. But are there any such powerful arguments?

No—or at least I've never seen any. There is the old chestnut according to which no immaterial object can cause changes in the hard, heavy, massive, massy (messy) physical world; there is the claim that dualism, or at least interactionistic dualism, violates the principle of Conservation of Energy; there is the charge that dualism is unscientific; there is the complaint that soul stuff is hard to understand; there is the canard that dualism is explanatorily impotent. None of these has any force at all.[26] However there is one that is perhaps not completely without promise. According to Nancey Murphy:

> In particular, nearly all of the human capacities or faculties once attributed to the soul are now seen to be functions of the brain. Localization studies—that is, finding regional structures or distributed systems in the brain responsible for such things as language, emotion and decision making—provide especially strong motivation for saying that it is the brain that is responsible for these capacities, not some immaterial entity associated with the body. In Owen Flanagan's terms, it is the brain that is the res cogitans—the thinking thing. (Brown, Murphy, and Malony 1998: 1)

Localization studies show that when certain kinds of mental activity occur, certain parts of the brain display increased blood flow and increased electrical activity. Paul Churchland goes on to point out that mental activity is also in a certain important way *dependent* on brain activity and brain condition:

Alcohol, narcotics, or senile degeneration of nerve tissue will impair, cripple, or even destroy one's capacity for rational thought. Psychiatry knows of hundreds of emotion-controlling chemicals (lithium, chlorpromazine, amphetamine, cocaine, and so on) that do their work when vectored into the brain. And the vulnerability of consciousness to the anesthetics, to caffeine, and to something as simple as a sharp blow to the head, shows its very close dependence on neural activity in the brain. All of this makes perfect sense if reason, emotion and consciousness are activities of the brain itself. But it makes very little sense if they are activities of something else. We may call this the argument from the neural dependence of all known mental phenomena. (Churchland 1984: 20)[27]

Of course it isn't true that it makes very little sense to say that activities of the immaterial self or soul are dependent in this way on the proper function of the brain; still, this argument from localization and neural dependence is perhaps the strongest of the arguments against dualism. That may not be much of a distinction; the other arguments, I believe, are without any force at all. But perhaps this argument has a little something to be said for it; at any rate dependence and localization phenomena do suggest the possibility that the brain is all there is. Taken as an argument, however, and looked at in the cold light of morning, it has little to be said for it. What we know, here, is that for at least many mental functions or actions *M*, there are parts of the brain *B* such that (1) when *M* occurs, there is increased blood flow and electrical activity in *B*, and (2) when *B* is damaged or destroyed, *M* is inhibited or altogether absent. Consider, therefore, the mental activity of adding a column of figures, and let's assume that there is a particular area of the brain related to this activity in the way suggested by (1) and (2). Does this show or tend to show that this mental activity is really an activity of the brain, rather than of something distinct from the brain?

Hardly. There are many activities that stand in that same or similar relation to the brain. Consider walking, or running, or speaking, or waving your arms or moving your fingers: for each of these activities too there is a part of your brain related to it in such a way that when you engage in that activity, there is increased blood flow in that part; and when that part is damaged or destroyed, paralysis results so that you can no longer engage in the activity. Who would conclude that these activities are really activities of the brain rather than of legs and trunk, or mouth and vocal cords, or arms? Who would conclude that your fingers' moving is really an activity of your brain and not of your fingers? Your fingers' moving is dependent on appropriate brain activity; it hardly follows that their moving just is an activity of your brain. Digestion will occur only if your brain is in the right condition; how does it follow that digestion is really an activity of the brain, and not an activity of the digestive system? Your brain's functioning properly depends on blood flow and on the proper performance of your lungs; shall we conclude that brain function is really circulatory or pulmonary activity? All of your activities depend upon your ingesting enough and the right kind of food; shall we see here vindication of the old saw 'you are what you eat'? The point, obviously, is that dependence is one thing, identity quite another. Appropriate brain activity is a necessary condition for mental activity; it simply doesn't follow that the latter just is the former. Nor, as far as I can see, is it even rendered probable. We know of all sorts of cases of activities *A* that depend upon activities *B* but are not identical with them. Why should we think differently in this case?

Perhaps a more promising way of developing this argument would go as follows. In science, it is common to propose *identities* of various kinds: water is identical with H_2O, heat and pressure with molecular motion, liquidity, solidity, gaseousness with certain properties of assemblages of molecules, and so on. This kind of identification, it might be argued, is theoretically useful in at least two ways; in some cases it provides explanations, answers to questions that are otherwise extremely difficult to answer, and in others it finesses the questions by obviating the need for answers, showing instead that the question itself is bogus, or ill-formed, or has a wholly trivial answer. Well, why not the same here? Suppose we identify mental activity with brain activity; more precisely, suppose we identify such properties as *being in pain* and *being conscious* with such properties as *having C-fibers that are firing* and *displaying activity in the pyramidal cells of layer 5 of the cortex involving reverberatory circuits.*[28] Then first of all, we don't have to answer the otherwise difficult questions, "Why is it that when someone is in pain, the C-fibers in her brain are firing?" Or "Why is it that when someone is conscious, his brain is displaying activity in the pyramidal cells?" (Alternatively, they might have answers, but the answer would be pretty easy: "Because being in pain *just is* having firing C-fibers and being conscious *just is* displaying pyramidal activity.") And second we will be able to answer some questions otherwise very difficult: for example, "Why is it that rapping someone smartly over the head interferes with her ability to follow a proof of Gödel's Theorem?" This identification, therefore, is theoretically fruitful and hence justified by the principle of inference to the best explanation (Block and Stalnaker 1999: 24, 45). Still further, of course, if mental properties are really identical with and thus reduced to neurophysiological properties of the brain, then dualism will be false. So here we have another objection to dualism.

Now first, note the language involved here: the suggestion is that *we identify*, say, the property of being in pain with the property of having firing C-fibers. That makes it sound as if it's just up to us whether these properties are identical—we can just identify them, if we find that useful. But of course it isn't just up to us, and we can't really do any such thing. All we can do is declare, perhaps loudly and slowly, that these properties are identical; but saying so doesn't make it so (not even if your peers let you get away with so saying).

More important, what about the fact that these properties— *being in pain* and *having firing C-fibers*, for example, or *being conscious* and *displaying activity in the pyramidal cells*—seem so utterly different? Pain and consciousness are immediately apprehended phenomenal properties; not so for firing C-fibers or active pyramidal cells. And as for that pyramidal activity, if that's what *being conscious* just is, then nothing, not even God, could be conscious but not have those pyramidal cells. So do we have here another shiny new argument for atheism, this time from neural science: God, if he exists, is conscious, but without a body; neuroscience shows that *being conscious* just is having active pyramidal cells; hence . . . ? On the face of it, these properties seem at least as different as *being chalk* and *being cheese*. In fact on the face of it they seem more different than the latter; at least any pair of things that exemplify *being chalk* and *being cheese* are clearly both material objects. How can being in pain be the same property as having firing C-fibers when it seems so utterly clear that someone could be in pain without having C-fibers that are firing, as well as have firing C-fibers without being in pain? Perhaps it's true that if these properties were identical, we would have answers to some otherwise difficult questions (and avoid some other questions): but isn't it obvious that the properties are not identical? Are not both

(1) Possibly, someone is in pain when no C-fibers are firing

and

(2) Possibly, C-fibers are firing when no one is in pain

wholly obvious?

Well, they certainly *look* obvious. Maybe identifying these properties would have a theoretical payoff; but the properties just don't seem to be identical. You might as well 'identify' Bill with his essence: concrete objects are so unruly and messy, after all. And why stop with Bill? Why not identify every concrete object with its essence, thus finessing all those annoying questions about the relation between concrete objects and abstract properties? There is a problem about how God knows future contingents: how does he know that tomorrow I will freely go for a bike ride? It hasn't happened yet, and since it will be a free action when it does happen, he can't deduce it from present conditions and causal laws. No problem, mates; just identify *truth* with the property *being believed by God.* How can we so blithely declare these properties identical when they look so different? How can we declare (1) and (2) false when they seem so obviously true?

Now here appeal will be made to Kripke and his celebrated thesis about necessary but a posteriori propositions. Block and Stalnaker and others suggest that the appearance of truth for (1) and (2) is like the appearance of contingency of such propositions as

(3) Water is H_2O,

or

(4) Gold has atomic number 79.

In these cases we have the appearance of contingency; but, so the claim goes, the appearance is shown by Kripkean considerations to be illusory. We initially think that these propositions are contingent; Kripke shows us that in fact they are necessary. As Sydney Shoemaker says in a similar context,

> Kripke . . . argued that the class of truths deserving this label [i.e., the label of being necessary] is much larger than had traditionally been supposed. And, in his most radical departure from the traditional view, he held that many of these truths have the epistemic status of being a posteriori. (Shoemaker 1998: 59)

Among these truths, of course, are (3) and (4). But then once we see that this is how it goes in the case of water and H_2O, and *being gold* and *having atomic number 79*, we can apply the lesson to neurophysiological and mental properties. Indeed, according to Block and Stalnaker,

> The crucial question for the issue we have been discussing in this paper is whether a relevant contrast can be shown between the relation between water and H_2O on the one hand and the relation between consciousness and some brain process on the other (Block and Stalnaker 1999: 43).

But such a relevant contrast, I believe, can easily be shown. Suppose we look a bit more deeply into the relevant Kripkean considerations. Kripke's principal thesis here, of course, is that natural kind terms—'tiger,' 'water,' 'gold'—function as *rigid designators;* they are not, for example, as Frege or Russell thought, disguised or abbreviated definite descriptions.[29] While there is a certain amount of controversy about the notion of rigid designation, what is clear is that the thesis in question is a *semantical* thesis, a thesis about the meaning or function of certain terms. And that should put us on our guard. A semantical thesis about how certain terms work is not, just by itself, of direct relevance to the modal question which *propositions* are necessary or contingent; what it *is* relevant to, is the question which propositions get expressed by which *sentences.* Pace Shoemaker, a semantical thesis can't by itself show us that the class of necessary propositions is larger than we thought; what it *can* show us is that sentences we thought expressed contingent propositions really express necessary propositions.[30]

Accordingly, consider the *sentences*

(5) 'Water is H_2O'

and

(6) 'Gold has atomic number 79';

what Kripke shows us is that these sentences, contrary to what we perhaps originally thought, really express necessary rather than contingent propositions. But it wasn't that we were clear about which propositions were in fact expressed by those sentences, and Kripke got us to see that those propositions, contrary to what we thought, were necessary. It is rather that he corrected our ideas about which propositions are expressed by those sentences: we mistakenly thought (5) expressed a certain proposition *P* which we correctly thought to be contingent; in fact (5) expresses a different proposition *Q*, a proposition that appears to be necessary. We might have thought that 'water' is synonymous with something like "the clear, tasteless, odorless stuff we find in lakes and streams," in which case the sentence (5) expresses a proposition put more explicitly by

(7) The clear, tasteless, odorless stuff found in lakes and streams is H_2O.

This is clearly contingent: it entails the contingent proposition that H_2O is found in lakes and streams. By way of a judicious selection of examples, however, Kripke gets us to see (if he's right) that the proposition expressed by (5) isn't (7) at all. What proposition does it express? That proposition can be put as follows.

(8) Consider the stuff actually to be found in the rivers and lakes: that stuff is H_2O.

That's the proposition expressed by (5). Alternatively, consider the stuff we do in fact find in lakes and rivers and name it 'XX'; then

(8) XX is H_2O.

Sentence (8) is at least arguably necessary:[31] it seems sensible to think that very stuff, i.e., H_2O, could not have failed to be H_2O. We are inclined to think, perhaps under the influence of mistaken views about the function of kind terms, that 'water' expresses such properties as *being clear, tasteless, and odorless* and *filling the lakes and streams.* Kripke gets us to see that 'water' does not express those properties, which could be had by very many different substances, but is instead a rigid designator of the stuff that actually has those properties, i.e., as I would put it, expresses the (or an) essence of that stuff. The difference is between, on the one hand, the term's expressing the properties we use to fix its reference, and, on the other, the term's being a rigid designator (I'd say expressing the essence) of what it denotes when its reference is fixed in that way. By analogy, return to those thrilling days of yesteryear, when Quine asked us to consider such sentences as

(9) Hesperus is identical with Venus.

This may look contingent: we might think 'Hesperus' expresses the property of being the evening star, i.e., of being the first heavenly body to appear in the evening. Surely it's not necessary that the first heavenly body to appear in the evening is Venus—any number of other heavenly bodies could have been (and I guess sometimes actually are) the first to appear in the evening. But what Kripke got us to see is that in fact 'Hesperus' does not express that property; it is instead a name or rigid designator (expresses an essence of) the thing that has that property, in which case (9), contrary to what we might have thought, does not express a contingent proposition after all.

How does this apply to the case in question, the case of the proposed identification of mental properties with neurophysiological properties? As follows: in the water/H_2O case, what we learn from Kripke is not that some proposition we had thought contingent is really necessary; what we learn instead is that some sentence we thought expressed a contingent proposition really expresses a necessary proposition. What we learn is a semantical fact, not a modal fact. It isn't that there is some proposition we thought to be contingent and is now seen to be necessary. It isn't that (3), the proposition, formerly appeared to us to be contingent, but then was seen, via Kripkean considerations, to be necessary; it is rather that (5) formerly seemed to express a contingent proposition and is now seen to express a necessary proposition. Our problem was not modal illusion, but semantical illusion. So what we have is not a reason for mistrusting modal intuition (more specifically, an intuition of possibility); it is rather a reason (if only a weak one) for mistrusting our ideas about the semantics of proper names and kind names.

But then there is a large, important, and crucial difference between the water/H_2O case and the pain/firing C-fibers case. In the former, as I've just been arguing, the proposed identification doesn't conflict with any modal intuitions at all. Indeed, (3) does seem intuitively to be necessary: that very stuff could not have been something other than H_2O. So here there isn't so much as a hint of conflict with modal intuition. In the latter case, however, the case of pain/C-fibers firing, there is a clear and wholly obvious conflict with intuition.

(10) Someone is in pain when no C-fibers are firing

appears for all the world to be possible; similarly, of course, for

(11) Someone is conscious when there is no pyramidal cell activity.

According to the proposed identification, however, these propositions are (of course) impossible. If pain just is the firing of C-fibers and consciousness just is pyramidal cell activity, then (10) and (11) are equivalent, in the broadly logical sense, to

(12) C-fibers are firing when no C-fibers are firing

and

(13) There is pyramidal cell activity when there is no pyramidal cell activity.

In other words, the proposed identification of water with H_2O goes contrary to no modal intuition; the proposed identification of pain with C-fiber firing, and consciousness with pyramidal cell activity, on the other hand, is wholly counterintuitive. The latter identifications go directly against strong modal intuitions; the former does not.

This objection to dualism, therefore, is no stronger than the others. No doubt splendid theoretical advantages would be forthcoming from the identification of mental with neurophysiological properties, as with the identification of concrete objects with their essences. But these theoretical advantages are surely outweighed by the fact that the proposed identifications are obviously false. Like the other objections to dualism, accordingly, this one is without any force. In conclusion, then: there are powerful arguments against materialism and none for it. Why, therefore, should anyone want to be a materialist?[32]

NOTES

1. See, e.g., Swinburne 1987: 2, 145. Aquinas's position on the relation between soul and body may be a special case of this view; see Plantinga 2007.

2. See, e.g., van Fraassen 2002: 50ff.

3. Although I can't help concurring with David Armstrong, no friend of dualism: "But disembodied existence seems to be a perfectly intelligible supposition. . . . Consider the case where I am lying in bed at night thinking. Surely it is logically possible that I might be having just the same experiences and yet not have a body at all. No doubt I am having certain somatic, that is to say, bodily sensations. But if I am lying still these will not be very detailed in nature, and I can see nothing self-contradictory in supposing that they do not correspond to anything in physical reality. Yet I need be in no doubt about my identity" (Armstrong 1968: 19).

4. See Plantinga 1993: ch. 6.

5. See, e.g., Zimmerman 2002: 504ff. Zimmerman himself seems attracted to the thought that "the mass of matter" of which one's body is composed is an object distinct from the latter, but colocated with it (although of course he is *not* attracted to the idea that a person is identical with such a mass of matter).

6. See ibid.

7. One such argument, for example, apparently has the following form: (a) many people who advocate *p* do so in the service of a hope that science will never be able to explain *p*; therefore (b) not-*p*. See Dennett 1995: 27.

Another seems to have the form (a) if you believe *p*, prestigious people will laugh at you; therefore (b) not-*p* (or perhaps (b*) don't believe *p?*). See Dennett 1991: 37.

8. "But on the kinds of figures that are coming out now, it seems like the whole brain must get recycled about every other month" (McCrone 2004).

9. Here I am indebted especially to Michael Rea.

10. See, e.g., Hershenov 2003: 33.

11. Complaint: this new 'part,' as you call it, isn't really a part, at first, anyway, because at first it isn't yet integrated into the organism. Reply: think of 'part' here as like 'part' in 'auto parts store.' Would you complain that the auto parts store is guilty of false advertising, on the grounds that none of those carburetors, spark plugs, and piston rings they sell is actually part of an automobile?

12. Here I'm indebted to Richard Fumerton.

13. No doubt this flexibility results from a principle of compounding for events: given any two successive events e1 and e2 occurring at roughly the same place, there is another event e3 compounded of them, an event that has each of them as a subevent. Short of such metaphysical extravaganzas as mereological universalism, clearly there is no corresponding principle for material objects. I stand in the corner from t1 to t2; then I leave and you stand in the corner from t2 to t3; it doesn't follow that there is a material object that stands in the corner from t1 to t3 and has my body and your body as successive parts.

14. See Zimmerman 2002: 510.

15. Here I am indebted to Nicholas Wolterstorff.

16. And hence strictly speaking, the argument doesn't require a thought experiment; it requires instead seeing that a certain state of affairs or proposition is possible. See Bealer 1998: 207.

17. Not strictly relevant, but of interest: could I perhaps be a *computer* (hardware), a computer made of flesh and blood? There are three possibilities here: I might be the hardware, I might be the program, and I might be the mereological sum of the hardware and the program. The first suggestion is vulnerable to the macroscopic Replacement Argument; on the other two, I would not be a material object. So no help for materialism there.

18. Realists will say that there can't be similarity without a property had by the similar things, thus resting on an alleged intuition of impossibility; nominalists will deny this claim, thus resting on an alleged intuition of possibility. In his argument for indeterminacy of translation, Quine claims that the native's behavior is consistent with his meaning 'rabbit state' or 'undetached rabbit part' or 'rabbit' by 'gavagai,' thus (despite his animadversions) relying on an intuition of possibility. Similarly for his and others'

claims about the underdetermination of theory by evidence. Further, anyone who proposes an analysis (of knowledge, for example) relies on intuition, as does someone who objects to such an analysis (by proposing a Gettier case, for example). In philosophy of mind we have Jackson's Mary example, Burge's arthritis example, twin earth arguments for a posteriori necessities and wide content, refutations of phenomenalism and behaviorism, and much else besides, all of which rely centrally and crucially on modal intuition. Most arguments for materialism rely on modal intuition (for example the intuition that an immaterial thing can't cause effects in the hard, heavy, massive material world). Indeed, take your favorite argument for any philosophical position: it will doubtless rely on modal intuition.

19. There is also the complex but powerful argument offered by Dean Zimmerman (2002: 517ff.).

20. Although there are speculative suggestions that quarks may in fact be composed of strings.

21. I've been assuming that there really are such things as beliefs. A materialist might demur, taking a leaf from those who accept 'adverbial' accounts of sensation, according to which there aren't any red sensations or red sense data or red appearances: what there are instead are cases of someone's sensing redly or being appeared to redly. Similarly, the materialist might claim that there isn't any such thing as the belief that all men are mortal (or any other beliefs); what there are instead are cases of people who believe in the all-men-are-mortal way. This may or may not make sense; if it does make sense, however, a person will presumably believe in the all-men-are-mortal way only if she harbors a neuronal structure or event that has as content the proposition *all men are mortal.*

22. See Dretske 1988: 54ff. See also Bill Ramsey's *Using and Abusing Representation: Reassessing the Cognitive Revolution* (presently unpublished). Materialists who try to explain how a material structure like a neuronal event can be a belief ordinarily try to do so by promoting indicators to beliefs; for animadversions on such attempts, see the appendix in Plantinga 2007.

23. Cf. Dretske 1988: 63.

24. That is (I take it), it seems to be necessary that material things don't have such properties. Van Inwagen's examples are such properties as being in pain and sensing redly; the same goes, I say, for properties like being the belief that *p* for a proposition *p*.

25. But couldn't a material thing also just directly think, without depending on the interaction of its parts? According to Pierre Cabanis, "The brain secretes thought as the liver secretes bile"; couldn't we think of this as the brain (or, if you like, the whole organism) directly thinking, not by way of the interaction of its parts? Well, if that's how a brain thinks, it isn't like

the way a liver secretes bile; the latter certainly involves the liver's having parts, and those parts working together in the appropriate way. Further, the idea of a physical thing's thinking without the involvement of its parts is even more clearly impossible than that of a physical thing's thinking by virtue of the interaction of its parts. Aren't those neurons in the brain supposed to be what enables it to think? You might as well say that a tree or my left foot thinks. Consider any nonelementary physical object—a tree, an automobile, perhaps a horse: such a thing does what it does by virtue of the nature and interaction of its parts. Are we to suppose that some physical object—a brain, let's say—does something like thinking apart from involvement of its parts? Talk about appealing to magic!

26. This may seem a bit abrupt; for substantiation, see Plantinga 2007: fn1.

27. See also Nagel 2002; in the course of a long, detailed, and subtle discussion, Thomas Nagel argues that there is a logically necessary connection between mental states and physical states of the following sort: for any mental state *M* there is a physical state *P* such that there is some underlying reality *R*, neither mental nor physical but capable of having both mental and physical states, which has essentially the property of being such that necessarily, it is in *P* just if it is in *M*. (And perhaps it would be sensible to go on from that claim to the conclusion that it is not possible that I exist when my body *B* does not.) Nagel concedes that it seems impossible that there be such a reality; his argument that nonetheless there really is or must be such a thing is, essentially, just an appeal to localization/dependency phenomena: "The evident massive and detailed dependence of what happens in the mind on what happens in the brain provides, in my view, strong evidence that the relation is not contingent but necessary" (Nagel 2002: 202), and "the causal facts are strong evidence that mental events have physical properties, if only we could make sense of the idea" (Nagel 2002: 204). The particular route of his argument here is via an argument to the best explanation: he suggests that the only really satisfactory explanation of those localization/dependency phenomena is the existence of such an underlying reality. (Of course if that is what it takes for a really satisfying explanation, it is less than obvious that there is a really satisfying explanation here.) This argument has also made its way into the popular press: see Pinker 2004: 78.

28. Cf. Block and Stalnaker 1999: 1.

29. Or if they are disguised descriptions, the descriptions they disguise express essences of their *denotata*.

30. Not everyone is prepared to distinguish propositions from sentences. Those who do not make that distinction, however, will presumably be able to make an equivalent distinction by noting the difference between coming to see that a sentence is necessary in virtue of discovering that it

doesn't mean what one thought it did, and coming to see that it is necessary without learning anything new about its meaning.

31. For the moment ignore the fact that it's contingent that there is any such thing as H_2O.

32. In addition to the people mentioned in the text, I thank Michael Bergmann, Evan Fales, Trenton Merricks, William Ramsey, and the members of the Notre Dame Center for Philosophy of Religion discussion group, in particular Thomas Flint and Peter van Inwagen, as well as others I have inadvertently overlooked. I'm especially grateful to Dean Zimmerman.

REFERENCES

Armstrong, David. 1968. *A Materialist Theory of Mind.* London: Routledge & Kegan Paul.

Bealer, George. 1998. "Intuition and the Autonomy of Philosophy." In *Rethinking Intuition*, edited by Michael DePaul and William Ramsey, 201–39. New York: Rowman & Littlefield.

Block, Ned, and Robert Stalnaker. 1999. "Conceptual Analysis, Dualism, and the Explanatory Gap." *Philosophical Review* 108:1–46.

Brown, Warren, Nancey Murphy, and H. N. Malony, eds. 1998. *Whatever Happened to the Soul?* Minneapolis: Fortress.

Campbell, Donald T. 1974. "Evolutionary Epistemology." In *The Philosophy of Karl Popper*, edited by P. A. Schilpp, 413–63. LaSalle, IL: Open Court.

Churchland, Paul. 1984. *Matter and Consciousness.* Cambridge, MA: MIT Press.

Dennett, Daniel. 1991. *Explaining Consciousness.* Boston: Little, Brown.

———. 1995. *Darwin's Dangerous Idea.* New York: Simon & Schuster.

Dretske, Fred. 1988. *Explaining Behavior.* Cambridge, MA: MIT Press.

Hershenov, David. 2003. "The Metaphysical Problem of Intermittent Existence and the Possibility of Resurrection." *Faith and Philosophy* 20: 24–36.

Leibniz, G. 1951. [*Monadology*]. In *Leibniz Selections*, edited by Philip Weiner. New York: Charles Scribner's Sons.

McCrone, John. 2004. "How Do You Persist When Your Molecules Don't?" *Science and Consciousness Review* [web-journal, June 2004, No. 1].

Nagel, Thomas. 2002. "The Psychophysical Nexus." In *Concealment and Exposure, and Other Essays*, 194–236. New York: Oxford University Press.

Pinker, Steven. 2004. "How to Think about the Mind." *Newsweek*, September 27, 2004.

Plantinga, Alvin. 1993. *Warrant and Proper Function.* New York: Oxford University Press.

————. 2007. "Materialism and Christian Belief." In *Persons: Human and Divine*, edited by Peter van Inwagen and Dean Zimmerman, 99–141. Oxford: Oxford University Press.

Shoemaker, Sydney. 1998. "Causal and Metaphysical Necessity." *Pacific Philosophical Quarterly* 79:59–77.

Swinburne, Richard. 1987. *The Evolution of the Soul.* Oxford: Clarendon.

Van Fraassen, Bas. 2002. *The Empirical Stance.* New Haven: Yale University Press.

Van Inwagen, Peter. 1995. "Dualism and Materialism: Athens and Jerusalem?" *Faith and Philosophy* 12:475–88.

————. 2002. *Metaphysics.* 2nd ed. Boulder, CO: Westview Press.

Wuketits, Franz. 1986. "Evolution as a Cognitive Process: Towards an Evolutionary Epistemology." *Biology and Philosophy* 1 (2): 191–206.

Zimmerman, Dean. 2002. "Material People." In *The Oxford Handbook of Metaphysics.* Oxford: Clarendon.

5

From Mental/Physical Identity to Substance Dualism

RICHARD SWINBURNE

1.

"Mental properties are the same as physical properties," "mental events are the same as physical events," "mental substances are the same as physical substances"—says many a physicalist. "Mental properties and events supervene on physical properties and events," and "mental substances supervene on physical substances"—says many another physicalist. Whether these claims are true depends first on what is meant by 'substances,' 'properties,' and 'events,' by 'mental' and 'physical,' and by 'supervene,' and then on what are the criteria for one property, event, or substance being the same as another.

The first issues can be dealt with quickly and to some extent stipulatively. I understand by a property a monadic or relational universal,[1] and by an event the instantiation of a property in a substance or substances (or in properties or events) at times. Any definition of a substance tends to beg philosophical questions, but I'll operate with a definition which does not, I think, beg the questions at issue in this paper. A substance is a thing (other than an event) which can (it is logically possible) exist independently of all other things of that kind (viz., all other substances) other than its parts.[2] Thus tables, planets, atoms, and humans are substances. Being square, weighing ten kilos, and being-taller-than are properties (the former two being monadic properties, the latter being a relational property which relates two substances). Events include my table being square now, or John being taller than James on March 30, 2001, at 10:00 a.m.

There are different ways of making the mental/physical distinction, but I propose to make it in terms of the privilegedly accessible/public.[3] I believe that my way of making the distinction highlights the traditional worries about how the mental can be connected with the physical; but some other ways of making the distinction may do so as well, and similar results to mine are likely to follow from these other ways. So a mental property is one to whose instantiation the substance in whom it is instantiated necessarily has privileged access on all occasions of its instantiation, and a physical property is one to whose instantiation the substance necessarily has no privileged access on any occasion of its instantiation. Someone has privileged access to whether a property P is instantiated in him in the sense that whatever ways others have of finding this out, it is logically possible that he can use, but he has a further way (of experiencing it) which it is not logically possible that others can use. A pure mental property may then be defined as one whose instantiation does not entail the instantiation of a physical property. So 'trying to raise one's arm' is a pure mental property, whereas 'intentionally raising one's arm' is not; for the instantiation of the latter entails that my arm rises.[4] My definitions have the consequence that there are some properties which are neither mental nor physical—let us call them 'neutral properties.' They include formal properties (e.g., 'being a substance') and disjunctive properties ('being in pain or weighing ten stone'). A mental event is one to which the substance involved has privileged access; normally this will consist in the instantiation of a mental property, but sometimes it may involve the instantiation of a neutral property (as, for example, does the event of me being-in-pain-or-weighing-ten-stone). A pure mental event is one which does not entail the occurrence of a physical event. A physical event is one to which the substance involved does not have privileged access. A mental substance is one to whose existence that substance necessarily has privileged access, and a physical substance is a substance to whose existence that substance necessarily has no privileged access, that is, a public substance. Since having privileged access to anything is itself a mental property, and someone who has any other mental property has that one, mental substances are just those for which some mental properties are essential. And we may define a pure mental substance as one for which only pure mental properties are essential (together with any properties entailed by the possession of pure mental properties).

I understand the supervenience of one (kind of) property on another in a sense derived from Kim's sense of 'global supervenience.'[5] A-properties supervene on B-properties iff there are no two possible worlds in each of which every substance has the same B-properties as some substance in the other, but not every substance has the same A-properties as some substance in the other which has the same B-properties as it (and no substance has A-properties without having B-properties). This leads to a natural definition of event supervenience as follows: A-events supervene on B-events iff there are no two possible worlds identical in their B-events but differing in their A-events. The difference between property and event supervenience lies in the fact that events are individuated in part by the substances in which the properties are individuated. If there can be two different substances (in different worlds) with the same B-properties (including relational properties), there could be event supervenience without there being property supervenience. For it could be that each substance S_n which had certain B-properties B_0 had to have determinate A-properties, but different ones for different substances—S_1 had to have A_1, while S_2 had to have A_2. Then there would be event supervenience. But there would still be two worlds in which two substances (S_1 in one and S_2 in the other) having all the same B-properties did not have all the same A-properties.

The natural extension of Kim's account of supervenience to substances is as follows: A-substances supervene on B-substances iff there are no two possible worlds identical in their B-substances but differing in their A-substances.[6]

So (pure) mental properties supervene on physical properties iff there are no two possible worlds in which every substance has the same physical properties as some substance in the other but not the same (pure) mental properties as some substance in the other which has the same physical properties as it (and no substance has mental properties without having physical properties). (Pure) mental events supervene on physical events iff there are no two possible worlds identical in their physical events but differing in their (pure) mental events (and no substance has mental properties without having physical properties). (Pure) mental substances supervene on physical substances iff there are no two possible worlds identical in their physical substances but differing in their (pure) mental substances.

A possible world is one which is metaphysically possible. I understand by a logically possible world, one whose full description entails no contradiction;[7] whether a world is a logically possible world is therefore something discoverable a priori. Thirty years ago Kripke and Putnam drew our attention to the fact that there were many propositions which seemed not to entail any contradiction but were necessarily true or necessarily false with a necessity as hard as that of logical necessity, and whose truth or falsity were discoverable only a posteriori. These propositions were said to be metaphysically but not logically necessary or impossible. Hence the notion of a metaphysically possible world as one which was different from a merely logically possible world; it had to be *both* logically possible *and* one whose full description (in terms of logically contingent propositions) involves no metaphysically necessarily false propositions. Thus "Hesperus is not Phosphorus" or "Water is XYZ" (where XYZ is different from H_2O) might seem to entail no contradiction, and yet they hold in no metaphysically possible world. However, I share Chalmers's view that the distinction between the logically and metaphysically possible "is not a distinction at the level of worlds, but at most a distinction at the level of statements. . . . The relevant space of worlds is the same in both cases" (Chalmers 1996: 68). That is, any logically possible world is a metaphysically possible world, and conversely. The Kripke/Putnam type of metaphysically (but not logically) necessary propositions are all ones in which some substance (or property, event, or time) is referred to by a rigid designator of a kind which is rather uninformative about the nature of what is referred to. A rigid designator of a substance, property, event, or time is a word which picks out that substance, property, event, or time in every possible world. Rigidifying any uniquely identifying description will yield a rigid designator, but it may tell you very little about what is designated. If 'water' is used to refer to whatever has the same chemical essence as the actual stuff in our rivers (and so used with what Chalmers calls its "secondary intension"), we can use the term to say something about that stuff without knowing what the stuff is and so without being able to identify instances of it except the ones in our rivers. However, we can describe logically possible worlds more informatively by using rigid designators of a special kind which I shall call "informative designators." For a rigid designator of a thing to be an informative designator it must be the case that someone who knows what the word means (that is, has the linguistic knowledge of how to use it) knows a certain set of conditions necessary and sufficient (in any possible world) for a thing to be that thing (whether or not he can state those conditions in words, or can in practice ever discover that those conditions are satisfied). Two informative designators are logically equivalent if and only if they are associated with logically equivalent sets of necessary and sufficient conditions. To know these conditions for the application of a designator is to be able (when favorably positioned, with faculties in working order, and not subject to illusion) to recognize where it applies and where it doesn't and to be able to make simple inferences to and from its application.[8] Thus "red" is an informative designator of a property, of which "the actual color of my first book" is a mere uninformative rigid designator. I can know what "red" means in the sense of being able to identify things as red, and make simple inferences using the word without knowing which things in our world are red. The ability to identify things as red can exist without the knowledge of which things are actually red. But knowing how to use the expression "having the actual color of my first book" does not give me the ability to recognize things other than my first book as having the color of my first book.

I am inclined to think that while being 'water' (as used in the eighteenth century) is an uninformative designator of a property, being 'H_2O' is an informative designator of a property. It is the property of being composed of molecules consisting of two atoms of hydrogen and one atom of oxygen. To be an atom of hydrogen is to be an atom consisting of one proton and one electron. Or rather we may allow that negatively charged hydrogen—hydrogen with an extra electron—is still hydrogen; and so are isotopes of hydrogen, in which there are one or more additional neutrons in the nucleus. A proton is a proton in virtue of its mass, charge, and so on; and an electron is an electron in virtue of its mass, charge, and so on. And I can know what it is to have certain mass or charge without discovering which things have what mass or charge, merely by knowing what people would observe (in this case using instruments) if things did have such and such mass or charge. A similar account should be given of what it is to be an atom of oxygen. But maybe physicists in the future would count something as an electron only if it was made of the same stuff as the electrons in the atoms of such-and-such a particular volume of H_2O, while it would be possible for something to have the same mass, charge, and so on as an electron and not to be so composed. In that case knowing what 'H_2O' means would as such no longer allow me to recognize new instances of it. To do this, I would need also empirical knowledge of the composition of some actual volume of H_2O. But I believe that the current rules for the use of 'H_2O' count anything as an electron which has the same mass, charge, and so on. Whether a word is or is not an informative designator is a matter of the rules for its use in the language.

A full description of a world will include descriptions of its events in terms of informative designators. If all the events so described are logically compatible, no metaphysically false propositions will be true of that world, for if one were, so would be the logically false proposition obtained by replacing any uninformative designator which it contains by an informative designator of the property or whatever so designated. If "Water is XYZ" were true of it, so would be "H_2O is XYZ"—yet that entails a self-contradiction. Hence all logically possible worlds are metaphysically possible.

This claim of course holds only for worlds where metaphysical necessity is analyzable as above. Anyone who makes a claim about what is metaphysically possible or impossible where this is not analyzable in the above way owes the reader an explanation of what "metaphysically possible" means. It may well be, as Gendler and Hawthorne say, that "the notion of metaphysical possibility . . . is standardly taken to be primitive," adding in a footnote "in contemporary discussions at any rate" (Gendler and Hawthorne 2002: 4). For myself, I simply do not understand what is meant by this notion, unless it is analyzable as above, or given some other technical definition. It is simply uninformative to say that it is the most basic conception of "how things might have been" (Gendler and Hawthorne 2002: 4–5). For since this "most basic conception" is supposed to be narrower than logical possibility, it is unclear how it is to be narrowed unless in the way I have analyzed.[9]

Given my understanding of a "possible world," whether the physicalist's claims of identity or supervenience are true now depends on the criteria for one property, event, or substance being the same as another. There are some identity criteria which will give him his result and some that won't. Ordinary usage provides no clear criteria, and different aspects of usage can be systematized to provide different criteria. We need a metacriterion for choosing which criteria to use.

Now the history of the world is the history of one thing and then another thing happening, in a sense of "thing happening" which includes both things remaining the same and things changing. I suggest that the things that happen and the only things that happen are events in my sense. The history of the world is this substance existing (which can be analyzed as it having its essential properties) for a period of time, coming to have this property or relation to another substance at this or that time, continuing to have it and then ceasing to have it. I have adopted the construal of properties as universals (instantiable in more than one different substance) rather than as tropes (particular properties), for the reason that—as far as I can see—there is not anything more or less to the difference between this (e.g.) redness and that one (of exactly the same shade and shape) except in terms of the substances (and times) in which they are instantiated. And I suggest, there are no other things that happen except events in my sense. Some have cited flashes and bangs as examples of things which happen but are not events in my sense. But they can easily be analyzed as the instantiation of properties in regions of space, or (if you do not think that regions of space are substances in my sense), as themselves substances which exist for a very short time.

So I suggest as a metacriterion that we individuate properties, substances, and times in such a way that if someone knows which properties were instantiated in which substances when, he is in a position to know everything that has happened. A canonical description of an event will say which properties, substances, and times it involves, by picking them out by informative designators—and conjointly the properties, times, and substances involved will form an informative designator of that event. Then it will be the case that someone who knows all the events that have happened under their canonical descriptions is in a position to know everything that has happened (and someone who knows all the events that have happened under their canonical descriptions in some spatiotemporal region is in a position to know all that has happened in that region). If you do not individuate properties, substances, and times in accord with a criterion derived from this metacriterion, then in order to give a full description of everything that has happened you would need additional metaphysical categories. It would need to be the case, for example, that as well as saying which properties were instantiated when, you would need to say which aspects or features those properties had. It is better not to multiply metaphysical categories beyond necessity. I predict that exactly the same kinds of issues would arise with a fuller system of categories as with the ones which I shall set out below using my system of categories, and that they would require exactly the same kinds of solutions. So I stick with my system of categories.

To give some person the knowledge of everything that has happened, it will suffice (given that that person has sufficient logical competence) to list any of many different subsets of all the events. For the occurrence of some events entails the occurrence of other events. There is one event of my walking from A to B from 9:30 to 9:45 a.m., another event of my walking slowly from 9:30 to 9:45, and a third event of my walking slowly from A to B from 9:30 to 9:45. But the third event is "nothing over and above" the first two events. To generalize—there is no more to the history of the world (or the world in a region) than any subset of events whose canonical descriptions entail those of all the events; and no less than any least subset which will do this. There are different ways of cutting up the history of the world into events, and there are many different sets of events such that there is no more or less to the history of the world than the occurrence of all the events of that set. All this suggests that we should count as the same event not merely two events which involve the instantiation of the same properties in the same substances at the same time, but also two events whose canonical descriptions (their informative designators) entail each other. For if you know that the one has occurred, that puts you in a position (if you have sufficient logical competence) to know that the other has occurred, and conversely. The occurrence of one event is then nothing in the history of the world 'over and above' the occurrence of the other event. Two events could involve the same substances, properties, and times and so be the same event, while having two different canonical descriptions which do not entail each other, if, for example, there could be two informative designators of a substance which are not logically equivalent (and that can happen if there can be contingent identity between substances—a possibility which I shall discuss later in the paper). Conversely, the canonical descriptions of two events may entail each other without the properties, substances, and events involved all being the same. One case of this is where a substance having some property entails and is entailed by some part of that substance having that property. For example, a table is flat if and only if that table's top is flat; but the former is not an occurrence in the history of the world additional to the latter, nor is the latter an occurrence additional to the former.

On a Humean picture of the world we need no relations other than spatiotemporal relations between substances to state the history of the world. The history of the world is just this substance (with its properties) coming into existence, acquiring now this monadic property, now losing that one, changing its spatial relations to other substances, and, finally, ceasing to exist; and a similar history for all the other substances. Causation for Hume is analyzable in terms of regularities in the temporal patterns of acquisition of monadic properties and spatial relations. But on an account of causation in which causation is unanalyzable and so not reducible to events of the former kind, the history of the world will involve not merely succession but causation. A substance or event causing an event is itself an event (of the instantiation of the relation of causation between the substance or event and the other event), and the history of the world will need then to include such events—though it need no longer mention as separate events, any events related by the relation of causation; their occurrence is entailed by the event of the one causing the other.

It is not, however, relevant to the present discussion whether a Humean or a non-Humean account of causation is correct. So—to return to the central theme—in order to satisfy my metacriterion how must we individuate properties and substances, so that someone who knew the canonical description of every event of some subset of events which entails the canonical descriptions of all the events would be in a position to know everything that had happened? (Our interest being only in the identity conditions for properties and substances which allow us to say whether there are mental as well as physical properties and substances, I shall not consider the interesting issue of what are the identity conditions for times—e.g., whether [if it is October 3, 2003, today] P being instantiated in S today is the same event as P being instantiated in S on October 3, 2003).

2.

To begin with properties—to satisfy my metacriterion each different feature of the world named by informative designators which are not logically equivalent has to count as a different property, though, since some entail others, we shall not need to mention them all in order to give a full account of the world. It is important to distinguish a description of a property P in terms of some property which it possesses, from an (informative or uninformative) rigid designator of P. 'Green' is an informative designator of the property of being green; it applies to it in all possible worlds, and someone who knows what 'green' means knows what an object has to be like to be green. 'Amanda's favorite colour' or 'the color of spring grass' may function as a description of the property green in terms of its properties, possibly (in our world) uniquely identifying descriptions. These words may be used to describe the property of being green by informatively designating a different property—the property of being Amanda's favorite color or the property of being of the same color as spring grass—which properties the property of being green possesses. "Green is Amanda's favorite color" is then a subject-predicate sentence where "Amanda's favorite color" informatively designates the property of being Amanda's favorite color and thereby (in our world) describes the property green. It says that the property 'green' has itself the property of being Amanda's favorite color. If it were (unusually) being asserted as a statement of identity between two informatively designated properties, it would be false. But any property name can be turned into an uninformative rigid designator of another property which has the first property. "Amanda's favorite color" can be used to rigidly designate that color which in the actual world is Amanda's favorite color. In that case "Green is Amanda's favorite color" will be a (true) identity statement. The device of rigidification allows us to turn any uniquely identifying description of something, including a property, into a rigid designator of that thing. But it does not make it into an informative designator of that thing. For someone who knows what the rigidified predicate "the color of spring grass" means need have no ability to identity any color property (other than that of spring grass) as being that color property—for they may never have seen spring grass.

It follows from all this that it is a purely a priori matter (a matter of logical entailment) whether one informatively designated property supervenes on other informatively designated properties. It follows straightforwardly that no mental properties (in the sense of properties which are such that necessarily their subject has privileged access on all occasions of their instantiation to whether they are instantiated in him) are the same properties as physical properties (in the sense of publicly accessible properties, such that no one substance ever has privileged access to whether or not they are instantiated in it)—for the simple reason that their informative designators are never logically equivalent. The property informatively designated by "being in pain" is just such a mental property. Others can find out whether I am in pain by studying my behavior and my brain states. But I too can study my behavior (on a film) or my brain states (via mirrors); yet I have a further way of knowing whether I am in pain or not which the others do not have—I can actually feel it. The same goes for all the "qualia" properties, and in my view also for the intentional properties of having such and such beliefs, desires, and purposes. On the other hand the properties informatively designated by "being square" or "weighing ten kilos," or the brain properties of patterns of electrochemical transmission, are physical properties in this sense. It follows for similar reasons that mental properties do not supervene on physical properties—since for any world in which some combination of physical and mental properties is instantiated, there is always a world in which the physical properties are instantiated but the mental ones are not. This follows because the canonical descriptions of the events of a world in which any combination of physical properties is instantiated never entail that mental properties are also instantiated, since what anyone can access equally can never entail what only one person can access in a privileged way. And since mental events are ones to which the substance involved has privileged access, and physical events are ones to which the substance does not have privileged access, no mental event can be the same as any physical event,[10] nor can it supervene on one. Clearly, too, both mental events (including pure mental events) and physical events occur, and so the former cannot be omitted from a full description of the world.

3.

I turn now to substances.[11] For a substance at one time t_2 to be the same substance as a substance at an earlier time t_1, two kinds of criteria have to be satisfied. First the two substances have to have the essential properties of the same species of substance which they are. Fairly clearly there are different ways of cutting up the world into species of substance, any of which would enable us to give a true and full description of the world. Suppose I have a car which I turn into a boat. I can think of cars as essentially cars. In that case one substance (a car) has ceased to exist and has become instead another substance (a boat). Or I can think of the car as essentially a motor vehicle, in which case it has continued to exist but with different (nonessential) properties. All three substances exist—the car which is essentially a car, the boat which is essentially a boat, and the motor vehicle which is essentially a motor vehicle. Yet I can tell the whole story of the world either by telling the story of the motor vehicle or by telling the story of the car and the boat.

The second requirement for a substance at one time to be the same as a substance at another time is that the two substances should consist of largely the same parts, the extent to which this has to hold varying with the genus of substance. At least five kinds of thing have been called "substances"—simples, organisms, artifacts, mereological compounds, and gerrymandered objects (such as the right top drawer of my desk together with the planet Venus). Despite the view of some[12] that only some of these are really substances, my metacriterion gives no justification for such an arbitrary restriction. For each of these genera of substance there is its own kind of identity criterion, varying with the extent of replacement or rearrangement of parts which is compatible with the continued existence of the substance (e.g., for a mereological compound, no replacement is possible; for artifacts such as a car, boat, or motor vehicle a small amount of replacement is possible). A full history of the world will need to mention only certain genera of substances—for example, if it tells us the history of all the fundamental particles (considered as mereological compounds), that might suffice (if we forget for a few paragraphs about obvious problems arising from substances having mental properties). There is no more to any substance than its parts, and the history of the substance is the history of its parts. It might sometimes be explanatorily more simple if one took larger substances, for example organisms, rather than their parts as the substances in terms of which to trace the history of the world; but the causal properties of large substances including organisms are just the causal properties of their parts, even if the latter have causal properties such that when combined with other parts, they behave in ways different from the ways in which they behave separately. Alternatively, instead of telling merely the history of fundamental particles, we could include in our history of the world organisms and artifacts, saying when they gained or lost parts, or their internal parts were rearranged. We might then need to describe the history of the fundamental particles only insofar as they did not form unchanging parts of the organisms or artifacts. And certainly we could do without describing the behavior of gerrymandered objects.

Being the same part may itself be a matter of having all the same subparts, and so on forever; or some replacement of subparts may be allowable, but in the end—if we are to operate with a sharp criterion of identity—we must define a level at which no replacement is possible if the subpart is to be the same subpart, a level of what I shall call ultimate parts. Being the same ultimate part will involve, as with any substance, having the essential properties characteristic of the kind—being this hydrogen atom will involve having a certain atomic mass, number, and so on. It will involve also something else, for it to be the same token of that kind—a principle of individuation.

What that principle is depends crucially on what sorts of thing substances are. One view is that substances are simply bundles of co-instantiated properties. The alternative view is that some substances have thisness.[13] A substance has thisness iff there could exist instead of it (or as well as it) a different substance which has all the same properties as it, including past and future related properties such as spatiotemporal continuity with a substance having such and such monadic properties.

If no substances have thisness, then the history of the world will consist of bundles of co-instantiated properties having further properties, including spatiotemporal relations to earlier bundles, coming into existence and ceasing to exist, and causing the subsequent existence and properties of other bundles. There are many different ways (equally well justified by our initial metacriterion for a system of metaphysical categories) to cut up the world into substances at a time, according to the size of the bundle and which members of the bundle are regarded as essential to the substance which they form. And, according to which members of the bundle are regarded as essential, so there will be different ways of tracing substance continuity over time. Ultimate parts will also be individuated by properties. The obvious such property for individuating parts which occupy space is spatiotemporal continuity with a substance having the same essential properties of the species, conjoined perhaps with causal continuity (that is, the earlier substance causing the existence of the later substance); for nonspatial substances, temporal plus causal continuity would seem to be the obvious requirement. And we need some uniqueness requirement, to ensure that at most one substance later than a given substance which satisfies both of these requirements is the original substance. But there are again alternative ways in which these requirements could be spelled out, any of which would allow us to tell the whole story of the world. If we make spatiotemporal continuity necessary for the identity of substances over time, then we shall have to say that if an electron disappears from one orbit and causes an electron to appear in another orbit without there being spatiotemporal continuity between them, they are different electrons. Yet if we insist only on causal continuity, then they will be the same electron. But we can tell the whole story of the world either way, and both stories will be true; electrons of both sorts will exist.

If, however, some substances have thisness, a full history of the world will have to describe the continuities not merely of bundles of co-instantiated properties, but of the thisness which underlies certain bundles (that is, of what it is which makes the difference between two bundles of the same properties with qualitatively the same history). So it must be a necessary condition of ultimate parts of substances being the same that they have the same thisness.[14.] For those physical substances which are material objects, thisness is being made of the same matter. We have then the hylemorphic theory that sameness of a material object requires sameness of essential properties of the species and sameness of underlying matter. We could, contrary to the Aristotelian model, insist that as well as sameness of matter, for an ultimate individual part to be the same individual some essential properties (in addition to those of the species) have to be the same. But it is more natural to insist only on preservation of the essential properties of the species; and in this way we can still tell the whole history of the world. In that case if (and only if) the electron in the new orbit is made of the same matter as the old electron, it is the old electron. Spatiotemporal continuity is now no longer an independent requirement for a substance continuing to exist, but probably (fallible) evidence that the same matter has continued to exist, and so (given that the other arbitrarily chosen essential properties of the species are preserved) that the same material object exists. Spatio-temporal continuity is evidence of sameness of matter insofar as the best (i.e., most probable) physical theory of how matter behaves has the consequence that it moves along spatially continuous paths. I shall in future assume that this theory is probably true.

We do not know whether the inanimate material objects of our world have thisness, and in this respect we do not know what would constitute a full description of our world.[15] If they do, then not any account of the world which describes the patterns of property distribution in the world will be a correct one. We need one which individuates the ultimate parts of inanimate material objects (picked out as such in some clear way) being the same substances only if they have the same matter. Then mereological compounds will have to have the same matter throughout their existence, while organisms may gradually replace matter.

Now, to give the full history of the world, I have claimed, involves listing all the events of some subset which entails all the events that have happened under their canonical descriptions. We saw in the case of properties that that involves picking out the properties involved by informative designators. And surely we need to informatively designate the substances too—merely giving a description of them, even a rigidified description, won't tell us what was green, or square or in pain. Informatively designating a property involves knowing a certain set of necessary and sufficient conditions for something to be that property. Similar considerations seem to apply to substances. But here we have to note that while we do know informative designators for many properties, we do not know informative designators for many substances. We often do not know the conditions necessary and sufficient for a substance to be that substance; for often we do not know what would make a later substance or a substance in another world that substance. The first reason for our inability to informatively designate substances is that we do not know with respect to some kinds of substances and in particular inanimate material objects, whether or not they have thisness (and so, for example, are to be individuated partly by their underlying matter) or whether they are to be individuated solely by properties, including (spatiotemporal and/or other) properties of continuity.

So in practice we often pick out material objects by uninformative rigid designators of a kind which we may call quasi-informative designators. They are words associated with a disjunction of two sets of necessary and sufficient conditions for a thing to be that thing (one disjunct applying if the substance has thisness, the other if it does not), but which in practice lead us to identify the same things in the actual world as the thing in question. Thus Hesperus is the actual planet which often appears in the evening sky. If material objects do not have thisness, then being Hesperus consists in being a planet which is a bundle of co-instantiated properties spatiotemporally continuous with those which constitute the planet which appears in the evening sky. If material objects do have thisness, then being Hesperus consists in being a planet made of a particular chunk of matter (i.e., with thisness). Since we do not know whether material objects have thisness, 'Hesperus' does not function as an informative designator. But although the nature of Hesperus differs in the two cases, we are likely (when positioned as favorably as we can be) to pick out the same planet as Hesperus on other occasions in both cases. For in the latter case we will use the criterion of spatiotemporal continuity with the matter of the actual planet as evidence of a chunk of matter being the same matter; but satisfying the criterion will be fallible evidence of the sameness of two planets, whereas in the former case it will be what constitutes sameness.

If material objects do not have thisness, then an informative designator of a substance will be a conjunction of informative designators of co-instantiated properties. If we learn that material objects do not have thisness, then we will be able to designate them informatively. 'Hesperus' can function as an informative designator of a planet spatiotemporally continuous with the planet (if any) which actually appears in the evening sky. 'Hesperus' is then an informative designator because I know what is involved in calling something Hesperus, and I can have the ability to identify things as Hesperus without having any empirical knowledge—I don't need to know that there are any planets in order to know what the informative designator means. But if material objects do have thisness and we learn this, in practice humans would still be unable to pick them out by names. This is because we would be unable to identify a planet (e.g., one in the morning sky) as Hesperus without knowing of what chunk of matter the planet which appears in the evening sky is made; we might have fallible knowledge that the same chunk was or was not present in Phosphorus, but we still wouldn't know what that chunk was, except in terms of its properties, which wouldn't enable us to distinguish it from another chunk (in another world) with the same properties. Maybe God can tell the difference between two such chunks, but we humans can only distinguish chunks by properties. There will still be a true description of the world using informative designators of substances, but it will not be accessible to us.

Note that if material objects do have thisness, there will be informative designators of the planets currently picked out by the quasi-informative designators 'Hesperus' and 'Phosphorus'; call them 'H' and 'P'. Then 'H is P' will be a logically necessary truth, because in each case what constitutes being that planet will be the same—being a planet made of such and such a chunk of matter. But if material objects do not have thisness and 'Hesperus' and 'Phosphorus' are used in the way described at the beginning of the previous paragraph, then 'Hesperus is Phosphorus' will be a contingent truth; the identity it reports will be a contingent identity. This is because being Hesperus is being spatiotemporally continuous with such and such a planet; and being Phosphorus is being spatiotemporally continuous with such and such a planet; and it would be a contingent matter whether each was spatiotemporally continuous with the other. There would be worlds in which each existed but they were not spatiotemporally continuous.[16] If we use 'Hesperus' and 'Phosphorus' only as quasi-informative designators, we will not know whether the identity is necessary or contingent.

However, having only an ability to pick out inanimate material objects by means of quasi-informative designators, we can still know quite a lot about which ones are or are not identical with or supervene on others. Merely knowing to which kind a substance belongs often enables us to say that two substances rigidly designated in different ways are not the same—since they do not satisfy some of the necessary conditions for sameness—even though we cannot nearly so often say that two substances are the same. This table may or may not be the same as the one that was here last week, but it is certainly not the planet Hesperus—for Hesperus is essentially a heavenly body and the table is not. And sometimes quasi-informatively designating may enable us to say that this kind of substance supervenes on that kind. Suppose that there can be just three kinds of motor vehicles— ones which can travel on land (cars), ones which can travel on water (boats), and ones which can travel in the air (airplanes); and suppose that we have some criterion for determining to which of these kinds a dual- or triple-use vehicle belongs. Then motor vehicles supervene on boats, cars, and airplanes—there are no two possible worlds with the same cars, boats, and airplanes, but different motor vehicles. But cars, boats, and airplanes do not supervene on motor vehicles—there can be two possible worlds with the same motor vehicles, but different cars, boats, or airplanes (if, for example, what was a car in one world has been turned into a boat in the other world).

4.

Now suppose that no substances have thisness, and so the bundle view of all substances is correct. Mental substances are those substances which have mental properties essentially. Then whether there are mental substances depends on how one bundles together bundles of properties into substances. Mental properties with physical parts (such as the property of intentionally raising one's arm) are naturally thought of as belonging to the substance to which the physical part belongs. But one may either put pure mental properties (such as the property of trying to raise one's arm) in the same bundle as the physical property to which it is most closely related causally, the one which causes it to be instantiated or whose instantiation is caused by it;[17] or, following Hume,[18] put the pure mental properties into a bundle with other pure mental properties to whose instantiation it is related causally (and perhaps also related by relations of similarity and apparent memory). On the Humean model clearly there will be mental substances, for some bundles of properties would be individuated by their mental properties. It might seem, however, that on the non-Humean model one could individuate substances solely by their physical properties and regard mental properties as merely contingent members of bundles, and then the only substances would be physical substances. Alternatively one could individuate substances at least partly in terms of mental properties, and then there could be mental substances. Either way of describing the world would yield a full description.

It is, however, not possible to have a full description of the world in which all substances are individuated only by physical properties. For it is an evident datum of experience that conscious mental events of different kinds (visual sensations, auditory sensations, etc.) are co-experienced, that is, belong to the same substance. Any description of the world which had the consequence that co-experienced events did not belong to the same substance would be a false one. Hence if the substance to which these events occur has physical properties and so a spatial volume, that spatial volume must include within it the total physical cause of those mental events. My having mental properties forces us to recognize as a substance something which (if it has physical properties) has spatial boundaries at a time and over time no narrower than those of the physical correlates of what I co-experience. The identity of the substance is thus constituted by a mental property, that its boundaries are no narrower than the boundaries of the physical correlates of what I co-experience. We cannot cut up the world in an arbitrary way and individuate substances solely by physical properties, and suppose that the mental properties are merely contingent properties of these substances. For even if (as seems not to be the case empirically) the brain basis of, for example, my visual sensations and my auditory sensations were the same, that would not still entail the datum of experience that they were both had by the same person. We can only include that datum in a full description of the world if we suppose that the identity of substances which have conscious mental properties is determined by whether the mental properties which they have at the same time are co-experienced.

It is also an evident datum of experience that certain mental events are had consecutively by the same person. Experiences take time—if only a second or two; and every experience which I have I experience as consisting of two smaller parts. I am the common subject of the experience of hearing the first half of your sentence and the experience of hearing the second half of your sentence. And yet the mere fact that these experiences are caused by events in the same part of the physical substance which is my brain does not entail that. It follows for both of these reasons that we cannot describe the world fully except in terms of mental substances which—if they have physical properties—are the substances they are both at a time and over time, whose boundaries are no narrower than those of the physical correlates of what a subject co-experiences.

It will be evident that it will make no difference to the fact that there are mental substances if the bundle theory of all physical substances is false, and inanimate material objects including brain molecules have thisness (and so being the same substance is not solely a function of properties, but of the matter in which those properties are instantiated). For still nothing would follow from that for which mental properties were co-experienced. We can describe the facts of co-experience only if we allow the existence of mental substances.

This conclusion is reinforced when we consider some well-known neurophysiological data and thought experiments. The crucial issue when a patient's corpus callosum is severed is whether (on the assumption that experiences are produced by both half-brains) the experiences produced by his left brain are co-experienced with the experiences produced by his right brain. It is not merely that some ways of dividing up the brain or defining when it began or ceased to exist would provide simpler explanations of how the brain or body behaves than do others, but that some ways would entail the non-occurrence of a datum of experience, whose occurrence would be evident to its subject or subjects—that a subject had both sets of experiences, or that he had only one set. Whether there is one person or two is not entailed by which experiences are connected with which half-brains, or anything else physical. To describe what is going on we need to individuate persons in part by the experiences they have, and not by the extent of the unity of a brain. Merely to describe, not to explain, experience, we need mental substances individuated at least in part in this way.

This conclusion is further reinforced when we consider the thought experiment of half-brain transplants. S's brain is taken out of his skull, it is divided into two halves, these halves are put into two different skulls from which brains have been removed, a few additional bits are added from a clone of S, the bits are connected to the nervous system, and we then have two functioning persons with mental lives. But if we know only the history of all the physical bits, described in terms of their properties (and, if required, their underlying matter) and which mental properties are instantiated in all the persons involved, there seems to be something crucial of which we are ignorant—which (if either) of the subsequent persons is S. Whether S has survived such a traumatic operation seems an evidently factual issue, and yet one underdetermined by the physical and mental properties associated with physical substances. Only if S is a mental substance (to whom the co-experienced experiences occur) can there be an unknown truth about whether or not S has survived this operation—which surely sometimes there will be.

It follows that mental substances are not identical with and do not supervene on physical substances, since there can be worlds in which the physical substances (brains and the extent of their continuity) are the same but there are different mental substances (two in one world, only one in another).

5.

My final claim is that human beings, you and I, are pure mental substances (which do not supervene on physical substances). Many thought experiments in the spirit of Descartes seem to describe conceivable situations and so to be strong evidence of the logical possibility of me existing without a body, or continuing to exist when my body is destroyed. Let us take Descartes's original thought experiment:

> I saw that while I could conceive that I had no body . . . I could not conceive that I was not. On the other hand, if I had only ceased from thinking . . . I should have no reason for thinking that I had existed.

From this I knew that I was a substance the whole nature or essence of which is to think and that for its existence there is no need of any place, nor does it depend on any material thing. (Descartes 1972: 101)

We can make sense of this and many similar suppositions (disembodied life after death, etc.); they do not appear to contain any contradiction—and that is strong evidence that what we appear to conceive is logically possible. But, says the objector, "maybe they are not 'metaphysically possible.'" However, that possibility only arises if 'I' (or 'Richard Swinburne' as used by me) is not an informative designator, but only an uninformative designator (such as a quasi-informative designator) of some substance whose identity is constituted by some underlying factors whose nature is unknown. But clearly it is an informative designator. For I do know the conditions necessary and sufficient for a substance to be that substance. I can recognize (with faculties in working order, favorably positioned, and not subject to illusion) when it applies and when it doesn't and make simple inferences from its application. For I can always pick out myself as the subject of experience and action—infallibly. In this I am, in Shoemaker's phrase, "immune to error through misidentification" (Shoemaker 1994: 82). I cannot recognize that a present conscious experience is taking place and yet misidentify it as yours when it is really mine, or conversely. I can misidentify myself if I pick out myself by means of a body—for example, believing falsely that the person seen in the mirror is me—but that will be a case of illusion.[19]

Of course I can still misremember what I did in the past, and indeed misremember how I used the word "I" in the past. But this kind of problem arises with every claim whatsoever about the past. "Green" is an informative designator of a property, but I may still misremember which things were green and what I meant by "green" in the past. The difference between informative and uninformative designators is that (when my faculties are in working order, I am favorably positioned, and I am not subject to illusion) I can recognize which objects are correctly picked out at a present time by informative designators, but not generally when they are picked out by uninformative designators (in the absence of further information). And I know what a claim about the past or future amounts to when it is made by informative designators, but not when it is made by uninformative designators. I know what would constitute a future or past experience being mine, what it is for some future or past person to be me. Not so with Hesperus or water. I don't know (in the sense defined) what would constitute past or a future substance being water or Hesperus if I am merely in the position of the 'water' user in the eighteenth century, or the 'Hesperus' user in the early ancient world; or even today—for reasons given above.

I conclude that, in the absence of some hidden logical (and I mean 'logical') contradiction in Descartes's description of his thought experiment—to suppose which would be immensely implausible—the experiment shows what it purports to show: Descartes is a pure mental substance. He could exist without anything physical existing, and so pure mental substances do not supervene on physical substances. Each of us can do the same experiment about ourselves and so show that we are pure mental substances.

There are, however, two kinds of pure mental substances—those which do not have a body as a contingent part, and those which do. Ghosts do not have bodies, for example, whereas human beings living on Earth do have bodies. But since the body which is currently mine could continue to exist as a living body without having any causal connection with any mental substance, or could become instead the body of a different mental substance; and since I could under such circumstances go on existing and have a mental life without a body, I now consist of two disjoint parts—my body (the contingent part of me) and the rest of me, which we can call my soul (the essential part of me). Since what is required for a mental life is the part of me other than my body, I have a mental life in virtue of my soul having a mental life. But that does not have the consequence that there are two events of thinking going on when I am thinking—my soul thinking and me thinking; since the two canonical descriptions of the event mutually entail each other, the events are the same. Human beings are thus a composite of substances of two genera—a soul which is, I suggest, a simple; and a body which is an organism.[20] We could therefore tell the whole story of the whole by telling the story of souls and bodies, and not mention human beings at all. But if you do include the story of human beings, and their souls and bodies part company, we shall then need to include their separate histories.[21]

For me to exist, I need only to have some pure mental property (for example, having privileged access to my beliefs). I do not need to have any particular mental properties. I pick myself out as the subject of certain currently experienced mental properties. But I would pick out the same substance if I used fewer or more of the properties of which I am currently aware as co-instantiated. Thus suppose I pick out myself as the subject of two separate sensations (say, visual and tactual sensations). But if at the same time I also had two other sensations (say, auditory and gustatory), I could have picked out the same myself by means of those latter sensations. And if I had done so, the fact that I had the former (visual and tactual sensations) would have been irrelevant to who was picked out. But then the same person would have been picked out had I not had those (visual and tactual) sensations at all, the only ones I did have. So I would have been the same person if I had had quite other sensations instead. And since I could have had different mental properties, clearly I could have had different physical properties too (which gave rise to the different mental properties). Or—to take a temporally extended example— suppose I say to myself, "It is 5:00 and time to stop work." I pick out myself as the substance who said all these words to itself. Now it would be the same substance if I had uttered only the first six words; and also the same substance if these had been followed by two different words—"It is 5:00 and time to work harder"; yet a quite different thought would have been had. The words uttered later cannot make a difference to who it was who uttered the earlier words. And it would have been the same substance if I had uttered only the last two words, and also the same substance if these had been preceded by six different words—"I am getting tired and must stop work." Words uttered earlier cannot make a difference to who it was who uttered the later words. Hence, very different sensations or thoughts can be had by the same person from the ones he actually has. And yet a substance might only exist long enough to have these particular sensations or thoughts. The examples therefore suggest that for a substance who exists for a longer period of time, there can be no principled argument for claiming that there are any limits at all to the kind and length of mental life which can be had by that substance. For there could be a sequence of overlapping experiences, each consisting of two parts, the later of which formed the earlier part of the next experience, from which it must follow that the same substance has all the experiences which form the chain, and the later members could be very different in character from the earlier members. So, since what makes me is not the particular mental or physical properties which I have and not the matter of which my body is made, I must have a further thisness which is independent of any thisness possessed by physical matter.

This point is brought out by the apparent conceivability of a world W_2 in which for each substance in W_1 there is a substance which has the same properties as it and conversely (and any physical matter underlying the properties is the same in both worlds), but where a person S who exists in W_1 does not exist in W_2. The person who lives in W_2 the life (physical and mental) which S lives in W_1 is not S. And surely this world could be different solely in the respect that the person who lived my life was not me. For it is not entailed by the full description of the world in its physical aspects and in respect of which bundles of mental properties are instantiated in the same substance that I, picked out as the actual subject of certain mental properties, have the particular physical or mental properties which I do and am connected with the body with which I am connected. Human beings have a thisness which is quite other than any thisness possessed by the matter of which their bodies are made. In consequence of this and earlier thought experiments the Humean view of personal identity as constituted by the causal (and other relational) connections between our actual instantiated mental properties must be rejected.

Since I am a pure mental substance, I may hope to continue to exist after the destruction of my body, and perhaps then to be given a new body. My acquiring a new body will consist in the new body being brought into causal interaction with the pure mental substance which is myself. The "resurrection of the body" of all humans at the "last day" (the "General Resurrection") is a central Christian doctrine. Catholics, Orthodox, and many Protestants also believe that the person continues to exist without a body in the period between death and the General Resurrection. Both these doctrines are fully compatible with the account of human nature which I have defended in this paper.

NOTES

This paper profited much from discussion at three workshops funded by a grant from The Pew Charitable Trusts. I am especially grateful to Howard Robinson for showing me what was wrong with a previous version of the final section of the paper. The opinions expressed in this paper are those of the author and do not necessarily reflect the views of The Pew Charitable Trusts.

1. I shall count as 'properties' only hard properties, that is, properties the truth conditions for whose instantiation in a substance at a time are a matter of how things are with that substance at that time. I limit the class of properties in this way because we do not need to suppose that there are any other properties in order fully to describe the world. Times are periods of time. Causal relations or relations of spatiotemporal continuity relate substances at a period of time.

2. "The notion of a substance is just this—that it can exist by itself without the aid of any other substance" (Descartes 1984: 159).

3. There are in the literature other ways of understanding the mental/physical contrast, the most common of which are the intentional/nonintentional and the nonphysical science/physical science contrasts. I expound this solely in terms of events. On the former account a mental event is one which involves an attitude towards something under a description—it is fearing, thinking, believing so-and-so, when the subject does not necessarily fear, think, believe something identical to so-and-so; a physical event is any event other than a mental event. On the latter account the physical is what can be explained by an extended physics, and the mental is what cannot be so explained. The former account has the unfortunate consequence that pains and color qualia are not mental events; yet these are the paradigmatic troublemakers for "mind-brain" identity, and must count as mental if we are to deal in any way with the traditional mind/body problem. The latter account is hopelessly vague, for it is totally unclear what would constitute a science incorporating present-day physics as still being a physics. Hence my preference for my way of defining 'mental' and 'physical' properties, events, and—analogously—substances.

4. Mental properties will include both conscious properties and continuing mental properties. Conscious properties are ones of whose instantiation in a subject, that subject is necessarily aware while they are instantiated—for example, having the thought that today is Tuesday.

Continuing properties are ones for which the exercise of the subject's privileged access depends on her choice to introspect, but which continue to characterize her while she chooses not to ask herself about them—for example, the beliefs we have while asleep or thinking about other things, and the desires we have which are not currently influencing our behavior.

5. See Kim 1993: 80–82.

6. The corresponding definitions in terms of Kim's other sense of modal "supervenience," "strong supervenience," are as follows. A-properties strongly supervene on B-properties iff in all worlds any substance with the same B-properties has the same A-properties (and no substance has an A-property without having a B-property). A-events strongly supervene on B-events iff for any substance in all worlds in which it has the same B-properties it has the same A-properties (and no substance has an A-property without having a B-property). The natural definition for strong substance supervenience turns out to be the same as the definition for global substance supervenience. For both properties and events, strong supervenience entails global supervenience but not vice versa. If there is no global supervenience of properties, events, or substances, it follows that neither will there be strong supervenience.

7. My definition of a 'logically possible world' as one whose full description entails no contradiction is more satisfactory than a definition which defines a 'logically possible world' as a world describable by propositions not provable to be inconsistent by 'logic.' For clearly no world can be logically possible if it harbors any contradiction at all. Yet there are innumerable entailments which we can recognize without the entailment being captured by any system of logic so far devised. "This is red" obviously entails "This is colored," but no system of logic so far invented will show that it does. Our very understanding of a proposition involves some ability to recognize what it entails (quite apart from any system of logic), what one who asserts it is committed to. The notion of entailment is more basic than the notion of a 'logic.'

8. More precisely, if you have linguistic knowledge of the rules for using an informative designator of an object (substance, property, or whatever), then you can apply it correctly to any object if and only if (1) you are favorably positioned, (2) your faculties are in working order, and (3) you believe that (1) and (2). Thus 'red' being an informative designator means that someone who knows what 'red' means can apply it to an object correctly when (1) the light is daylight and he is not too far away from the object, (2) his eyes are in working order, and he believes that (1) and (2). Someone is subject to illusion if *either* {(1) and (2)} and not-(3) *or* {either not-(1) or not-(2)} and (3). By contrast, I shall argue (the designator words having their premodern senses), however favorably positioned you are and

however well your faculties are working, you may not be able to identify correctly some liquid not in our rivers and seas as 'water,' or some planet not in the evening sky as 'Hesperus.'

9. I myself have used "metaphysically necessary" to mean (roughly) whatever is the ultimate cause of things or is entailed by the existence of that ultimate cause; and so the 'metaphysically possible' is whatever is compatible with the existence of the actual ultimate cause. I give a more precise definition in Swinburne 1994: 118–19. But this is certainly not the sense which most writers who use the term have in mind.

10. It may be useful to compare my argument with Kripke's somewhat similar argument for the falsity of "my pain is my being in such-and-such a brain state." I analyze the version in Kripke 1971. Kripke claims, first, that "my pain" (which I shall understand as "me being in pain") and "my being in such and such a brain state" (which I shall understand as "me being in such and such a brain state") are "both rigid designators" (Kripke 1971: 162). Kripke and I are entitled to use these expressions in this way, and that is surely their normal use. But a conclusion will only follow about whether or not they rigidly designate the same event given an understanding of what it is for some event to be the event it is. In this case, Kripke claims, we pick out the events "by essential properties." That is, being a pain is essential to the first event and not the second event; and being a brain state is essential to the second event and not the first event. On my view (for which I have given reasons) an event is the event it is in virtue of the substances (or events), properties, and times involved in it. Since the substances and (I assume) times are the same in the events in question, the issue turns on whether the properties designated are the same. The conclusion that the two events are not the same will follow only if "being in pain" and "being in such and such a brain state" are being used not merely as rigid designators of properties, but as informative designators of the properties of being in pain and being in such and such a brain state—that is, do not designate some underlying property by means of its properties of being in pain or being in such and such a brain state. I am using the words in this way, and I would claim it to be the most natural understanding of them; and I am clearly entitled to use the words in this way. Kripke is equally entitled to think of the properties involved in the events as essential—but only given my view that we are entitled by definition to say which properties are essential to an event. Kripke's argument seems to be relying on an intuition that the properties stated are essential to the event; but there is no need for him to do that. He can make it a matter of definition. The conclusion of the nonidentity of the pain and the brain state does, however, need a further argument. It will only follow, given my criterion (or some similar criterion) for property identity—that to be identical two properties have to have logically equivalent informative

designators, that is, logically equivalent sets of necessary and sufficient conditions for their application (and I have given reasons for using that criterion). From that it will follow that the properties involved in the two events are not the same, and so the events are not the same. Without this an opponent of Kripke might say that the property of being in pain just is the property of being in such and such a brain state. I think that Kripke would be sympathetic to this final move, but he does not actually make it.

11. I shall assume for the sake of simplicity of exposition that substances "endure" rather than "perdure" through time; that is, in the case of the material objects of our world, that they are three-dimensional (spatial) objects rather than four-dimensional (three spatial and one temporal) objects. But I believe that this assumption can be dropped without any damage to the main argument.

12. See van Inwagen 1990: §13; and Merricks 2001. Van Inwagen considers that mereological compounds, artifacts, and gerrymandered objects do not exist, and so of course they cannot be substances.

13. For a more detailed account of thisness and of what would be evidence that material objects do or do not have thisness, see Swinburne 1995. This article has been subject to some detailed criticisms by John O'Leary-Hawthorne and J. A. Cover in their "Framing the Thisness Issue." One quite unjustified criticism which they make is that my "principle concerns intraworld duplication *solo numero*" and that "it is surprising that Swinburne does not explicitly address inter-world versions of his principle" (O'Leary-Hawthorne and Cover 1997: 104). However, I did make it explicitly clear that all the principles which I discussed (including, therefore, that principle in terms of which I defined thisness) "concern not merely the identity of individuals in a given world, but across possible worlds" (Swinburne 1995: 390).

14. If ultimate parts have the same thisness, then the substance composed of these will have a thisness constituted by these and conversely. I thus reject a view which Gallois calls "strong haecceitism," the view that two objects (O in world w, and O* in world w*) could yet be different, even if they have all the same properties and are composed of identical constituents. See Gallois 1998: 250–51.

15. See Swinburne 1995 on how physics may provide evidence on whether material objects do have thisness.

16. It is only identity over time (transtemporal identity) which can be contingent. Rejecting the necessity of identity for substances of certain kinds though preserving it for others requires understanding Leibniz's law in a more restricted way for the former. It remains the case that necessarily if a=b, φa if and only if φb, only so long as φ is a nonmodal property. On how this is to be spelled out, see Gallois 1998: ch. 6. In espousing contingent identity, I do not commit myself to the stronger thesis of occasional

identity—that two objects can be the same at one time but different at an-other. Gallois brings out that this can only be maintained if transtemporal identity (identity between an object and an object at another time) is not identity (that is, if the relation is not transitive and symmetrical). See Gallois 1998: 113–17. The possibility of contingent identity arises because of the possibility that some substances are mere bundles of instantiated prop-erties, and so the identity of a substance at another time will consist in the spatiotemporal continuity with it of some similar bundle. Contingent iden-tity then allows the possibility that the same substance may be picked out by names that are not logically equivalent (because it is not a matter of logical necessity which bundles are continuous with which other bundles). Given that only hard properties count as properties (See note 1), the same pos-sibility does not arise for properties.

17. As proposed by, for example, Shaffer (1961).

18. "The true idea of the mind, is to consider it as a system of different perceptions or different existences, which are linked together by the relation of cause and effect, and mutually produce, destroy, influence, and modify each other" (Hume, *Treatise* 1.4.6).

19. The need for some sort of qualification on Shoemaker's phrase is the subject of recent discussion. See Coliva 2003.

20. In Olson 2001, Erik T. Olson argues that there are two serious dif-ficulties for 'compound dualism' (the view that the person who I am has two parts—body and soul) which are not difficulties for simple dualism (the view that I am my soul). The first is that mentioned in the text—that if we (em-bodied on earth) are not souls, although souls think, then there are two thinking things—me and my soul. In the text I argue that this is unpara-doxical, since there is only one act of thinking going on—I think in virtue of my soul thinking. Olson admits (2001: 76) that "there are some properties we have in a derivative sense. We are tatooed insofar as our skin is tatooed," but seems to think this unimportant. But innumerably similar examples can be adduced (I give the example of the table and its top on p. 155), and it is all-important. Why these examples don't have paradoxical consequences, is because the events are the same: me being tatooed just is my skin being ta-tooed. We have seen earlier that there are many different ways of describing the world, but some of them don't describe anything "over and above" oth-ers of them. The other difficulty which Olson finds in compound dualism is that it has the "absurd consequence that one could come to be identical with something that was previously only a part of one" (Olson 2001: 81). Suppose I am embodied on Monday, but my body is then destroyed and I continue to exist in a disembodied state on Tuesday; then, Olson claims, (1) I on Mon-day am the same as I on Tuesday, (2) I on Tuesday am the same as my soul on Tuesday, (3) my soul on Tuesday is the same as my soul on Monday, from

which there follows a conclusion incompatible with compound dualism, (4) I on Monday am the same as my soul on Monday. But the false premise is (2). I on Tuesday have one and only one part on Tuesday, my soul. But I on Tuesday am not the same as my soul on Tuesday. This would be occasional identity, which runs into the problem mentioned in note 16. Clearly a substance (of many genera) gains or loses parts while remaining the same substance: and there is no good reason to deny that a substance might come to have only one part. The "absurd consequence" does not follow.

21. Our normal understanding of ourselves which I analyze in the text is that the parts of our bodies—arms, legs, and so on—are parts of ourselves; and so, given the arguments of this paper, we must think of whole bodies also as parts of ourselves. But, given that bodies are only contingent parts of human beings, we can think instead of ourselves merely as souls causally connected to bodies. Descartes himself seems to oscillate between these two ways of talking. For examples and commentary, see Smart 1977: 63–66.

REFERENCES

Chalmers, David. 1996. *The Conscious Mind.* Oxford: Oxford University Press.

Coliva, Analisa. 2003. "The First Person: Error through Misidentification, the Split between Speaker's and Semantic Reference, and the Real Guarantee." *Journal of Philosophy* 100:416–31.

Descartes, René. 1972. "Discourse on the Method." In vol. 1 of *Collected Works of Descartes.* Translated by E. S. Haldane and G. R. T. Ross. Cambridge: Cambridge University Press.

———. 1984. "Replies to the Fourth Set of Objections." In vol. 2 of *The Philosophical Writings of Descartes.* Translated by J. Cottingham, R. Stoothof, and D. Murdoch. Cambridge: Cambridge University Press.

Gallois, A. 1998. *Occasions of Identity.* Oxford: Clarendon.

Gendler, T., and J. Hawthorne, eds. 2002. *Conceivability and Possibility.* Oxford: Oxford University Press.

Kim, Jaegwon. 1993. "'Strong' and 'Global' Supervenience Revisited." In *Supervenience and Mind.* Cambridge: Cambridge University Press.

Kripke, Saul. 1971. "Identity and Necessity." In *Identity and Individuation,* edited by M. K. Munitz. New York: New York University Press.

Merricks, Trenton. 2001. *Objects and Persons.* Oxford: Clarendon.

O'Leary-Hawthorne, J., and J. A. Cover. 1997. "Framing the Thisness Issue." *Australasian Journal of Philosophy* 75:102–8.

Olson, Erik. 2001. "A Compound of Two Substances." In *Soul, Body and Survival*, edited by K. Corcoran. Ithaca: Cornell University Press.

Shaffer, Jerome. 1961. "Could Mental States Be Brain Processes?" *Journal of Philosophy* 58:813–22.

Shoemaker, Sydney. 1994. "Introspection and the Self." In *Self-Knowledge*, edited by Q. Cassam. Oxford: Oxford University Press.

Smart, Brian. 1977. "How Can Persons Be Ascribed M-Predicates." *Mind* 86:49–66.

Swinburne, Richard. 1994. *The Christian God*. Oxford: Clarendon.

———. 1995. "Thisness." *Australasian Journal of Philosophy* 73:389–400.

Van Inwagen, Peter. 1990. *Material Beings*. Ithaca: Cornell University Press.

Is Materialism Equivalent to Dualism?

WILLIAM HASKER

Is materialism equivalent to dualism? Clearly not, if the question is taken in its most natural sense, as referring to the entire families of philosophical views known respectively as dualism and materialism. These two are rightly regarded as rival explanations, or types of explanations, of the nature and status of mind and its relationship to the human organism. This does not, however, preclude the possibility that some particular version of materialism should prove to be equivalent, or nearly equivalent, to a particular version of dualism. The burden of this paper is to point out a version of materialism, or quasi-materialism, and a version of dualism for which this is indeed the case. I believe, though I shall not be able fully to argue this here, that the versions in question represent the *best* versions of their families—that the kind of dualism and the kind of materialism presented here are the best and most credible versions of dualism and materialism respectively. If this is so, the range of plausible choices for a solution to the mind-body problem is narrowed in an interesting way. But even apart from this more ambitious claim, the near-equivalence of the two views should be of considerable interest.

My procedure will be as follows: I begin by setting out briefly the version of dualism and the version of materialism that are under consideration, with some indication of why each may be deemed superior to its intrafamilial rivals. I will then discuss the objections proponents of each of these views have offered to the other. This will lead in turn to a further development of one of the views, a development which will enable the similarities between them to be displayed.

1. EMERGENT DUALISM

The dualistic view to be considered is emergent dualism, a conception I have expounded in Hasker 1999 and other writings.[1] (The clearest historical precursor for the view is Karl Popper.)[2] According to emergent dualism, the human person originates from a chunk of organized physical stuff; emergence then functions at two different levels. First there are *emergent causal powers* of the physical stuff: powers that, latent in every grain of sand and drop of water, nevertheless manifest themselves only when the matter is taken up in certain of the extremely complex functional configurations characteristic of animate beings. It is these powers that enable the manifestation of the typical psychic properties of consciousness, sensation, thought, desire and aversion, active choice, and the like. But second, what emerges is not merely powers and activities, but a *new substance*, one that is not composed of the particles of microphysics. It is this new substance, which is generated and sustained by the biological organism and continually interacts with the organism, which is the subject of conscious awareness and of cognitive and affective states, and is the agent-cause of our free actions. A suggestive analogy to the emergence of the self (it can be no more than that) is found in the generation by a magnet of a magnetic field.

The chief competitors of emergent dualism from the dualist family are those views which posit the direct creation of the soul by God: mainly Cartesian-type dualism and some versions of Thomistic dualism. Broadly speaking, views of these sorts have difficulty in giving plausible accounts of the kinds of relationships between the mind/soul and the world of nature that are indicated by the empirical evidence. Cartesian dualism has great difficulty in accounting for the souls of nonhuman animals, unless one is content (like Descartes himself) to deny them souls, and thereby any sort of conscious existence at all. Cartesian dualism also has difficulty in accounting for the extremely close dependence of our mental lives on the integrity and functioning of various parts of the brain; certainly this sort of dependence is unexpected given the nature of the "thinking thing" as described by Descartes. Thomistic dualism is arguably better off in this respect, but in making the soul the principle of biological life it is committed to a vitalism which is emphatically rejected by contemporary biology. Neither Cartesian dualism nor Thomistic dualism fits at all comfortably with evolution and the common ancestry of life on earth. But these and related difficulties can only be gestured at here; their full development must be found elsewhere.[3]

2. Emergentist Materialism

The version of materialism to be considered is adapted from a view developed in various writings by Timothy O'Connor, as well as in a recent article coauthored by O'Connor and Jonathan D. Jacobs.[4] Actually the status of the view as "materialist" is somewhat problematic. I have given it this label in view of O'Connor's and Jacobs's endorsement of the claim that a person "is entirely constituted by the simples comprising his body" (O'Connor and Jacobs 2003: 540). However, they reject the other doctrine, typical of materialist views, that "a person's having conscious experience is constituted by complex states in his nervous system" (O'Connor and Jacobs 2003: 540). Instead, they view the experiential states as *emergent from*, but not reducible to or constituted by, those states of the nervous system. Such a view may perhaps be characterized as "emergentist materialism," though O'Connor and Jacobs do not use that label.

The conception of property emergence developed by O'Connor is congruent with (and in fact served as a model for) the corresponding conception as found in emergent dualism. The following summary will help to fix the relevant concepts in place:

> I am indeed a biological organism, but some of my mental states are
> instantiations of simple, or non-structural, properties. A property is

'non-structural' if and only if its instantiation does not even partly consist in the instantiation of a plurality of more basic properties by the entity or its parts. . . . Emergent features are as basic as electric charge now appears to be, just more restricted in the circumstances of their manifestation. Further, having such emergent states is, in general, a causal consequence of having the requisite type of intrinsic and functional complexity. The emergent state is a "causal consequence" of the object's having this complexity in the following way: in addition to having local influence in a manner familiar from physical theories, fundamental particles and systems also naturally tend (in any context) towards the generation of the emergent state. Their doing so, however, is not detectable in contexts lacking the requisite macro-complexity, because each such tending is, on its own, incomplete. It takes the right threshold of complexity for those tendings, present in each micro-particle, to achieve their characteristic effect jointly, the generation of a special type of holistic state. (O'Connor and Jacobs 2003: 541–42)

It remains to be added that these emergent states exert "downward causation" on the simples that have given rise to them, thus resulting in behavior different from what would be predicted on the basis of the laws of physics alone. Furthermore, the novel causal influence thus provided for renders the theory hospitable to the doctrines of libertarian freedom and agent causation. Much more can be said about such emergent states, but this should be sufficient to fix the basic direction of O'Connor's thought on the subject.

In his earlier writings, O'Connor was content with this doctrine of property emergence. In the article with Jacobs, however, a second layer of emergence is added, termed by them "substance emergentism." Here, one might think, the parallel with emergent dualism threatens to collapse into identity, but this is not the case. They reject the view of emergent dualism, which they explain by stating that "a new object emerges and continues to depend for its existence on the structure that generated it: The underlying composite system and the new thing none the less interact with each other as distinct units . . . so that the emergent object affects other things in its environment only via affecting the originating system" (O'Connor and Jacobs 2003: 548). They hold, on the contrary, that "the new object *is itself the composite system:* the simples jointly compose the object, which has a distinctive thisness and some distinctive features" (O'Connor and Jacobs 2003: 548, emphasis added).

It is clear that O'Connor and Jacobs have avoided falling into the pit of dualism, but one might be inclined to ask, what is really *emerging* in this scenario? If the "new object" just *is* the composite system, what's new about it? Wasn't the system there already, prior to the alleged "emergence"? The answer to this can be appreciated only by taking into account the ontology within which they are working, described as an ontology of "immanent universals."[5] On this ontology a basic object, such as an electron, has as constituents such features as spin, charge, mass, and so on. These features are "in" the object rather than transcendent, but they exist in many other objects (e.g., other electrons) as well, so they cannot be what confers particularity on the electron. That is contributed, rather, by a *"particularity* or *thisness,* a non-qualitative aspect necessarily unique to" the electron (O'Connor and Jacobs 2003: 546). These universals and the thisness are bound together in a non-mereological structure called a "state of affairs."

So much for basic objects, but what about composite objects, such as (for instance) molecules? Do they also possess thisnesses of their own? Here we are cautioned to exercise restraint, lest there be "a bewildering variety of particularities instanced during every boring episode one may observe" (O'Connor and Jacobs 2003: 547). In order to avoid this, we "should posit distinctive particularities only in mereological simples and those composites that exhibit some kind of objective, substantial unity" (O'Connor and Jacobs 2003: 547). Molecules, like buildings and heaps of sand, are not real, substantial unities but rather mere aggregates of the simples of which they are composed. The "objective, substantial unity" required for the possession of a thisness is found in entities possessing "ontologically emergent properties" which do real causal work. And this applies in particular to persons: "Their holistic mental states . . . confer on them a substantial unity as thinking biological substances, requiring one to treat persons as wholes in any adequate characterization of the dynamics of the world" (O'Connor and Jacobs 2003: 548). In view of this, "the particularity of persons is primitive, rather than deriving from the primitive particularity of their parts, since those are constantly changing" (O'Connor and Jacobs 2003: 548). Here, then, we have the answer to the question, what is it that emerges in substance emergentism? It is precisely the *person as substance* that emerges; prior to the emergence there was only an aggregate of simples, even if the arrangement of the simples was very similar to that of the bodily parts of a person.

This exposition should already have made it evident why emergentist materialism is preferable to other, more widely accepted versions of materialism. The versions that treat mental states as "constituted by complex states in the nervous system" are simply unable to acknowledge mind and consciousness for what we find them to be. (Witness the heavy labors of materialists over the last generation in seeking to overcome this intractable difficulty.) Views that insist on strict supervenience of the mental on the physical, and on the causal closure of the physical domain, may acknowledge the existence of the mental life but end up by denying it any real causative role in the goings-on in the world. (Note the continuing struggles to capture some sort of causal relevance for mental states.) Emergentist materialism, on the other hand, retains at least a minimal materialist commitment in that human beings are composed of physical stuff and nothing else, but the view is able to recognize the reality and importance of the mental in ways that other materialist views are not.

3. CRITIQUE OF EMERGENT DUALISM

So much, then, for an initial characterization of the two competing views; we turn now to the criticisms of each of the views offered by partisans of the other. We begin with the objections offered by O'Connor and Jacobs to emergent dualism, which they judge to be "not conclusively ruled out . . . but not terribly attractive either" (O'Connor and Jacobs 2003: 549). On this view, they say,

> one is apparently asked to contemplate a composite physical system's giving rise, all in one go, to a whole, self-contained, organized system of properties bound up with a distinct individual. Applied to human beings, the view will imply that at an early stage of physical

development, a self emerges, having all the capacities of an adult human self, most of which, however, lie dormant owing to immaturity in the physical system from which it emerges. (O'Connor and Jacobs 2003: 549)

Now, emergent dualism will indeed posit the emergence of the conscious self "all at one go," in the sense that there is a threshold stage, early in the development of the organism, before which the self is absent and after which the brain and nervous system give rise to the emergent self—yet (we are supposing) that self immediately acquires capacities which are far beyond the present stage of the development of that same brain and nervous system. This may not be flatly inconsistent, but it is certainly (as O'Connor and Jacobs have noted) far from being plausible or attractive.

But why attribute such a view to emergent dualism? On that view, material stuff is anything but psychically inert, so there is no need for all of the potentialities to be present in the self from the beginning—except, to be sure, in the sense that the nascent self is the *kind of thing* that is able, given favorable development, to arrive at the possession and exercise of the powers in question. But since the self is not only generated in the first place but is also constantly sustained and empowered by its organic base in the brain and nervous system, why should we not suppose that its powers and capacities naturally grow in consequence of the brain's own development? On this conception, O'Connor and Jacobs's criticism fails for lack of a target.

In another article, O'Connor seeks to rule out this move. In addition to repeating the criticism given above, he writes, "For we cannot say, as we should want to do, that as the underlying physical structure *develops*, the emergent self does likewise, as there doesn't seem to be conceptual space for changing mereological complexity within a nonphysical simple" (O'Connor 2003: 3). This is an interesting argument, but it contains two dubious assumptions within the space of a single sentence. The sense in which the emergent self is "simple" is something that needs to be carefully investigated, not taken for granted. It is quite true that, as will be pointed out below, the self that is the subject of experiences must function as an undivided unity and not as a system of parts. But this does not immediately carry with it all the freight traditionally attached to metaphysical doctrines of the "simplicity of the soul." I have repeatedly argued, for example, that the emergent self could under certain circumstances be divided—for instance, by the fission of the generating organism. (Arguably the famous cases of "brain bisection" through commissurotomy constitute partial examples of this possibility.)[6]

Even more obviously unwarranted, however, is the assumption that growth in the powers of the emergent self must come about through "changing mereological complexity"—that is, through the *addition of parts* to the mind/self/soul. I submit that this is entirely gratuitous; nothing we know about the ways in which persons, and their minds, grow and develop provides a basis for such an assumption. I conclude that O'Connor's attempt to shore up his objection is a failure, and the objection itself should be relegated to the dustbin.

It should not be supposed, however, that O'Connor would be reconciled to emergent dualism were he to recognize the failure of the objection we've been discussing. In still another article he gives a lucid characterization of the view, and admits that it provides a solution for the "pairing problem" for Cartesian dualism urged by Jaegwon Kim. But he goes on to say, "The present sort of emergence . . . would involve the generation of fundamentally new substance in the world—amounting to creation ex nihilo. That's a lot to swallow" (O'Connor 2000b: 110). Especially in a theistic context, this seems to be a forceful objection. Creation ex nihilo has always been viewed as a uniquely divine prerogative; to attribute such a power to creatures goes very much against the grain of theistic sensibilities. But is the attribution fair? On the view under consideration, the physical stuff of the world has been *endowed by its Creator* with the capacity—indeed, with the necessity—to generate an emergent mind in the appropriate combination of circumstances. Given this, the production in question is simply a matter of physical stuff's *fulfilling its divinely ordained destiny*—and how could its doing so amount to the usurping of a divine prerogative? As a parallel, many believers have felt strongly that the theory of organic evolution, which attributes the genesis of new life-forms to the material processes of the world, is a denial of the dignity of the Creator—but many other believers have come to understand that it is no such thing. Note also that it is not excluded that the production of the emergent self is a process that *consumes energy;* the idea that energy is convertible into physical substance has come to be recognized as scientifically sound and theologically unproblematic, so why should it not be convertible into mental substance?[7] Finally, we may wonder why the generation of mental substance is theologically suspect but the generation by matter of completely new kinds of states and properties, differing fundamentally from those in the inorganic world (as is postulated by O'Connor's emergentist materialism) is supposed to be unproblematic. If a divinely implanted "tending" is sufficient to deflect the charge of heresy in one case, why not in the other?[8]

For all that has been said, I do not suppose for a moment that I have removed all objections to emergent dualism or overcome the resistance many will feel to this view. This is not, after all, the simplest or most obvious solution to the mind-body problem. It's just that (as Winston Churchill said about democracy) it begins to look better, the more one considers the alternatives!

4. Critique of Emergentist Materialism

The principal objection an emergent dualist might urge against emergentist materialism is found in the unity-of-consciousness argument which is derived from Leibniz and Kant. In a familiar passage Leibniz writes,

> In imagining that there is a machine whose construction would enable it to think, to sense, and to have perception, one could conceive it enlarged while retaining the same proportions, so that one could enter into it, just like into a windmill. Supposing this, one should, when visiting within it, find only parts pushing one another, and never anything by which to explain a perception. Thus it is in the simple substance, and not in the composite or in the machine, that one must look for perception. (Leibniz 1991: 19 [*Monadology* 17])

The problem Leibniz is pointing out here does not lie, as many have supposed, in the limitations of seventeenth-century technology. If instead of his "parts pushing one another" we fill the machine with vacuum tubes, transistors, or for that matter with neurons, exactly the same problem remains. The problem does not lie in the pushes and pulls but rather in the *complexity* of the machine, the fact that it is made up of many distinct parts, coupled with the fact that *a complex state of consciousness cannot exist distributed among the parts of a complex object.* The functioning of any complex object such as a machine, a television set, a computer, or a brain consists of the coordinated functioning of its parts, which working together produce an effect of some kind. But where what is to be explained is *the having of a thought,* a state of consciousness, what function shall be assigned to the individual parts, be they transistors or neurons? Even a fairly simple experiential state—say, your visual experience as you look around the room—contains far more information than can be encoded in a single transistor, or a single neuron. Suppose, then, that the state is broken up into bits in such a way that some small part of it is represented in each of many different parts of the brain. Assuming this to be done, we have still the question: *Who or what is aware of the conscious state as a whole?* For it is a fact that you *are aware* of your conscious state, at any given moment, as a unitary whole. So we have this question for the materialist: When I am aware of a complex conscious state, what *physical entity* is it that is aware of that state? In order to be viable, emergentist materialism needs to provide an answer to that question.[9]

Here is a relatively simple formal presentation[10] of the unity-of-consciousness argument against materialism:

1. I am aware of my present visual field as a unity; in other words, the various components of the field are experienced by a single subject simultaneously.

2. Only something that functions as a whole rather than as a system of parts could experience a visual field as a unity.

3. Therefore, the subject functions as a whole rather than as a system of parts.

4. The brain and nervous system, and the entire body, is nothing more than a collection of physical parts organized in a certain way. (In other words, holism is false.)

5. Therefore, the brain and nervous system cannot function as a whole; it must function as a system of parts.
6. Therefore the subject of experience is not the brain and nervous system.

To the best of my knowledge O'Connor has never published a reply to this argument, but he is well aware of it and presumably must have satisfied himself that it poses no threat to his position. In view of this, it becomes necessary for us to attempt to discern what his response to it could be. An initial thought might be that the need for a unified consciousness is met by the postulation of a "thisness" that is present in the person but lacking in composites that are mere aggregates without novel causal powers of their own. This, however, would be a mistake. The presence of the thisness guarantees that the person is a real, substantial unity, contributing novel causal powers to the way the world operates. But the thisness does not itself change the mode of operation of the elements of the system in which it inheres; at least, nothing has been said that would indicate that this is the case. Furthermore, it is the *person* that undergoes conscious experiences, not the thisness—and the person, according to emergentist materialism, is precisely *the composite system*—a whole consisting of many, many parts.

Consider again the formal argument given above. Premise 1 is obviously true, and premise 2 seems above reproach; it simply formulates the evident fact that a complex state of consciousness cannot exist distributed among the parts of a complex object. Steps 3, 5, and 6 are each validly inferred from previous steps in the argument. It seems, then, that the only feasible recourse for the materialist will be to deny step 4, and to claim that the brain and nervous system are indeed something more than a collection of physical parts organized in a certain way. But what would this amount to? In order to satisfy the requirements of the situation, the brain[11] *as an undivided whole* must experience all of what is phenomenally "going on" in the person at a given time, and must do this in such a way that there is no "dividing up" of the phenomenal experience between different parts or subsystems of the brain. At the very same time, the brain must *also* function as a system of parts, since a great many different parts of the brain are playing their respective roles in providing the information which is contained in this unitary experience. Trying to think all of this together may well occasion in us a certain dizziness—is this really coherent, really conceivable? If we suspect that it is not, this may be because so much of what we have learned about the brain depends on regarding and treating it as a system of parts. This is certainly true of recent scientific work on the brain, and is reinforced by the ubiquitous computer models of the brain. However, there is not lacking in physics itself the suggestion that this "atomistic" approach may not be telling us the entire story.[12] I am thinking, for example, of the phenomenon of "quantum entanglement," in which two objects (normally elementary particles) are linked together in such a way that what happens to one instantaneously determines the fate of the other, no matter how far apart they are. This certainly is a kind of holistic phenomenon, in which two apparently discrete objects are in fact intimately connected. Now, quantum entanglement in itself is hardly the solution to the materialist's problem with the unity of consciousness; it just is not the case that, for example, all of the elementary particles in the brain, or in any significant subregion of the brain, are quantum-entangled with each other. However, it does demonstrate that holistic phenomena are not as such alien to the nature of the physical world, and thus lends some plausibility to the holistic behavior of the particles in the brain that must be affirmed by emergentist materialism.

The emergentist materialist, then, will assume that the functioning of the brain has two distinct aspects: there is the *particulate aspect*, in virtue of which the different subunits of the brain act and interact in the way studied by neuroscientists, and there is the *holistic aspect*, in virtue of which the brain as a whole is aware of whatever may be the contents of phenomenal consciousness at any given time. *If* such a "dual-aspect theory" of the brain is genuinely possible (I am inclined to strengthen this to "if and only if"), then emergentist materialism may provide a viable solution for the mind-body problem.[13]

5. SOME ADDITIONAL QUESTIONS

So far, I have been attempting to expound O'Connor's position, or when necessary to draw reasonable inferences with regard to how it should be developed in response to a particular objection. In what follows, I shall be setting out on my own and can lay no claim to his authority or endorsement. I hope nevertheless that, if what has gone before is accepted as at least reasonably plausible, the ensuing reflections may retain a certain degree of credibility. What needs to be done at this stage is to investigate further the nature of the "particulate aspect" and the "holistic aspect" of brain function—especially the latter, since the particulate aspect is already being intensively studied by brain scientists.

An initial question of some interest is the following: *What is the location* of the events and processes comprised in the brain's holistic aspect? It has sometimes been held that mental events and processes are unlocatable, and that it is a category mistake to speak of them in spatial terms at all. But on the view we are now pursuing this can't be right; the events and processes occur to and in *a material object*— namely, the brain—and physical objects are not without location. Nor, on the other hand, can we say that (for example) the awareness of a person's skin color occurs in *this* bit of brain tissue, the awareness of shape in *that* bit, and the awareness of facial expression in that other bit. Without doubt the various parts of the brain play crucial roles in processing the data that eventually comes to consciousness, as brain scientists are continuing to discover. But to locate the *awareness* of these features in the brain regions that process the data flies in the teeth of the unity-of-consciousness argument; it will leave us precisely in the impossible situation where the (necessarily unified) awareness of a complex experience is distributed among the parts of a system.

What must be said, apparently, is that the awareness occurs in the *whole* of the brain without being distributed among the brain's parts. But that still leaves us with an interesting choice to make: Does the awareness occur in *all* of the space occupied by the brain? Or does it occur in just the same space as is occupied by the brain's particles? The reason these are not the same is that, as has been known for the past century or so, the actual particles that compose the brain (or any other ordinary physical object) occupy only a tiny fraction of the space occupied by the object as a whole. (This is the source of Eddington's famous remark that stepping on a plank is like stepping on a swarm of bees.) Upon consideration, it seems more plausible to pre-fer the second alternative, according to which the holistic aspect of the brain exists only in the actual particles. It's true that we normally assume that everyday objects occupy continuous volumes of space, regardless of "empty space" that may be included in those volumes. (A Swiss cheese occupies the volume defined by its external dimen-sions, without there being additional "stuff" that fills up the holes.) But these ordinary objects are not ontologically fundamental; the fundamental causal powers they exemplify must in the final analysis be attributed to the particles of which they are composed—the "sim-ples" of O'Connor and Jacobs's account of the person. So one would think that it is to these particles that awareness must be attributed, and it will follow that the awareness must occur in the space that is occupied by the particles. These particles must then be assumed to be linked together in an instantaneous connectedness analogous to quantum entanglement. An interesting side-question concerns the topology of these connections—is each particle linked directly to each other particle? Or only to the particles in its immediate vicin-ity? Or is it sufficient that each particle be linked to at least one other, so long as the system as a whole remains connected?

But leaving this aside, we may ask, what is the role played by each individual particle in the holistically connected array? (That is, what is the role played by each particle *in the experience of phenomenal consciousness?* As already noted, the role of the particles and of the brain systems composed of them in processing data is not in ques-tion.) We've already seen that we cannot assign to each particle a *part* of the conscious experience; shall we then say that the phenomenal field *as a whole* is experienced by each quark and each electron in the brain? This simply cannot be right; to say this would be to attribute to the simplest elements of physical reality the capacity for an ex-perience containing virtually unlimited internal complexity. So we cannot say of the particles *either* that each of them experiences some part, however minute, of the entire phenomenal field, *or* that each of them experiences the field in its entirety. Which is to say: the parti-cles do not experience anything at all, *and yet* there is nothing to do the experiencing except for the brain, which is, by hypothesis, the ob-ject composed exclusively of these very same particles!

At this point, I think we are forced to reconsider our previous conclusion that it is to the particles that awareness must be attributed. We shall have to say that there is "something else" in the brain, something besides the particles, to which the awareness is attributed. And since the "something else" is not particulate, there is no remaining reason to suppose that its spatial extent is limited to the region occupied by the particles. The "something else," whatever it may be, will be an emergent entity that functions holistically, in that phenomenal awareness is attributed to it *as a whole* and not as a collection of parts.

The time has come for us to take an overview of the (amplified) theory of emergentist materialism. It is postulated that the human brain[14] (and that of other animate life-forms) has both a particulate aspect and a holistic aspect. In its particulate aspect it performs the incredibly complex and sophisticated functions that are being studied by brain science. In its holistic aspect, on the other hand, it functions as an undivided whole in experiencing the person's states of phenomenal consciousness. It is in virtue of having such a holistic aspect that the brain is able to perform such crucial activities as conceptual thought, sensory experience, voluntary choice, and the like. The potential for such a holistic aspect and for these kinds of experience is present in ordinary matter, but both the holistic aspect of the brain and the particular experiences emerge only given the right sort of organized complexity in the structure and functioning of the brain. We have seen, furthermore, that the brain's holistic aspect needs to be something objectively distinct from the particles of which the brain is composed, since those particles cannot be supposed to experience either the phenomenal field as a whole, or some particular part of that field.

But is the "something else" still physical? (One colleague suggested that if the subject of experience exists in more space than the particles do, "it looks like dualism.") This, it seems to me, is a nice question! It is not particulate, but we are (I trust) well past the point of supposing that the physical realm must be limited to particles. Over the centuries, the limits of what was previously considered to be physical have been repeatedly transgressed; first by Newton's mysterious gravity, then by electrical and magnetic forces, and more recently by quantum fields, strings, dark matter, and dark energy. The outcome of these transgressions has generally been that the supposedly "nonphysical" entities have been swallowed up by physics, with no indigestion resulting. (In view of this history, O'Connor and Jacobs's reference to "simples" may best be taken as meaning "the ultimate constituents of physical reality, whatever those constituents may turn out to be.") So the holistic aspect of the brain might be just another chapter in that same story.

Still, there is no gainsaying the similarity of the brain's holistic aspect to the emergent mind/self/soul as described by emergent dualism. It is not entirely clear, in fact, whether any substantive difference remains between the two views. One potential difference concerns a topic that has not surfaced until now: the possibility for the emergent individual to persist beyond bodily death. It has been argued elsewhere that this is at least logically possible for the self of emergent dualism. That self is ontologically distinct from the body and brain, even though causally dependent on them. But the causal dependence is logically contingent, so it may be that a sufficiently powerful and knowledgeable being (e.g., God) could maintain the self in existence during a period when the brain and body are no longer available to play their ordinary causal roles in sustaining it. Can a similar case be made for emergentist materialism? I believe that it can, though the conclusion may not be quite as clear-cut. Is the holistic aspect of the brain ontologically distinct, and potentially separable, from the particulate aspect? The distinctness is clear if we say (as I have argued that we ought to say) that the holistic aspect occupies all of the space of the brain, whereas the particles occupy only a minute portion of that space. Separability may seem more questionable. But recall that, in the brain's holistic functioning, we were unable to assign any distinctive role to the particles; we cannot say that each particle is aware either of the whole of the conscious state, or of some part of it. The only role assignable to the particles is their causal role in the brain function that supports the state—and as noted above, such causal dependence is logically contingent; whatever causal contribution is needed could be supplied in a different way by a sufficiently wise and powerful being. It would seem, then, that the brain's holistic aspect and its particulate aspect may well be separable, at least by divine power.

Is materialism equivalent to dualism? More precisely, is emergentist materialism equivalent to emergent dualism? The descriptions of the two views are not logically equivalent, but deeper analysis might remove some of the differences. It may not matter all that much, for instance, that the self of emergent dualism is said to be immaterial, whereas the "holistic aspect" of emergentist materialism is an aspect of a material object, namely the brain. The self of emergent dualism is not a Cartesian soul: it is generated by a physical object and is itself spatially located, and it is not simple in the way that a Cartesian soul is simple. And on the other hand, the holistic aspect of the brain is in many ways unlike our ordinary conception of matter; especially this is so if, as was argued in the preceding paragraph, it is capable when sustained by divine power of existing without the particles of which the brain is composed. On either of these two views the line between "physical" and "mental" needs to be redrawn, and once this has been done the opposition between them will be narrowed and may even disappear entirely.

6. Conclusion: Materialism and Dualism

Still, it may be that not all of the differences can be made to disappear. The emergence of a new substance seems different from the emergence of a new aspect of a substance, even if the aspect is supposed to be capable of separate existence. The need to accept that physical stuff is able to function holistically in the way called for by emergentist materialism may continue to be an obstacle for some. (But isn't there the same problem for the self of emergent dualism? Not quite; the problem for emergentist materialism is that the holistic behavior is attributed to something we already know a great deal about, almost all of which lends itself to being understood in atomistic fashion.) On the other hand, it is quite a bit more obvious in the case of emergentist materialism that the charge of creation ex nihilo doesn't apply. As we've seen, the possibility for the self to exist separate from the brain and body is clearer for emergent dualism than it is for emergentist materialism; those who find the doctrine of resurrection through reassembly or re-creation plausible and attractive will not, however, be concerned about this. But it is not my purpose in this essay to sort out all of the remaining differences; what is intriguing is that the differences are as narrow as they are. Is emergentist materialism equivalent to emergent dualism? Not quite, perhaps, but near enough!

NOTES

My thanks to Dean Zimmerman for his comments on an earlier version of this essay.

1. Cf. Hasker 1999, 2004, 2005, and 2010.

2. See Popper's contributions to Popper and Eccles 1977.

3. See Hasker 1999: ch. 6.

4. See O'Connor 1994, 2000a, 2000b, and 2003 and O'Connor and Jacobs 2003.

5. They also discuss the prospects for such an emergentist view within a trope ontology. This approach, however, is clearly less favored by them than the ontology of immanent universals, and it will not be pursued further here.

6. See Hasker 1999: ch. 7 and Hasker 2010.

7. For a dualist view that posits exchange of energy between the physical and mental realms, see Hart 1988.

8. An intriguing light is thrown on this topic by theologian Michael Lodahl. Commenting on the depiction of creation in Genesis 1, he writes, "There is even an apparently playful punning in the Hebrew that may well reinforce this idea of creation's creativity: the earth is called upon by God to 'put forth' (*tadshe*) vegetation (*deshe*) and the waters are called upon to 'bring forth' (*yishretsu*) swarming creatures of the sea (*sherets*). *Tadshe Deshe*—the earth, we might say, is called upon to produce produce, to implant itself with plants. *Yishretsu Sheres*—the seas, we could say, are called upon to swarm with swarms of swimmers. Creaturely elements are invited to contribute their distinctive energies and capacities to what God is doing in the labor of creation" (Lodahl 2009: ch. 3). My thanks to Michael Lodahl for permitting me to use this draft of work in process.

9. Consider the following from Dean Zimmerman: "Thus the unity of consciousness supports the view that whatever is the bearer of psychological properties must be a single substance capable of exemplifying a plurality of properties. Its unitary nature consists in the impossibility of its having a 'division of psychological labor' among parts. If a single thinker can recognize the difference between sounds and colors, this thinker does not enjoy

the ability to compare the two simply by having one part that does its see-ing and another that does its hearing, even if these parts are tightly bound together. As Franz Brentano remarks, this 'would be like saying that, of course, neither a blind man nor a deaf man could compare colors with sounds, but if one sees and the other hears, the two together can recognize the relationship'" (Zimmerman 2007). Zimmerman correctly points out that this does not entail that the subject of experience must be absolutely simple, having no parts at all.

10. This version is adapted from a formulation by Paul Draper, who in turn was summarizing the argument as given in chapter 5 of Hasker 1999.

11. In the interest of convenience I shall from this point on refer simply to "the brain," while recognizing that the relevant part of the organism might be either more or less than the entire brain. The points made will apply in any case.

12. The relevance of this data to the mind-body problem was pointed out to me by Robin Collins.

13. The word "aspect" has a certain ambiguity which may actually be useful in the present case. Different aspects of a thing are often distin-guished subjectively, in terms of the "point of view" from which the matter in question is considered. But different aspects can also be objectively dif-ferent parts of the item in question: the "northern aspect" of a building can be physically and structurally distinct from its "southern aspect." We shall need to determine whether, and if so, how, this ambiguity is relevant to the case of the brain.

14. The reader is reminded that "brain" is used here as a shorthand for whatever portion of the anatomy turns out to be relevant, which may be ei-ther more or less than the actual brain. It is not excluded that something similar may occur in primitive life-forms that lack a recognizable brain.

REFERENCES

Hart, W. D. 1988. *The Engines of the Soul.* Cambridge: Cambridge University Press.

Hasker, William. 1999. *The Emergent Self.* Ithaca: Cornell University Press.

———. 2004. "Emergent Dualism: Challenge to a Materialist Consensus." In *What about the Soul? Neuroscience and Christian Anthropology,* edited by Joel B. Greene, 101–15. Nashville: Abingdon.

———. 2005. "On Behalf of Emergent Dualism." In *In Search of the Soul: Four Views of the Mind-Body Problem,* edited by Joel B. Green and Stuart Palmer, 75–100. Downers Grove, IL: InterVarsity.

————. 2010. "Persons and the Unity of Consciousness." In *The Waning of Materialism: New Essays*, edited by George Bealer and Rob Koons, 175–90. Oxford: Oxford University Press.

Leibniz, Gottfried. 1991. [*Monadology*]. In *G. W. Leibniz's "Monadology": An Edition for Students*, edited by Nicholas Rescher. Pittsburgh: University of Pittsburgh Press.

Lodahl, Michael. 2009. *Readers of the Scripture*. Grand Rapids: Brazos Press.

O'Connor, Timothy. 1994. "Emergent Properties." *American Philosophical Quarterly* 31:91–104.

————. 2000a. *Persons and Causes*. Oxford: Oxford University Press.

————. 2000b. "Causality, Mind, and Free Will." In *Action and Freedom*, edited by James E. Tomberlin, 105–17. Philosophical Perspectives 14. Oxford: Blackwell.

————. 2003. "Groundwork for an Emergentist Account of the Mental." *Progress in Complexity, Information and Design* 2.3.1 [October 2003]: 1–14.

O'Connor, Timothy, and Jonathan D. Jacobs. 2003. "Emergent Individuals." *Philosophical Quarterly* 53:540–55.

Popper, Karl R., and John C. Eccles. 1977. *The Self and Its Brain: An Argument for Interactionism*. New York: Springer-Verlag.

Zimmerman, Dean. 2007. "Dualism in the Philosophy of Mind." In *The Encyclopedia of Philosophy*, 2nd ed., 113–22. New York: Macmillan.

7

Benign Physicalism

A. D. SMITH

This essay may seem an odd one to be included in the present collection, since in it I argue that a certain form of physicalism may be true. I always used to think that physicalism, in any form, could not possibly be true—either epistemically or metaphysically. Recently, however, I have come to think that there is a physicalist account of things that is not, at least, demonstrably false. I have not relinquished any of my intuitions about the nature of consciousness—in particular, its "irreducibility"—that I formerly regarded as invalidating physicalism. The form of physicalist theory to be developed here, therefore, respects all such intuitions. Because of this, I term it "benign physicalism." It is, I believe, the *only* form of physicalism that stands any chance whatsoever of being true—or, at least, of being a way things might have been.

1.

A core element in the physicalist theory to be developed here is *topic-neutrality*, in J. J. C. Smart's sense. This notion is, however, here employed in a way that is the precise inverse of Smart's. Smart contended that our grasp of "mental" items—such as sensations, on which he focused—is topic-neutral in character. He suggested, for example, that seeing a yellowish-orange afterimage is adequately rendered as "something going on which is like what is going on when . . . I really see an orange" (Smart 1959: 149). Smart's suggestion was that, since all that may be going on when I see an orange is that certain brain processes take place, the way is cleared for the "mind-brain identity theory." Like many others, I found, and still find, this idea preposterous. Sensory experiences are as "topic-specific" as you can get—and manifestly so. They have their irreducible intrinsic, qualitative character; and we are aware of this through apperception. Smart's topic-neutrality thesis was an early expression of what has come to be known as "functionalism" in the philosophy of mind. As I have urged elsewhere (Smith 1993: 230–31), what is fundamentally wrong with this theory is not that given kinds of experience lack specific "causal roles." The point is, rather, that, even if it were essential to a given kind of experience that it sustain a certain causal role, and even if such a causal role were (necessarily) unique to such a kind of experience, something about the experience—something, moreover, that we know and know to be essential to it—would be left out, namely, how the experience is for the subject—or, as we might say, how it experientially (and hence essentially) *is*.[1]

My current employment of the notion of topic-neutrality is, as I say, the inverse of this. It is our concepts of *physical* objects, states of affairs, properties, and so on that are topic-neutral. As many have urged, and as I have argued elsewhere (Smith 1990; 2002: 13–17, 62–64), a physical realist must accept the primary/secondary quality distinction. The distinctively sensory qualities that feature in our perceptual experience of the world are actually qualities of experiences—qualia—and not inherent qualities of any merely physical non-conscious entities. If this is the case (and I shall assume that it is), although everyday experience may give us an appreciation of the spatial and temporal properties of physical objects, it gives us no insight into *what* it is that is arrayed in space and that physically persists through time. In some sense, of course, everyday character-izations of the physical world do offer us a plethora of ways of speci-fying what is thus arrayed in space. It may, for instance, be a table, or a cucumber, or gold. However, as far as the physical *nature* of such things is concerned, perceptual experience leaves us in the dark. If we are to gain any such insight, we must turn to science. When we turn to science, however, we find that what we are offered is but, as Bertrand Russell (1927: 391) nicely put it, "the causal skeleton of the world." It, too, fails to give us any appreciation of the *intrinsic nature* of anything physical. There are, indeed, certain theoretical reductions that are commonly, and no doubt rightly, seen as involv-ing identifications. Heat (of a certain sort) with molecular kinetic en-ergy, for example. But what is kinetic energy? Scientists characterize (some kinds of) electric current in terms of electrons. But what are electrons? Our understanding of electrons is exhausted by our grasp of the fundamental physical properties that we attribute to them—such as charge. But what is charge? Our grasp of such fundamental physical properties (and forces) is exhausted by our understanding of the physical theories in which they feature: theories that tell us how things *behave*. Charge, for example, as well as kinetic energy, is *what-ever it is* that makes, or would make, certain theories true: theories that are all, ultimately, about functional dependencies. We have, and can have, no grasp of what charge may be "in itself" over and above the causal role that is attributed to it by some physical theory. Our concepts of such fundamental physical properties are, and must re-main, as Colin McGinn has recently put it (2006: 93), essentially *functional* concepts. So, the claim that the physical is ultimately only topic-neutrally specifiable is the claim that at the ultimate (not-further-to-be-reduced) level, all physical concepts are (necessarily) merely functionally specifiable. John Foster (1982: 51–66; 2008: 42–82), and before him Eddington (1928: 251), have called this the *inscrutability* of the physical—a term I shall adopt. Although this claim is not uncontroversial, since it has been expounded at length by many others I shall not go into a defense of it here, but assume its truth.[2]

Before moving on, I do, however, want to make four points about the notion of inscrutability that will be in play in this paper. First, to say that the physical realm is ultimately inscrutable is to imply that it does indeed have some intrinsic nature, though one that it is impossible to "get at" save by way of topic-neutral, functional characterization. So, the view that some have held, according to which the physical world may *ontologically* be a matter of dispositions, or powers, "all the way down," is rejected as incoherent. Foster (1982: 67–72), and others as well, have argued against any such possibility; and I concur with them in rejecting it.

Secondly, although I have endorsed Russell's claim that we can only ever get at the "causal skeleton" of the physical world, the kind of merely "structural" knowledge to which Russell seems (at one time) to have thought we are limited is much more restrictive than the kind that I—together with everyone else, today, who holds similar views—have in mind. Russell seems to have thought that the structure of the physical world that we can come to know is one that can be characterized only formally and mathematically.[3] Such a claim was soon shown to be almost trivial, since any sufficiently populous domain can be shown to possess any and every merely formally or mathematically specified structure that one can dream up.[4] The knowledge that Russell allows us is far more exiguous than that to which I claim we are restricted. For one thing, as Galen Strawson (2003: 57–60) has suggested, our experience of *space* may give us some firsthand appreciation of what physical space may be in itself—something that goes beyond any merely mathematically defined notion of a "space." Perhaps he is right. And perhaps the same goes for time. To be sure, a doubt may arise about how much a grip our experience of space and time gives us on the nature of the "space-time" of relativity theory; but it would be absurd to deny that we possess, or could possess, knowledge, at least to some degree of accuracy, of the locations and relative positions of some physical entities. Even more importantly, I do not deny that we can attain knowledge of the *causal relations* that hold between physical entities. Indeed, without this ingredient, our knowledge would hardly be of the *causal* skeleton of the world at all. Given this, there is no threat of triviality to the present proposal. Indeed, the task of delineating the causal structure of the physical world is a massive undertaking: one that may not be fully achievable, even in principle. To the extent that we do attain a

scientific understanding of the world, we come to some understanding of the actual causal relations that hold between spatiotemporally
located items. All that is being rejected here as absolutely impossible
is that we should have any conception, other than a merely topic-
neutral one, of the intrinsic nature of anything non-conscious that
could be in space or time, and that could causally interact.[5]

Thirdly, inscrutability is to be distinguished from the kind of
"humility" concerning the nature of the physical world that David
Lewis (2009) has enjoined upon us.[6] This is because it is an essential
part of Lewis's case for cognitive humility that the very same patterns of causal interaction that are actually sustained by entities with
certain natures could have been sustained by entities with different
natures (or fundamental properties), or, alternatively, that certain natures could have sustained different patterns of causal interaction
from those they actually do. In other words, there are different "possible worlds" that embody the same causal structure (including the
same spatiotemporal distribution of causal powers) while yet differing either in the fundamental natures that are exemplified, or in the
precise causal roles that they sustain. Since science can tell us only
about the structural and locational facts concerning powers, we cannot possibly know which of these worlds is actual. It is precisely *this*
fact, according to Lewis, that forces "humility" on us. By contrast, the
proposal to be developed here is weaker than this, in that it relies on
no such presumption that it is possible to dissociate natures and their
causal powers. "It is one thing to know that a role is occupied, another thing to know what occupies it," writes Lewis (2009: 204). Not
only is this true, it is true without qualification. More particularly, it
remains true even if it is essential to the thing in question that it fulfill this role, and even if it is not possible for this role to be fulfilled by
anything else. Indeed, it remains true even if we know these "essentialist" facts.

Fourthly, although I adopt the term "inscrutable," it may mis-
lead. For it may suggest merely that, although non-conscious physical entities have an inner reality, we can never get to know what that
is in itself. The question of possible knowledge is not, however, what
is of crucial importance here. The important point is not that such an
inner reality is unknowable—though that is true—but that it is nec-

essarily *unconceptualizable* by scientific means. We cannot even *surmise* what such intrinsic natures may be if they are the natures of non-conscious entities. Not only is it the case that our appreciation of our conscious experiences is not topic-neutral in character; it is the *only* "topic-specific" appreciation of anything that is possible. This fact invalidates Daniel Stoljar's recent attempt to defend physicalism. He accepts that physical science offers us only causal roles and not the intrinsic natures (or "categorical grounds," as he puts it) of the things that have such roles. But, he claims, there is a possible cognition of such natures. Moreover, anyone who had such knowledge would be able to understand, a priori, how the physical sustains consciousness (Stoljar 2001: 273–75). There is, however, no *conceivable* way in which such knowledge could be attained.[7] One can come by a concept of a nature that something located in space can possess in only two ways: experience and theory. Although experience may give us direct awareness of physical objects, as far as the nature of what it is that we are thus acquainted with as located in space is concerned, experience offers us only *experiential* qualities, or qualia.[8] As Stoljar makes abundantly clear, it is not these that he takes to be the currently unknown natures of things. He insists that the latter are non-conscious (Stoljar 2001: 257n10 and 273). Theory, however, necessarily gives us but topic-neutrally specified natures. These are the only two *possible* avenues to cognition; and their respective features— experientiality and topic-neutrality—are *essential* to them. Stoljar's proposal is, I contend, an incoherent pipe dream.

2.

Given physical inscrutability, the following possibility emerges: that the intrinsic natures of some physical entities, in virtue of which they sustain the causal roles they do in the world, and, hence, in virtue of which various (topic-neutrally) specified physical properties—or, as I shall call them, *physicalistic* properties—are ascribed to them (correctly, let us suppose), are *experiential states* (and events and processes). To employ a natural extension of the language of functionalism familiar from the philosophy of mind, we may say that it is possible that what *realizes* a functionally specified physical property (a physicalistic property) is some kind of experiential state. So—though this is an illustration of the idea, and not a serious suggestion—perhaps positrons are a certain kind of Leibnizian monad. What sustains the causal interactions on the basis of which we attribute, say, positive charge to positrons is a certain sort of experiential state. A certain type of experience would be the *intrinsic nature* of positive charge as possessed by positrons. Less fancifully, I suggest that perhaps *our* conscious experiences, which we know do exist, are the intrinsic natures of (instantiations of) certain physical, functionally specified properties. If this were so, the inner nature of some physical things would be "scrutable," though only because of the firsthand, immediate, apperceptive awareness we have of the character of our own experiences.[9]

This suggestion that experiences may be what certain physical entities intrinsically and ultimately are, so that certain (instantiations of) qualities of experience realize certain physicalistic properties, should be distinguished from a superficially similar suggestion that has been made by Michael Lockwood.[10] He, too, bases his account on the inscrutability of the physical; and he even explicitly employs the idea of inverting Smart's topic-neutrality thesis, as have I (Lockwood 1981: 156; 1989: 160). For Lockwood, however, it is not qualities of experiences (qualia) that are the ultimate realizers of at least some physicalistic properties, but "phenomenal qualities."[11] Crucially, Lockwood does not regard an instantiation of such a quality as an essentially conscious affair. When we have, say, a visual experience of red, according to Lockwood, the phenomenal quality redness has an instantiation, and there is an episode of awareness. The two are, however, distinct. Lockwood (1989: 162) proposes what he terms a "disclosure view" of phenomenal qualities: a kind of naïve realism with respect to such qualities. In other words, he embraces an act-object analysis of sensory awareness of the kind proposed by early sense-datum theorists. When I am visually aware of redness, on this view, red is not a quality *of* my conscious state (nor do I "sense redly"). Rather, the redness is something distinct from the awareness of it, and can exist without being an object of awareness at all. According to Lockwood, when I experience red, I am immediately aware, in virtue of my being acquainted with this instance of redness, of an intrinsic quality of some physical entity: in fact, of my brain, or current brain state. But this brain state, with its qualitative character, is not *itself* a conscious state. It is only my awareness *of* it that is conscious.

I reject this account on two grounds. First, for reasons that it would take too long properly to present here, but which I have sketched elsewhere (Smith 2002: 55–57), I find the act-object analysis of sensory awareness implausible.[12] Lockwood does, it is true, offer two arguments in favor of the view; but they trade on an ambiguity in the notion of being an item of consciousness. To illustrate the first argument, consider what Fred Dretske has termed *non-epistemic (or simple) seeing* (e.g., Dretske 1969 and 1979).[13] Something features in my visual field in a discriminable way, but I entirely fail to notice it. If it features in my visual field, it does so, I am assuming, because my visual experience is characterized by a certain quale, or phenomenal quality. If, however, we are dealing with a case of non-epistemic seeing, I will not be *aware of* or *conscious of* this quality (or of the quality of the physical object of perception that the occurrence of this quale serves to manifest in my experience). Lockwood concludes from this that instances of phenomenal qualities are not essentially conscious affairs: that they could be realized without the occurrence of experience at all. The ambiguity, however, should be clear. If there is, as I believe there is, such a thing as non-epistemic seeing, then things can be "in" consciousness, in the sense that they are qualities of conscious states, without our being conscious "of" them. We can help to avoid the ambiguity that is in play here by saying that the qualities in question are essentially *experiential qualities:* qualities of experiences (specifically sensory experiences). Such a quality can be realized in a subject's experience without that subject's attention being in any way directed to it (or to a corresponding physical object or quality), even minimally and incidentally. Lockwood writes that "the traditional view would have it that a given quality ceases to be realized in one's visual field, when one ceases to be conscious of it (even dimly)" (1989: 163). It is clear that Lockwood is here employing the "attentional" sense of being conscious: it is a matter of being conscious *of* something. So, what Lockwood is attributing to the traditional view that he opposes is the idea that attention *creates* its objects (or at least aspects of experience that subjectively manifest objects). Few "traditional" writers accepted such a view, however; and I regard it as absurd. Sensory experience can be a certain way even if it is entirely overlooked.

Lockwood's second argument is equally unpersuasive. He infers from the supposed fact of the non-transitivity of subjective indiscriminability that two phenomenal qualities can be "objectively" distinct even though the subject who is aware of them is incapable of distinguishing them, and hence that "we should allow phenomenal qualities quite generally to outrun awareness" (Lockwood 1989: 165). The notion of outrunning awareness is once again ambiguous, however. If it means that there may be differences in conscious experience *of* which we may not be aware, it should be accepted—as in the Dretske cases. But this in no way implies, or lends support to, the idea that such differences can exist in the absence of any conscious experience at all—which is what Lockwood supposes. To this it might be replied that I am failing to appreciate the full force of the relevant experimental findings. They do not show, it may be suggested, merely that subjects fail to make certain discriminations, but that they are utterly incapable of making them. Surely, however, the idea that there should be differences in conscious experience (in my sense) that cannot even in principle be appreciated by the subject is a highly obscure and dubiously coherent one. To this I would, in turn, make two replies. The first is that the idea that experiences can have a phenomenal character that may not be detectable, even "in principle," by the subject of the experience is not dubiously coherent. Indeed, as I have argued at some length elsewhere (Smith 2008), I believe it is true. The second is that, in any case, the experimental findings do not force this strong interpretation on us.[14] Indeed, there are two other possible interpretations. The first, which I have already intimated, is that, although subjects fail to detect certain differences in their experience, they could in principle have detected them. The actual experimental findings do not conclusively rule this out. The second is that there may be no such differences to detect. Just because a subject fails to detect any qualitative difference between stimuli X and Y, and none between stimuli Y and Z, though he or she does detect a difference between X and Z, where X, Y, and Z are "objective," "physical" stimuli, does not demonstrate that X and Y look (or sound, or whatever) exactly the same to the subject in the two contexts in which they feature. All that experimental procedures can guarantee is identity of *physical stimulus*. For at least these reasons I suggest that Lockwood's second argument for his act-object analysis of sensory experience is, to put it no more strongly, inconclusive.

The second problem with Lockwood's proposal is that it does not escape the case against more familiar physicalist theories. Since, for Lockwood, the realization of phenomenal qualities does not constitute or suffice for consciousness, such a realization is, in and of itself, a non-conscious affair. So, Lockwood's account of consciousness really concerns the act of awareness that is directed upon (or "discloses") such qualities. In this, and this alone, does consciousness reside. What, then, can a physicalist, who, like Lockwood, respects our anti-reductionist and anti-eliminativist intuitions about consciousness, say about this state or process of awareness itself? What Lockwood himself does is to apply the topic-neutrality claim—now in a form closer to Smart's original one—to awareness itself. Since we have, he claims, no "transparent" conception of awareness, but only of the phenomenal *objects* of awareness, there is nothing to prevent us from identifying conscious awareness with some kind of physical process in the brain—though he admits that "it remains profoundly mysterious, in physical terms, what form such a process could take" (1989: 169). Indeed it does. So, Lockwood's particular way of inverting Smart gets us nowhere. Instances of phenomenal qualities are not themselves conscious. Acts of awareness are conscious; but they are just physical processes in the brain that themselves are constituted by non-conscious items. This, as I say, is no real advance on more familiar forms of physicalism. Consciousness is supposed to be constituted by what is non-conscious. And that, I maintain, is impossible.

Lockwood presents his view as being at least a close cousin of *neutral monism*—particularly as developed by Russell. It is, perhaps, worth briefly stating how the position to be developed here differs from such monism. As the very term suggests, the metaphysically ultimate elements in neutral monism are not intrinsically conscious items. They are *neutral* (as between the conscious and the nonconscious). And because they are fundamental, they are *prior* to the distinction between the mental and the physical. On such a view, therefore, consciousness is not an ultimate, irreducible feature of reality. Consciousness, rather, emerges as a result of intrinsically non-conscious (because neutral) elements coming to stand in certain relations to each other. Such a view, therefore, tries to conjure consciousness out of non-consciousness just as much as do the usual forms of materialism, and is equally unacceptable for this very reason.

3.

My own proposal is that at least some physical entities may, in their ultimate nature, be conscious *experiences*. Although the intrinsic nature of the physical is mostly cognitively closed to us, in having conscious experiences and appreciating their nature we are, uniquely, acquainted with the intrinsic nature of something physical. As Lockwood himself says, we transparently know the intrinsic character of certain physical states "by living them, or, one might almost say, by self-reflectively *being* them" (1989: 159). It is, however, the conscious experiences *themselves* that we are thus acquainted with and that constitute the inner nature of some physical item.

This proposal, as such, is nothing new. Eddington (1928), Maxwell (1970, 1978), and Strawson (2003, 2006b), for example, have propounded it. What all such proponents have in common, however, is that they present conscious states as the intrinsic natures of things *already recognized as physical*. In particular, they all propose that in being immediately acquainted with the phenomenal character of our own experiences, we are acquainted with the intrinsic nature *of our own brains* (or of our brain activity).[15] Now, a brain is a physically complex thing.[16] It is *constituted* by its parts; it is "nothing over and above" such constituents arranged and interacting in a certain way. (And the same goes for brain activity.) The question now is, are the constituent elements of a (working) brain themselves conscious or not? If not, then we have the problem that faces more familiar kinds of physicalism. Consciousness is constituted by unconsciousness.[17] According to Strawson, we must therefore opt for the other alternative and embrace "micropsychism," and perhaps even panpsychism.[18] There is, that is to say, consciousness "all the way down," at least as far as the relevant constituents of higher animal brains are concerned.

As a number of critics (e.g., Goff 2006, Carruthers and Schachter 2006) have pointed out, there is as much of a problem with this proposal as there is with the idea of consciousness being constituted by what is not conscious. This time the problem is with the idea that *my* consciousness should be constituted by conscious experiences that are not mine. On this view, neurons in my brain—or, if neurons aren't "ultimate" enough, some constituents of neurons—are little centers of consciousness. Even if these were not a part of my (or anyone else's) brain, they would still be little centers of consciousness—for otherwise we should be faced with the previous problem of conjuring consciousness out of unconsciousness. Strawson's proposal is that when a host of such experiencing items come together in the right spatiotemporal and causal manner, they just are *my* consciousness at that time (or yours). This, however, falls foul of a point that is often made in discussions of Kant's doctrine of the transcendental unity of apperception. One cannot conjure a *unitary* consciousness out of initially discrete centers of consciousness by any form of juxtaposition or causal relatedness. Relatedly, as Carruthers and Schachter (2006: 38) point out, Strawson's suggestion is undermined by Ned Block's famous counterexample to functionalist accounts of consciousness (Block 1978). Functionalists hold that consciousness is just a matter of individual elements—it doesn't matter what they are—causally behaving in a certain way. Block suggested that for any proposed functionally organized system, we can suppose that the population of China could instantiate such an organization. But, Block claims, surely they would not constitute a *single consciousness*, even though each element is conscious. If the idea that the Chinese would indeed constitute a unitary consciousness is absurd, as surely it is, so is Strawson's proposal. Strawson is aware of this kind of objection, and even quotes a characteristically incisive expression of it by William James. I find his response to it (Strawson 2006a: 246–62) utterly inadequate, however. Indeed, what he writes hardly constitutes a reply to the objection at all. He seems simply not to appreciate its force.

My own proposal, by contrast, is that consciousness may be *autonomously* physical: not, that is to say, physical in virtue of being the intrinsic character of (to put it somewhat tendentiously) *something else* that is recognized as physical—such as a functioning brain. Perhaps conscious states (all of them) have their *own* distinctive functional roles, patterns of causal interaction, that suffice for them to be physical: a functional role that is different from that of brains (or neurons, or constituents of neurons). But if so, what, it may be asked, is the relation between the (functioning) brain and experience? The most natural answer, for a physicalist, is that it is causal. Since our intuitions about conscious experiences indicate that they are radically and irreducibly different in kind from anything non-conscious, they cannot be reductively explained by, supervene upon, be constituted by, or, as I have put it elsewhere (Smith 1993: 249), "radically emerge" from what is non-conscious. I cannot, however, see why they may not be *caused* by what is non-conscious.[19] It is not, after all, that such *causally* emergent novelty is foreign even to the account of things offered by current physical science. In certain circumstances, for example, a photon gives rise to, indeed gives way to, a positron and an electron pair. Both of the latter possess charge and mass, whereas the photon from which they are created possesses neither.

4.

It is perfectly clear, I hope, that the account I am proposing is "benign." Less clear, so far, is why it counts as a form of physicalism. In order to establish this we need to determine what it means to say that something is physical. In an earlier paper of mine on the topic of physicalism (Smith 1993), I suggested that this can be done only negatively: by means of a certain contrast with what is experiential, or conscious. It suffices for something to count as physical, I suggested, that it be "concrete" (i.e., not "abstract," like numbers and propositions) and *wholly non-conscious.* Such a thing I termed "merely physical." A *property* is merely physical, I suggested, if it is a non-formal, non-categorial property that a merely physical thing can have.[20] Something is then physical—that is, *wholly* physical, though perhaps not "merely" so—if and only if it either is merely physical or is but a complexion of—is entirely constituted by—such merely physical things (as structured, and perhaps causally interacting, in a certain way). With a qualification to be introduced below, this is, I continue to hold, the only adequate way of spelling out what it is for something to be physical.

Given this account of what it is for something to be physical, I argued in my earlier paper, on the basis of considerations that are similar to those that have since become familiar through the writings of others—for example, Chalmers (1996: 32–51, 104–8) and Strawson (2006b:12–21)—that physicalism could not possibly be true (either epistemically or metaphysically). In a nutshell, the argument was that since conscious experiences are clearly not "merely" physical, they can be (wholly) physical only if they are wholly constituted out of, are "nothing over and above," merely physical things. But, given that the qualitative experiential character of consciousness is absolutely irreducible, this is impossible. Consciousness cannot be constituted by what is non-conscious. I now think that this argument can be blocked, if we bear the inscrutability (or topic-neutrality of our concepts) of the physical firmly in mind. For I take it as uncontroversial that a thing is wholly physical *if all its (non-formal and non-categorial) properties are physical.* I formerly claimed that a property is "merely" physical if a non-conscious thing could have it. But the "merely" now appears too strong. Consider again my (fanciful) supposition of Leibnizian "monadic" positrons. Let us also suppose, as of course we do, that *protons* are wholly non-conscious entities. Both positrons and protons possess positive charge. So, positive charge, since it can be possessed by wholly non-conscious protons, and is neither "formal" nor "categorial," formerly would have counted for me as merely physical. However, the positive charge of a Leibnizian positron, since it is realized by a conscious state, is not "merely" physical, but is mental "as well." Nevertheless, it seems to me that positive charge as such—even when possessed by a conscious positron—counts as at least a *physical* property, since it (topic-neutrally construed, of course) can be possessed by a non-conscious thing—such as a proton. A Leibnizian positron would, therefore, be *wholly* (though not "merely") physical if *all* its properties were physical in this way:

if, that is to say, there were no aspect of its ultimate conscious nature that did not sustain patterns of causal interaction in a way that suffices for possession of some topic-neutrally specified physical property that a non-conscious thing could possess.

The case of monadic positrons is still meant only as an illustration. If taken seriously, it would be too close to Strawson's micropsychism. On the present account there is no need to attribute consciousness to any subject other than those associated with complex nervous systems.[21] Note: "associated with"—not "identical to." The form of physicalism that I am proposing as conceivably true is not a form of "identity theory," since such a theory, in my view, always tries to identify experience with *something else*. Experiences are identical only to themselves; and it is these experiences themselves, my suggestion is, that may be physical in their own right in virtue of being the intrinsic character of instantiations of physicalistic (topic-neutrally specified) properties. What I am suggesting is that experiences may have a set of physicalistic properties of which we are currently unaware as physicalistic properties—as, that is to say, functionally, causally defined properties—because we are as yet unaware of the causal roles that they fulfill. If experiences sustain causal interactions that can be made sense of only by (correctly) postulating entities with certain physicalistic properties, so that experiences are the ultimate intrinsic natures of such entities, and their experiential properties are the realizers of the physicalistic properties in question, and if *everything* about experiences as such had such a causal significance and thereby sustained a correct attribution of such physicalistic properties, experiences would be wholly physical.

5.

The suggestion that something is wholly physical if and only if all of its properties are ones that a non-conscious thing can possess can be spelled out in different ways that it is perhaps worth investigating— since some are stronger, and perhaps less defensible, than others.[22] On its strongest reading the claim is that something is (wholly) physical only if each of its *determinate* physicalistic properties is a property that a non-conscious thing can have. This suggestion raises a number of worries. One worry is that if a determinate physicalistic property can be "ultimately realized" both consciously and non-consciously, the instantiation of the property in these two cases could be caused by exactly the same kind of physical event. One effect will, however, be conscious, and the other unconscious. But will this not infringe some acceptable version of the same (total) cause/same effect principle? Of course, at the merely physicalistic, topic-neutral level, the two effects are qualitatively identical, so there is no infringement. One may yet feel that the causal principle is being infringed at some deep metaphysical level. In fact, it need not be. There would, for instance, be no such infringement if, whenever the scenario in question occurs, at least one physicalistic property of the cause of the non-conscious effect is *itself* differently realized from the way the property is realized by the cause of the conscious effect.[23]

Another worry is that the proposal infringes the perhaps mandatory causal account of the individuation of physical properties. There is, it may be held, no difference that does not *make* a difference.[24] If a certain (functionally specified) physicalistic property can be realized both consciously and non-consciously, this difference must itself have some possible causal expression. But then there would be a causal *divergence*, arising solely from the ultimate natures of the things concerned, and we cannot be dealing with two instantiations of the *same* physicalistic property, since physicalistic properties are individuated precisely in terms of causal role. This objection, too, can, however, be answered, if we bear firmly in mind the distinction between functionally specified physicalistic properties and metaphysically ultimate properties. Two instantiations cannot, indeed, be instantiations of the same *physicalistic* property if they sustain causal interactions that are different in terms of *their* physicalistic character. Conversely, if such physicalistically specified causal interactions are identical, we are dealing with two instantiations of the *same* physicalistic property. Such a physicalistic identity of causal role is, however, compatible with there being a divergence at the ultimate metaphysical level. It could be, for example, that *conscious* realizers of a certain physicalistic property give rise to *conscious* realizers of physicalistic properties in a way that onscious realizers do not, even though the *same* physicalistic

properties are in question. Even if every difference makes a difference, the difference need not emerge at the merely physicalistic,
topic-neutral level.

There is, however, one final worry that will, for some, be the
most worrying. For the current suggestion does not exclude in principle the possibility of something at least analogous to "zombies"—
something that physicalists typically regard as incompatible with
their position.[25] Although it is no part of even this strongest version
of the present proposal that a conscious entity, in order to be physical, must share *all* its physical properties with some possible nonphysical entity—but only that *each* such property could be had by
some non-conscious entity or other—it does not, as such, exclude
the possibility in principle of exact physical (i.e., physicalistic) duplicates, one of which is conscious and the other not.[26] When, however,
physicalism is understood as it is here, the possibility of "zombies" is
not incompatible with physicalism. For, on the present view, two entities can be wholly physical, physically (i.e., physicalistically) identical, and yet differ in nature. This is because a physicalistic characterization of an entity, since it is merely topic-neutral in import, is not a
metaphysically fundamental or ultimate characterization of it. Lying
beneath all such characterizations are the intrinsic natures of physical things: natures that can vary without any physicalistic difference,
so long as the variants sustain the same patterns of causal interactions at the physicalistic (topic-neutral) level. The whole idea behind the present proposal is that science, and "common sense," give
no insight at all into the metaphysically ultimate nature of physical
reality. From the metaphysical point of view, science and common
sense are superficial—indeed, nugatory. It may be that there are ultimate *differences* that are inscrutable both for common sense and for
science.

Although this first, strong form of the present proposal does not
rule out the possibility of "zombies" in principle, it is yet compatible
with the proposal that such zombies are, indeed, metaphysically impossible. The impossibility in question may lie in the ultimate natures of the kinds of physicalistic processes that alone can *give rise to*
things that sustain the patterns of causal interaction that conscious
experiences sustain. It may be that, in a way that is not a priori deter-

minable, the actualization of such natures can give rise *only* to conscious experiences, and that *only* they can sustain the pattern of causal interaction that they manifest. If this were so, then although, on this first version of the present proposal, any physicalistic property possessed by a conscious entity is such that it could be possessed by some non-conscious entity, it is metaphysically excluded that a conscious experience should possess *only* the physicalistic properties that a single non-conscious entity could possess. A certain *combination* of physicalistic properties would then be (necessarily) distinctive of conscious experiences.

It is, however, not necessary, in order that conscious experiences should be themselves physical, to claim that all their *determinate* physicalistic properties are ones that non-conscious entities could exhibit. It may be, for instance, and it may be necessary, that experiences, and only they, exhibit physicalistic properties that, although generically common to them and non-conscious entities, are possessed by conscious entities *to a degree* that no non-conscious entity does (or could) possess them—just as two entities can both possess electric charge, but one possess a greater charge than the other. If this were the case, experience would again be physicalistically distinctive. Since the distinctiveness here in question is not, as it was in the previous paragraph, a matter of a distinctive *collection* of properties, but is a matter of the distinctive determinate realization of particular properties, this present form of the theory wholly avoids the problems concerning the same cause/same effect principle, the causal individuation of physical properties, and the "zombie" question that attached to the first and stronger version of the theory.

Even this, however, is stronger than is necessary for the coherence of the present proposal, and for an adequate account of what it is to be physical. Consider, again, the creation of a positron and an electron from a photon. Physics can make sense of this event, despite the fact that a photon does not even determinably possess charge and mass, as do positrons and electrons, because there is a story to be told in terms of energy. Given a principle such as $e=mc^2$, we do not require the common possession of even determinable "properties" to make physical sense of causal interactions. I am not suggesting that physical science must work with the notion of energy. Perhaps it will cease to feature in future science (though that seems unlikely). The point is that something like energy, in virtue of being such a high-level physical concept, *can* underwrite and intelligibly connect specific (even determinable) physical properties, such as charge. And perhaps at least something like this is necessary for science to hang together in an intelligible way. Energy (or its possible future replacement) is, of course, something that non-conscious things possess (or are equivalent to). But, as we know, energy can be manifested in different ways, with different correlated properties. So, conscious states do not need to possess any (and only) physical "properties" that non-conscious things can possess in order to count as physical. Their properties can be unique to the conscious domain, so long as they have "energy-equivalents," or are themselves specific manifestations of energy.[27]

6.

I have referred to the possible causal powers of conscious experiences, on the basis of which topic-neutrally specified physical properties may be attributed to them. But what, it may be asked, could these powers be? As things stand, we recognize at most two sorts of causal interaction involving experiences. They give rise, at least given certain other attendant conditions, to other mental states and to behavior; and they are themselves caused both by physical stimuli and by other mental states.[28] If this is granted, we must attribute to experiences physicalistic properties that are sufficient to account for these causal roles. Similar causal roles are, however, also attributed (and let us suppose correctly) to brain states and activities. Sensory stimuli cause brain activity, brain activities give rise to other brain activities, and some give rise to behavior. Neurons, and constellations of neurons, are assigned physical properties, in part, on the basis of such roles (or on the basis of relatively "micro" roles that sustain such roles). If, as on the view I am proposing, experiences are distinct from any brain states and processes, their causal roles will have to be different from those of neurons, and their physical properties will have to be different, in part at least, from those possessed by neurons and neuronal activity.[29] If such a causal involvement of experiences is granted, neurophysiology is necessarily an incomplete science if my version of physicalism is true. On at least some occasions, the originating physical causes of efferent nerve impulses that lead to bodily movement are not patterns of neuronal activity, but experiences: experiences that have their own physicalistic properties in virtue of which they can play this originating role. And whenever afferent nerve impulses give rise to experiences, they do so *in addition* to any neuronal states and processes they give rise to; and such experiences will have a physical nature that makes them apt for being so caused. Thus, whenever neurophysiology posits a brain state that is both the final effect of an afferent chain and the first cause of an efferent chain of impulses, this brain state will, in fact, whenever experience is causally involved, be neither: it will be the penultimate link in the afferent chain (since it is itself the cause of an experience), and it will not be the causal instigator of the efferent chain at all (for it is the experience that is that). This picture is, of course, somewhat similar to that offered by traditional forms of interactionist dualism. It differs, however, in that experiences are seen as having a physical nature, and as causing neuronal activity physically, in virtue of their being realizations of distinctive physical properties.

Another possibility is that experiences have no cerebral effects. This is, no doubt, not an attractive view; but I explore it, since it is not ruled out by the present account as such. This would be somewhat similar to epiphenomenalism. Once again, however, there is an important difference. On the present account, experiences would not be epiphenomenal to the *physical* order, of course, since they are themselves physical. They would be epiphenomenal merely to the cerebral. More significantly, this "epiphenomenalist" version of the present proposal escapes what I regard as the serious metaphysical objection to ordinary epiphenomenalism, namely, that it postulates causal "dead-ends." Surely nothing in nature is without any possible effect.[30] Since, on the present proposal, experiences are physical, their properties are topic-neutrally specified by their passive *and active* causal powers. If experiences have no effects on the brain, they will have effects, currently unknown to us, on other physical—perhaps non-conscious—things. For all we know, experiences have causal effects of a kind of which we have no inkling. If there are such effects, discovering them and explaining them by attributing physicalistic properties to "theoretical entities" would be postulating entities the intrinsic nature of which would be conscious experiences.

On either version of the present proposal—"interactionist" or "epiphenomenalist"—experiences are something "over and above" brain activity, and they have a physical nature that is different from that of any brain, brain state, or brain activity. When physical scientists investigate experiences, they not unnaturally investigate the animal body, and, in particular, the animal brain and central nervous system. If physicalism is true—that is, if the present form of physicalism, which is the only possibly true form of physicalism, is true—they are doomed to miss their target. If the "interactionist" version of physicalism is true, they will discover its truth only by seeing that their present approach offers an account that is (necessarily) incomplete. Only by postulating physical items in addition to neurons and neuronal activity will they attain a theory that is fully "joined up." If the "epiphenomenalist" version of physicalism is true, the animal body is simply the wrong place to be looking for the physical presence of experience. Perhaps we will stumble upon it elsewhere—as, over a century ago, we stumbled across X-rays and radioactivity.

7.

I have stated that my opposition to familiar sorts of physicalism arises in large part from the fact that the brain is composite, having parts that are not themselves conscious. The same goes for brain activity. Consciousness cannot, therefore, be (or supervene upon, or be "nothing over and above") what is cerebral, for then consciousness would, absurdly, consist of non-consciousness.[31] If the present proposal is not to be subject to a devastating *tu quoque*, the physical nature of consciousness must be dissimilar to the physical nature of the brain in this respect. In particular, the physicalistically specified entities, the inner natures of which are conscious experiences, must not themselves be physicalistically decomposable into physicalistic items that lack conscious realization. Nor, as we saw earlier in connection with Strawson's micropsychism, can they be decomposable into physicalistic items the inner natures of which, though experiential, are not experiences of the same subject as the original experiences. In this sense, experiences must be irreducible or fundamental *even physicalistically.* Experiences cannot, physicalistically conceived, have anything like a particulate structure. I assume that this is fairly obvious. But even if experiences are conceived, as doubtless they must be, not as anything like "substances," but as dynamic states and processes, they cannot be resultants of states and processes in independently existing elements. Rather than the way that most physical objects are composed out of atoms, or the way that brain activity is constituted by the activities of neurons, a better analogy would be the way in which, say, a magnetic field is generated by a moving charge. Something like a field may be complex, or internally differentiated, yet not in virtue of being composed of elements that can exist independently of the field. Again, it may well be that any experience necessarily realizes *several* physicalistic properties. But it is not as if a combination of properties were like a composition out of elements. An entity that possesses a plurality of properties is not *constituted* by them.

What, however, of these physicalistic properties themselves, where conscious realizers are in question? Galen Strawson believes that at this point we are faced with the following choice: "Either experiential properties, being natural physical properties, are reducible to other natural physical properties, in something like the way we take physical properties like liquidity or acidity to be, or they are not. But if they are not so reducible, then at least some of them must themselves be fundamental physical properties, like electric charge, not reducible to (or theoretically explicable in terms of) any other physical properties" (Strawson 1994: 60). Strawson quite rightly rejects the first alternative.[32] But what exactly does the second commit us to? Strawson clearly means by it that some experiential properties— such as, for example, red and green qualia—will have to be physically fundamental. Moreover, he takes this to mean that such properties will be properties of physically fundamental entities. In short, he takes the only reasonable answer to the present question to be "micropsychism," at least.[33] Now, in the context of the present proposal, to say that such qualia are physical properties is to say that they are the inner nature of some physicalistically specified properties. The qualia *red* and *green* are not going to feature in any physical theory, however, but only certain physicalistic properties of which they are the realizations.[34] In the present context, the question is, therefore, whether such *physicalistic* properties must be "fundamental," given that the qualia that realize them are irreducible. When the question is interpreted in this way, the issue is somewhat less straightforward than it is for Strawson himself.

There is, it seems to me, one way of so interpreting Strawson's argument according to which it is sound. Suppose that a certain simple experiential property were the intrinsic nature of some physicalistic property P.[35] Suppose, furthermore, that our physical theory states that possessing P is "nothing over and above" possessing physicalistic property (or properties) Q. Now, perhaps Q itself can be realized both consciously and non-consciously. It cannot, however, be that a conscious realization of P should be nothing over and above a non-conscious realization of Q, for then we should have the sort of "reduction" of the experiential to the non-experiential that both Strawson and I reject. So, if any conscious instantiation of P is nothing over and above some instantiation of Q, the latter must itself be consciously realized. Since, however, realization, in the present sense, is nonreflexive, the experiential quality that realizes Q must be a different quality from that which realizes P. But the experiential property that realizes P was supposed to be simple; and it is nonsensical to suppose that the realization of one experiential property is nothing over and above the realization of some *different* experiential property. P, therefore, must be a fundamental physicalistic property if it is so much as *possible* for it to be realized by an irreducible experiential property. This is because physical theory will not distinguish between conscious and non-conscious realizations of any physicalistic property. Being merely topic-neutral in its import, science is constitutionally incapable of making any such discrimination. So, in the context of physical theory, P as such is either nothing over and above Q as such, or it is not. If it is, any *possible* conscious realization of P

would be nothing over and above some possible instantiation of Q. But that, as we have just seen, is impossible—whether Q itself be consciously or non-consciously realized.

This conclusion, however, is considerably weaker than that which Strawson draws in the present context. Moreover, no stronger conclusion is forced on us. For one thing, a certain experiential property, even a simple one, may, in each case in which it is exemplified, be the ultimate realizer of more than one physicalistic property. This would be the case, for example, if such an experiential property sustained two (or more) irreducibly different kinds of causal interaction. Even if each of the physicalistic properties that the experiential property realized were physicalistically fundamental, two or more of them taken together—a co-instantiation of them—would not be. Another possibility, as we have seen, is that any experiential property should realize some physicalistic property only when the latter is exemplified *to a certain degree*. At lower degrees the property is non-consciously realized. In neither of these two scenarios would an experiential property be represented by what is physicalistically fundamental; and yet "reductionism" would be avoided. Furthermore, since the experiential is not, as such, represented by what is physicalistically fundamental, micropsychism is avoided, since it may be that only highly complex physical processes can give rise to entities that exemplify a certain combination of physicalistically fundamental properties, or to entities that exemplify a certain physicalistically fundamental property to a given degree.

A final possibility is that each experiential property realizes one and only one determinate physicalistic property that is in some sense fundamental. This may seem to grant Strawson all he wants. In particular, one might ask, how can the instantiation of what is physically (and metaphysically) fundamental be caused, as I am suggesting may be the case, by that which is physically (and metaphysically) complex? Indeed, since what is complex is reducible to its constituents (and their relations), we may rephrase this challenge more forcefully: how can what is fundamental be caused by what is not fundamental? This may seem absurd. But what exactly is meant by "fundamental" here? May more than one sense of this notion be in play here? At this point we should bear in mind the third, and weakest, form of the present proposal outlined above—that which appealed to the notion of energy (or its possible future surrogate). Recall the production of things that have mass and charge (e.g., positrons and electrons) from things that do not (e.g., photons). Charge, let us suppose, is fundamental.[36] But fundamental in what sense? It may be fundamental in the sense that it is ineliminable from any viable or "complete" scientific account of the world. And yet, even if it is, in some sense *energy* is more fundamental. It is not that charge is "reduced" thereby. It is, or may be, a fundamental way in which energy is expressed: that is, it may not be reducible to any other expression of energy.[37] And "expression" does not imply reduction. Scientists do not treat charge, or mass, as simply "nothing over and above" energy. They do not regard them as being "forms" of energy. Heat is a form of energy, but not mass or charge. The latter, rather, have energy "equivalents." Moreover, I can find nothing incoherent in the idea that a certain irreducible expression of energy should be produced by, and perhaps only by, a complex cause. Perhaps the physicalistic properties of which experiences are the inner nature are such expressions of energy. Micropsychism is, thereby, once again avoided.

8.

The physicalist theory that I have presented lacks certain features that I, for one, regard as characteristic of *philosophical* theories. If true, it is not knowable a priori, since its being true depends upon the actual causal structure of the world. Moreover, if it is metaphysically possible for given natures to have different causal powers from those they actually have, then this theory, if true, is only contingently true, since experiences might have lacked the causal roles that sustain the attribution of physicalistic properties to them; and if false, it is contingently false, since experiences might have had the requisite causal roles.[38] Indeed, it is, perhaps, debatable whether the theory I have offered is, strictly speaking, a philosophical theory at all. Although some philosophy is required to articulate it, its truth ultimately boils down to questions of causal structure; and that is hardly a distinctively philosophical, or metaphysical, issue. I must confess to having some lingering reservations about the ultimate coherence even of the form of physicalism I have presented here. One thing I am sure of, however, is that no other form of physicalism has any chance whatsoever of being true. I suggest, therefore, that physicalism, as such, is either false or philosophically somewhat uninteresting.

NOTES

1. I realize, of course, that many are unmoved by such considerations. What I have just written is not meant as an argument to convince anybody, but merely as a statement of my position.

2. In addition to Russell, Foster, and Eddington, see, for example, Maxwell 1968 and 1970 and Strawson 2003. In Smith 1990 I also, in effect, argued for the position.

3. I say that Russell "seems" to have thought this, since, although he wrote that we can know only the structure of the physical world, and that "structure is what can be expressed by mathematical logic" (Russell 1927: 254), he also wrote, "I had not really intended to say what in fact I did say, that *nothing* is known about the physical world except its structure" (Russell 1968: 176).

4. The original criticism was due to Max Newman (1928). It was influentially revived by Demopoulos and Friedman (1985).

5. Some writers propose a "substantialist" account of space-time. If space-time itself is a "thing" with a nature, indeed a variable nature, this definitely does exceed the "intuitive" appreciation of space of which Strawson speaks. Here we have again entered the domain of the merely topic-neutral.

6. Although, as I write this, Lewis's paper is still to be published, versions of it have been circulating for a number of years, and his view has already received considerable discussion in the literature.

7. Moreover, even if, *per impossibile*, a knowledge of the intrinsic natures of non-conscious physical entities were attainable, it would not put one in a position to understand how they could embody or entail consciousness, as Stoljar proposes—precisely because they are non-conscious.

8. Some proponents of "structural realism," such as Russell and Maxwell, feel the need to reject direct realism in order to sustain their position. There is, in fact, no such necessity. In Smith 2002 I give a (conditional) defense of a form of direct realism that I regard as wholly compatible with structural realism.

9. In saying that the inner nature of something physical would, in such a case, be "scrutable," I am not implying that we would, or perhaps even could, *know* that the experienced natures of our conscious experiences were the inner natures of some physical things. All that I am claiming, at a minimum, is that in such a case we would be acquainted with what is in fact the inner nature of something physical.

10. Lockwood's proposal has been endorsed by Peter Unger (1999).

11. It is no part of the position to be developed here that the conscious character of an experience is just a matter of "qualitative character": of featuring qualia. Certain experiences are both conscious and yet nonsensory. A sudden realization is one example—as is the whole domain of the apperceptive. Since, however, this issue is still somewhat controversial, I shall focus on the "qualitative" character of conscious experience in this paper.

12. Not only is it implausible, but, as I have also argued elsewhere (Smith 2002: 13–17, 54–64), an act-object analysis of sensory awareness is incompatible with direct realism, and direct realism is the only form of physical realism that is tenable.

13. In Smith 2001 I defend (and develop) the idea.

14. For a discussion of the issues, see, for example, Martin 2004: 76–79.

15. Such writers do not restrict the claim that conscious experiences are, or may be, the inner nature of some physical entities to the brain. The important point for the moment is that their position at least involves this.

16. Some physicalists think that focusing on the brain is too narrow, and would rather direct our attention to the central nervous system. Others propose a yet wider physical base: one that involves an animal-in-an-environment. These differences are not relevant to the points I shall be making, so I continue, just for simplicity's sake, to refer to brains and their activity.

17. This slogan is (of course) just a gesture towards a more fully articulated argument against familiar forms of physicalism. For the fuller argument see, for example, Smith 1993 and Strawson 2006b.

18. Strawson 2003 advocates micropsychism—the view that at least some "physical ultimates" are conscious; Strawson 2006a and 2006b advocate panpsychism—the view that they all are. The difference between these two positions is, however, not relevant to the present argument, since it is what these have in common—the idea that there must, in relevant respects, be consciousness "all the way down" if physicalism is to respect our convictions about the irreducible character of consciousness—that I shall be objecting to.

19. Strawson, as far as I can see, never considers causation as a possible source of radical novelty. By contrast, Chalmers (1996: 124–29) carefully distinguishes between "logical supervenience" and "natural supervenience."

20. Spelling out what "formal" and "categorial" mean is a significant task that I cannot begin to undertake here. The basic idea, however, is that some properties, such as *being self-identical*, are irrelevant to the metaphysical kind to which their possessors belong. So are some others that are not quite so "abstract": such as *being a substance* (or property, or state, or process), *being a cause*, and *being temporal*. I would also add here the property *being spatial*. Although, of course, it has not been beyond dispute that experiences may be spatial in nature, I assume in this paper that this is a possibility.

21. The present account is not, as such, committed to this restriction. My point is, rather, that this account does not need (somewhat implausibly) to exceed it, and that exceeding it solves no problems.

22. It should be borne in mind that the postulated physical properties need not be properties that we already know some non-conscious thing to possess. Perhaps the properties are as yet unknown to us (because the causal roles are unknown to us) *even where non-conscious things are concerned.* Indeed, it is not even part of the present proposal that any non-conscious entity does actually possess any of the relevant physical properties. The claim is only that it is possible that one should.

23. The difference in the nature of the causes need not be that one is intrinsically conscious and the other non-conscious in nature. That would eventually lead to something like micropsychism. All that is required is there be *some* difference in the two causes: but that may be a difference in two sorts of ultimate *non-conscious* natures.

24. See, for example, Shoemaker 1980. To allow that this may be an acceptable account of the individuation of properties, even experiential properties, is not to embrace a merely topic-neutral account of them. Recall my remarks on functionalism in section 1 above.

25. Specifically, it allows "Australian zombies," as Strawson (2006b: 22n37) has termed them. For an explanation of the term, see Strawson 2006a: 271–72. In brief: an "Australian" zombie is a non-conscious entity that is not merely behaviorally, but physically, identical to some conscious entity.

26. This scenario is somewhat different from the usual "zombie" one, in that the physically identical entities here in question are not animal bodies or functioning brains, but things caused by brain activity. One could, of course, make the present issue closer to the usual "zombie" one by supposing that the two physically identical items in question could be caused by physically identical bodies or brains, and by considering the bodies and the relevant effects together. Either way, the basic philosophical issue involved is the same.

27. The account of what it is to be physical that I offered in Smith 1993 is hereby modified, and weakened, though the general idea that the physical can be specified only in terms of something that can hold of non-conscious entities is preserved.

28. I have tended to use sensory experiences as examples of conscious experiences, and such experiences are not thought to be caused by other mental states and processes, but only by physical stimuli. I do not, however, for a minute suppose that sensory experience is the only type of conscious experience; and we do naturally take it that some other types of conscious experience—such as a feeling of disgust, or the conscious realization of something—may be occasioned by other mental states and occurrences.

29. Barring, that is, not only massive causal over-determination, but reduplication. I exclude this as a possibility, since, for reasons that I will not go into here, I reject the possibility of causal over-determination in the strict sense that would be required here.

30. Traditional (i.e., dualist) epiphenomenalism, as such, of course requires only that experiences have no *physical* effects. So, it may be suggested, it can avoid the "dead-ends" objection by postulating that they have non-physical mental effects. This, however, would—unless one accepts causal over-determination, which I do not—conflict with the idea that *all* mental realities are caused by physical realities. If an (ordinary) epiphenomenalist did not endorse this idea, he or she would allow the mental to "go its own way" in a manner that was, in principle, wholly unanswerable to what goes on in the brain—something that runs counter to the spirit of epiphenomenalism.

31. Once again, in case it needs saying, this is a mere sketch of my opposition to familiar forms of physicalism. I am not simply cheerfully embracing the "fallacy of composition." Consciousness is unique in such a way that there is no "fallacy" here. The fuller story is contained in Smith 1993.

32. In case it is not obvious, Strawson makes it clear that the "other" physical properties in question are "nonexperiential physical properties" (Strawson 1994: 61).

33. For the "at least," see n15 above.

34. Strictly speaking, it is *instantiations* of qualia that realize *instantiations* of physicalistic properties.

35. Or, more precisely, that some instances of the experiential property were the intrinsic nature of *at least some* instances of *P*.

36. Of course, what is regarded as fundamental at one time is not at another time. Just let us treat charge as a placeholder for something that is physicalistically fundamental. In fact, I believe that the search for what is physicalistically absolutely fundamental is an incoherent search. But that is another story.

37. "Expression" is meant to include both specific forms of energy—such as kinetic and electromagnetic—and things that have an energy "equivalent," such as mass.

38. This is a big "if," and I do not commit myself to it. Recall my remarks on David Lewis's "humility" above.

REFERENCES

Block, N. 1978. "Troubles with Functionalism." In Savage, *Perception & Cognition*, 261–326.

Carruthers, P., and E. Schechter. 2006. "Can Panpsychism Bridge the Explanatory Gap?" *Journal of Consciousness Studies* 13:32–39.

Chalmers, D. 1996. *The Conscious Mind*. Oxford: Oxford University Press.

Demopoulos, W., and M. Friedman. 1985. "Critical Notice: Bertrand Russell's *The Analysis of Matter*: Its Historical Context and Contemporary Interest." *Philosophy of Science* 52:621–39.

Dretske, F. 1969. *Seeing and Knowing*. London: Routledge & Kegan Paul.

———. 1979. "Simple Seeing." In *Body, Mind, and Method*, edited by D. F. Gustafson and B. L. Tapscott, 1–15. Dordrecht: Reidel.

Eddington, A. S. 1928. *The Nature of the Physical World*. Cambridge: Cambridge University Press.

Foster, J. 1982. *The Case for Idealism*. London: Routledge & Kegan Paul.

———. 2008. *A World for Us*. Oxford: Oxford University Press.

Goff, P. 2006. "Experiences Don't Sum." *Journal of Consciousness Studies* 13:53–61.

Lewis, D. 2009. "Ramseyan Humility." In *Conceptual Analysis and Philosophical Naturalism*, edited by D. Braddon-Mitchell and R. Nola, 203–21. Cambridge, MA: MIT Press.

Lockwood, M. 1981. "What *Was* Russell's Neutral Monism?" *Midwest Studies in Philosophy* 6:143–58.

———. 1989. *Mind, Brain and the Quantum*. Oxford: Blackwell.

Martin, M. G. F. 2004. "The Limits of Self-Awareness." *Philosophical Studies* 120:37–89.

Maxwell, G. 1968. "Scientific Methodology and the Causal Theory of Perception," in *Problems in the Philosophy of Science*, edited by I. Lakatos and A. Musgrave, 148–60. Amsterdam: North-Holland Publishing.

———. 1970. "Structural Realism and the Meaning of Theoretical Terms." In *Theories & Methods of Physics and Psychology*, edited by M. Radner and S. Winokur, 181–92. Minnesota Studies in the Philosophy of Science 4. Minneapolis: University of Minnesota Press.

————. 1978. "Rigid Designators and Mind-Brain Identity." In Savage, *Perception & Cognition*, 365–404.

McGinn, C. 2006. "Hard Questions: Comments on Galen Strawson." *Journal of Consciousness Studies* 13:90–99.

Newman, M. H. A. 1928. "Mr. Russell's 'Causal Theory of Perception,'" *Mind* 37:137–48.

Russell, B. 1927. *The Analysis of Matter*. London: Kegan Paul, Trench, Trübner.

————. 1968. *The Autobiography of Bertrand Russell: Vol. 2 (1914–1944)*. London: Allen & Unwin.

Savage, C. W., ed. 1978. *Perception & Cognition: Issues in the Foundations of Psychology*. Minnesota Studies in the Philosophy of Science 9. Minneapolis: University of Minnesota Press.

Shoemaker, S. 1980. "Causality and Properties." In *Time and Cause*, edited by Peter van Inwagen, 109–35. Dordrecht: Reidel.

Smart, J. J. C. 1959. "Sensations and Brain Processes." *Philosophical Review* 68:141–56.

Smith, A. D. 1990. "Of Primary and Secondary Qualities." *Philosophical Review* 99:221–54.

————. 1993. "Non-Reductive Physicalism?" In *Objections to Physicalism*, edited by H. Robinson, 225–50. Oxford: Clarendon.

————. 2001. "Perception and Belief," *Philosophy and Phenomenological Research* 62:283–309.

————. 2002. *The Problem of Perception*. Cambridge, MA: Harvard University Press.

————. 2008. "Disjunctivism and Discriminability." In *Disjunctivism: Perception, Action, Knowledge*, edited by A. Haddock and F. Macpherson, 181–204. Oxford: Oxford University Press.

Stoljar, D. 2001. "Two Conceptions of the Physical." *Philosophy and Phenomenological Research* 62:253–81.

Strawson, G. 1994. *Mental Reality*. Cambridge, MA: MIT Press.

————. 2003. "Real Materialism." In *Chomsky and His Critics*, edited by L. Antony and N. Hornstein, 49–88. Oxford: Blackwell.

————. 2006a. "Panpsychism? Reply to Commentators with a Celebration of Descartes." *Journal of Consciousness Studies* 13:184–280.

————. 2006b. "Realistic Monism." *Journal of Consciousness Studies* 13:1–31.

Unger, P. 1999. "The Mystery of the Physical and the Matter of Qualities: A Paper for Professor Shaffer." *Midwest Studies in Philosophy* 22:75–99.

8

Qualia, Qualities, and Our Conception of the Physical World

HOWARD ROBINSON

1. The Real Power of the Knowledge Argument

The Initial Predicament

The dialectical situation in which the knowledge argument (KA) for property dualism is usually taken to be located is the following.[1] It is taken as agreed that physicalism gives an adequate account of non-conscious reality, and that this part of reality constitutes almost 100 percent of the universe. Despite this overwhelming success, however, the physicalist account struggles to accommodate certain features of mental life, namely the 'what it is like' or qualia of certain conscious states. These qualia constitute the qualitative nature of sensations and probably of secondary qualities, but have nothing to do with our robust conception of the physical as it applies to the vast mindless tracts of reality. These awkward entities constitute what Chalmers called "the hard problem" for physicalism (Chalmers 2003). But the fact that they also constitute such a tiny part of the world is implicitly understood as being a strong prima facie reason for thinking that there must be some way of reconciling their apparent existence with the otherwise triumphant and clearly adequate physicalist account of the world: if it were not for the qualia that occur in a few corners of reality, the adequacy of physicalism would not in any way be in dispute.

I think that this interpretation of the situation constitutes a radical misunderstanding of and understatement of the problem that faces physicalism and the role that the knowledge argument plays in bringing out that problem: the dialectic is quite different from the way it is represented in the previous paragraph. To see why and how this is so, one must direct attention at our conception of matter and the physical, rather than at our concept of mind. Science, whether of the macroscopic or the microscopic, is very largely concerned with measurement and quantification and with the expression of its findings in mathematics, as far as is possible. But the resultant abstract—we might call it Platonistic—conception of the physical cannot, we think, wholly capture our concept of the physical, especially as it is conceived in our naïve or commonsensical conception of the world. Taken in this abstract form, the concept of the physical is insufficiently concrete. But what concretizes it is the addition of qualities—essentially sensible qualities—that figure so importantly in our naïve or commonsensical conception of the world. These are essential to our ability to 'cash' or 'model' or 'interpret' the abstract, mathematical conception.

Physicalism's real predicament, as has been brought out by the KA, can be represented in two propositions.

(1) Standard physicalism cannot capture the *qualitative* nature or aspect or reality.
(2) The qualitative is an essential feature of any conception of the physical that goes beyond the purely abstract and mathematically expressed.

These two together entail

(3) Standard physicalism cannot capture any conception of the physical that goes beyond the purely abstract or mathematically expressed.

This is, of course, a much stronger conclusion than that which the normal understanding of the 'hard problem' attributes to the knowledge argument, namely

(4) Standard physicalism cannot capture the qualitative nature of certain mental states.

On my reinterpretation of the situation, what the knowledge argument really shows is (1). I take (2) to be independently plausible, possibly analytically true and probably largely uncontested. Propositions (1) and (2) together show that standard physicalism is not merely incomplete, failing to cope with consciousness, but something more like incoherent, because it cannot give a coherent account of the physical itself.

In the next two sections I shall do the following. First, I shall show that the knowledge argument, if sound, proves that physicalism cannot capture the qualitative at all: that is, I shall try to prove (1). Second, I will argue that this does not merely strengthen the knowledge argument's conclusion, but also undercuts all known attempts to refute the argument, for they all rest on the assumption that the physicalist's conception of the purely physical is itself unproblematic; that is, they rest on the assumption that the physicalist's conception of the physical would not be inadequate if it were not for the need to explain consciousness.

Extending the Scope of the Knowledge Argument

The knowledge argument as traditionally stated appears to concern only the nature of mental states. This appearance is founded on two factors. First, the argument concerns 'what it is like' to have certain experiences, and this expression clearly names something subjective. This alone is not enough to confine the topic to the mental world. If one is talking about *what it is like* to feel pain or jealousy, then this might seem to be purely internal, but *what it is like* to see color or to hear sound is directly connected with our notion of *what color is like* or *what sound is like*, as those things are, or as we naïvely conceive them to be, in the external world. There is an irony here. It is a feature of the accounts many physicalists present of experience that it is transparent. This means that the only feature that characterizes the experience *qua* experience is the apparent presence of some objective or external property. So *what it is like* to experience red or C-sharp is no different from *what red is like* or *what C-sharp is like*. This transparency alone is not enough, however, to show that the knowledge argument concerns our conception of the external or physical world, because the qualities that are invoked in the argument are secondary qualities and, at least since Locke, it is standard within the scientific form of physical realism to treat secondary qualities, insofar as they are not just powers or dispositions but monadic qualities, as subjective. This leaves the physical world untouched, for that is characterized wholly by primary qualities.

Once one has reached this point, it ought to be becoming clear why the argument does not concern secondary qualities alone. 'Red' is defined in terms of what it is like to perceive the color red; 'square' is not defined in terms of what it is like to perceive a square. But someone's conception of 'square' is not independent of what it is like for him to perceive (see, touch, or whatever else possible sense) square things, for if it were it would be wholly axiomatic and mathematical. Using Sellars's convenient terminology, we can say our 'manifest image' of the world is a projection of what it is like to perceive it, in respect of both primary and secondary qualities. The secondary qualities are attached to a particular form of experience, the primary are not. But without any experience—in our case, visual or tactile or both—there would be no conception of spatial properties beyond the wholly mathematical.

What the knowledge argument really brings out is that only experience of the appropriate kind can reveal the qualitative, as opposed to purely formal and structural, features of the world. What the standard modern physicalist fails to notice is that the kind of thing that Jackson's Mary (Jackson 1982; Ludlow et al. 2004) did not know, generalized from color vision to all the other sensible qualities, is essential to any contentful conception of the world, and hence that

physicalism without it would lack any empirical content. The generalization of the knowledge argument can be expressed as follows.

Take any property *P* which is a quality or has a qualitative aspect;
then of any subject *S* who has no experiential grasp on that qualitative aspect but otherwise has full knowledge of all matters relating
to *P*, it will be true that *S* lacks knowledge of *P*'s qualitative aspect.

I call this the *generalization* of the argument, but one might, with
equal justice, say that it is the principle underlying the argument.
The thought experiment merely makes its truth clear.

It is vital to appreciate that this rationale applies to primary
qualities as much as to secondary. The fact that it is easier to describe
a thought experiment in which someone has experience like ours except that chromatic color is missing than it is to imagine experience
like ours without spatial features (if that is possible at all) does not
affect the fact that an empirically contentful (as opposed, say, to a
purely axiomatic) conception of space depends on visual or tactile or
some other experience of a spatial field to give us a conception of
what space might be empirically like, and that this is dependent on
what it is like to perceive it in some particular way. P. F. Strawson
(1959) argued that a purely auditory universe would not be enough
to generate a conception of space, however the sounds were managed
and organized. Whether he was right in thinking hearing alone could
not generate a conception of space is not something we need now
consider. What matters for present purposes is that, whether or not
there could be a purely auditory and genuinely spatial world, we can
certainly make prima facie sense of a mind with auditory experience,
where the sounds are organized in a way which could not sustain a
conception of space, and which lacks any other senses that might be
sufficient to contribute a sense of space. The sounds it hears are
simply those, say, of verbal discourse. If such a mind could be taught
orally all the proofs of geometry and of relativity theory, it seems
clear that its resultant grasp on the nature of empirical space would
be no better than Mary's on color. This mind would have a purely
scientific or formal conception, in a way that did not guarantee he
would have any conception of what space was, or might be, like in

itself or qualitatively. I want to emphasize that any worries one might have about whether there could be such a mind as this are not to the point.[2] The prima facie intelligibility of the suggestion is enough to bring out the point that our conception of primary qualities as more than purely formal is not independent of what it is like to experience them. So, though the knowledge argument is most easily stated in terms of secondary qualities, which are seemingly easily relegated into the dustbin of the mind, the principle of the argument can be carried through for primary qualities that are fundamental for our conception of physical reality. Our conception of these is, at bottom, no more independent of what it is like to perceive them than is our conception of the secondary qualities. I say "at bottom" because primary qualities are not dependent on any particular form of experience, but this does not mean that we can have an interpreted or modeled conception of them without some form of qualitative content derived from experience. Furthermore, the doctrine of the 'transparency' of perception applies as much to primary as to secondary qualities, so what it is like to see square is only the obverse of what squareness is visually like.

Our own experience in fact bears this out. I suggested above that a mind with no spatial experience could not gain a better-than-abstract conception of space on the basis of learning geometry, relativity theory, and the like. But this is not so far from our situation. Insofar as our own grasp on four and above spatial dimensions, or on relativistic or bent space, is not purely mathematical, it depends on trying imaginatively to extend the two and three dimensions of which we have actual experience. This attempt is only very limitedly successful: we do not really achieve a grasp on what four and more dimensions, or other spatial exotica that go beyond experience, could actually be *like*. The narrative of *Flatland* makes plausible the thought that creatures that lived in two dimensions would have a similar difficulty to the one we have with more than three dimensions, in giving imaginative content to three dimensions.[3] In none of these cases is the problem a lack of 'theoretical knowledge': it is a lack of the kind of experience that could give interpretation to that knowledge.

The correct way of looking at the rationale of the knowledge argument is to see it as granting content to the physicalist hypothesis only for purposes of argument. "Even if we grant," it says, "that physicalism could cope with the rest of reality, it still cannot cope with what it is like to experience things." But once one recognizes the connection between what it is like to experience the world and what we can conceive the world we experience to be like, one can see that if physicalism cannot capture the former, it cannot capture the latter: one cannot have an adequate conception of the physical which does not include those qualitative components that are the 'transparent' projections of the qualitative nature of experience. Seen in this way, the knowledge argument begins to look as if it cannot fail to be right, for if there were not some special kind of content that is revealed only in experience, then we could not have an empirically significant conception of the physical in the first place. So, if you are tempted to think that physicalism might somehow be able to defuse the intuition that Mary learns something substantive and new, you need only direct your attention to the way that any nonformal conception of the physical is dependent upon the qualitative nature of reality as revealed uniquely in experience to see that this could not possibly be true. If, in general, the acquisition of experience did not teach something new, then a purely descriptive account of reality ought not to lack anything essential. In sum, the argument draws our attention to the fact that a physicalism that depends on a notion of the physical that is somehow independent of the qualitative nature of experience can present us only with a world that is so formal as to be empirically contentless.

How All Objections to the Knowledge Argument Miss the Point

A natural response to the argument so far might be as follows. It might be conceded that the KA, *if sound*, has a much stronger conclusion than has previously been thought. This merely emphasizes the need to show that it is not sound and increases the incentive to support one of the considerable set of objections that have been made to it.

This response is overoptimistic, however, from the physicalist's perspective. All the responses to the KA of which I am aware assume that the physicalist's conception of the material world is or could be adequate for the nonmental realm and then explain how, starting from this basis, Mary's apparently new knowledge can be accommodated. I do not find these responses plausible, even in their own terms. But not merely does the KA challenge the physicalist's assumption that he has an adequate conception of the physical; it does so in a way that it is difficult to see that the physicalist, once the situation is drawn to his attention, can deny.

No one, I think, would wish to deny the following:

(1) Our naïve, commonsensical or manifest image of the physical world essentially has qualitative features: that is, in addition to formal or mathematical features it has qualitative features which cannot be reduced to the formal ones.

From what has already been argued, it is clear that

(2) These qualitative features derive, via the 'transparency' of perception, from the nature of qualia.

As qualia contribute an essential component in the commonsensical conception of the physical, it would seem that

(3) The nature of qualia cannot be *analyzed* as some function of, or on, the operations of the physical, naïvely conceived.

This is relevant to the usual responses to the KA. Two of the most popular responses are the *abilities* response and the *phenomenal concept* response. Both these strategies take for granted the adequacy of a conception of the physical that does not essentially rely on the qualitative nature of experience to give it content, and then try to explain the latter—the qualitative nature of experience—in terms of this autonomous conception of the physical. In the case of the *abilities* account, the explanation of experience is in terms of behavioral abilities of physical organisms. In the case of the *phenomenal concept* strategy, it is in terms of a special form of conceptualization of certain physical states, nonmentally conceived. But if the qualia in experience are foundational for our notion of the physical, there is no autonomous conception of the physical; so experiential states cannot be conceived in terms of some function on the physical as autonomously conceived.

This consequence might be taken as suggesting that the knowledge argument is set up in a way that is unfair to physicalism. It might seem to be unfair because it saddles the physicalist with having a purely descriptive or intellectual account of reality, and surely he is not denied the resource of sense experience in forming his conception: something must have gone wrong in our understanding of what physicalism or materialism requires.

Nothing, however, has gone awry. Of course, the physicalist is allowed to rely on perception to explain the acquisition of particular information about the physical world. But he is not allowed to draw essentially on the subjective dimension of experience—on what it is like to experience the world—in forming his conception of the physical nature of the world, for his conception is one committed to the availability of a purely objective account of the world. Insofar as the qualitative content of our conception of the world—that part which goes beyond what can be wholly captured descriptively—is a reflection of 'what experience is like,' it is a resource denied to the physicalist. This is the point at which traditional empiricism and physicalist realism as a metaphysical theory diverge. It is a starting point for empiricism that the qualitative components of experience are, or are among, the building blocks from which our conception of the physical world is constructed. Physical realists, on the other hand, simply ignore the role of perceptual experience, not simply in giving us information, but in giving our empirical concepts content. Whilst this can be thought of as an oversight, it is also essential to the orthodox physicalist project, for if the physicalist were to allow that *what it is like* to experience features of the world played an essential constitutive role in our conception of *what the world is like in itself,* he would have to abandon his fundamental project of assimilating the mental into, or reducing it to, the physical as autonomously conceived, for there is no such autonomous conception.

The way the argument undermines physicalism can be put even more comprehensively. A standard statement of physicalism is that it is the theory according to which phenomenal (and other mental) states supervene with metaphysical necessity on physical states. Supervenience is an asymmetric dependence relation. It presupposes that the nature of the supervenience base does not essentially depend on that which supervenes on it: one can at least conceive of the base in the absence of the supervenient properties. But the KA shows that the physical cannot be conceived autonomously of elements dependent on the mental.

Now the physicalist might be tempted to argue that this is just a clash of intuitions: the proponent of the KA, as I interpret it, says there is no autonomous conception of the physical, and he, the physicalist, denies this. But I do not think this is true: the physicalist does not deny the role of the qualitative in any more-than-formal conception of the physical; he simply fails to notice the connection between this and the qualitative nature of experience and hence between it and qualia.

It is more or less explicit for the physicalist that

(i) we can have a grasp on the nature of the physical in scientific terms.

What I suspect most physicalists accept but which is not discussed in this context is

(ii) our concept of the physical is not purely mathematical and formal but involves a qualitative component.

Once one recognizes (ii), and one considers both or either of the KA (as I have re-expressed it) and the apparent transparency of at least some features of our experience, it is difficult to deny

(iii) we can have a clear grasp on a quality—be able to imagine what it is like—only if it is ultimately based on qualia: a quality is a 'transparent' projection or reflection of [some aspect of] a quale.

From this it follows

(iv) our conception of the physical is conceptually tied to or dependent on the nature of qualia.

From this it follows that

> (v) qualia or qualia possessing states cannot be analyzed or expli-
> cated in terms of some function of or operation on the physical, as
> independently conceived.

2. THE NEUTRAL MONIST/TYPE-F MONIST RESPONSE

So, What's New?

I have talked as if there is at least a modicum of originality in my interpretation of the KA, but is it not essentially the same point as is
made by Russell (1927), Maxwell (1978), Lockwood (1989), Galen
Strawson (2006, 2007), and Stoljar (2006), who think that the scientific conception of matter is too abstract to accommodate consciousness and that this is what arguments such as the KA bring out?
Certainly, I am moving in the same territory as Russell and these
more recent philosophers, for we have in common the belief that a
purely scientistic physicalism fails to accommodate something which
is essential to our overall conception of the world, namely those
qualitative features of which we are consciously aware. This is in
the vicinity of the theory labeled "neutral monism" by Russell and
"type-F monism" by Chalmers (2003). It is valuable, however, to bear
in mind the variety of tasks for which the qualities that standard
physicalism cannot accommodate have been employed. My argument
above has drawn attention to two.

(i) Without the special role of quality there could be no commonsense or manifest-image conception of the world, either in its primary or secondary quality aspects, and without this there could be
no scientific image either. There could be no science without perception, no perception without sensible qualities, and no grasp on them
without qualia, so even if there need have been no qualitative content
in the subatomic world (as (iii) and (iv) below insist there must),
quality must figure irreducibly in the world of experience.

(ii) Quite apart from the manifest image, our conception of the
scientific world must include quality in its spatial properties. We
might think we proceed as follows. We form a mental picture of the

web of causal powers that constitute the standard physicalist picture by imagining lines of influence and force similar to those by which we characterize a magnetic field. Then we ask ourselves whether this requires supplementing by qualities, as argued in (iii) and (iv) below. But the pure causal web is imagined in a (visual) qualitative space, even if it is imagined as an ontology of pure powers. In other words, quality comes in not just as a feature of the commonsense objects in space, but as an essential feature of the spatial medium itself, even in the scientific image. Space cannot be realistically conceived as purely mathematical, even in a world of pure energy and fields.[4]

These are the essential qualitative features that I have tried to indicate above, and they are concerned with our conception of the macro, not the micro, world. The post-Russellian tradition is mainly concerned with the role of quality at the micro level and how it can be deployed in the philosophy of mind.

(iii) Some philosophers, such as Armstrong (1968: 85–88) and Foster (2008: 71–72), have held that dispositional states must have categorical owners or bases. As science uncovers only structural and causal properties, these categoricals must be monadic and, in that sense, qualitylike.

(iv) The scientific account seems to construct the world from powers—forces, fields, energy—and there is a dispute about whether a world that consists purely of powers is incoherent. Those who claim that it is argue that powers to produce powers to produce powers . . . *ad infinitum* constitute a vicious regress. The point here is not that powers must be *owned* by something categorical—pure unowned powers or fields may be a possibility, according to this objection— but that they must, ultimately, result in some effect that is categorical. Again, the only clear candidate for this is something qualitative.[5]

(v) The neutral monist or type-F materialist project is to appeal to the qualitative nature of matter as a way of explaining the qualitative content of consciousness. In the world of consciousness, we are simply aware of the intrinsic qualitative nature of our brains, which science, as essentially the view from the outside of mere structural and relational properties, cannot reveal.

I am not convinced of the force of (iii)—maybe there can be unowned powers—but the necessity for qualities as specified in (i), (ii), and (iv) seems to me to be conclusive. But it is (v) which matters for the philosophy of mind. The crucial issue in the philosophy of mind is whether the appeal to qualities deployed in any of (i) to (iv), which all purport to be, in some broad sense, features of the physical world, can be deployed in the articulation of a modified kind of materialism, which can be used to solve the mind-body problem.

I do not think that anyone would suggest that the possession of a qualitative nature by space could, on its own, at least, contribute to an analysis of the phenomenology of experience: so (ii) is not central to the issue. The qualitative nature of the manifest world is taken by some direct realists as helping to dissolve the mind-body problem: if the new quality Mary experiences when she leaves her room is a feature of the external world, then it is not an internal constituent of her mental state and so does not count against that state's being physical.[6] This, as a strategy for reconciling experience and materialism, faces three problems. The first concerns the problematic nature of attributing secondary qualities to matter as intrinsic, mind-independent features. The second concerns the plausibility of direct realism, especially when charged with the task of being deployed to cope with *all* the kinds of qualities that we perceive and not just the obviously perceptual ones. Discussion of these two points would take me too far afield from the present discussion.[7] The third difficulty is that direct realism of the kind being countenanced here is surely not a materialist theory. The relation between the perceiving subject and the objects and qualities he perceives would have to be a sui generis relation of awareness, and this is not part of a materialist ontology. Any attempt to replace this relation with something materialistically acceptable—say, some kind of purely causal relation—would leave one with a reductive account of experience: that is, if being aware of an external quality consists simply in the quality physically causing some physical process in the brain, that would render the presence of the quality phenomenologically irrelevant. It is not surprising, therefore, that it is the imputation of qualities to micro matter, as in (iii) and (iv), that has played a part in attempts to state type-F materialism.

Chalmers states this position as follows.

Russell pointed out that physics characterizes physical entities and properties by their relations to one another and to us. For example, a quark is characterized by its relation to other physical entities, and a property such as mass is characterized by an associated dispositional role, such as the tendency to resist acceleration. At the same time, physics says nothing about the intrinsic nature of these entities and properties. Where we have relations and dispositions, we expect some underlying intrinsic properties that ground the dispositions, characterizing the entities that stand in these relations. But physics is silent about the intrinsic nature of a quark, or about the intrinsic properties that play the role associated with mass. So this is one metaphysical problem: what are the intrinsic properties of fundamental physical systems?

At the same time, there is another metaphysical problem: how can phenomenal properties be integrated with the physical world? Phenomenal properties seem to be intrinsic properties that are hard to fit in with the structural/dynamic character of physical theory; and arguably, they are the only intrinsic properties of which we have direct knowledge. Russell's insight was that we might solve both these problems at once. Perhaps the intrinsic properties of the physical world are themselves phenomenal properties. Or perhaps the intrinsic properties of the physical world are not phenomenal properties, but nevertheless constitute phenomenal properties: that is, they are protophenomenal properties. If so, then consciousness and physical reality are deeply intertwined. (Chalmers 2003: 130)

There are at least four problems with this type-F or neutral monist strategy, the fourth of which has not, as far as I can tell, received serious discussion. They are as follows. (i) How is one to move from the attribution of *quality* to matter, to endowing it with phenomenal *consciousness?* (ii) One must try to find a plausible account of what qualities or protoqualities (or phenomenal qualities or protophenomenal qualities) can be attributed to the elementary constituents of matter. (iii) How can one account for the unity of consciousness on the basis of the phenomenal/qualitative core of individual particles or events? The neglected one is (iv): More and more anti-reductionists seem to think that intellectual consciousness—states of conscious thinking— as well as sensory-type experiences, are irreducible. How can one apply the type-F strategy to these?

From Quality to Consciousness

At first sight, there would seem to be no reason why a qualitative core to atoms should provide any explanation of how consciousness emerges. Some defenders of neutral monism, for example Galen Strawson, try to solve the consciousness problem by adopting panpsychism. It is noteworthy, however, that earlier protagonists, such as Russell and Lockwood, thought that they could avoid compromising their physicalism in this way. For Russell, the qualities themselves are equivalent to the contents of *unconscious* mental states, and consciousness of them is given something close to a behavioral analysis: "A percept differs from another mental state, I should say, only in the nature of its causal relations to an external stimulus. 'Unconscious' mental states will be events compresent with other mental states, but not having the effects which constitute what is called the awareness of a mental state" (Russell 1927: 385). Consciousness is, in effect, quality plus appropriate effect on behavior. If one is not satisfied with this account of awareness, the problem of consciousness remains a major one.

Lockwood is not so behavioristic, but his original account of awareness seems to end up having, in its application of the concept of topic-neutrality to consciousness, more in common with Smart or Armstrong (1968) than one might expect from a neutral monist.

> To the extent that we have a transparent grasp on the concepts that we bring to bear on our mental lives, those concepts may be seen as capturing certain intrinsic attributes of brain states. To the extent, however, that they are topic neutral, they represent no obstacle to an identity theory anyway. Moreover, *this goes for the concept of awareness itself.* For it seems to me that we cannot be said to have a transparent conception of awareness. . . . If that is right, then it follows that there can be nothing in our concept of awareness, such as it is, that could debar us from identifying awareness with some kind of physical process in the brain—albeit that it remains profoundly mysterious, in physical terms, what form such a process could possibly take. (Lockwood 1989: 169; emphasis original)

These are strange remarks. If our grasp on awareness is really topic-neutral, then it could be identical with any physical state that performs the right role. We may be ignorant of this, but there is no reason why its nature should be "profoundly mysterious." Like many other philosophers, Lockwood seems to be confusing the fact that awareness is a simple, unanalyzable, and *transparent* relation with the idea that our concept is an empty one, waiting to be filled by some scientific theory. If the latter were true, then one could have a straightforwardly reductive account of mind, of a broadly causal or functionalist kind.

As Chalmers points out in the quotation above, neutral monism tries to kill two birds with one stone. A crucial gap is detected in our concept of matter, and this is remedied by deploying the concept of quality that derives from our ordinary experience to fill this gap. By importing these qualities, which might be thought of as qualia, neutral monism hopes to endow matter with the resources for generating experience. But if the qualitative element is genuinely neutral between mental and physical—'merely qualitative'—then there is no explanation of how or why this should result in conscious states: we do not think of a red patch as being *per se* conscious. If one is to build the consciousness into the qualitative element that one is importing into the matter, then one has lost the neutrality and moved over to a panpsychism, which makes the core of matter at least minimally conscious. Russell and Lockwood seem to want to avoid doing that, but instead seem to end up with an account of consciousness which is somewhere between straightforwardly reductive and elusive. The source of the idea that the distinction between quality and consciousness can be blurred is, of course, Hume. The hope is that impressions are sufficiently phenomenal to be the building blocks for mind, without this phenomenality presupposing mentality as a principle in addition to their qualitative content. It is fairly clear, I think, that this cannot be done.

Imputing (Phenomenal) Qualities to the Fundamental Constituents of Matter
There are two ways of categorizing the fundamental constituents of matter. The most natural is to treat them as objects of certain kinds—

protons, electrons, quarks, gluons, and so on. These objects would have to have a qualitative core. The crudest version of this theory would think of these particles as consisting of little patches of color, or of sounds, itches, and so on, with these conceived of as not simply physical qualities but phenomenal or protophenomenal. The other option is to follow Russell and Maxwell in regarding the names of these so-called particles as names for groups of pure events. Maxwell thinks that the latter option is the only one that makes sense.

> If C-fiber activity is thought of as consisting of threadlike pieces of matter . . . waving around and perhaps stroking each other, then any attempt to identify such activity with pain (as felt in all its excruciating immediacy) does become patently absurd. However, if we recognize that C-fiber activity is a complex causal network in which at least some of the events are pure events and that neurophysiology, physics, chemistry etc., provide us *only* with the *causal structure* of the network, the way is left open for the neuropsychologist to theorize that some of the events in the network *just are pains* (in all their qualitative, experiential, mentalistic richness). (Maxwell 1978: 386; emphasis original)

Maxwell does not explain why he thinks that the event ontology is so much more amenable to his theory, but one might imagine the reasons to be as follows. Pains are occurrent events, but C-fibres or complex brain states endure no doubt for a long time. If the pain is identical with the qualitative nature of the constituents of the fibers or cells, which overwhelmingly remain the constituents whether activated or not, why is the sensation not there for just as long? But it is not clear that an event ontology really gets round the problem. A brain process is, from the perspective of the subatomic, a massive and complex event. The pain must be a compound from the qualitative natures of the micro events that go up to compose it. But the ontology of particles cannot simply be ignored. Such things according to Russell, and of necessity if one has an exclusive ontology of events, must be compounds of events. The theory is not that it is a *mistake* to say that there are electrons, photons, and so on; rather, the theory is that such things are constructed from events. If we think of an electron that endures from t_1 to t_n as constituted by events e_1 to e_n, then one might assume that, as the electron remains the same electron, its intrinsic nature does not change. Indeed, one might expect all electrons to have similar intrinsic natures. In this case there will have to be a consistency in the intrinsic nature of the events that compose it. The alternative appears to be that the qualitative nature of elementary particles—whether or not constructions from events— changes according to the nature of the large-scale causal net into which they are placed, and even though their causal contribution does not (electrons have always the same mass, the same charge, etc.). This would seem to be a very strange top-down phenomenon.

It is difficult to avoid the suspicion, from reading the passage quoted above from Maxwell, that he thinks of the pain event as a primitive, not something constructed from more primitive events.[8] The same is true about Russell's (1927: 137) statement that in experience one is perceiving the inside of one's own head, as if the qualitative content of our sense data were what constituted the matter. There is, I suspect, an empiricist impulse to crunch together a phenomenalist and a physical realist conception of the world, without paying enough attention to the fundamental problems with this project. The introduction of the term 'protophenomenal' to characterize the qualitative nature of the elementary particles seems to me to name a problem, not to propose a solution. It amounts to no more than the suggestion that there must be something such that, if you get enough of it, you get a real experience, whilst hiding from the question of whether this involves moving from the non-experiential to the experiential. It is very difficult to form a conception of the consciousness of an earthworm—indeed to decide whether or not one can ascribe consciousness to it at all. What meaningful minimal consciousness-involving content is to be ascribed to a quark, or to one of the events that, as a group, constitute a quark?

The Problem of the Unity of Experience

On any type-F materialist strategy, the qualities which are supposed, in the end, to explain consciousness belong to the most elementary particles or events. When these qualities do constitute consciousness, they are bound together in unified sense-fields and in total cross-media consciousness. How are we to explain this unity by reference to the phenomenal core of the individual elements? Notice that this is not the so-called grain problem, which is concerned with why a smooth and continuous consciousness should emerge from particles that are spatially distant from each other. The implication of the grain problem is that we should expect consciousness to be 'grainy'—a crude picture full of holes, gaps, and blanks. What I have called 'the unity problem' is the problem of explaining why there should be an overall picture at all, of whatever quality. This puzzle is strengthened if one considers what happens in other hunks of matter outside a limited area in brains. The lower brain, the kidney, and the table are all made up from matter which has a qualitative core, but no one seems inclined to attribute a unified subjectivity to them. If one followed Russell in treating consciousness as simply a matter of causal consequences, then there would be an answer to this problem, but such an approach to consciousness is no different from reductive functionalism.[9] I quoted Lockwood above as seeming to adopt a reductive view, but in a later article he says that "it is difficult to see how *awareness itself* could be anything other than an emergent phenomenon" (Lockwood 1993: 280). Indeed, the bonding of the phenomena into a unity, though no doubt supervenient on functional organization, cannot be wholly explained by it, as liquidity is explained by atomic structure, and so must be emergent. But if awareness is emergent, what is achieved by attributing its objects to the matter of the brain? That awareness must be emergent is also attested by the following consideration. The individual elements have, at best, only the dimmest consciousness. Supposing them to be united into one consciousness, why should that not be equally dim? On what principle is the quality of consciousness accumulated?

Type-F Materialism and Intellectual States

The discussion of neutral monism is usually conducted with reference to the sensory *qualia* of consciousness, and most of the original protagonists of the theory were radical empiricists with reductionist accounts of thought. They tended to be imagists, associationists, or, later, behaviorists or functionalists about intellectual activity. More recent proponents of the theory tend not to share this reductionism.

Strawson, for example, rejects such reductionism, together with reductionism about sensory experience (1994: 4). The elementary entities, therefore, must possess not just protophenomenal qualities, but
proto-intellectual content. This problem is easily overlooked because
of the historical emphasis on the irreducibility of sensation rather
than thought. Because perception gives us a conception of the physical world as being saturated with sensible qualities, it is natural for
us to think of matter as essentially characterized by such qualities,
and even, with some imaginative-cum-conceptual effort, by more
primitive analogues of the same. The idea that minute matter mani-
fests similar proto-intellectual features is harder to grasp. One might
just about make a gesture in this direction by conceiving of the electron as possessing a protoconceiving of its own protophenomenal
nature. This, however, will not be adequate to build up the distinctive
character of thought unless all our thinking is built up logically from
the concepts whose contents are restricted to the qualities they directly capture. This would be equivalent to a form of conceptual
logical atomism, as found in linguistic phenomenalism. Such a program is both demonstratively impossible and presumably not what
Strawson or the other contemporary Type Fs intend. One cannot
build, without brute emergence, thoughts about Manchester United,
the Trinity, or even our normal physical world from self-conceiving
protophenomenal patches.

Explicit Panpsychism

Galen Strawson (2006, 2007), unlike Russell, Maxwell, and Lockwood, opts for the panpsychist solution. He calls his position "real
physicalism," but this label is misleading because 'real' does not
qualify 'physicalism'; rather the point is that the position is a physicalism that asserts the irreducible *reality of experience*. The use of
'physicalism' is also broad. Any concrete object that occupies space-
time is physical, and this includes conscious animals such as ourselves. The bite in calling this 'physicalism' is a commitment to the
idea that all the properties of such concrete objects, including the
conscious states of those that are conscious, somehow flow from their
nature as physical; that is, from the properties of the ultimate parts.

Strawson's argument for panpsychism can be reconstructed as follows (2006: 3–31).

(1) Reductionism about experience is false.
(2) Physicalism is true.
(3) If reductionism about experience is false, and if physicalism is true, then, if "physical stuff is, in itself, in its fundamental nature, something wholly and utterly non-experiential," there must be "brute emergence" of the experiential.

Therefore

(4) If "physical stuff is . . . utterly non-experiential," then there must be brute emergence of the experiential.
(5) Brute emergence is an incoherent idea.

Therefore

(6) Physical stuff is not in its fundamental nature utterly non-experiential.

The argument is valid. Strawson regards (1) as intuitively obvious, but it is also *ex hypothesi* at the current state of the argument in this paper. The strategic situation is that, if (5) is true, either matter is essentially experiential or one must abandon physicalism and accept that consciousness is an essentially different nature or substance from matter, as the dualist claims. Why is Strawson so convinced of (5)? There are, I think, two reasons. First, he argues that what are usually cited as cases of emergence—for example, liquidity arising from atoms that are not themselves liquid—are not cases of brute emergence, because the nature and the behavior of the atoms rationalize and entail the liquid product. Once you understand how the atoms behave, you are in a position to see that the macro phenomena could not fail to be liquid. Second, he thinks that the belief that there could be such a thing as brute emergence derives from an exaggerated conception of what it is for causal relations to be contingent, which itself derives from a misunderstanding of Hume: once one is purged of this error, then one will see that brute emergence is a nonsense.

I cannot here discuss causation in general or the interpretation of Hume, but it is generally accepted that the emergence of consciousness involves an 'explanatory gap' not present in cases such as liquidity. It therefore follows for the physicalist that either the seeds of experience are in matter in the panpsychic sense, or experience emerges in so unique a way as might be thought to constitute a form of dualism.

Suppose we agree that a physicalist who accepts the irreducible reality of experience is obliged to be a panpsychist. Why should we not regard this as a reductio of physicalism rather than an argument for panpsychism? Why, in other words, does Strawson think that it is so plausible to claim that physicalism can absorb the experiential? The answer is that he thinks that, given the topic-neutral nature of our scientific conception of matter, physicalism that accommodates irreducible experience is common sense. He approvingly quotes Eddington, who is asking whether there is anything in our knowledge of matter that prevents attributing mental properties to it.

> In regard to my one piece of insight into the background, no problem of reconciliation arises; I have no other knowledge of the background with which to reconcile it. . . . *There is nothing to prevent the assemblage of atoms constituting a brain from being a thinking [conscious, experiencing] object in virtue of the nature which physics leaves undetermined and undeterminable.* If we must embed our schedule of indicator readings in some background, at least let us accept the only hint we have received as to the significance of the background—namely that it has a nature capable of manifesting itself as mental activity. (Eddington 1928: 259–60; quoted in Strawson 2006: 11; emphasis original)

Strawson believes that the experiential and the scientific conception of the physical slot easily together and that treating them dualistically pointlessly offends against Ockham's razor. This of itself, of course, does nothing to answer the four problems I raised above for type-F monism, so how does Strawsonian panpsychism fare on these?

The first problem—how one moves from qualitative content to consciousness—does not arise for a theory that is explicitly panpsy-

chist. On the second problem—the mental life of quarks and strings—
I see no helpful guidance in Strawson.

This problem is to say what kind of mental life a quark or a proton is supposed to possess. There are two forms of panpsychism, and
Strawson's physicalism commits him to the less plausible. The more
plausible version is holistic, in that it sees the whole of the material
universe as somehow pervaded or infused by mind or intelligence.
This 'world spirit' is a property of the whole and is not constructed
from the mental features of the parts. The other version is atomistic—
Strawson calls it 'smallism'—and seeks to attribute to each atom an
appropriately minute form of consciousness and to build more sophisticated consciousnesses out of this material. The mentality in the
former case, though no doubt mysterious, is at least modeled on
mind, spirit, and intelligence as we know it. In the latter case, it is
utterly obscure what the atomic materials could consist in. When
setting out this problem, I said that the consciousness of an earthworm—a massively complex organism by subatomic standards—is
hard enough to conceive and asked what it might mean to attribute a
suitably diminished version of consciousness to an electron. I suggested that it might be impossible to imagine or give theoretical content to such an idea. It is important that it is not just a matter of
imagination, in the way that it might be impossible to imagine what
it is like to be a dog, even though one is quite confident that there is
something that it is like. It is plausible to maintain that being conscious involves a certain complexity of structure: one is taking something in a certain way and responding to it. This is true of a dog and
just possibly of an earthworm. 'Responding' need not mean external
behavior: it could be any mental affective or cognitive response. But
the occurrence of a single, minimal qualitative content, in association
with an undifferentiated external causal response (for example, in
the case of an electron, unalterably exercising the influence of the
mass of $1/1860$ of a proton and of a negative charge), cannot constitute any inner consciousness. It seems to me reasonable to think that
the existence of any kind of subject presupposes a certain movement
of mind and hence the active grasp on more than one content. Strawson says that the experiential is always active, not passive, but the
only activities that he can ascribe to the electrons, strings, and so on

are the kinds of external, unvarying properties I have cited for the electron: this is not mental activity.

Strawson has more to say about the unity of nonsimple consciousnesses, which he calls "the composition problem."[10] There are in fact three components to this problem. First, there is the issue of why and how the inner core of separate simples could or should merge into one consciousness. Second is the issue of why and how the very dim and different contents of simples come to make up the kind of conscious experiences we have, given that they can come together at all. Third is the issue of how separate *subjects* can make one subject, especially whilst escaping detection to introspection.

It is not clear to me that Strawson distinguishes the first two problems. On the first problem, he cites William James as having gone from believing that composition was impossible to believing in a "not-rigidly-particulate, field-quanta-friendly form of Composition" (Strawson 2006: 248). The rationale is as follows. Provided that one has a field, rather than a particulate, conception of the simples, the thought that they overlap and 'flow into' each other to form a new unity does not seem so unnatural. Furthermore, this helps with the second problem, because this intermixing might explain how they can produce contents that are significantly different from those of the elements that mix—their fusion is more like something chemical than like mere physical combination. These thoughts seem to be backed up by two general principles. One is the optimistic belief that "we know it is actual so it must be possible," and the other is that "unintelligible experiential-from-experiential emergence is not nearly as bad as unintelligible experiential-from-non-experiential emergence" (Strawson 2006: 250).

We have now moved a long way from the original position, where the role of the qualitative/mental was to provide the monadic intrinsic properties of matter, to which the causal properties discoverable by physical science could belong. The mental atoms have now developed a chemistry of their own which does not seem to follow from the physical laws which were originally conceived to be their only powers. One has disposed of the obligation to make any sense of how or why the mental developments come from their elements. We are much nearer to a holistic idealism than we were at the start of the project. Perhaps one is near to thinking of the whole process as having some mind-serving teleological focus.

The third problem of composition was how many selves can form one. This itself has two subproblems. One of these, raised by Goff (2006), is how, given the transparency of consciousness, we could fail to notice that we were constituted "like the eye of a fly." Strawson's reply to this specific point seems to me to be adequate. He says that transparency of consciousness does not guarantee awareness of all its features. I would put it by saying that we are aware of qualitative content but not metaphysical structure. As an analogy, it could be pointed out that simple introspection does not reveal the correct philosophical ontology of perception, only its qualitative phenomenology. The more serious problem, I think, concerns how one subject can be aware of the logically private contents of another mind. Either what I am aware of is, in some fused way, identical with the contents of all the lower-level subjects, or it is a causal product of these. The former option infringes logical privacy; the latter is a case of brute emergence. Strawson prefers conscious-to-conscious brute emergence over unconscious-to-conscious, but this seems to me a pretty desperate position.

On the fourth general problem—the emergence of thought—the original problem remains for any version of panpsychism that seeks to have a tight and systematic account of how thought can develop from minimal qualitative consciousness. Whether the allowance of Jamesian flowings and fusings really makes this any better is hard to estimate.

The Appeal to Ignorance

Daniel Stoljar (2006) gives what might seem to be an alternative to Strawson's panpsychism. Stoljar's starts from the Russellian position that there is something about the nature of matter that current science cannot tell us and of which we are ignorant. He does not claim that this gap is filled by the qualities revealed in experience, but he does believe that it is filled by something which, were we to come to know its nature, we could see how it gives rise to experience. Stoljar, therefore, circumvents Strawson's direct move to panpsychism, whilst accepting his rejection of brute emergence in favor of the belief that the underlying nature of matter must be able to provide an explanation of the development of consciousness. We are just ignorant of what this underlying feature is. He believes that this appeal to ignorance, which has other parallels in the history of science, is more plausible than reifying our ignorance into dualism.

Stoljar recognizes that the main opposition to the suggestion that we are simply ignorant of what it is about matter that enables it to produce consciousness comes from the conviction that, in principle, nothing that was any sort of physical feature could constitute an explanation of mentality. And he recognizes that the principal reason behind this conviction is that, to be physical, a feature must be objective, that is, equally available to anyone, and that no such feature could explain subjectivity—which consists in features available in a special way only to the subject who has them (Stoljar 2006: 153–62). The crucial part of his positive argument, therefore, consists in his attempt to show that this divide can, in principle, be crossed. He has a two-pronged argument for this conclusion.

First, Stoljar argues by counterexamples (2006: 157–62). He argues that

(i) John is in pain

is a subjective statement, and that, therefore,

(ii) John is not in pain

is also subjective because it "contains the same constituents" as (i). Moreover,

(iii) John is a number

is an objective statement, but it is true that

(iv) if John is a number then John is not in pain

is a true entailment. So statements with objective subject matter can entail statements with subjective subject matter.

In case one finds something linguistically odd about (iv), he runs a parallel argument through for

(v) if John does not exist then he is not in pain,

to which the same objection cannot be raised.

The initial reaction to this line of argument is to be suspicious of the way it deploys negatives. The fact that certain categories necessarily exclude each other seems not to throw light on whether they might positively entail each other, and if so, how. This suspicion is correct, for this negative strategy, if sound, would prove far too much. It is true that

(vi) if seven is a number then it is not spatially extended

and

(vii) if John does not exist he is not spatially extended.

It would be bizarre, however, to take these propositions as giving any kind of support to the hypotheses that there might be a feature of abstract objects or a feature of nonexistents of which we are currently ignorant which could explain how some or all of them might actually possess, or have possessed, spatial or other physical properties.

In fact Stoljar's principle of argument seems to entail the following absurdity.

(viii) If an object's belonging to category X (possessing X-type properties) logically excludes its possessing Y-type properties, then it follows that another object belonging to category X might possess properties that entail that it does possess Y-type properties.

But it surely cannot be right that the fact that one object in a certain category, X, is conceptually excluded from belonging to another category Y entails that there must be something else in X which is not so excluded.

What this shows is that entailments of exclusion do not throw light on the possibility of positive entailments.

Second, Stoljar presents a diagnosis of why we mistakenly think
that no objective fact could ever seem fully to explain experience
(158–62). He thinks that we confuse two things. ('N' represents the
physical feature of which we are currently ignorant, and 'E' the experiential state.) They are

(1) Even if you were to know N, you would still not thereby know E.

And

(2) Even if you were to know N, there would still appear to you to be
an element of contingency in the relation between N and E.

The mistake is thinking that (2) follows from (1), whereas (1) is true
and (2) is false. The issue turns on whether "if N then E" is what
Stoljar calls *synthesizable*, which it is if and only if understanding N
involves understanding E. It is because that conditional is not synthesizable that (1) is true. It does not follow, however, that the relation would appear to be contingent, as claimed in (2).

I think that this diagnosis is false. Synthesizability seems to be
more or less equivalent to definability of E in terms of N, because it
requires that understanding of N is itself sufficient for understanding
E. This contrasts with the case in which you independently understand both and can see how N is sufficient for E. Taking 'A' to stand
for the atomic structure that makes something a liquid,

if A then x is a liquid

is not synthesizable, for someone might, theoretically, have the vocabulary of atomic or molecular science without having the concept
of a liquid. One can nevertheless see how A is adequate for constituting something as a liquid. But this is not the problem with experience. Before the chemistry of liquidity was uncovered, sophisticated
people would not have thought that liquidity was the kind of phenomenon for which no possible physical and mechanical constitution
could be found. Standard scientific reductions are not synthesizable,
but that did not create resistance to the prospect.

In short, it seems to me that Stoljar fails to undermine the intuition that no kind or kinds of objective facts could be seen as sustaining experiential states in a way analogous to that in which facts about atoms can be seen as sustaining facts about liquidity. But furthermore, the point about intellectual states I raised against Strawson applies against Stoljar. Even if some unknown feature could rationalize in a bottom-up way the emergence of sensory experiences, can we really believe that it could do the same for our intellectual states, however subtle or abstract? Stoljar does discuss intellectual character, but only in the context of Descartes's antiphysicalist argument that a machine could not think *because it was inconceivable that its behavior should show the appropriate subtlety* (124–25). Stoljar cites this as a historical parallel to his own argument, because later science revealed that matter does possess the relevant property. This suggests that Stoljar, like Russell and, earlier, Lockwood, but unlike Strawson, is satisfied with a reductionist (in this case, a computer functionalist) account of thought. This essentially ignores the phenomenology of thought.

Stoljar, therefore, in my opinion, fails to vindicate type-F materialism by an appeal to our ignorance.

■ One might summarize the argument of the second part of this paper as follows.

The knowledge argument shows

(1) there can be no adequate account of the conscious mind in standard physicalist terms.

It follows from this that, unless one accepts a uniquely brute form of emergence,

(2) if mind is to be explained from a materialist perspective at all, there must be some feature of matter in addition to those contained in a standard physicalist account which, unlike the standard ones, does provide an explanation of the generation of the conscious mind.

(3) This further feature must itself be either mental or protomental (conscious or protoconscious)

because

(4) nothing that was purely and simply physical—nothing that was essentially accessible from a third-person perspective—could conceivably explain the generation of the subjective and hence the mental.

This last is what Stoljar denies, but I have tried to refute his arguments.

(5) The attribution directly to elementary matter of full-fledged mental properties, the same kind of properties as figure in our experience—colors, sounds, itches, and so on—is totally bizarre. This is even more especially true in the case of the contents of intellectual conscious states.

Maxwell, we have seen, tried to get around this problem by locating these qualities (the sensible, not the intellectual, which he does not mention) at a relatively macro level, but Lockwood shows that this makes his theory a standard version of emergentism.
Therefore,

(6) the materialist needs proto-mental, or proto-conscious, states.

But

(7) no clear sense has been given to the notion of such proto-mental or proto-conscious states that differentiates them from *whatever it is* that adequately explains the generation of mind. It does not help in understanding what sort of thing might provide such an explanation, what such a thing might be like, or that there could be such a thing.

Furthermore,

(8) there is no remotely plausible account of how proto elements might combine to produce full or normal conscious states. One would be forced back to emergence. This is especially true of intellectual states.

Overall, the theory-based physicalism of the physicist cannot capture the qualitative nature of the world and so is condemned, as a total worldview, to be incoherently abstract. This cannot be remedied by any version or development of neutral monism, which tries to load what is missing in the physicist's world into a richer conception of matter. If there is a physical world independent of our experience, it cannot provide an explanation of why that experience should exist. There cannot be a materialist, or a materialistically based, monism that is adequate to the phenomena.

NOTES

1. The literature on the knowledge argument is vast, but classic pieces can be found in Ludlow et al. 2004.

2. In case one is worried by the apparent impossibility of such a case, one might consider the following. Imagine someone who had developed with normal spatial experience, but then suffered brain damage that destroyed all memory of the spatial features of his experience whilst not harming his general and mathematical intelligence. There was then an attempt to teach him scientifically the properties of space. This would lead to the same situation.

3. See Abbott 1884/2006.

4. For a demonstration of this, see Foster 1982: 176–88.

5. The dispute about the powers conception of reality has a growing literature. Examples are Robinson 1982: 108–23; Robinson 2009; Foster 1982: 67–72; Blackburn 1990; and Molnar 2003.

6. This general line has been strongly defended in discussion by my colleague Hanoch Ben-Yami. I am very grateful for his contribution to the development of my ideas in this paper.

7. They are discussed in Robinson 1994.

8. Maxwell remarks that perhaps it is "this 'middle sized' realm that provides the relevant context for investigation of mind-brain identities" (1978: 399). Lockwood takes this as suggesting that the neutral monism

applies only at a relatively macroscopic level, and shows that such a theory is no different from a standard sort of emergence (Lockwood 1993: 280–81).
    9. Some empiricists—for example, A. J. Ayer—seem to think that it is possible to be non-reductionist about qualia, but reductionist about our cognition of them. For an argument that this is impossible, see Robinson 1982: 105–7.
    10. For discussion of this issue, see Strawson 2006. The discussion by Goff in that volume is very clear and helpful. Strawson's reply is at 248–52.

REFERENCES

Abbott, E. A. 1884. *Flatland: A Romance of Many Dimensions.* London: Seeley and Co. Repr., Oxford: Oxford University Press, 2006.
Armstrong, D. M. 1968. *A Materialist Theory of the Mind.* London: Routledge & Kegan Paul.
Blackburn, S. W. 1990. "Filling In Space." *Analysis* 50:62–65.
Chalmers, D. 2003. "Consciousness and Its Place in Nature." In *The Blackwell Guide to the Philosophy of Mind,* edited by Stephen Stich and Ted Wardfield, 102–42. Oxford: Blackwell.
Eddington, A. 1928. *The Nature of the Physical World.* New York: Macmillan.
Foster, John. 1982. *The Case for Idealism.* London: Routledge & Kegan Paul.
———. 2008. *A World for Us.* Oxford: Clarendon.
Goff, P. 2006. "Experiences Don't Sum." In G. Strawson et al., *Consciousness and Its Place in Nature,* edited by A. Freeman, 53–61. Thorverton: Imprint Academic.
Hume, D. 1978. *A Treatise of Human Nature.* Edited by L. A. Selby-Bigge, revised P. H. Nidditch. Oxford: Clarendon.
Jackson, F. 1982. "Epiphenomenal Qualia." *Philosophical Quarterly* 32:127–36. Reprinted in Ludlow et al., *There's Something about Mary,* 39–50.
Lockwood, M. J. 1989. *Mind, Brain and the Quantum.* Oxford: Blackwell.
———. 1993. "The Grain Problem." In *Objections to Physicalism,* edited by H. Robinson, 271–91. Oxford: Clarendon.
Ludlow, P., Y. Nagasawa, and D. Stoljar. 2004. *There's Something about Mary: Essays on Phenomenal Consciousness and Frank Jackson's Knowledge Argument.* Cambridge, MA: MIT Press.
Maxwell, G. 1978. "Rigid Designators and Mind-Brain Identity." In *Perception and Cognition Issues in the Foundations of Psychology,* edited by C. Wade Savage, 365–403. Minnesota Studies in the Philosophy of Science 9. Minneapolis: University of Minnesota Press.
Molnar, G. 2003: *Powers: A Study in Metaphysics.* Oxford: Oxford University Press.

Robinson, H. 1982. *Matter and Sense*. Cambridge: Cambridge University Press.

————. 1994. *Perception*. London: Routledge.

————. 2009. "Idealism." In *The Oxford Handbook to the Philosophy of Mind*, edited by Brian McLaughlin, Angsar Beckermann, and Sven Walter, 189–205. Oxford: Oxford University Press.

Russell, B. 1927. *The Analysis of Matter*. New York. W. W. Norton.

Stoljar, D. 2006. *Ignorance and Imagination: On the Epistemic Origin of the Problem of Consciousness*. Oxford: Oxford University Press.

Strawson, G. 1994. *Mental Reality*. Cambridge, MA: MIT Press.

————. 2006. "Realistic Monism: Why Physicalism Entails Panpsychism" [keynote paper] and reply to commentaries. In G. Strawson et al., *Consciousness and Its Place in Nature*, edited by A. Freeman, 3–31. Thorverton: Imprint Academic.

————. 2007. *Real Materialism, and Other Essays*. Oxford: Oxford University Press.

Strawson, P. F. 1959. *Individuals*. London: Methuen.

9

Groundwork for a Dualism of Indistinction

BENEDIKT PAUL GÖCKE

Although "most contemporary analytic philosophers [endorse] a physicalist picture of the world" (Newen et al. 2007: 147), it is unclear what exactly the physicalist thesis states. I briefly argue that a coherent presentation of physicalism entails the thesis that every particular in the actual world essentially exemplifies properties the exemplification of which does not conceptually entail the existence of conscious beings. I then argue for the theses that, firstly, I am not identical with the human being 'Benedikt Paul Göcke' and that, secondly, there is no particular in any possible world with which I could be identified at all. In contrast to more traditional versions of dualism, I thus establish not a dualism between different ontic kinds to be found within a possible world, but an ontological difference between the *I* and possible worlds. I continue to argue that precisely because physicalism's scope is restricted to the actual world, physicalism is irrelevant when it comes to the *I* and its relation to the world, which, as I argue, is a relation of indistinction. Even if every particular in the actual world were a physical particular, that would not affect the truth of my dualism of indistinction. Because a certain understanding of possible worlds and of the relation between conceivability and possibility is crucial for my argument, I start the essay with these preliminary issues.

1. Possible Worlds as Maximally Consistent Co-exemplifications of Individual Essences

For the argument to come it is crucial that we have an intelligible account of why conceivability should entail metaphysical possibility. It is futile, however, to argue that conceivability entails metaphysical possibility without further specification of what one assumes the realizers of metaphysical possibilities to be, that is, without what one takes possible worlds to be. I begin by presenting an account of possible worlds, which circles around the premise that possible worlds are composed of states of affairs.[1]

A state of affairs is a constituted abstract entity: it consists of a particular p combined with a property of a particular F, and it is in "no way dependent for [its] being upon the being of concrete, individual things" (Chisholm 1976: 114). Although states of affairs compose possible worlds, not all combinations of states of affairs do. They have to obey rules of consistency. These rules are expressed in terms of inclusion and exclusion. According to Plantinga, "a state of affairs S includes a state of affairs S' if it is not possible that S obtain and S' fail to obtain [and] a state of affairs S precludes a state of affairs S' if it is not possible that both obtain." Deploying the rules of inclusion and exclusion, we can define what it is for a state of affairs S to be maximal: a state of affairs S is maximal if for every state of affairs S', S includes S' or S precludes S'. On these premises, a possible world is "simply a . . . state of affairs that is maximal" (Plantinga 1974: 44–45).

Maximal states of affairs obtain or do not obtain. The actuality of the actual world is ontologically significant in that it is the only possible world which in fact obtains. Other possible worlds might have obtained but in fact do not. To be clear, nonobtaining possible worlds exist "just as serenely as your most solidly actual state of affairs" (Plantinga 2003: 107), but they do not obtain.[2]

Because possible worlds are composed of states of affairs which are constituted by a particular p combined with a property of a particular F, and because the same particular is constitutive of different states of affairs, which in turn are part of different maximal states of affairs, it comes as no surprise that according to this conception of possible worlds one and the same particular can be said to exist in more than one possible world.[3] In order to account for the properties particulars exemplify in different possible worlds from a point of view independent of which world in fact obtains, we introduce the notion of world-indexed properties: a property P is world-indexed if "there is a world w and a property Q such that P is equivalent to the property of having Q in w or to its complement—the property of not having Q in w" (Plantinga 2003: 69).

Deploying the notion of world-indexed properties, we can specify the properties a particular would have exemplified if a certain possible world had been actual independently of which world is in fact the actual world: that a particular p exemplifies the world-indexed property of being F in the possible world w means that if w had been actual, the particular would have exemplified F. If w is in fact the actual world, then the particular exemplifies F and trivially also the world-indexed property of being F in w.

The notion of world-indexed properties leads to a nontrivial notion of individual essences. Individual essences consist of "properties essential to an object and essentially unique to that object" (Plantinga 2003: 196).[4] Consequently, a particular p exists in a possible world w if and only if p's individual essence is exemplified in w. Furthermore, because a particular exemplifies its world-indexed properties essentially—that is, because, independent of which world is in fact the actual world, if the particular exists in that world, then it exemplifies its world-indexed properties—the individual essence of a particular entails the particular's world-indexed properties.[5]

In general, individual essences are maximally consistent exemplifiable modal determinations of particulars. Firstly, because a particular cannot exemplify a property F in the same respect in which it does not exemplify F, it follows that if an individual essence is exemplified in a possible world w, then it does not entail a contradiction that it is exemplified in w. Secondly, because particulars exemplify world-indexed properties, it also follows that if an individual essence is exemplified in a possible world w, then no contradiction is involved, either, in reference to the exemplification of the particular's world-indexed properties. No particular exemplifies both the world-indexed property of being F in w and its complement of being non-F in w. Therefore, if we assume that a particular p is F in a possible world w, then either p's being F in w is part of the individual essence of p, or we obtain a contradiction by assuming that p is F in w.

In the framework introduced, we can reduce possible worlds to maximally consistent co-exemplifications of maximally consistent modal determinations of particulars, or, for short, we can reduce possible worlds to maximally consistent co-exemplifications of individual essences. Here is why: because states of affairs are constituted by a particular and a property of a particular, and because possible worlds are maximal states of affairs, it follows that possible worlds are constituted by maximally consistent combinations of particulars and their properties: whichever properties a particular p existing in a possible world w exemplifies, it does not contradict the exemplification of any property of another particular p^* coexisting with p in some possible world. Since which properties particulars exemplify is determined in turn by their respective individual essences, possible worlds turn out to be maximally consistent co-exemplifications of individual essences. The actual world is the exemplified maximally consistent co-exemplification of individual essences, and it is since the individual essences constitutive of this world are constitutive of other possible worlds that "the actual world is a modal world" (Ellis 2002: 117).

2. Conceivability, Individual Essences, and Possibility

Conceivability is crucial to metaphysical argument; it is our most useful means of getting in contact with the realm of possible worlds. As Chalmers says, "one argues that some state of affairs is conceivable, and from there one concludes that this state of affairs is possible" (Chalmers 2002: 146).[6] But are conclusions like this in fact justified? Does conceivability in fact entail metaphysical possibility?

Or is Mill right to argue that "our capacity or incapacity of conceiving a thing has very little to do with the possibility of the thing in itself; but is in truth very much an affair of accident" (Mill 1851: 265)?

We have to clarify some features of conceivability which will help to answer this question. First of all, conceiving as I understand it is an a priori affair which is independent of our knowledge of the actual world. It is instead concerned with the question of whether a certain particular or combination of particulars possibly or necessarily exemplifies a certain property.[7] By way of conceiving the exemplification of a property by a particular, we thus want to know whether it is in fact part of the particular's individual essence that in some possible world the particular exemplifies the property in question (or, respectively, in all worlds in which it exists). Because to try to conceive whether it is entailed by an individual essence that the corresponding particular possibly exemplifies some property F is to attempt to obtain insight into that very individual essence, the objects of our acts of conceiving turn out to be individual essences themselves.

In this context, there are two relevant means by which we might conceive individual essences: propositional conceiving and state-of-affairs-like conceiving.

Propositions are expressed in sentences and statements. For instance, the sentence "The table in the room is green" and the sentence "Der Tisch im Raum ist grün" express the same proposition that the table in the room is green. Propositions are abstract entities, and I assume that they are structured entities, constituted by a particular combined with a property of a particular.[8] What distinguishes propositions from states of affairs is that propositions do not obtain (or not). Instead, they are true or false, where a proposition of the form that p is F is true if and only if the exemplified individual essence of p entails that p is F.[9] Because both, states of affairs and propositions, are constituted by a particular combined with a property of a particular, and because both which propositions are true in a certain possible world and which states of affairs obtain in this world are entailed by the relevant individual essences which constitute that world, it follows that to speak of the (possible) truth of a proposition and the (possible) obtaining of a state of affairs are two different ways to account for individual essences.

In more detail, in propositional conceiving we deal with individual essences as they are conceptualized as propositions which can be true or false. When we propositionally conceive whether p possibly exemplifies F, we conceive whether the proposition that p is F is possibly true. The way we do this is by understanding that the putative truth of the proposition constituted by p and F is consistent with reason alone, that is, by way of seeing that it does not contradict reason that the individual essence entails the particular's being as conceived. To conceive propositionally by way of understanding what it means for a proposition to be true is thus to allocate possible truth-values to propositions.

State-of-affairs-like conceiving is not concerned explicitly with the question whether the truth of a proposition is consistent with reason but rather with the question whether we can positively imagine that the corresponding state of affairs obtains. In order to state-of-affairs-like conceive whether a particular p possibly exemplifies the property F we have to positively imagine in a certain way the obtaining of the corresponding state of affairs that p is F; that is, we have to imagine p's being F.[10] While propositional conceiving succeeds when we cannot find a contradiction, state-of-affairs-like conceiving succeeds if we can positively imagine the obtaining of a state of affairs.[11]

How determinate does state-of-affairs-like conceiving have to be? In a sense, not very: "There is a world of difference . . . between imagining [a particular] as determinate—as possessing determinates for each its determinables—and determinately imagining it—specifying in each case what the underlying determinate is" (Yablo 1993: 28). For state-of-affairs-like conceiving, only the first way of determination is asked for, not the second. In order to conceive the obtaining of a state of affairs, we do not have to determinately imagine everything the obtaining of that state of affairs implies. If I state-of-affairs-like conceive a blue table, I do not have to imagine all the properties of the table in order to succeed in my act of conceiving. It is enough if I suppose that the obtaining state of affairs is "fully determinate [while] determinate properties are left more or less unspecified" in the act of imagining (Yablo 1993: 28).

Now that we have distinguished two different ways by means of which we may attempt to illuminate individual essences, we are in a position to state two slightly different theses about the relation between conceivability and metaphysical possibility. That conceivability entails metaphysical possibility means either (a) that the state-of-affairs-like conceiving of a particular exemplifying a certain property entails that there is a maximally consistent co-exemplification of individual essences which entails the particular as imagined or (b) that the propositional conceiving of the broadly conceptual consistence of a proposition with reason alone entails that there is a maximally consistent co-exemplification of individual essences such that the proposition is true in that co-exemplification.

Both theses about the relation between conceivability and metaphysical possibility are correct. On our conception of possible worlds, possible worlds are constituted of maximally consistent combinations of individual essences which at the same time are the objects of our acts of conceiving. That is to say, individual essences are at once the objects of our acts of conceiving and the elements of which possible worlds are constituted; they are the link between conceivability and modality, because they are what conceivability and modality are all about. If we propositionally conceive a certain particular in a certain state—that is, if we conceive a certain proposition to be possibly true—then we are *eo ipso* dealing with a certain element of a possible world, and the same is true of state-of-affairs-like conceiving. Because we can find a maximally consistent combination of individual essences for any single, even partly available, individual essence, we know that the individual essence we conceive of is also part of some maximally consistent co-exemplification of individual essences. Therefore we know that it is possible that the particular is as we conceive it. For instance, because we can state-of-affairs-like conceive that the green table in the room is blue, we know that it is part of the individual essence of the table that it is blue in certain circumstances. And if we know this, even if we know nothing else about the individual essence of the table, then we know, because individual essences are maximally consistent determinations of particulars, that there is a maximally consistent co-exemplification of individual essences which entails that the table is blue.

3. Physicalism and Individual Essences

Let me briefly clarify the physicalist thesis. In order to do so, I start by way of drawing a distinction between physical and nonphysical particulars, which entails distinguishing between physical and non-physical individual essences. Because individual essences are maximally consistent modal determinations of particulars, they are all abstract entities. The distinction between physical and nonphysical individual essences thus does not mean that there are literally physical and nonphysical individual essences; I just call the individual essence of a physical particular a physical individual essence, and the individual essence of a nonphysical particular a nonphysical individual essence.

Regarding physical individual essences, it is a *contradictio in adjecto* to assume that a physical particular can exist without exemplifying any physical property. A physical particular therefore necessarily exemplifies at least one physical property in all the possible worlds in which it exists, which means that there is no possible world w in which the individual essence of a physical particular p is exemplified while p does not exemplify a physical property in that world. By contrast, a nonphysical particular can exist in a possible world w without exemplifying any physical property in w. Nonphysical individual essences can be exemplified in possible worlds in which no physical property is exemplified at all.

The distinction between physical and nonphysical particulars is exhaustive, although it does not preclude that the individual essences of physical and nonphysical particulars entail the same non-world-indexed physical and nonphysical properties to be exemplified by the respective particulars in a world in which they coexist. There is no contradiction involved in assuming that a physical particular exemplifies nonphysical properties, and neither is there a contradiction involved in the assumption that a nonphysical particular exemplifies physical properties. Therefore, there might be particulars which exemplify the same non-world-indexed properties in a certain possible world w while one of the particulars has a physical and the other one a nonphysical individual essence. In order to determine whether a particular in fact has a physical individual essence or not, we have to take all the possible worlds into account in which the particular's individual essence is exemplified.

This being said, here is an argument why physicalism in fact should be a thesis about particulars: it should be a thesis about particulars because the existence of a nonphysical particular clearly is a refutation of physicalism, whereas the exemplification of a nonphysical property in the actual world no longer is understood to be a problem for the physicalist's position in general: that there is a property ontologically not reducible to, and hence not identical with, but otherwise dependent on physical properties is precisely the claim of nonreductive physicalism according to which "psychological properties depend on, but are irreducible to, physical properties" (Moser and Trout 1995: 187).

Physicalism ought not to be a thesis about particulars *tout court*, however, because neither the thesis that every particular in any possible world, nor the assumption that every particular in some possible world, is physical is able to catch the physicalist's metaphysical intuition. Physicalism should therefore be the thesis that every particular in the actual world is a physical particular, which means that for the physicalist, the obtaining world is a maximally consistent co-exemplification of physical individual essences.

First of all, the only case in which it is true that every particular in any possible world is a physical particular is the case where no nonphysical particular could have existed. Because there is no contradiction in propositionally conceiving that there is a possible world in which at least one nonphysical individual essence is exemplified, I take it that there is in fact a possible world in which at least one nonphysical particular exists.

Should the physicalist plainly deny the possibility of there being nonphysical particulars, then he would beg the question in favor of physicalism. It would be trivially and trivially necessarily true that every particular in any possible world is a physical particular. In this case, to use a phrase coined by Crane and Mellor (1990), "there is no question of physicalism."

Secondly, the physicalist should not assume, either, that all his thesis comes to is that every particular in some possible world is physical. Because there is no contradiction in the assumption that there is such a world, this thesis is true but far from being substantial. It is true even if in the actual world not every particular is physical. One plausible option remains: the physicalist should assume that every particular in the actual world is a physical particular. This respects our intuition that nonphysical particulars could exist, and it is not a trivial claim.[12]

The thesis proposed, however, is vague until we have an account of physical properties. It is only if such an account is at our disposal that we can tell whether particulars belong to the class of physical particulars or not, in virtue of the way they exemplify physical properties in possible worlds. However, we cannot just open up a book of current physical theory and look for an enumeration of physical properties, because, as Hempel (1980: 194–95 and 1969: 183) has shown, a dilemma obtains. The first horn of Hempel's Dilemma is this: if one assumes that physical properties are in fact the properties of current physics, then physicalism is probably false. Based on pessimistic meta-induction, it is probable that current physics is false. A physicalism which relies on a probably false physical theory in order to bestow content on the notion of a physical property is itself probably false. One cannot escape this conclusion by assuming that physical properties are those invoked by true or final physics. According to the second horn, if by 'physical properties' one means the properties invoked by true or final physics, then physicalism as a metaphysical thesis here and now is vacuous. One does not know which properties true or final physics will deal with, if there can be such a physics. It would therefore be vacuous to state that every existing particular is physical, because we could not tell physical from nonphysical individual essences.

There is a very effective way to circumvent the dilemma. Both horns presuppose that the physicalist should accept the authority of physics as a means to demarcate a set of physical properties. However, as I have shown elsewhere (cf. Göcke 2009), on this assumption, Hempel's dilemma is indeed a rock which we cannot climb but which we cannot set aside either. So what happens if we reject the presumption that physics has this authority? Because physics would be the best candidate out of all the natural sciences, rejecting the assumption that the physicalist in fact should rely on physics in this respect

274   *Benedikt Paul Göcke*

means rejecting that there is a useful a posteriori account of physical properties provided by the sciences.

That there is no useful a posteriori account of physical properties might be devastating for those who believed that the natural sciences are able to provide answers to daunting philosophical questions. It is not much of a problem if we suppose that physicalism is a purely philosophical thesis. In this case, we can rely on an a priori criterion of physical properties, and, following the *via negativa*, according to which we can bestow content on the notion of physical properties by way of contrasting them with mental ones, I assume that physical properties are those and only those which we can identify as non-mental properties. So what can we say about mental properties? At least the following: mental properties are those properties of which we know a priori that their exemplification conceptually entails the existence of a conscious being, because it is a contradiction in terms that a mental property is exemplified without there being a conscious being whose property it is. Pursuing the via negativa, we thus obtain that physical properties are those properties which do not conceptually entail the existence of conscious beings. This gives us the plausible result that geological, biological, chemical, and, say, astronomical properties are all to be classified as physical properties (or as combinations of physical properties), since their exemplification does not entail the existence of conscious beings, while, say, sociological and economical properties would be classified as mental properties because they cannot be exemplified without conscious beings around. A physical individual essence, then, is an individual essence which entails that the corresponding particular exemplifies at least one property in any possible world in which it exists that does not conceptually entail the existence of a conscious being. Physicalism as a purely philosophical thesis with no intrinsic relation to physics claims that every exemplified individual essence is a physical one in the sense specified.

4. I Am No Particular

Keeping the above conception of possible worlds as well as the present thesis of physicalism in mind, we begin to ask whether I myself am part of the actual world. If physicalism is true, then in order for me to be a part of the actual world, there would have to be an exemplified physical individual essence which is mine: there would have to be a physical particular that I am. Furthermore, on physicalist premises, I am not just any particular, but the most likely candidate for me to be is the human being which is known by my name or perhaps the brain of the human being which is known by my name, but I focus only on the human being for the sake of brevity. Because on physicalist premises I am a certain human being, I exist in a possible world if and only if the individual essence of the human being Benedikt Paul is part of the maximally consistent co-exemplification which constitutes that world: that world could not be actual while I myself had no being at all.

Such a possible world is, however, clearly propositionally and state-of-affairs-like conceivable. Because these kinds of conceivability are sufficient for metaphysical possibility, we know that there is in fact such a possible world. We can reconstruct it beginning with an empty space of possibility which step by step we fill with items taken from the actual world. First of all, we take all the exemplified individual essences to be found in the actual world, and copy and paste them into the empty space of possibility. This done, we seal the world for further individual essences. This ensures that in the case that the reconstructed world should obtain, the same particulars as in the actual world would exist. Since the individual essence of a particular entails that the particular exemplifies different non-world-indexed properties in different possible worlds, we further assume that all of the particulars in the reconstructed world exemplify the same properties as in the actual world. Because a possible world is nothing over and above a maximally consistent co-exemplification of individual essences, these assumptions guarantee that the reconstructed world is, although another possible world, nevertheless a duplicate simpliciter of the actual world.

If the physicalist conjecture that I myself am Benedikt Paul is true, then, because Benedikt is part of the duplicate simpliciter, it has to be true that I myself have being in the case that that world is in fact the actual world. However, and this is crucial to understand, it is not settled whether I myself have being in this case or not, because it does not entail a contradiction to claim that I myself have no being if the duplicate world in fact should obtain. Perhaps I have being in this case, or perhaps not. Let me explain: in the duplicate world, there is the human being Benedikt with his entire psychophysical life, and, because the existence of a psychophysical life entails that there is someone who is the subject of mental states, there is some mind's *I* which is Benedikt's in that world, but it is not of necessity I myself who am playing this role. The duplicate simpliciter could be actual while I am not related to that world in any way. Someone else could live my life. Therefore, I am not identical with the human being Benedikt Paul. As Priest says, "I might not have been that psychophysical human being born in a certain place at a certain time in England. . . . That very psycho-physical human being might well have existed, but it could have been someone else" (Priest 1999: 210).

The argument entails more than the conclusion that I am not identical with Benedikt. Although it seems that he would be the best candidate to identify myself with either way, the argument entails an even stronger conclusion: it entails that there is no particular whatsoever in any possible world with which I could be identified. For any particular which one might suggest, that particular could have existed while I had no being. *Therefore, I am no particular.* More generally: the *I* itself is no particular, and since it is only particulars that have an individual essence, it follows that the *I* itself does not have an individual essence. Given my conception of possible worlds as maximally consistent combinations of particulars and their properties, the conclusion that there is no particular in any possible world with which the *I* could be identified further entails that there is no possible world in which the *I* exists at all: the *I* could exist in a possible world if and only if the *I* were a particular the individual essence of which is exemplified in a possible world. This conclusion follows analytically from my conception of possible worlds. According to my account, existence in a world is a property uniquely tied to particulars, and a particular exists in a possible world if and only if its individual essence is exemplified in that world.

The following picture emerges: on the one hand, we have all the possible worlds as maximally consistent combinations of particulars and their properties, and on the other we have the *I*, which is not to be identified with anything in these possible worlds. This dualism between the *I* and possible worlds is not to be compared with more traditional variants of dualism according to which the human being is composed of a physical and a nonphysical particular, that is, body and soul. Those kinds of dualism argue for an ontic difference among distinct kinds of particulars to be found *within* possible worlds, not for an ontological difference between the *I and* possible worlds. It is crucial to keep in mind this ontological difference. It does not, however, entail that the *I* cannot be *related* to a particular in a possible world. In fact, there is a certain particular in a possible world to which the *I* that I am is intimately related. It is of course that particular which in ordinary thinking we take ourselves to be, namely a certain human being with a certain well-defined individual essence. In order to understand the nature of this relation, I first state in which ways the *I* cannot be related to this human being.

Since the *I* is not identical with any particular in any possible world, we can exclude the relation of identity from the set of putative candidates. That is to say, in whichever way the *I* is related to a certain human being, it cannot be a relation of identity. If the *I* were identical to a certain human being, then it would be identical to a certain particular, which in turn would contradict our above conclusion that the actual world could be as it is while, for instance, I had no being in it. However—and here is the argument to explain why the dualism I propose is a *dualism of indistinction*—precisely because the *I* is not identical with *any* particular in any possible world, neither can it be distinct from any particular in a possible world in the way in which particulars are distinct from one another. In order for the *I* to be distinct from some particular it is not identical with in this way, it would have to be identical with another particular. This follows from both my account of possible worlds and the logic of identity and distinction as applied to particulars. On these premises, the negation of the property of being identical to a certain particular is being distinct from that particular. Being distinct from a certain particular, however, entails being identical to some other particular. Since we already showed that there is no particular the *I* could be identified with, it follows that the *I* cannot be distinct from any particular. In other words, if the universe of discourse consists of particulars, as it does in our case, since particulars and their individual essences constitute possible worlds, then, if *a* is not identical to *b*, *a* is distinct from *b*. If *a* is distinct from *b*, then *a* has to be a particular in the universe of discourse itself. The relation the *I* can bear to a human being thus is neither identity nor distinction as we know these to hold *among* and *within* possible worlds.

One could object that this makes no sense if "being distinct from" simply means, as it does, "being not identical to."[13] This could be taken to be a problem because one could assume that, necessarily, for any property *F*, something exemplifies either *F* or non-*F*. According to this assumption, we obtained a contradiction in assuming that the *I* is neither identical to nor not identical to a certain particular. My response is as follows: I take distinction and identity to be relations that hold among particulars existing within possible worlds and a fortiori to be relations among individual essences, that is, individual sets of properties. Since the *I* itself is not identical to any particular existing in a possible world and hence does not possess an individual essence, it follows that neither the term 'is identical to' nor the term 'is not identical to' can be applied to the *I* itself. Therefore, it is not the case that either the *I* is identical to a certain human being or the *I* is distinct from a certain human being, which just means that the *I* is neither distinct from nor identical to a certain human being. I am not arguing that the *I* itself exemplifies the properties both of being identical to and of not being identical to a certain human being, but rather that these properties uniquely belong to particulars and their individual essences existing within possible worlds, and that since the *I* is no such particular, we can speak neither of the *I*'s being identical to a certain particular nor of the *I*'s being distinct from a certain particular. Any such statement would commit us to assume that the *I* is a particular in a possible world after all (which is where all the problems of traditional substance dualism start). In other words, I am not denying generally that for every particular and every property *F*, the particular is either *F* or non-*F*, but denying, rather, that the *I* is that kind of thing which could exemplify either *F* or non-*F*. The *I* is not that kind of entity that can be distinct from or identical to a certain particular in a possible world.

With identity and distinction excluded from the set of possible relations between the *I* and a particular in a possible world, I now state a positive way to describe the relation. Phenomenologically speaking, the relation the *I* bears to a certain particular in a possible world is one which draws the *I* into the psychophysical life to which it is related. By this I mean that the *I* is not some exterior observer of the psychophysical life it is related to but is instead the actual, although contingent, subject of that psychophysical life, such that, for instance, the pain of the human being it is connected to is this *I*'s pain, the joys of the human being are this *I*'s joys. Simply put, the relation between the *I* and a certain human being is one in which that human being's existence is an issue for the *I*. Because the relation which makes that human being's existence an issue for the *I* is neither identity nor distinction, but nevertheless draws the *I* into the psychophysical life of that human such that it is an issue for the *I*, it follows that the relation between the *I* and a human being has to be *a relation of indistinction*. Whenever there is a psychophysical life which is an issue for the *I*, the ontological difference between the *I* and the human being can be addressed as a dualism of indistinction between the *I* and the human being in which the *I*, because it is no particular, is distinct from the particular through indistinction.

Let me end the article by returning to the physicalist thesis. The physicalist might object that his thesis is a thesis about the actual world and the particulars existing within that world. He might say that I did not show that physicalism is false, because I did not show that there is a nonphysical particular existing in the actual world, and that this is what would be needed in order to refute physicalism. Insofar as it goes, I grant this objection to the physicalist. But does he gain much? Suppose the physicalist has an argument to show that every existing particular essentially exemplifies properties the exemplification of which does not conceptually entail the existence of conscious beings. Even if every existing particular were to be a physical particular, that would not in any way affect the dualism I have argued for here. That is, even if the arguments for physicalism are entirely sound, my dualism of indistinction remains true. Physicalism is simply irrelevant when it comes to the *I* and its relation to the world.

APPENDICES

I have presented the groundwork for a dualism of indistinction, which in a monograph I plan to spell out in more detail. There is a lot more to say about every topic scratched, about the ontology of possible worlds in terms of individual essences, about conceivability as directed upon individual essences, about physicalism, and also about the ontological difference and what I really am: the *I* that is indistinct from the human being Benedikt. In the appendices I very roughly spell out points of major concern. In the first appendix, I deal with the consequence that obtains in reference to our ability to propositionally grasp the *I*—an ability which is not straightforwardly given according to my framework. In the second appendix I try to dissolve a problem which often, although with less and less force, is proposed to be lethal for the thesis that conceivability entails metaphysical possibility, the problem of the a posteriori necessities. In the last appendix, I briefly and semiformally spell out in more detail than in the text how to state different notions of *de re* and *de dicto* modality within the possible-worlds framework presented.

Appendix 1: The I as the Absolute and the I as Nonexistent

That the *I* is no particular in any possible world has consequences when it comes to our ability to speak about the *I*. Because propositions are constituted by a particular combined with a property of a particular, and since the *I* is no particular, it follows in a straightforward way that there are no propositions about the *I*. We cannot speak about the *I* simpliciter but only *secundum quid*. We did so when we spoke about the *I* as being the actual, although contingent, subject of a certain psychophysical life, or when we argued that in a duplicate simpliciter of the actual world I myself might have had no being because another *I* might have been the subject of the psychophysical life of Benedikt. These were all assertions about the *I* insofar as it is related, or might not have been related, to particulars, not about the *I* simpliciter.

That it is impossible to speak about the *I* simpliciter is an insight we find in multiple traditions both in Western and in Eastern philosophies, where, roughly, the propositional unavailability of the *I* leads either to the identification of the *I* and the Absolute, or to the putative contradiction of that identification, the denial of the existence of the *I*. I briefly show how the dualism of indistinction elaborated here can account for both seemingly contradictory ways of dealing with the *I* simpliciter.

According to the Advaita Vedanta tradition in Hinduistic philosophy, we cannot speak about the *I* simpliciter because of the *I*'s nature as pure subjectivity. Every attempt to propositionally grasp the *I* would prevent us from seeing the true nature of the *I*. In the Advaita Vedanta tradition, at least according to Sankara, this feature of the *I* leads to the insight that the *I* of the ontological difference, that is, Atman, is ontologically identical with the Absolute, that is, Brahman (cf. Flood 2006: 241). A similar relation between the propositional unavailability of the *I* simpliciter and the *I*'s identification with the Absolute is also to be found more or less in the writings of the German idealists and their followers, who had no problems with granting the *I* the ontological status of the Absolute in reference to the being of the world. According to my dualism of indistinction, the identification of the *I* with the Absolute is an intelligible option. If the Absolute is that which is beyond affirmation and negation, if the Absolute is that of which we cannot ask how it came to be, if the Absolute is that which figures most in there being a world for us, then the *I* of the ontological difference is indeed the Absolute: it is beyond affirmation and negation because it is beyond propositionality; it is that of which we cannot ask how it came to be because to ask this is to demand an intelligible propositional explanation, which again is not available in reference to the *I* simpliciter; it is, finally, that which figures the most in there being a world for me because there is a world for me if and only if I myself am related to a particular life through indistinction.

The Hindu and the Idealist traditions are not the only ones which my dualism of indistinction helps to understand. While in these traditions one is tempted to identify the *I* with the Absolute, there are other traditions, for instance some Buddhist traditions, in which apparently the contradictory move is made when the *I* is said not to exist at all. According to my dualism of indistinction, seeing the *I* as having no existence at all is very often just the other side of that coin which identifies the *I* with the Absolute. Keeping the ontological difference in mind, it is literally false to assert that the *I* exists if we use "exists" to mean that a particular's individual essence is exemplified. The *I* does not have an individual essence and consequently cannot be said to exist in this way.

In each kind of tradition, the balance point of interest rests on a different side of the ontological difference between the *I* and maximally consistent combinations of particulars and their properties. While the Hinduist/Idealist tradition illuminates the relation between the *I* and the world from the side of the *I* simpliciter and its unavailability, the Buddhist tradition starts from the other side, that is, by way of firstly seeing how the world is constituted and, secondly, by way of arguing how the *I* therefore cannot be like ontologically. However, the impossibility of propositionally speaking about the *I* simpliciter in either tradition does not exclude that there are other ways in which it can be disclosed. In order to disclose the *I* simpliciter, the psychophysical life of the human being whose existence is an issue for the *I* has to be bracketed, which means that its consciousness has to be emptied of all things. When there is nothing that it is to be a certain human being, then there is everything it is to be the *I* simpliciter. As Pseudo-Dionysius says, "Being neither oneself nor someone else, one is supremely united to the completely unknown by an inactivity of all knowledge, and knows beyond the mind by knowing nothing" (Pseudo-Dionysius 1987: 137 [1001A]).

Appendix 2: A Confusion of Naming and Necessity

On the account developed above, conceivability understood as propositional or state-of-affairs-like conceivability entails metaphysical possibility because of the link ensured by individual essences. However, Kripke argued that there are metaphysically necessary truths which are a posteriori as well as metaphysically contingent truths which are a priori. In what follows, I bracket the a priori contingencies because the main point of interest in reference to the conceivability-entails-metaphysical-possibility thesis concerns the a posteriori necessities. The problem with these is that metaphysically necessary a posteriori statements are often said to be counterexamples to the thesis that conceivability entails metaphysical possibility.

I provide a brief outline of Kripke's basic terms and ideas, starting with the notion of a rigid designator: a rigid designator is a designator which has the same designation in any possible world in which it has a designation at all (Cf. Kripke 1980: 48). According to Kripke, proper names like 'Hesperus' and 'Phosphorus' are rigid designators, as are terms for natural phenomena and for natural kinds like 'water' and 'heat' (cf. Kripke 1980: 134). For the sake of brevity I speak only of 'names.' In contrast to names, definite descriptions are nonrigid designators: in different possible worlds they denote different things. However, we can fix the rigid reference of a name by help of a definite description: "We can let the name pick out across possible worlds whatever the description picks out in the actual world" (Gendler and Hawthorne 2002: 28). When we do so, "the only use of the description will have been to pick out to which [(kind of) particular] we mean to refer [rigidly]" (Kripke 1980: 57). It is irrelevant whether the particular to which we thus fixed the rigid reference exemplifies the property with the help of which we in fact fixed the reference in other possible worlds in which it exists or not, because "the name denoting that object is . . . used to refer to that object, even in referring to counterfactual situations where the object doesn't have the properties in question" (Kripke 1980: 106). Reference fixing of a name with the help of definite descriptions is like Wittgenstein's ladder.

Next to the distinction between rigid and nonrigid designators, Kripke argues for the thesis that the notions of the necessary and the a priori "are dealing with two different domains, two different areas, the epistemological and the metaphysical" (Kripke 1980: 36). A-priority concerns the way in which the truth of a statement is justified; necessity concerns the possible worlds in which the statement is true. According to Kripke, it is natural to confuse the two terms. In the case of necessarily true statements, we tend to think that if a statement is necessarily true, then, "just by running through all the possible worlds in our heads, we ought to be able with enough effort to see . . . that it is necessary, and thus know it a priori" (Kripke 1980: 38). And in the case of a priori justifiable statements, we tend to think that "if something is known a priori it must be necessary, because it was known without looking at the world. If it depended on some

contingent feature of the world, how could you know it without looking?" (Kripke 1980: 38). Thus, in order to show that "it's not trivial to
argue on the basis of something's being something which maybe we
can only know a posteriori, that it's not a necessary truth" (Kripke
1980: 39), Kripke argues that there are metaphysically necessarily
true but only a posteriori justifiable statements. His examples concern (a) identity statements involving names and (b) statements concerned with theoretical identifications in the sciences.

(a) Identity statements involving two rigid designators are necessarily true, if true (cf. Kripke 1980: 98). The reason is that rigid
designators have the same designation in any possible world in
which they have a designation at all: if there is one world in which
they co-refer, then they co-refer in any world. However, according to
Kripke, "we do not necessarily know a priori that an identity statement between names is true" (Kripke 1980: 101). All we know a priori is the truth of the conditional "if an identity statement between
names is true, then it is necessarily true." That is, in the cases in
which the rigid reference of each name involved in the identity statement is fixed by a respectively different definite description recurring to a different contingent property of the referent, "we . . . are in
no position to find out the answer except empirically" (Kripke 1980:
104). We need experience to know whether the names in fact co-
refer; we need experience to know whether the statement in question
is necessarily true. For instance, to pick up one of Kripke's examples,
if we fix the reference of the name 'Hesperus' by saying that it is a
certain star seen in the evening, and the reference of 'Phosphorus'
with help of the definite description that it is a certain body seen in
the morning, then we do not know a priori whether 'Hesperus' and
'Phosphorus' co-refer, because there might be two distinct objects in
the sky. Once we know through empirical research that both names
in fact refer to Venus, we know that 'Hesperus' and 'Phosphorus' necessarily co-refer, and hence that it is necessary that, as we use the
terms, 'Hesperus' and 'Phosphorus' both refer to Venus in any possible world in which Venus exists.

(b) Theoretical identifications in the sciences "are necessary,
though not a priori" (Kripke 1980: 138). The difference from the kind
of necessity a posteriori mentioned above is that in the case of theo-

retical identifications, only one name involved is such that its rigid reference is fixed by contingent features of the referent, namely the natural kind term. The other name rigidly refers to the underlying structure of the natural kind in question. Because we do not know this structure a priori, we need to rely on scientific research: it is "science [which] attempts, by investigating basic structural traits, to find the nature . . . of the kind" (Kripke 1980: 138). Therefore, theoretical identifications are necessities a posteriori as well (cf. Kripke 1980: 140).

The statement that water is H_2O, is, on Kripke's view, an example of an a posteriori necessity of theoretical identification. The reference of the natural kind term 'water' is fixed by help of a priori available definite descriptions: a priori we know that we call 'water' whatever stuff it is which in the world which is the actual world fills the rivers and oceans surrounding us (that it fills the rivers and oceans is the contingent mark of the object referred to). However, although we know a priori which kind of stuff we call water, we do not know its underlying structure a priori. Scientific research discovered that it is H_2O. Because H_2O is a rigid designator itself, it is necessary but a posteriori that water is H_2O.

On the semantic framework introduced we are suddenly confronted with putative illusions of possibility. Although we know that identity statements of the two types mentioned are necessarily true, if true, it is conceivable that they are false, even if we know that they are in fact true. As Putnam says in reference to water, "We can perfectly well imagine having experiences that would convince us . . . that water isn't H_2O. In that sense, it is conceivable that water isn't H_2O. It is conceivable, but it isn't [metaphysically] possible! Conceivability is no proof of [metaphysical] possibility" (Putnam 1973: 709). If metaphysical impossibilities are clearly conceivable, then how can we assume that conceivability in fact entails metaphysical possibility?

The answer to this question is simple: it is not metaphysically necessarily true that water is H_2O, or that Hesperus is Phosphorus. The putative modal illusions are due to a confusion between naming and necessity. In the case of Hesperus and Phosphorus, where the reference of the names 'Hesperus' and 'Phosphorus' is fixed by definite descriptions recurring to contingent features of the particular referred to, it is a priori consistent to assume that a world is actual in which the definite descriptions we use to fix the references have different designations from the ones they actually have. If a different world had been actual, then the particulars for which the descriptions fix the rigid reference might have been different as well. The statement that Hesperus is Phosphorus is false if one considers a possible world as actual in which the star seen in the morning is not the star seen in the evening, because if that world had been actual, then although the reference of the names 'Hesperus' and 'Phosphorus' would still have been fixed with the nonrigid definite descriptions of the form 'the object seen in the morning sky' and 'the object seen in the evening sky,' respectively, the statement that Hesperus is Phosphorus then would have expressed the false proposition that a certain particular is identical with another (cf. Kripke 1980: 143–44). Once we fixed the reference of 'Hesperus' and 'Phosphorus' in the actual world, we settled—deploying the names of which we fixed the reference—how to describe certain features of possible worlds considered as counterfactual. Our semantic decision to call 'Hesperus' and 'Phosphorus' whatever in the actual world satisfies the definite descriptions 'the star seen in the evening' and 'the star seen in the morning,' respectively, binds us to describe certain features of maximally consistent co-exemplifications of individual essences in which the star seen in the evening is not the star seen in the morning considered counterfactually as worlds in which some other object than Hesperus is seen in the morning, but not as worlds in which we would say that it is false that "Hesperus is Phosphorus" (cf. Kripke 1980: 109).

But all this is a matter of semantic necessity, not of metaphysical possibility. It is a matter of naming, not of metaphysical necessity. It is a matter of correlating semantic items (rigidly referring names) to metaphysical items (individual essences) with the feature that the way we correlate these names depends on which world turns out to be the actual world.

A priori we can know all about maximally consistent co-exemplifications which there is to be known. Otherwise we could not even specify what it means that a name would have had another reference if another possible world had been actual. Because possible worlds are maximally consistent co-exemplifications of individual essences, it follows that there is a priori no corresponding individual essence for proper names and names for natural phenomena which are such that their respective rigid reference is of necessity fixed a posteriori. There is an individual essence of H_2O, XYZ, and Venus because a priori we know the referent of the terms 'H_2O,' 'XYZ,' and 'Venus.' The individual essence of H_2O entails, for instance, in which worlds it is the stuff in the rivers and oceans; correspondingly, the individual essence of XYZ entails in which worlds it is the stuff in the rivers and oceans. Consequently, it is a priori not a proposition that water is H_2O or that Hesperus is Phosphorus, because a priori it is neither true nor false that water is H_2O or that Hesperus is Phosphorus: as we use the term 'water' and as we fix its reference, it is a priori just not settled which (kind of) individual essence it refers to. Illusions of possibility, therefore, are not illusions of metaphysical possibility, but concern solely the way in which we counterfactually are able to describe certain features of possible worlds. To say otherwise is to confuse naming and necessity.

APPENDIX 3: A ROUGH ACCOUNT OF MODALITIES AND ESSENTIAL EXISTENCE

De re modalities are modalities of particulars. Because in the possible worlds framework elaborated these are a matter of their respective individual essences, I can state de re modalities as follows, where I bracket world-indexed properties:

Essential property exemplification: A property F is essentially exemplified by a particular p if and only if p's individual essence does not entail that in some maximally consistent co-exemplification of individual essences p exemplifies non-F.

Contingent property exemplification:	A property F is contingently exemplified by a particular p if and only if p's individual essence entails that there are maximally consistent co-exemplifications of individual essences in which p is F and such in which p is non-F.
Possible property exemplification:	A property F is possibly exemplified by some particular p if and only if p's individual essence entails that p is F in some maximally consistent co-exemplification of individual essences.

De dicto modalities are modalities of propositions. While we can specify de re modalities in terms of single individual essences, we have to specify de dicto modalities in terms of maximally consistent co-exemplifications of individual essences. We are able to do so because propositions are constituted by a particular combined with a property of a particular.

Necessary truth of a proposition:	A proposition of the form that p is F is necessarily true if and only if any maximally consistent co-exemplifiable modal determination of particulars entails that p's individual essence is exemplified in that maximally consistent modal co-exemplification of individual essences and entails that p is F in that world.
Possible truth of a proposition:	A proposition of the form that p is F is possibly true if p's individual essence is exemplified in at least one maximally consistent modal determination of particulars such that p is F in that determination.

Consider the following diagram:

	p	q	r
w	F, G		non-F, G
w^*	F, non-G	F, G	non-F, non-G
w^{**}		F, non-G	non-F, G
w^{***}	F, non-G	F, G	non-F, non-G

According to the diagram, if w, w^*, or w^{***} obtains, then p exists, because p's individual essence is exemplified in these worlds but not in w^{**}. The individual essence of p exists in w^{**}, but it is not exemplified in that world. According to the diagram, we obtain the following de re modalities: p is essentially F because no matter which world is the actual world, if p exists in the world which is actual, then p is F; p is contingently G because in w p is G while in w^* and w^{***} it is non-G. As regards q and r, we can see that q's being F is sufficient but not necessary for r's being non-F. It is sufficient because in any possible world in which q is F, r is non-F, while there is a world, w, in which r is non-F without q existing in that world. As regards propositions, the proposition that r is non-F is necessarily true, because any of the four maximally consistent modal determinations of particulars entails that r's individual essence is exemplified such that r is non-F. The proposition that q is G is contingently true, because there are possible worlds in which q is G and such in which q is non-G. In effect, the diagram consists of three individual essences in terms of which we can specify all relevant de dicto and all de re modalities. The columns give us de re modalities, and the horizontal rows give us the de dicto modalities. Modality is all about individual essences and their combinations.

In the framework introduced here, particulars exist essentially, although not necessarily. Particulars exist if and only if their individual essence is exemplified; that is, the existence of a particular is nothing but the exemplification of its individual essence. The particulars existing in the actual world are those and only those the individual essence of which is exemplified. Because all the properties a particular exemplifies are fixed by its individual essence, a particular can exemplify properties only if its individual essence is exemplified, that is, if the particular exists. If there is a possible world such that the obtaining of that possible world does not entail that the particular's individual essence is exemplified, then the particular does not exemplify any properties in that world. Since it is not the case that any maximally consistent modal determination of particulars entails that p's individual essence is exemplified, it is not necessarily true that p exists. However, because there is no world in which p's individual essence is exemplified without p existing, p exists essentially.

Thus far we have ignored world-indexed properties in reference to the analysis of states of affairs as regards their obtaining and the analysis of propositions as regards their being true. Suppose that w^{**} as specified in the diagram above is the actual world. The individual essence of p is not exemplified in w^{**}, which means that p does not exist in the situation at hand. If it is a proposition that p is F-in-w, then it seems that we should say that this proposition is true, because if w were to have been the actual world, then p would have been F, which is just what the proposition states. But then we could no longer state that a proposition is true if the corresponding state of affairs that p is F-in-w obtains, because that would amount to the claim that p exemplifies in w^{**} the property of being F-in-w, which in turn would mean that, contra our assumption, p has to exist in w^{**} after all. Because what this leads to is that all individual essences are exemplified in whichever world is actual, we should reject it and rethink whether there are really propositions of the form that p is F-in-w. This, however, is no easy matter, because in the case of q, we do not have this problem: that q is F-in-w^* is true because q exemplifies this world-indexed property. It seems that if we do not accept propositions of the form that p is F-in-w, which leads to a contradiction, then we cannot accept propositions of the form that q is F-in-w^*, which are unproblematic.

The problem consists in the fact that p's individual essence is not exemplified in w^{**}, but nevertheless exists. In saying that p is F-in-w^*, we are in fact not talking about p, but about an entailment of p's individual essence, namely that in a certain maximally consistent modal determination of particulars, p's individual essence is exemplified and entails that p is F in that co-exemplification. Therefore, propositions about particulars the individual essence of which is not exemplified should be analyzed as de dicto modalities: that p is F-in-w^* means that it is possible that p is F, which in turn just means that if w^* had been the actual world, then p would have been F. In the case of exemplified individual essences this problem disappears, or at least does no harm, because no contradiction arises in saying that the existing particulars exemplify world-indexed properties, although, here again, we could also analyze their exemplification of world-indexed properties in terms of de dicto modalities.

NOTES

1. For an introduction into the philosophy of modality see Loux (1979). In what follows, I more or less follow Alvin Plantinga's conception of a possible world. Cf. Plantinga (2003) for a collection of his essays on this subject.

2. For the purpose of this essay I take it as a basic fact that a certain possible world is actual. That is, I bracket the question of why a certain possible world is the actual world. Ultimately, my answer to this question is theological. That this world and no other is the actual world is true because God causes this world to be the actual world.

3. For instance, the table in front of me is constitutive of the state of affairs that there is a blue table, and it is also constitutive of the state of affairs that there is a wooden table. We thus have two distinct states of affairs of which the table is constitutive. This given, it follows that there are also different possible worlds such that if one of these worlds had been actual, then the two states of affairs would have obtained. Just think of the actual world and of a possible world which differs from the actual world only in the obtaining of a state of affairs independent of the states of affairs that the table is wooden and that the table is blue. Therefore, one and the same particular is constitutive of different states of affairs which in turn are part of different possible worlds.

4. Cf. also Ellis (2002: 12): "The individual essence of a thing is the set of its characteristics in virtue of which it is the *individual* it is." Although I am going to focus on individual essences, my account is compatible with the existence of kind essences. However, for my purpose, I ignore kind essences. For an analysis of these, cf. Ellis 2002 and Oderberg 2007.

5. Here is a more formal argument why the individual essence of a particular entails its world-indexed properties. Suppose a particular p exists in w and in w^* and that in w it is F while in w^* it is non-F. If w is the actual world, then p exemplifies F and also the world-indexed properties of being F in w and of being non-F in w^*. If w^* is the actual world, then p exemplifies non-F, but also the world-indexed properties of being F in w and of being non-F in w^*. Therefore, independent of which world is actual, a particular exemplifies its world-indexed properties in any world in which it exists. The individual essence of a particular also entails the property of being self-identical, if it is possible that there are two distinct particulars p and p^* which exemplify the same world-indexed properties. As regards p and p^*, there would be no possible world in which the one exists without the other. The existence of p would be a sufficient and a necessary condition for the existence of p^*, and, of course, vice versa. The only property which p would exemplify that p^* would lack is the property of being identical to p. Although this property as such appears to be a trivial property because anything exemplifies self-identity, it is not trivial in this case because it is what in fact would distinguish particulars with the same world-indexed properties.

6. A paradigm example of metaphysical argument involving conceivability as a ticket to the realm of possible worlds concerns identity and distinction: if it is conceivable that the existence of p is neither necessary nor sufficient for the existence of q, then we conclude that there is no possible world in which p and q are identical.

7. That a particular p possibly exemplifies a certain property F, on our account of possible worlds, means that there is a maximally consistent co-exemplification of individual essences such that p is F in this co-exemplification. A particular p necessarily exemplifies a property F if p is F in any maximally consistent co-exemplification of individual essences of which it is a part. There are other ways to understand the notion of conceivability. Gendler and Hawthorne provide the following characterizations: "rationally intuiting that it is possible that P, realizing that not-P is not necessary, imagining (that) P, conjecturing that P, accepting that P for the sake of argument, describing to oneself a scenario where P obtains, pretending that P, make-believing that P, supposing (that) P" (Gendler and Hawthorne 2002: 7). However, I see no philosophical use for a notion of conceivability which is not interested in trying to obtain insight into possibilities, which is why I specified conceivability as I did.

8. Particulars and properties thus are propositional building blocks. They are "the entities from which propositions are built up via certain recursive rules" (Schiffer 2002: 81).

9. Consequently, a proposition is possibly true if and only if it is true in some maximally consistent co-exemplification of individual essences, and it is necessarily true if true in all such co-exemplifications.

10. That we are able to imagine the obtaining of a state of affairs does not entail that the things imagined have to be perceptible. As Chalmers says, "One can imagine situations that are unperceivable in principle: for example, the existence of an invisible being that leaves no trace on perception. And one can imagine pairs of situations that are perceptually indistinguishable: for example, the situations postulated by two scientific hypotheses that make the same empirical predictions, or arguably the existence of a conscious being and its zombie twin" (Chalmers 2002: 151).

11. What about the relation between propositional and state-of-affairs-like conceiving? Ultimately, I do not think it probable that we can state-of-affairs-like conceive something which is propositionally inconceivable. However, following Chalmers (2002: 155), I do think that our ability to conceive propositionally of an individual essence in a certain state does not *eo ipso* entail that we are able to state-of-affairs-like conceive that individual essence in a certain state.

12. Cf. Göcke 2009 for an argument that this thesis of physicalism entails that every minimal physical duplicate of the actual world is a duplicate simpliciter of the actual world.

13. This objection is due to an anonymous referee, to whom I am grateful for pointing this out to me.

REFERENCES

Chalmers, David. 2002. "Does Conceivability Entail Metaphysical Possibility?" In Gendler and Hawthorne, *Conceivability and Possibility*, 145–200.

Chisholm, Roderick. 1976. *Person and Object: A Metaphysical Study.* London: George Allen & Unwin.

Crane, T., and D. H. Mellor. 1990. "There Is No Question of Physicalism." *Mind* 99:185–206.

Ellis, Brian. 2002. *The Philosophy of Nature: A Guide to the New Essentialism.* Chesham: Acumen.

Flood, Gavin. 2006. *An Introduction to Hinduism.* Cambridge: Cambridge University Press.

Gendler, T. S., and J. Hawthorne, eds. 2002. *Conceivability and Possibility.* Oxford: Oxford University Press.

Gillett, C., and D. Witmer. 2001. "A 'Physical Need': Physicalism and the Via Negativa." *Analysis* 61:302–9.

Göcke, Benedikt Paul. 2009. "What Is Physicalism?" *Ratio* 22:291–307.

Hempel, C. 1980. "Comments on Goodman's 'Ways of Worldmaking.'" *Synthese* 45:193–99.

————. 1969. "Reduction: Ontological and Linguistic Facts." In *Science and Method: Essays in the Honor of Ernest Nagel*, edited by Sidney Morgenbesser et al., 179–99. New York: St. Martin's Press.

Kripke, Saul. 1980. *Naming and Necessity*. Cambridge, MA: Harvard University Press.

Loux, Michael. 1979. *The Possible and the Actual: Readings in the Metaphysics of Modality*. London: Cornell University Press.

Mill, J. S. 1851. *A System of Logic Ratiocinative and Inductive: Being a Connected View of the Principles of Evidence, and the Methods of Scientific Investigations*. London: John W. Parker.

Moser, Paul, and J. D. Trout. 1995. "Physicalism, Supervenience and Dependence." In *Supervenience: New Essays*, edited by E. Savollos and Ü. Yalcin, 187–217. Cambridge: Cambridge University Press.

Newen, A., V. Hoffmann, and M. Esfeld. 2007. "Preface to Mental Causation, Externalism and Self-Knowledge." *Erkenntnis* 67:147–48.

Oderberg, David. 2007. *Real Essentialism*. London: Routledge.

Papineau, David. 2002. *Thinking about Consciousness*. Oxford: Oxford University Press.

Plantinga, Alvin. 1974. *The Nature of Necessity*. Oxford: Clarendon.

————. 2003. *Essays in the Metaphysics of Modality*, edited by Matthew Davidson. Oxford: Oxford University Press.

Priest, Stephen. 1999. "Aquinas' Claim 'Anima Mea Non Est Ego.'" *The Heythrop Journal* 40 (2): 209–11.

Pseudo-Dionysius. 1987. *The Complete Works*. New York: Paulist Press.

Putnam, Hilary. 1973. "Meaning and Reference." *The Journal of Philosophy* 70:699–711.

Schiffer, Stephen. 2002. "Meanings." In *Meaning and Truth: Investigations in Philosophical Semantics*, edited by J. K. Campbell and M. O'Rourke, 79–104. New York: Seven Bridges Press.

Yablo, Stephen. 1993. "Is Conceivability a Guide to Possibility?" *Philosophy and Phenomenological Research* 53:1–42.

10

The Unconditioned Soul

STEPHEN PRIEST

There is a distinction to be drawn between conditioned and unconditioned philosophy. Unconditioned philosophy entails ultimate explanation of how philosophical problems may be formulated. Conditioned philosophy is the attempt to solve philosophical problems without disclosure of their fundamental possibility. A philosophical problem is one we have no method of solving.

In section 1, "The Conditioned Paradigm," and section 2, "Deconditioning," I identify some of the components of the conditioned/ unconditioned distinction in a preliminary way. In section 3, "Deconditioning and Problems in the Philosophy of Mind," I roughly outline applications of the distinction to the following questions: what personal identity consists in, whether the mind is the brain, what the difference is between the past and the future, and how free will is possible. I do not pretend there is not much more to be said. There is. However, a result of even these tentative explorations is that physicalism and materialism are clearly false and any plausible theory of the mind entails the existence of the soul.

1. The Conditioned Paradigm

There are conditioned patterns of thinking and conditioned dogmas, both of which impede the disclosure of the soul. Conditioned patterns of thinking include the following:

Means-to-end thinking and perceiving. Although conducive to the manipulation of nature for the perpetuation or destruction of biological life, means-to-end thinking and perceiving are inimical to *being brought up sharp with the existential reality of one's own existence.* We are lost in regret for the past and hope or fear for the future. Always *on the way*, we are never *all here now.* Noticing this 'all,' this 'here,' and this 'now,' and not just moving on, is necessary for the disclosure of the soul.

Thinking and perceiving in generalities. Often perpetuating a theoretical totalitarianism which masquerades as a profound understanding, thinking and perceiving in generalities is an obstacle to the revelation of the soul. In the philosophy of mind, problem solving is made impossible by using the anonymous 'the mind,' 'persons,' 'the brain.' Even 'the self' and 'the soul' are inadequate tools for problem solving, even if necessary heuristic bridges.

It is your own particularity *as you* which is most difficult to explain about you. This *own-most* particularity not only exceeds any empirical identity and difference but is not even exhausted by 'this very' human being's having the modal properties of being self-identical and numerically distinct from any other. The fact of someone's *being you* cannot be generalized. You escape the language of anonymity. You are the opposite of anonymous.

Scientific thought. Although useful for the predictive description of physical objects in motion, science faces away from the soul. For all its admirable rigor, its detached observations, its careful reporting, its mathematical modeling and predictive power, science is limited by a catastrophic mistake: *Science construes its subject matter as only other.*

In understandably adhering to objective *methods,* science has excluded the study of subjective *subject matter.*

On one level, you are of course another: You are another to another. However, you infinitely exceed what can be observed of you from the standpoint of exteriority. Becoming aware of this infinite interiority is becoming aware of the soul.

Scientific objectivity has caused ob-ject-ivity: the worship of objects. Dispassionateness has caused eliminatory ideology. If not tempered by spirituality, science will extinguish the last vestige of meaning from the world, recognizing only silent matter in motion.

Third-person thinking. Third-person thinking leaves no room for first-person singular psychological ascriptions, let alone spiritual ascriptions. Such ascriptions *seem* not to add any new information because re-couching a first-person sentence in the third person does not alter its truth conditions. For example, 'I am conscious' and 'He is conscious,' said of the same human being, are true or false under the same conditions.

However, the use of the first-person singular pronoun (or cognate devices) is possible only because there is something it consists in to be someone, the person who one is, as opposed to not being any of the people one is not, or no one. The ontological bifurcation between self and other makes possible the bifurcations between grammatical persons, not vice versa. (The power of language was massively overrated by twentieth-century philosophy.) One's own existence qua one's own is omitted from any purely third-person description.

Conditioned dogmas include:

Everything real is other. We could call this the 'suicidal method' in the philosophy of mind and action. To do conditioned philosophy of mind, you treat yourself as though you do not exist. At best, you unquestioningly accept that conclusions about others are easily extrapolated to one's own case. In particular, you do not inquire into how this cosmic chasm between you and everyone else could obtain in the first place.

Science is fundamental. For all its mathematical rigor and predictive power, science has only ever told us about matter in motion. In fact, scientists have not the faintest idea what energy is, what gravity is, what consciousness is, what it means to say something 'exists,' or even, most shockingly, what matter is.

Science rests on metaphysical assumptions. Science is powerless to answer an infinite number of profound questions, including the following: Why is there anything? Why does anything happen? Why are there laws of nature? What is the scientist? Why is someone you? Why is the time now? Science provides us with only a narrow window onto the world. It is not the best window we have. Inference to the best explanation is not inference to the best scientific explanation. Inference to the best explanation is inference to the ultimate explanation.

The present is not real. The growth of science entails the suppression of presence. Physics has no conceptual room for presence, either in the sense of 'now' or in the quasispatial senses of 'presence to' and 'presence of.' Scientific thought is characterized by a complete disregard for the referents of 'I,' 'now,' and 'here.' Science is a subject without a subject. (The deconstructive idea that Western thought is characterized by a *privileging* of presence and 'the subject' is the reverse of the truth.)

If it exists, it can be quantified over. In modern materialist society, the value of anything is essentially its financial value. If it cannot be readily counted, or quantified over, it cannot be bought or sold. If beauty, truth, the soul, God, cannot be readily enumerated, it is *as though* they do not exist. Quantification is blind to the first-person/third-person distinction. (Historically, religion did not facilitate the rise of capitalism. Capitalism supplanted religious *knowledge* and left religious *belief* [or the lack of it]).

Anything knowable is empirically observable or rationally provable. One obstacle to philosophical progress is the dogma that in order to come to know something it is necessary to exercise either the senses or the intellect or both. Despite the lengthy debate over rationalism and empiricism, the idea that there could be a third epistemology is lacking.

The fundamentals *slip between* rationalism and empiricism. For example, although some things that exist can be detected rationally or empirically, their *existence* is not empirically or rationally detectable. Although spatiotemporal processes, and numbers of things, can be detected empirically, *space, time,* and *numbers* cannot. Nor can they be discovered just by thinking. Although *present things* can be perceived, their *presence* cannot. Although the human being you take yourself to be can be sensed, the fact of its being you (rather than no one or someone else) cannot. Nevertheless, all these phenomena, or realities, are *intuited* or are *present.* If they are experienced or thought, then that is in a very broad sense of 'experienced' and 'thought.'

All experience is sense experience. It is a conditioned dogma that experience is either introspection or sense perception, and that if there is introspection, it depends on sense perception. Yet in fact, there is much experience that is neither introspection nor sense perception: mystical experience, meditation, the pure experience which makes both introspection and sense perception possible.

All explaining is explaining away. According to this dogma, the exquisite rendering of Mozart's Clarinet Concerto is 'nothing over and above' sound waves. My anguish at the death of my loved one is 'nothing over and above' atoms in motion in my brain.

Yet the claims of 'scientific reductionism' are self-evidently false. I mean by 'self-evident' (or 'self evidently true') that

> p is self-evident if and only if perceiving the truth of p is a necessary condition for understanding p.

I mean by 'self-evidently false' that

> p is self-evidently false if and only if perceiving the falsity of p is a necessary condition for understanding p.

If anyone understands the claims of 'scientific reductionism,' they know them to be false. If they do not know them to be false, they do not understand them.

This set of views is 'practical' and 'realistic' and 'genuinely explanatory.' I am right. One of the delusions of the conditioned state is that it appears to be a state of knowledge but is in fact a state of ignorance. It says: "How can I be wrong if I am at the cutting edge of scientific progress? I depend upon hypothesis formulation and strict and dispassionate observation. These could not possibly lead me astray, could they? I am a scientist who tests hypotheses open-mindedly by evidence, and I am willing to give the hypotheses up if the evidence falsifies them. Theologians are fools who only follow blind dogma *whatever* the evidence. *Aren't they?*"

Well, no. Theologians simply do not assume that everything to be found out can be found out only by hypothesis formulation and empirical testing. In particular, the fundamental philosophical questions cannot be answered in this way. (Imagine criticizing a mathematician for not proceeding by experiment.)

This 'I am right,' which has an ethical connotation also of 'I am *in* the right,' because the intellectual procedures I have learned are the only truly respectable ones, is an expression of outward confidence. This 'I am right' in the attitude of philosophers is haunted by a dread: the possibility that philosophy is really what I thought it was before I was taught it, the possibility that I am a sophist who has betrayed something terribly important.

■   These patterns of thinking and conscious or unconscious dogmas keep the soul hidden. From the conditioned point of view, there seems to be only *belief* in the existence of the soul (as there seems to be only *belief* in the existence of God). From the unconditioned point of view there is *knowledge* of God and the soul.

A mistake of the conditioned view is to assume the existence of the soul is the positing of something *extra* to the world we know. In fact the soul is disclosed through the world we know when we know that world for what it really is. The 'extra' is extra to our knowledge, not to what our knowledge is knowledge of. The 'extra' is not extraneous. It is in fact intimately present. The difficulty in knowing the soul is not that it is too remote. It is too proximal. You are it.

To the conditioned mind, the findings of mysticism and theology look like extravagant postulates, the products of fanciful imagination and wishful thinking. They appear to be add-ons to the empirical world, which is assumed to be self-sufficient. In fact, God and the soul are fundamental presuppositions of the empirical world. Theology divulges reality shorn of the contents of space-time. If all the physical objects were subtracted from existence, God and the souls would be left over. Theology reveals the fundamental ground. Science is not fundamental. Theology is fundamental.

What is it to be conditioned? There are different senses in which conditioned knowledge is conditioned.

1. A condition is a state, so conditioned knowledge is a state of knowledge, defined by what it includes or excludes. The condition of philosophy is a philosophical standpoint. Something can be in good condition or in bad condition. Within the conditioned paradigm we think our knowledge is in good condition. It is in bad condition.

2. 'Condition' can have the sense of 'necessary condition' or 'prerequisite.' Conditioned knowledge is conditional upon not only its own hidden entailments but upon ignorance. The known presupposes the unknown. Conditioned knowledge is an edifice: the sustaining of conditioned knowledge is a condition for further conditioned knowledge.

3. In its etymology, 'condition' is derived from the Latin 'dicere,' 'to say,' and the prefix 'con,' 'with.' Although etymology is clearly not an infallible guide to current meaning (because "What did it mean?" is a different question from "What does it mean?"), in this case, as in many others, etymology provides insight into truth. The colleagues are *speaking together*. The con-dition is a shared ideology.

    In its French etymology 'ignore' is derived from 'ignorer,' which means 'to be ignorant of.' Conditioned philosophy ignores that which it is ignorant of. The mind-body dualist, the idealist, the theist, the mystic (no matter how logically rigorous) is not attacked but ignored.

4. The condition is a premise: a premise which unwittingly rests on other premises.

5. 'To condition' is to impose a character on. The conditioned presupposes the unconditioned. Conditioned knowledge is constrained knowledge.

6. 'Conditional' means 'not absolute.' Conditional knowledge is true because knowledge is truth entailing. Although relativism is a naïve and ultimately self-refuting doctrine, it gestures towards an insight into conditioned knowledge: much knowledge which appears to be of intrinsic properties of entities is knowledge of relations or processes. (For example, if to say someone is tall is to say they are taller than most people, then 'tall' tacitly means 'taller than.' More controversially, 'exists' means 'exists now,' but 'now' means 'when I am,' so 'exists' means 'exists when I am.') Unconditional knowledge is knowledge of what is the case *come what may*.

7. Conditioned knowledge is conditioned and reactive in the way of a conditioned reflex: a quick response which is only through habit. In conditioned philosophy, the instinct to refute overrides the care to understand (or even hear).

8. Conditioned knowledge is subject to conditions, subject to what other people say. Conditions are the contents of stipulations or commands: "On this condition . . ." The parameters of the conditioned paradigm are implicit prohibitions and commands: "Do not endorse a theological view. That is superstitious"; "Do aspire to the detachment or objectivity of science. That is academically respectable"; and so on.

It is a historical rather than a philosophical question why the conditioned paradigm exists. It has *levels* of origin—economic, pragmatic, biological—but finds its *ur* source in desire. Desire is essentially a distraction from the present, but it is precisely the disclosure of presence which facilitates the disclosure of the soul.

2. Deconditioning

Different philosophies exhibit different degrees of understanding. Here I restrict the taxonomy to theories which bear closely on the philosophy of mind.

Conditioned philosophies include:

Materialism (def.) Everything is physical. This view is conditioned by the third-person perspective. The materialist has not noticed his own existence.

Physicalism (def.) Everything is either physical or reducible to the physical. This view is conditioned by the third-person perspective. Anything spiritual or inner is identified with the physical and outer.

Functionalism (def. 1) What anything is, is what it is for. This view is conditioned by means-to-end thinking. It is an ideological legitimation of capitalism and, ultimately, survivialism.

Functionalism (def. 2) Anything is either a cause or an effect or both.

Essentialist functionalism (def.) Anything is essentially what it is for.

Logical behaviourism (def.) The inner is reducible to the outer. The psychological is reducible to the behavioral. This view is conditioned by the third-person perspective. Anything private or inner or spiritual has to be rewritten as publicly observable, which means, in effect, physical.

Atheism (def.) God does not exist. This view is conditioned by the assumption that the existence of God is a matter of belief or disbelief based on evidence. Not seeing any evidence, the atheist understandably chooses, not just not to believe, but to disbelieve.

Philosophies that break with conditioning include:

Buddhism (def.) Suffering can be ended by realizing enlightenment. Through detachment, meditation, and leading an ethical life, the Buddhist is freed from means-to-end thinking and the third-person perspective.

Phenomenalism (def.) Any sentence or set of sentences about physical objects may be translated into a sentence, or set of sentences, about sense contents, without loss of meaning.

Phenomenology (def.) The description of what appears to consciousness, as it appears, with no commitment to its reality. The conditioned is part of the natural attitude so is suspended by the *epochē*.

Existentialism (def.) The attempt to solve fundamental problems of human existence. Confronting one's own freedom and the responsibility it entails, facing death, becoming aware of one's own existence, is a shedding of conditioning and a being brought up sharp with the here and now.

Solipsism (def.) Only my mind exists. At a conditioned level, solipsism is a laughably improbable conjecture or a kind of conceit. To feel the plausibility of solipsism is to feel the terror of solipsism.

Agnosticism (def.) Neither 'God exists' nor 'God does not exist' is certain. Perhaps because there are unanswered metaphysical questions, the agnostic chooses not to disbelieve in God even though he does not believe in God.

Pantheism (def.) There is nothing that is not either God or a part of God. A crucial stage in deconditioning is the endorsing of pantheism: the ascribing of the properties of God to reality as a whole. After all, if anything does everything, if anything is infinite, then these properties seem most plausibly ascribed to the totality of what is.

Fundamental ontology (*Fundamentalontologie*) (def.) The attempt to answer the question of Being (*Seinsfrage*). The break with the ontic is a break with conditioning. The clarification of the question of being and the disclosure of Being are only possible by a suspension of ordinary means-to-end thinking.

Deconditioned philosophies include:

Mind-body dualism (def.):
(i)   Both minds and physical objects exist.
(ii) No mind is a physical object and no physical object is a mind.
(iii) No mind depends upon a physical object for its existence.
(iv) No physical object depends upon a mind for its existence.

This view does justice to both the third person and the third-person perspective on the person.

Idealism (def.) Everything is mental or reducible to the mental. This view does justice to the first-person perspective on the person but does not retain the conditioned and third-person view of physical objects as mind-independent.

Theism (def.) God exists. To the conditioned mind, God seems like an extravagant postulate. To see the plausibility of theism, consider the much stronger claim, 'Necessarily, there is a God,' and then deduce 'God exists' from that. 'Necessarily, there is a God' is derived from the conjunction of the unconditioned insight that, necessarily, Being is the being of God and, necessarily, there is not nothing. Being is necessarily the being of God because Being qua being has all and only the essential properties of God essentially.

Fundamental theology (def.) The attempt to answer the question of Being (*Seinsfrage*) theologically. It is a deconditioned insight that Being is the being of God. Being qua being has all and only the properties of God. This truth is not obvious at a conditioned level, because there it is hard to draw a clear distinction between Being and beings and therefore hard to inspect the properties of Being.

What Is the Relationship between Conditioned and Unconditioned Philosophy?

There is a hierarchy of understanding between levels 1 (conditioned philosophies), 2 (philosophies that break with conditioning), and 3 (deconditioned philosophies). For example, a philosopher operating at level 1 will think all the philosophies at level 2 false. However, they will consider philosophies at level 3 not only false but grossly implausible. They will find it utterly incomprehensible why anyone should subscribe to them, and they will put this down to wish fulfillment, fantasy, or ignorance of science. Philosophy at level 1 seems to its practitioners the most sophisticated and explanatory philosophy. It is in fact the most naïve.

A philosopher operating at level 2 has some insight. Perhaps through aesthetic experience, they have seen the falsity, the limitations, of the philosophies at level 1. They have seen that the prospects for a scientific explanation of everything are nil. They have seen that the philosophies at level 1 are not even scientific but are pseudoscientific. A level 2 philosopher has begun to notice their own existence but does not yet know what they are. They realize that they are the living refutation of level 1 philosophies, but their understanding is still only egocentric. Philosophy at level 2 is of extreme interest and importance, because it breaks up the assumptions upon which conditioned philosophy, level 1, relies.

A philosopher at level 3 can fully understand the plausibility of levels 1 and 2 and is able to explain them as part of the truth. Philosophy at level 3 seems to the conditioned mind to be the most naïve and groundless and extravagant philosophy. In fact it approaches the truth. It seems the most abstract but is in fact the most concrete. It deals with what exists, not with what is only thought to exist. Level 3 philosophy is unconditioned knowledge, that is, unconditional knowledge.

Level 1 philosophers are not capable of grasping philosophical questions. Level 2 philosophers are capable of grasping philosophical questions but regard them as unanswerable. Level 3 philosophers grasp philosophical questions and have techniques for answering them.

This tripartite taxonomy seems unwarranted to philosophers operating at level 1. It should be pointed out, firstly, that the faith in science and dismissal of metaphysics at level 1 is largely unargued at level 1. The justification is at best an inductive faith in science. Secondly, a good reason for preferring one theory over another is that one can explain what the other cannot. Levels 1–3 are increasingly explanatory. Level 3 includes level 2, and level 2 includes level 1. Finally, in the case of philosophy, the test is problem solving. Level 3 philosophy can answer philosophical questions unanswerable at levels 1 and 2.

Conditioned philosophies are not so much false as incomplete. They are true in their positive theses, false in what their practitioners deny (even though *p* may be rewritten as *p salva veritate* and vice versa). They mistake part of the truth for the whole of the truth about the relevant domain.

For example, it is just about possible to believe materialism is true of any human being, *except one:* yourself. It is in one's own case that one is presented with a constellation of mental events, saturated with emotion and meaning. Conditioned philosophies *seem* to be genuinely explanatory because they are explanatory *at their own level*. For example, physicalism works as an explanation of events within the physical world. It breaks down straight away as an explanation of consciousness. Trying to understand thinking in terms of the brain activity which is its empirical and contingent prerequisite is as absurd as trying to learn mathematics by studying the sound waves emitted from mathematicians' bodies when they speak. The level of explanation is completely wrong.

Conditioned and unconditioned philosophies rely, tacitly or explicitly, on different root metaphors. Conditioned philosophers think of themselves as going forwards, making progress. Unconditioned philosophers think of themselves as going down to the more and more fundamental, the primordial.

How Is Deconditioning Possible?

For any individual, there is a distinction between

(1) their worldview, that is, the constellation of words, beliefs, symbols, and images (however rigorously ordered or however loose and impressionistic),

and

(2) the stark existential reality of their being-all-here-now.

The worldview is abstract but masquerades as concrete. Being-all-here-now is concrete but is abstract, or even undetected, from the standpoint of the worldview. We are lost in thought. Being-all-here-now is repressed by the worldview, but it makes the worldview possible. Deconditioning requires breaking with the worldview and being-all-here-now (which is to arrive where you have been all along, to arrive intellectually where you are existentially). In authentic philosophy, existentialism and metaphysics coincide.

There are many methods of deconditioning. They include the asking of philosophical questions, the having of mystical or religious experiences, the revelatory use of imagination, and meditative techniques (which are not ways of thinking).

The Asking of Philosophical Questions
Conditioned ontology rests on metaphysical assumptions. Although it is part of doing level 1 philosophy to assume metaphysical questions are senseless (as though they were like "What is north of the north pole?"), the questions force themselves upon level 1, on pain of

inauthenticity (that is, denying what you presuppose): Why is there anything? Why are there laws of nature? What caused the big bang? And so on.

Level 2 philosophy rests on metaphysical assumptions as well. Although it is part of doing level 2 philosophy to regard metaphysical questions as genuine but unanswerable, they are forced on level 2 on pain of inauthenticity. Why do you exist? What is the space in which sensations arise and subside? (Plus all the metaphysical questions put to level 1.)

Some questions are too proximal, too close, for conditioned philosophy and science to answer, some too macroscopic, too remote. "Why is someone you?" is too proximal. "Why does anything happen at all?" is too remote. Unconditioned philosophy does not let go of these questions until they are answered.

The Having of Spiritual Experiences

There is spiritual knowledge by acquaintance, not just by description. (Spiritual knowledge cannot be 'explained away' by neurology. Neurology is powerless to explain how even ordinary, day-to-day awareness is related to atoms in the brain. A fortiori, it tells us nothing whatsoever about mystical or religious experience.)

Acquaintance with the soul is self-intimating (like the rare acquaintance with God granted to some individuals). By 'self-intimating' I mean that it is not possible to be in the state without realizing the state is veridical:

(i)   Anyone in the state believes they are in the state.
(ii) Anyone in the state believes the state is veridical.
(iii) The belief of anyone in the state that the state is veridical is true.

These hold because, at the unconditioned level, there is no distinction between appearance and reality. The distinction between appearance and reality paradigmatically applies to perception of the physical world, although, obviously, one might make a mistake in mathematics; or, less obviously, from the fact that one is in a mental state it does not follow as a matter of logic that that belief is true. (I am not saying there are not exceptions: "I possess at least one belief," for example.)

The Use of Imagination
There is a conditioned and an unconditioned use of the imagination. The conditioned use of the imagination is inventive or playful: the generation of mental images of empirical objects which might or might not exist. This use of imagination is familiar; it is thought useful for artistic creation and for doing inventive science. However, it is not normally considered knowledge generating per se.

The unconditioned use of the imagination is the reverse of the conditioned use. Its function is to discover, in the sense of dis-cover, not to invent. The imagination is not used to generate mental images but to 'experience' the infinity of Being, the unbounded expansiveness of one's own psyche. Why is this imagination? Because it is the deployment of the same faculty used in generating images of the empirical.

The conditioned use of the imagination is known to both the conditioned and the unconditioned mind. The unconditioned use of the imagination is beyond the grasp of the conditioned mind. It is utterly incomprehensible and so will seem ridiculous fancy or, at the very least, not knowledge yielding. There is knowledge and ignorance of what the mind is capable of.

Self-Knowledge
A step in self-knowledge is feeling the plausibility of solipsism. Your own existence is a clue, a portal, to the unconditioned. At the conditioned level we glide over our own case in an instant and think of 'the' person, 'the' mind, 'the' brain, and so on. Deconditioning requires being-all-here-now, being brought up sharp with one's own existence in the present or, more profoundly, as the present. For this, we cannot validly extrapolate from third-person cases to our own case. (Of course, to the conditioned mind it looks as though we can. This is thinking by habit, which is hardly thinking at all.) Everyone has to realize their own existence for themselves. By 'realize' is meant both 'understand' and 'make real,' 'real-ize.' Although the inner space of the soul is a discovery, this uncovering is in a sense a making real. The uncovering is not only epistemological but, because it is a change in you, ontological. There is an ontology of the epistemological. You are hidden from yourself at the conditioned level. By deconditioning you are dis-closed.

Doing History
Doing history produces a sense of the deep contingency of the world as it appears in the present. Taking this contingency seriously is a kind of deconditioning. What is constant and what is variable? What is permanent and what is impermanent? Physical objects, for example, are impermanent.

Philosophy has a 'commonsensical' starting point (which engages 'the' skeptic). This 'common sense' is historically constituted. How did it look a thousand years ago? How will it look in a million years' time? This should affect our attitude to science. How will science look in a million years' time?

Discovering Portals
There are *portals* or *gaps* in the empirical world, portals to the unconditioned, for example,

(a) your own existence
(b) space
(c) now
(d) being
(e) fear of death
(f) the aesthetic
(g) being disconcerted
(h) that which you exclude, deny, (profess to) treat with contempt, dismiss as impractical or delusional.

The empirical world as a whole is a portal, because it is not complete, not self-sufficient, not a substance. The empirical world as a whole does not exhaust reality as a whole.

Meditation
Meditation is not a kind of thinking. Meditation is not introspection. If the many practices called 'meditation' have anything in common, it is the peaceful or relaxing disclosure of the emptiness, or inner space, or zone of Being, which is the originary synthesis of one's own existence and essence. It is in this boundless inner space that thoughts and experiences arise and subside. Techniques of meditation range

from the Zen 'just sitting,' through the repetition of a mantra, or the focus of attention on a flame, or tantra, to numerous Yogic or quasi-yogic breathing exercises. Meditative states are not states of hypnosis, nor are they states of sleep, or half sleep. Meditative states typically involve great relaxation of the body but sharp alertness of the mind. Meditation is a third state which is neither being awake nor being asleep. If you have not learned how to meditate, you have little reason to believe this. It is outside your experience.

Mysticism

The spiritual practices of the world's great mystics are, inter alia, methods of deconditioning:

(1) The mind is turned away from the senses.
(2) The world is apprehended as an aesthetic whole.
(3) The senses are revealed as limited.
(4) There is a dissolution of the physical world.
(5) There is a dissolution of the psychical world.
(4) There is the stillness of being-all-here-now.
(5) The infinite inner space of the soul is disclosed.

Deconditioning and the following of an ethical life are routes to moral knowledge, as opposed to moral opinion. These are paths to acquaintance with your own soul, paths to God.

Conditioned knowledge is knowledge of the changing. Unconditioned knowledge is knowledge of the unchanging. For example, in the case of the soul, what you are looking for is already here, but it is not what you think it is. You are what you are looking for, but you do not know what you are.

Conditioned and Unconditioned Meaning

Is the unconditioned ineffable? God and the soul infinitely exceed any description of them in empirical terminology. One of the difficulties of doing deconditioned metaphysics or theology is that ordinary language is geared to making intelligible the world of physical and psychophysical processes. In metaphysics, this language is stretched beyond the bounds of sense in the sense of 'sense experience' but not beyond the bounds of sense in the sense of 'meaning.' Metaphysical meaning makes empirical meaning possible. Empiricist theories of meaning are not false but incomplete, metaphysically inadequate. The conditioned can be described, in scripture, in great mystical writing, in poetry. However, unconditioned writing can be understood only by an unconditioned mind.

Is the soul ineffable? Is space ineffable? Are you ineffable? Is the you-ness of being you ineffable? Is absolute interiority ineffable?

We can understand an explanation only if it is couched in concepts we already have. Understanding the unconditioned cannot be done using conditioned concepts. If we use the same old ways of thinking, the same old pigeonholes, it will be impossible to learn anything new. Conditioned concepts keep us at the conditioned level.

The soul can be described, but we need to deploy a terminology which breaks with the conditioned secularism of physicalism. In its Old English etymology 'soul' is derived from 'sawel' (saw[el], -ol, -ul), which is etymologically related to the notion of *sea* or *lake* through the German 'See.' The German for soul is 'Seele.' The Dutch for 'soul' is 'ziel.' As usual, etymology is a clue to profound metaphysical meanings covered over by contemporary empirical use. The soul is sea-like. The soul is sea-like because the soul is the expansive space of your own being. The soul is oceanic. The soul is where sensations and the events of mental life happen, as the sea is where waves happen. Although the soul is infinite, unbounded, and any sea is finite, the soul and the sea are broad and deep. There are depths of the soul. The soul is the *sol:* the ground and the sun.

It is therefore meaningful to talk about unconditioned souls. Prima facie, if meaning is public and rule governed and outer, meaning does not extend to the private and inner. However, the theory that meaning is public rule following is only half a theory of meaning. The language of exteriority is inadequate to the inner life, because experience is necessary for understanding first-person singular psychological ascriptions.

On an empiricist theory of meaning, meaningful terms either refer to the immediate contents of experience or are members of chains of sequentially defined terms terminating in those referring to the immediate contents of experience. At the level of the soul, the distinction between empiricism and metaphysics breaks down. In the broad sense of 'experience' there is experience of the soul. There is experience of the soul insofar as the soul is disclosed, insofar as the soul is presence. Although on any metaphysically antirealist view, the truth or falsity of sentences does not outstrip the capacity to know their truth or falsity, there is knowledge of the soul, so there are truth-valued claims about the soul.

The criteria for counting souls are the criteria for counting spaces. In particular, it is impossible to be mixed up about which soul is one's own soul. (One might be mixed up about which fingers are one's own in playing the children's game of intertwining fingers.) One is only ever directly presented with one absolute interiority: the one that one is.

Certain concepts admit of both a conditioned and an unconditioned use, an empirical and a metaphysical deployment. For example:

(1) Empirically, your own existence is the existence of a certain human being, born in a certain place of just those parents, socialized and educated in just those ways. Metaphysically, your own existence consists in this human being 'being' you. I place 'being' in single quotation marks here because the relation between you and this human being is not identity. You view the world from this human being. You are partly where it is. You control it. You are present through it.

(2) Empirically, 'now' is an indexical expression. (For example, the word 'now' in 'I am speaking now' picks out the time at which I am speaking.) Metaphysically, there is no time that is not now. The past does not exist, because it is over. The future does not exist, because it does not exist yet. The metaphysical now, or Now, is when anything happens. The now is the eternal present.

(3) The empirical concept of being or existing is used to refer to particular things that exist. The metaphysical concept of existence or Being is used to refer to whatever it is that the existing of the particular things that exist consists in.

(4) Empirical space is a totality of spatial relations between physical objects or processes. Metaphysical space is either Newtonian space or the subjective phenomenological space in which one's

own experiences are located. Understood as including the visual field, the tactile field, the olfactory field, the auditory field, and where thoughts happen, this could be called the 'field of experience' or 'consciousness.'

The intuitive idea of space, or the intuition of space, is a heuristic for the soul. Phenomenological space, devoid of contents, is the soul. The soul is a private space but not a place. Places are spatially related, so putatively distinct places are in fact parts of one and the same space. Private spaces are not spatially related, and are therefore distinct spaces. As a space,

(i)   the soul is infinite;
(ii) the soul is immaterial;
(iii) the soul 'contains' phenomena;
(iv) the soul is an atom.

Space qua soul is not quite void (*kenòn*, *vacuum*), not quite emptiness, but no-thing-ness. Space qua the soul is a private, quasiabsolute (Newtonian) space, not a relational (Leibnizian) space. Space, in this sense, is what we normally understand by 'consciousness.' Although there is a difference between being conscious and being unconscious, space is the background against which changes take place. Newtonian space being empty or containing physical objects is analogous to the space of the soul being empty or containing phenomena. Numerically distinct souls are numerically distinct inner spaces individuated by privacy; by the ontological analogue of privacy, absolute interiority; and by qualitative difference. Each soul is qualitatively distinct from every other soul. For example, the *you-ness* which saturates the inner space of your soul is qualitatively distinct from the *me-ness* of my soul.

No-thing-ness

There is an ontological and theoretical distinction between *thing-ness* and *no-thing-ness:*

Thing-ness. Whatever exhibits thing-ness may be readily individuated, discriminated in thought or perception, in principle singled out, especially as an object, 'there,' or 'over there.' In a mainly automatic and unacknowledged way, thing-ness is exhibited by any thing in front of me, paradigmatically: physical objects, but derivatively, physical and psychophysical processes. (Through a tenuous psychological projection of physical metaphors, even mental processes, numbers, sets, and members of sets are construed on the model of thing-ness.) Thing-ness is an individuated synthesis of form and content.

The construal of any subject matter on the model of thing-ness is partly a derivation from acquaintance with physical objects, partly a product of technology, of manipulation, of control, of counting, of buying and selling, of imposition. Thing-ness as a worldview is the result of the sword, the masculine. It appears strong but is fragile.

No-thing-ness. No-thing-ness is a property of whatever does not admit of straightforward individuation: space, time, God, the soul, Being, Nothingness, consciousness, presence, Now. The world of no-thing-ness is the world of God and Being. No-thing-ness does not admit straightforwardly of a distinction between form and content. No-thing-ness is disclosed by openness, by revelation, by relinquishing control, by letting go. No-thing-ness is the opening of the flower, the feminine. It appears fragile but is strong.

From the conditioned point of view, that is, from the point of view of thing-ness, no-thing-ness is either mistaken for nothing at all or misconstrued on the model of thing-ness: Space is a container or nothing. Consciousness is a mechanism or nothing. Time is motion or nothing. God is a huge intelligence the other side of the sky or nothing. Thing-ness allows no ontology of the subtle. No-thing-ness seems to be nothing but it is nearly everything.

For present purposes, the crucial application of the distinction is this: You think of yourself on the model of thing-ness. You have to understand yourself on the model of no-thing-ness. Your essential being is not that of a thing. Your essential being is an unbounded inner space or presence.

Even now, immense caution is needed not to misunderstand these claims. I do not mean a space construed on the third-person model: a kind of vapor, or cloud, or a place enclosed by surfaces;

something individuated on the model of thing-ness. I mean: You are the inside of unbounded space. Similarly, when I say you are a presence, I mean just that. I do not mean *that which is* present but the presence itself. Your idea of yourself as one flesh-and-blood human being among others is a product of third-person and generalized thinking. Thing-ness is recuperated and self-imposed. This imposition, on an empirical level, is not false. It is, however, a distraction from your true nature. You are a presence. You are the inside of space. You are the inside of time.

The transition from thing-ness to no-thing-ness is effected by the techniques of deconditioning (see above, under *"How Is Deconditioning Possible?"*). There is an intermediary ontology in which some of the properties of both thing-ness and no-thing-ness are exhibited. Processes are individuated, but their essential entailment of change precludes their being physical objects, the paradigmatic things. Sensations are roughly individuated but have an amorphous phenomenology characteristic of no-thing-ness. Numbers are sharply individuated but not objects. The subatomic constituents of matter cannot be straightforwardly singled out in space-time. Matter is mainly emptiness. Appreciation of realities which are not straightforwardly thing-like effects the transition from taken-for-granted thing-ness to the disclosure of no-thing-ness.

Thing-ness is temporal. No-thing-ness is atemporal. Thing-ness is changing. No-thing-ness is the unchanging, the permanent. Thing-ness is plurality. No-thing-ness is unity in the sense of *one-ness:* a unity that is not a bundle of parts; a unity that does not in principle admit of plurality. The dependencies between no-thing-ness and thing-ness are as follows:

(i)   No-thing-ness is necessary for thing-ness.
(ii) Thing-ness is not necessary for no-thing-ness.
(iii) Thing-ness is sufficient for no-thing-ness.
(iv) No-thing-ness is not sufficient for thing-ness.

The Disclosure of the Soul

There are stages of that deconditioning which is revelatory of the soul:

(1) You are surrounded by physical objects on every side. You view the world from the physical object you call your body. You have a worldview, a picture, or a complex representation of what there is. This is ordinary, conditioned existence at the level of thing-ness.

(2) Your worldview is, ontologically speaking, a constellation of thoughts and emotions. (This tells us nothing about which parts of it are true or which false.)

(3) It is as though phenomenalism is true (even though phenomenalism might be false).

(4) It is as though solipsism is true. A distinction may be drawn between kinds of solipsism. Firstly, solipsism is the doctrine that only I have a mind, a subjective point of view, a psychological interiority. Others are pure exteriority. They have no subjectivity, no point of view, no mental life. Secondly, solipsism is the doctrine that only I exist. I include what is presented to me. That is, I include what someone who is not a solipsist would count as what is presented to them, not as part of themselves.

Both doctrines are false but disclose an important truth which is not solipsism. Solipsism is false because the other (unless dead) is never presented as a pure exteriority. The other is presented as living, breathing, speaking, gesturing, threatening, ingratiating, subservient, and so on, with a reality which cannot be reduced to behavior, to matter in motion. The other is the presence of the other. This presence of the other is the kind of presence you feel yourself to be as you view the world from your body. It is in fact this presence which is absent from the body in death. In the appearance of a corpse the *presence* of the other is absent.

The important truth disclosed by solipsism is that your own existence is the existence of a substance. That your own existence qua your own depends upon nothing empirical is the explanation of the plausibility of solipsism. This substance which is your own existence is a subjective space. To perceive the plausibility of solipsism is to reveal the phenomenological space where sensations arise and subside, the space where events take place.

(5) Inner space is still (there) when sensations no longer arise and subside.

(6) Inner space is the space of no-thing-ness. The space of no-thing-ness is unchanging, because all becoming has ceased.

(7) Inner space is a form of intuition.

(8) Inner space is the field of transcendental subjectivity which survives the *epochē*.

(9) Inner space is the originary synthesis of the fields of the sensory modalities as one field, that is, the field in which phenomena arise and subside: the phenomenal field, the *phield*.

(10) Inner space as no-thing-ness is the site or the *Lichtung* or the zone in which Being is disclosed to Being.

(11) Inner space is *Hiersein*. I say 'Hiersein,' not 'Dasein,' because the being of inner space as no-thing-ness is not being-in-the-world but pervasion of the world. We could call this 'being in the world' (unhyphenated) to signal both the fact that this 'in' is not an 'in' of inclusion and the fact that whatever being in the world pertains to inner space pertains to it contingently.

(12) Inner space, as no-thing-ness, has all and only the characteristics of the soul. It is immaterial, immortal, a thinking substance, someone, unchanging, always now, private, an inner space, an absolute interiority. I define each of these terms below.

Immaterial (def.): (i) Not physical. Not composed of matter nor of any of the constituents of matter. (ii) Not amenable to natural destruction. (iii) If existing at a time then existing at any time later than that time.

Thinking (def.) Capable of engaging in doxactic activity. ('Thinking,' despite its present continuous tense, is used in a dispositional rather than occurrent sense.)

Substance (def.): (i) That which depends upon nothing natural for its own existence. (ii) That which bears properties but is not itself a property. (iii) That which can be meaningfully said to possess a separate existence.

Someone (def.) A being rightly mentioned in answer to the question 'Who?' For example: (the lived existential reality of) you. The being you are. Any being truly called 'you' or 'I.'

Unchanging (def.) Not gaining or sheding any properties.

Always now (def.) The timeless present.

Inner space (def.) Where the experiences of one, and (under normal circumstances) only one, person always take place.

Private (def.) Given to only one subject. Known by acquaintance by only one subject.

Absolute interiority (def.) An inside without an outside.

The site of the disclosure of Being to Being (def.): (i) The space in which what is is dis-closed. (ii) The space in which the being of what is is dis-closed.

Soul (def.): both (i) immaterial, immortal, thinking substance and absolute interiority which is someone; and (ii) unchanging and private space which is the site of the disclosure of Being to Being.

The soul is a simple immaterial finite presence. Your soul is essentially you, therefore logically necessary and sufficient for your existence. The soul is not intrinsically mental or physical. The soul is not of this world, so it is not a natural entity. The soul is a kind of presence, and so accounts for your own presence in, or as, this human being. The soul is immaterial, simple, and invisible. This is one's own true nature revealed by deconditioning. Spiritual development is possible beyond this. It is possible to know God.

Fantastic as it seems to conditioned thought, you are not included in the physical universe. You peer into the universe from outside it. The idea that you are a member of the physical universe is a sophisticated achievement of that conditioned thinking which construes everything as other. You have perceived human beings. You have had the thought "I am one of those," and you have imposed the picture of the human being as another on yourself. Many layers of psychophysical conditioning constitute this recuperation, this rewriting of the self as other, as just another member of the public. From a third-person perspective the person appears to be included in the world. The third-person perspective is radically incomplete. The universe is not anonymous.

Nevertheless, with sensitivity, the presence or absence of the soul can be discerned in the third-person case. When a human being is dead, something is lacking in their appearance:

(i)   The presence of the other is absent.
(ii) The subjectivity of the other is absent.
(iii) Movement is replaced by stillness.

The soul is the presence which is absent from a corpse. Subjectivity can be essentially understood only from your own case. Nevertheless, in life, anyone's subjectivity is their pervasion of a body (as opposed to that person being only a complex physical object). The soul is invisible in the way that space is invisible but present in the way that space is present. In death there is a transition from becoming to being. The human body and mind are temporal. The soul is timeless.

The existence of a soul is necessary and sufficient for the existence of a person qua that person.

Your being is only partly and contingently being in the world, because your being is essentially being-out-of-this-world. I hyphenate the expression 'being-out-of-this-world' to signal the ontological inseparability of the terms of this relation. I leave 'being in the world' unhyphenated to signal the ontological separability of the terms of that relation. The 'here' of *Hiersein* is a subjective space, not an empirical location. Being in the world and facing the world are conditioned states (even though immensely psychologically compelling while one is in them). The conditioned state is being in time. The unconditioned state is being out of time, or being in eternity, that is, being in the eternal Now.

In being in the world, the world is revealed and God is hidden. In being-out-of-this world, God is revealed but the world is hidden. Presence is the presence of God. In the world, presence as the presence of God is hidden by the presence of the things the world makes present. Out of the world, presence as the presence of God is overwhelming.

Is the Soul a Substance?

Having broken with the conditioned paradigm of level 1, how do we know that we should not simply stop at level 2 and, say, engage in pure phenomenology and not the metaphysics of level 3? How can we be certain that the soul is a substance? To decide this we have to decide how to decide whether anything is a substance.

Suppose matter is a substance. In this case, we are willing to say that something is a substance if, no matter how thorough the inspection, nothing is found which this depends upon. The materialist does not say that matter is not a substance because it could, under further investigation, be found to depend upon something else. Suppose the totality of what is, whatever is, is a substance. Suppose God is a substance. In these cases, it is necessary and a priori that they are substances, so the search for extraneous necessary conditions is logically futile. To the conditioned mind it looks as though the soul could turn out *not* to be a substance ("Doesn't all this depend on the brain?"). To the unconditioned mind it is necessary and a priori that the soul is a substance in the sense that it depends on nothing empirical. It is not a substance in the sense that it is necessary and a priori that the soul depends on God, rather as it depends on reality as a whole.

Suppose a substance is something that can be meaningfully said to possess a separate existence. For example, a physical object might depend upon the physical universe but be a substance in this sense. Newtonian space and time depend upon God yet are substances in this sense. The soul is a substance in this sense. The soul can be meaningfully said to possess a separate existence. It is given as though it could be all there is.

Knowledge of the Soul

The disclosure of the soul is between rationalism and empiricism. To see this, consider that there is in a sense apprehension of space, of time, of the being of what is. This apprehension is not the same as perception of spatial things, perception of temporal things, perception of actual things, perception of existent things. It is not right either that this apprehension is a kind of detection by thought, a kind of intellectual intuition. Rather, space, time, actuality, and existence *are present* in any experience of spatial, temporal, or existent things. They are not sensed in the sense of 'perceptually discriminated from items of the same type with which they are not identical.' This *presence* is an entailment of perception, or knowledge by acquaintance. The acquaintance in knowledge by acquaintance is presence. The disclosure of the soul is the presence of the soul. Presence is presupposed by both thought and experience as ordinarily understood. Therefore presence is presupposed by rationalism and empiricism. It infinitely exceeds both.

Incredible as it might seem, observation and thought reveal the world only at a conditioned level. Presence is the revelation of the world at the unconditioned level. So, is there experience of the soul? There is not experience of the soul as one thing among others.

Unconditioned knowledge of the soul is not only propositional knowledge but knowledge by acquaintance. Acquaintance with the soul entails the presence of the soul. The presence of the soul is not something extra to a certain presence. For example, by 'your presence' I mean what sees these words on the page now. I do not mean the image this presence has of itself as one human being among others in the world. That is to lapse back into the old habits of third-person and generalized thinking.

If we construe experience as only sense experience, then the logico-epistemological status of unconditioned claims is synthetic a priori. Unconditioned claims are knowable to be true independently of sense experience and so a priori in that sense. On the other hand, they are knowable through experience only in the broad sense of 'experience' which admits mystical and meditative states. In a wide sense of 'a posteriori' they are therefore a posteriori. On the other hand, their truth is a necessary condition for any experience whatsoever, and so in that sense of 'a priori' they are a priori.

Knowledge of the soul is synthetic because informative, not merely tautologous. The soul is present but not perceived, apprehended but not sensed as a discriminable particular, so a being devoid of sensory faculties could in principle acquire unconditioned knowledge.

The soul does not necessarily exist even though there is a necessary inference to the existence of the soul from the existence of oneself. The soul is necessary *for* the world as it is presented in experience; therefore the world as it is presented in experience is sufficient for the soul. This does not show that the soul necessarily exists in any strong or logical sense. The denial of the existence of the soul is not contradictory, but it is self-refuting. "The soul exists" is necessary in this weaker sense: nothing empirical can refute the existence of the soul, because the existence of the soul is necessary for the empirical world (qua object of experience). The existence of the soul is in this sense a priori.

3. Deconditioning and Problems in the Philosophy of Mind

When we engage in philosophy, including philosophy of mind, we operate with a set of background, taken-for-granted pictures of the subject matter under investigation. I call these pictures 'thought pictures.' They seem necessary for understanding philosophical problems, but their inaccuracy, or at least the philosophical assumptions embedded in them, prevents the problems' solution. Here I sketch some constraints on solutions to the problem of personal identity, the mind-body problem, the problem of distinguishing between the past and the future, and the problem of freedom and determinism. I show in each case how the formulation of the problem rests on a thought picture: a conditioned and contingent constraint. I then suggest that any plausible solution to each problem entails the existence of the soul: an unconditioned and essential constraint.

What Does Personal Identity Consist In?

In trying to solve the problem of personal identity we habitually operate with a taken-for-granted picture of what it is to be a person. We think of a person as one human being among others, paradigmatically, somebody who is not oneself but someone else. They are pictured as distinct from but situated within their environment. They think or experience. Because the problem is about identity over time, we entertain a picture of a person at one time, and of a qualitatively distinct person at a distinct time. We think of the person as extended between the two times. We rightly wonder what the necessary and sufficient conditions are for the earlier person being the later person. The problem of personal identity is, then, really 'the problem of the identity of the human being over time,' especially 'the problem of the identity of the human being who is somebody else, over time.' Crucially, this picture is essentially the residue of perceptual encounters with human beings other than yourself. As in the case of so many philosophical problems, to solve the problem of personal identity, you have to bring yourself into the picture.

Physical and psychological solutions to the problem of personal identity fail because they provide no account of the reality of one's own existence. They do not entail necessary and sufficient conditions for the identity of 'the' person over time because they eschew the soul.

If the spatiotemporal continuity of the body is what personal identity consists in, then the later person is the earlier person if and only if a certain human body exists at the earlier time, exists at the later time, and exists at all intervening times. The body is a space-time continuant, and an earlier and a later person being the same person is their being (necessary and sufficient for) slices or portions of that continuant.

The spatiotemporal continuity of the body is not sufficient for personal identity, because there is no contradiction in the supposition that numerically distinct subjects of consciousness should occupy the same body over time (where a subject, for example, views the world from that body). The inference from '. . . is the same body as . . .' to '. . . is the same person as . . .' fails.

It is often assumed that the spatiotemporal continuity of the body at least provides a necessary condition for the identity of the person over time. This is, however, not the case because there is no contradiction in the notion of intermittent existence. Suppose we are perceptually presented with a human being. Suppose then that human being ceases to exist and we therefore cease to perceive them. Suppose next a human being qualitatively similar to the one who ceased to exist begins to exist and is perceptually presented to us. In this case, we would be presented with a conceptual choice. We either say that spatiotemporal continuity has not been preserved, so the later person is not the earlier person, or we say the later person is the earlier person because they say they are, they are where the earlier person was, they look and behave in the same ways, and so on. The fact that nothing compels us to choose the first way shows that the continuity of the body is not a necessary condition for personal identity.

Personal identity does not consist in a memory criterion holding. From the fact that I remember someone it does not follow that I am the person whom I remember, so the memory criterion is not sufficient for personal identity. From the fact that I cannot remember a certain person it does not follow that that person was not I. If the inference were valid, then I did not exist for any periods of my life that I am unable to remember, and I did not perform any actions that I cannot remember myself performing. These entailments are false. Therefore the memory criterion is not necessary for personal identity. Although some of the conceptual resources essential to the formulation of the memory criterion are derived from the first-person singular case, the question "What remembers?" is only superficially answered.

The literature on personal identity contains a fatal error. It takes lasting as what identity over time fundamentally consists in. Lasting, however, is not the fundamental concept. Lasting itself needs explanation. To see this, ask: *What lasts?* It is the numerical identity of something between an earlier time and a later time which explains how something can last between those times. Lasting presupposes identity. It is not what identity consists in. Continuity presupposes identity, but identity does not presuppose continuity. Identity consists in the existence of something changeless.

On one definition of 'changeless' anything is changeless if it lasts but does not gain or shed any properties over time. The definition captures one sense of 'changeless' but not one adequate to your own changelessness. That a *person* changes presupposes an inherently changeless subject of change: that which changes in the sense of that which *undergoes* change.

By deconditioning, it is revealed that despite the coming and going of thoughts and experiences, there is something utterly unchanging which is the core of your own being. This is the eternal now, inner space, you-ness, a disclosure of Being, no-thing-ness. The unchanging has all and only the properties of the soul, so the soul is the changeless. Personal identity consists in the existence of a soul. In referring to the soul at different times, reference is made to the changeless reality which is the essence or innermost being of the person. That the same timeless reality is referred to at different times does not entail that the reality referred to is in fact not timeless. A timeless being is simply referred to at different times. Leibniz's Law is preserved, and the problem of personal identity solved. It will not be solved in any other way.

What Is the Relationship between the Mind and the Body?

As in the case of the problem of personal identity, in trying to solve the mind-body problem we paradigmatically operate with a background picture of a human being who is somebody other than oneself, distinct from their environment but embedded within it. Because the mind-body problem is that of stating the relation between the mind and the brain, we entertain a crude picture of the brain and of mental life 'above' it, perhaps like a cloud. Compared to the sophistication of our attempts to think the relation between them, the picture of the *relata* is primitive.

It is the existence of the soul which makes the mind-body problem hard. It is the existence of the soul which provides the mind-body problem with its solution.

The existence of the soul makes the mind-body problem hard for two kinds of reason. Firstly, the mind-body problem depends upon a more profound problem for its formulation: Why are human beings divided into two mutually exclusive but jointly exhaustive categories: the category which has only one member, oneself, and the category with many members, everyone else? Understanding this dichotomy is necessary for understanding how the mind-body problem is thinkable. We are conditioned into thinking of persons in the abstract, as psychophysical wholes or human beings. By deconditioning, that is, by reversing conditioning, we can become aware of the component parts of the human being which we assimilate to form the conditioned picture. One part is one's own first-person psychology and the inner space of the soul in which it takes place. The other part is the physical exteriority of the other, and their intimidating or inviting presence (which makes it impossible not to believe in other minds).

Materialism, logical behaviorism, physicalism, and other secular views are derived from a picture of the person as 'other' as 'not oneself.' Mind-body dualism and various kinds of idealism are derived from a model of the person as oneself. In their conceptual possibility, in their conceivability, materialist philosophies are third person. Philosophies of consciousness are first-person singular. (This dichotomy is fully consistent with the truth that the same facts may be reported about the same human being in both first- and third-person terms: "I am thinking" said by me is made true by the same fact as "He is thinking" said by you when you are referring to me, and so on.) If people were only *other* people, materialism would look plausible (even if ultimately refuted by the glow of the other's presence). It is one's own existence which introduces directly the following: consciousness, subjectivity, agency, free will, me-ness, and all the other phenomena which resist materialist analysis.

The dichotomy between being someone, the person who you are, and not being all the people you are not, exists because your soul exists and other souls exist. The soul is your presence. Your presence in the world contrasts with the presentation of the exteriority of the other to you. The dichotomy of self and other makes the mind-body problem hard. The existence of the soul creates the dichotomy of self and other. Therefore, the existence of the soul makes the mind-body problem hard.

The second way in which the existence of the soul makes the mind-body problem hard is this. The soul bestows on mental states some of the properties which make them mental. In particular, the privacy of mental states exists because the soul is an inside without an outside. The absence of any exteriority to the soul, which is to say, the absence of any physical property from the soul, makes the soul (ordinarily) undetectable from a third-person standpoint. Mental events qua mental are episodes within the phenomenological space of the soul and so are equally undetectable from the standpoint of exteriority.

Before showing that the soul is the solution to the mind-body problem, I say something briefly in criticism of materialism and physicalism.

Materialism is false because, ontologically, from the point of view of what exists, the body is only billions of atoms moving in empty space. It is absolutely self-evident that there is more to a human being than that. I think, therefore materialism is false.

The existence of mentality is a necessary condition for denying mentality. Materialism entails the denial of mentality, so materialism is self-refuting. Therefore materialism is false.

Physicalism either collapses into materialism or collapses into mind-body dualism. Physicalism collapses into materialism if it is, for example, the doctrine that everything is physical or the doctrine that the mental is ontologically, semantically, or otherwise 'reducible' to the physical. In those cases physicalism is false because materialism is false. Physicalism collapses into mind-body dualism if it entails even the tiniest bit of mentality. For example, the doctrine that the only substances are physical substances but there are mental properties is a mind-body dualist doctrine. The doctrine that mental events in various senses 'supervene' on physical events is a mind-body dualist doctrine. To fail to realize this is to fail to realize that the brain is only billions and billions of atoms in motion in empty space. So-called physicalist views, so sustaining of modern secularism, leave wholly unexplained the relation between thoughts and experiences on the one hand and billions of atoms in motion on the other. Physicalism presupposes the mind-body problem. It is not its solution.

Materialism and physicalism are grossly implausible positions in the philosophy of mind. Even though great logical ingenuity went into *formulating* materialism and physicalism, there are no good logical arguments for them. They are in fact advocated on ideological grounds: either through the massive misconception that these philosophies are genuinely scientific, or through the current rage for secularism, the wish to deny the existence of God and the soul.

The relationship between mental and physical events is psychophysical causal interaction: mental events cause physical events, and physical events cause mental events. Any solution to the mind-body problem has to do justice to these facts:

(1) *Some physical events are sufficient for some mental events.* Standing barefoot on the sharp end of a nail causes a sharp pain in the foot. Drinking claret, a physical liquid, revises one's perceptual world.

(2) *Some mental events are sufficient for some physical events.* Other things being equal, my belief that this bus goes to the city center, conjoined with my desire to reach the city center, precipitates my stepping onto this bus.

(3) *Some physical events are necessary for some mental events.* Well-functioning eyeballs, connected by optic nerves to a living brain, are needed for seeing. A well-functioning living brain is a necessary condition for thinking.

(4) *Some mental events are necessary for some physical events.* If I had not felt angry, I would not have stormed out of the room. If I had not seen him, I would not have crossed over the road.

Any putative solution which entails that psychophysical causal interaction does not occur is false. Accommodating psychophysical causal interaction is a requirement of any solution to the mind-body problem.

It is an elementary logical principle that if *a* is necessary for *b*, then *b* is sufficient for *a*, and if *a* is sufficient for *b*, then *b* is necessary for *a*. Applying this principle to the four tenets shows that (1) and (4) are logically equivalent and (2) and (3) are logically equivalent.

These consequences, although soundly derived, are counterintuitive. We balk at the consequence that a pain in the foot is a necessary condition for the treading on the nail which predates it, or that thinking a thought is a sufficient condition for the whole history of the universe prerequisite to it. Nevertheless, neither the logic of the entailments nor the truth of the premises can be plausibly challenged.

The solution is to adopt a plausible view of causation on which causes, when they are causally efficacious, are *simultaneous* with their effects. Then, if a physical event is necessary for a mental event, that mental event is sufficient for that physical event, and for anything necessary for that physical event, but *causally* sufficient only for the prerequisite events it is simultaneous with. If a mental event is necessary for a physical event, then that physical event is sufficient for that mental event, but *causally* sufficient only because it is simultaneous with it.

How does consciousness push atoms around? To understand the relation between the soul and the human being, we need a new concept: 'pervasion,' which we may define as follows:

a pervades *b* if and only if *a* is at least where *b* is, and *a* is not *b*.

The soul pervades the human being. For example, you are at least *where* your body is, but you are not *identical* with your body. 'At least' is required because you do not end where your body ends. Inner space infinitely exceeds the exterior of the body.

Agent causation is explained by the existence of the soul. Insofar as the first-person singular pronoun (or cognate forms in other languages) is used in true ascriptions, there is a secret reference to the soul. At a conditioned level, or empirically, 'I' is a word that each English speaker uses to refer only to him- or herself. (I say 'a' word because there are other such words: 'me' and 'mine' for example.) Also, insofar as it is true of someone that they *do* something, as opposed to events simply taking place in them, they act as a soul. The agent is the soul. It is not wrong to say the human being is an agent, but they are an agent only because there is a soul.

It is often said that there cannot be mental causation, because it would violate the Third Law of Thermodynamics, according to which the amount of energy in the universe remains constant. The existence of mental causation is, however, no threat to this law. If something physical causes something physical, then energy is displaced or transferred from cause to effect. There is no reason why mental causation should not merely *displace* energy and neither add to nor subtract from the quantity of energy in the universe.

I suggest we replace the term 'consciousness' with the term 'soul.' How does the soul move atoms? The soul moves atoms by being where they are but not being them. You pervade your body as an initiator: you cause without being caused to cause. What is this causation like? You have direct experience of this kind of causation when, for example, you raise your hand or your head. You move your hand by moving your hand. You move your head by moving your head. The conditioned model of causation, one billiard ball colliding with another, is inapplicable to mental causation.

What Is the Difference between the Past and the Future?

We think of the past as 'behind' us. We think of the future as 'in front' of us. Why?

I venture the following explanation of the picture. It is caused by travel. In this explanation I make use of the case of travel by train. Nothing rests on this. Travel on foot would also work, but the explanation is simply clearer and more obvious in the case of travel by train (because it is fast but not too fast).

If you are traveling, in a train, facing forward and looking out of the window, say to the left, the objects in the landscape are visually presented momentarily in front of you, and then alongside you, and then they have passed behind you. Because the train is moving, the objects are presented as event-like as though the objects, or set of objects at a time, are moving to the rear. Although still known to be objects, they are sometimes presented as stretched or blurred in the direction of the back of the train, the opposite direction of the direction of travel. As this happens, clock time of course moves from earlier to later. When the objects are in front of you, but not yet visible, they are in the future. As you perceive them, they are in the present. When they are behind you, and no longer visible, they are in the past. This experience ties the future to what is in front, and the past to what is behind. It should now be easy to see how the picture of the past as a trail left behind oneself is mentally built up. One's route through the world does map a physical trail or a line, with witnessed objects along it. The continued appearance of new objects causes one to acquire the picture of the future as in front.

The picture is a conditioned picture. Shorn of the conditioned picture, only the changing contents of the present remain. From an unconditioned point of view, only the present exists. The unconditioned content of the present is Heraclitean. The unconditioned present itself is Parmenidean. What happens in the present constantly replaces itself. The present when this happens is utterly unchanging. (Even at a conditioned level we can see that the past did exist but does not and that the future will exist but does not. Therefore the past and the future do not exist.)

This present is the presence of the soul, or, to put it another way, now is the time it is within the soul. At the unconditioned level, one is not presented with *two* realities: both inner space and the unchanging now. On the contrary, inner space is the space of the now, and the now is the eternal now of inner space. Within the unchanging present of the soul, events replace one another, and this gives rise to the conditioned ideas of past and future. In fact it is only ever now. You personally demarcate everything that has happened from everything to come. Any event that is not yet has not been simultaneous with an event in the soul. Any event that is over has been simultaneous with an event in the soul. (Every event is necessarily simultaneous with itself.) If the soul did not exist, events would nevertheless be ordered by the before/simultaneous-with/after relation. Now is the time it is inside the soul. You are the difference between the past and the future.

How Is Freedom of the Will Possible?

In order to understand freedom of the will it is necessary to contrast

(A) *the linear sequence of events in which each event is the effect of the predecessor events*

with

(B) *The exploding spontaneity of the present.*

(A) is a conditioned thought-picture. (B) is existential reality. The exploding spontaneity is the constantly changing events replacing one another in the eternal present. The present is a fountain. The linear sequence is our conditioned picture of this. We mis-take the picture for reality. The linear picture is not fundamental but itself takes place in the present.

It follows that the present, not the past, is the source of what happens. That the present is conditioned by the past is a conditioned idea. It is not wrong at an empirical level, but if we remain with this picture, we miss the source of what is. If this seems odd, consider reality as a whole. It has no cause except itself. If we ask who or what does everything, it is not too misleading to say 'the whole.' Analogously, the soul is an independent reality.

I said above that the soul is an initiator. It causes actions but is not caused to cause those actions. At the unconditioned level it is disclosed both that the soul is the cause of its own actions and that there is always the possibility of not acting, or acting otherwise, which is to say the soul has free will. At a conditioned level the following objection naturally arises: "You do not know that there are no *hidden* causes of every action you seem to initiate. Your so-called choices might well be the inevitable result of your neurology. You are simply not aware of the neurology." This is not right. The objection takes the dependence of mind and action on the brain from the conditioned level and applies it to the unconditioned. This is to fail to realize that the unconditioned massively undercuts the conditioned. Science is not fundamental. The empirical is not fundamental. The unconditioned is fundamental. The unconditioned is the level of Being, Now, spiritual space, no-thing-ness. The unconditioned is necessary for the empirical world, but the empirical world is not necessary for the unconditioned. There are no beings without Being, no empirical events without now, no persons without spiritual spaces, no agents without initiators, no neurologists without souls. The converse dependencies do not hold.

I consider one more objection to free will. It is sometimes argued that my behavior could in principle be predicted, given enough knowledge of the prior state of the universe, and it is concluded, from these premises, that determinism is true.

The inference from predictability to determinism is invalid. From the fact that you can predict my behavior it does not follow that I do not behave freely. Perhaps I exercise my freedom in regular patterns with which you have been acquainted. Perhaps you are thereby able to inductively infer my future actions. None of this entails determinism.

The soul is the source of freedom of the will. The exercise of freedom of the will consists in being a cause without being an effect. I am free because I am the uncaused cause of my actions.

■ None of these problems admits of solution unless the soul exists. To the conditioned mind, the soul is a groundless conjecture, a product of wishful thinking or fear of death, a meaningless pseudoconcept, an indeterminate figure without solidity cast a priori over nothing. The unconditioned mind has knowledge of the soul: self-knowledge.

Benedikt Göcke asked me to write about mind-body dualism for his book. A sound proof of the existence of the soul is not sufficient for the truth of mind-body dualism, even if souls are minds, because it is consistent with idealism. Here I offer no proof of the existence of the physical world, and so offer only reasons for accepting a necessary condition for the truth of mind-body dualism (in the sense of 'substance dualism').

Most philosophy, however ingeniously argued, is done at the conditioned level, so its prospects for solving fundamental philosophical problems are slight, even though at the conditioned level there might, for example, be true belief in God and the soul. Fundamental philosophical problems exist because some problems understood by the conditioned mind can be solved only by the unconditioned mind.

Modern philosophy made a catastrophic mistake in taking its dominant models of problem solving from the natural sciences. In order to solve philosophical problems, it is necessary to synthesize scientific models with the theology on which they ultimately depend. Synthesizing science and theology requires deconditioning. In this paper I have outlined some of the applications of unconditioned thought to the philosophy of mind. There are many more applications. Unconditioned knowledge is ultimately knowledge of God, in both senses of 'knowledge of God.'

NOTE

I am grateful to Daniel Came, Benedikt Göcke, Michael Inwood, Grahame Lock, Alexander Norman, and the Dominican Brethren and Fellows of Blackfriars Hall, Oxford, for discussion of the issues raised in this paper. I thank His Holiness the Dalai Lama for discussion of transience and permanence. I owe a debt to the late A. J. Ayer for discussion of free will and predictability.

11

Beyond Dualism?

The Track-Switch Model of Resurrection

THOMAS SCHÄRTL

1. RESURRECTION IN A MATERIALIST'S WORLD

It is not impossible to be a materialist and to believe in the resurrection of the dead. As Hudson pointed out, in a number of publications,[1] a materialist still has some tools in his bag of tricks to reconcile materialism with a Christian worldview. The materialist's possibilities look like this:

(1) replica,
(2) fission,
(3) divine body preservation,
(4) constitution,
(5) four-dimensionalist connection of detached person-stages,
(6) no criteria of identity.

The list of alternatives to a dualistic account of resurrection is pretty impressive. But, as one can easily figure out and as was discussed in

literature also, each solution has a price tag attached to it: The replica theory, which holds that God might create a simulacrum of my
self[2] at the end of days, has to deal with the fact that it severely jeop-
ardizes the requirements of personal identity. The fission model,
which says that my body, or, to be more precise, the simples that
make my body, undergo some sort of fission at the moment of death,[3]
has to implement a closest-continuer theory of identity and has,
therefore, to cope with the fact that there is a rival entity competing
with the resurrected or "saved" entity, namely the corpse in the tomb.
The idea of "body preservation" was introduced famously by Peter
van Inwagen.[4] Basically, it says that at the moment of death God miraculously takes my body and replaces it by a replica corpse for the
piety of those who are left behind. The problem of this view is that
it looks like an ad-hoc theory which is pretty counterintuitive. The
constitution view, on the other side, allows some liberty, since it
states that the physical body constitutes the person but is not identical with the person.[5] It is therefore conceivable that at the moment of
death my physical body is replaced with another (nonphysical?) body.
The question remains, however, whether the result of such a rather
unnatural replacement is still a *human* being. A four-dimensionalist's
account grants us some alternative liberty. Within its categories, it is
conceivable that interrupted person-stages belong, nevertheless, to
one and the same person if there is still some sort of metaphysical
rope (immanent causation, God's miraculous action) that ties these
stages together.[6] However, the four-dimensionalist's notion of resurrection has to deal with the nominalistic underpinning of its theoretical premises: If, from a certain point of view, any summation of
stages is allowed, how can we avoid the introduction of *too many persons* that might claim to be me or to be my four-dimensionalist coun-
terpart? The last theory on the list holds that, since there are no
criteria for personal identity over time, we do not need any for the
identity issue related to resurrection beliefs. Although this is an elegant way of weaseling out of the metaphysical problems, it can be
seen as an unjustified move that jumps from a philosophically rather
miserable situation to some sort of theological optimism: God might
know what to do and how to do it when it comes to resurrection—
even if we have no clue what this might look like.[7]

A sober look at the questions provoked by a materialist's account of resurrection will make one wonder why we shouldn't endorse dualism, that is, substance dualism, as a better alternative. Although some scholars, like Alvin Plantinga, think that Christians cannot proceed without dualism,[8] we have to be aware of two heavy-weighing difficulties. I am inclined to sum these difficulties up—instead of repeating them in further detail—and to distinguish between two categories of problems attached to dualism: there is a general metaphysical problem, and there is a specific metaphysical problem which is brought to light under the pressure of eschatological questions. The first problem has to do with everything scholars have written about the problem of mental causation: if there are two layers of reality within the finite universe, their interaction is a pure mystery. We can broaden the perspective and say that dualism forces us to acknowledge two very heterogeneous layers of reality. To say that Christians who believe in the existence of God must accept, at any rate, the existence of a nonphysical being[9] will not help here, since there is a severe category-problem involved: God, as an infinite being, has to be—based on the premises of classic theism (which, in my eyes, has been questioned but has not been refuted yet)—immaterial. But what a substance dualist wants to declare is that we have to believe in the existence of immaterial finite entities (called "souls"). It is perfectly consistent to believe in the existence of a nonmaterial infinite being and to postulate, on the other side, that finite entities have to be material entities. I am absolutely aware that the latter statement is a metaphysical claim which cannot be proven; but it is a claim which has certain pragmatic advantages, since it also postulates a metaphysical unity of finite existence. Maybe even the talk about angels and demons can be reconciled with such a worldview.[10]

The second metaphysical problem has to do with the notion of a disembodied soul. Although I see no reason to claim that such a notion is self-contradictory or inconceivable (it becomes inconsistent only in a materialistic worldview, and one might ask why we should hold such a view), it generates a further problem: If the soul can be without a body, why do we need the body anyway? And if the soul can be separate from the body—you might want to call it an unnatural stage (if you are a Thomist) or not; it is the *possibility* of separation which counts as the origin of the problem—what gives identity to the body? Wouldn't the body be in need of another identity-granting principle—something which resembles an Aristotelian soul (rather than a detachable Cartesian soul)? And if this is true, what is the benefit of having a soul substance in addition to a living, animated, and formed body? Theologically, a closer look at biblical anthropology—despite the provocative findings and statements of John Cooper[11]—might tell us that we don't *need* substance dualism (of course, the Bible does not *exclude* substance dualism) in order to believe in resurrection. You can have a multilayered concept of human existence,[12] but you don't really need to be a Cartesian.

The following considerations discuss the metaphysical requirements of Christian eschatology. They are meant to offer a modification of the so-called fission model of resurrection. And they try to do so without ontological commitments to substance dualism. However, it will become clear along the way that we cannot and will not be able to get too far away from dualism as such. The moment we say goodbye to substance dualism, we might have to deal with another, less obvious, but still significant form of dualism: the dualism of what is realized and the means of realization.

2. The Track-Switch Model of Resurrection

Let me right at the beginning introduce three dogmas, which I regard as basic for the following considerations (although I know that some of my estimable colleagues will attack these dogmas):

(1) 'Gappy' existence is a metaphysical riddle and atrocity.[13]
(2) Identity-claims without an account for criteria of identity are unjustified.
(3) The concept of resurrection shall not rely on notions that are metaphysically and logically impossible.

All of these dogmas still leave us with a variety of options to develop a consistent concept of resurrection. The spectrum of so-called materialistically underpinned concepts of resurrection is relatively wide: it ranges—as we have seen—over Peter van Inwagen's "Body-Snatch

Theory"[14] and Kevin Corcoran's idea of bodily "fission"[15] to Lynne Baker's constitution view.[16] So, why shouldn't we sign off on one or the other theory of the introduced spectrum, instead of looking for an additional alternative? Why isn't van Inwagen's, Corcoran's, or Baker's view sufficient already?

Van Inwagen, as summarized earlier, proposed the idea that at the time of death my body is miraculously and invisibly removed by God and replaced by a corpse that resembles my body.[17] Although it is philosophically somewhat hazardous to claim that events fall through the cracks of evidentialist requirements, the bigger problem in van Inwagen's approach is that humans are somehow stuck with the bodies they have at the time of death. Ironically, Billy Joel's song "Only the Good Die Young" seems to be a justified expression of preferences here, because no one I know desires to spend eternity in the shape of, let's say, a ninety-year-old. And what should we do with Augustine's christologically motivated idea that we will be raised with bodies that have the age of the risen Lord[18] in order to honor the glory of our savior? Van Inwagen might have no room for the necessary transformation and glorification of earthly bodies unless he thinks that God is some kind of advanced St. Barbara surgeon whose skills in rejuvenating people surpass human technologies by far. But it is hard to believe that these bodies could ever have qualities that are ascribed to the body of the risen Lord with the help of a powerful imagery: the risen Lord isn't subject to the conditions and laws of time and space any longer.

On the other side, Kevin Corcoran's fission theory allows some liberty for a good deal of transformation taking place in the afterlife. However, there is a mereological undertone in Corcoran's proposal that destroys the smooth melody. But let's listen to his leitmotif first:

> It seems possible that the causal paths traced by the simples caught up in the life of my body just before death can be made by God to fission such that the simples composing my body then are causally related to two different, spatially segregated sets of simples. One of the two sets of simples would immediately cease to constitute a life and come instead to compose a corpse, while the other would either continue to constitute a body in heaven or continue to constitute a body in some intermediate state. In other words, the set of simples

along one of the branching paths at the instant after fission fails to perpetuate a life while the other set of simples along the other branch does continue to perpetuate life. (Corcoran 2001: 210)

Several questions have to be raised here. To clarify the path of debate let us call the products of the fission entity *a* and entity *b* and their metaphysical predecessor *a**. The fission story tells us that entity *a** underwent a procedure we might want to call *body-swelling*. Immediately after or simultaneously with this swelling the fission occurs with *a* and *b* as its resulting entities. According to Corcoran, entity *b* is the corpse left behind at the moment of death. Let us illustrate this in a manner that looks at this story from a four-dimensionalist's perspective:

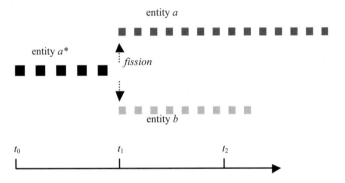

If we look at this chart, we may wonder: where did entity *a* go? The above-presented chart insinuates that *a* exists simultaneously to *b*. But, in reality, this is—at least *quoad nos*—not the case. The only answer one could come up with is Dean Zimmerman's idea, which, basically, says that *a* was miraculously transported or transferred to heaven or to the future, which would explain why *a* is no longer copresent with *b*, and so on. To make sense of this theory and its accordance with dogma (1) we would have to do what the plain resurrection-in-death theorist is required to do: we would have to work with two budgets and books for the existence *in* time, namely with a viewpoint from eternity and a viewpoint from inside of time. But from the perspective of anybody who is subject to time, the situation still looks like this:

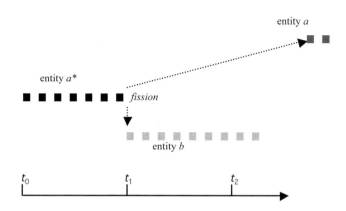

And it is yet another question whether a closest-continuer theory, which is required[19] to keep the so-called fission model going and to stick to dogma (2), could tolerate and handle the use of two different "books" and "budgets" which are the implication of the apparent (apparent to beings in time) gap between the last stage of a person in time and the first heavenly stage of a person in the future. Well, a third problem is more mind-boggling: If at the time t_1 of an individual x's death the simples, which are parts that form a whole (let's express this in a rather vague interpretation of 'forming a whole'[20] for the time being), have spatiotemporally instantiated attributes, it is quite likely that the products of the fission (entities a and b) at t_2 have spatiotemporally instantiated attributes as well. This conclusion is still unproblematic, and Corcoran's as well as Zimmerman's model might be able to underline its validity. But the real problem is waiting between the lines if we assume that (i) being the product of a fission is a spatiotemporally instantiated attribute and that (ii) whatever has spatiotemporally instantiated attributes is (broadly speaking) subject to sense experience. Let's just assume for a moment that claims (i) and (ii) are intuitively plausible. Thus, especially, (i) will put some pressure on the theory of fission because, in one way or another, it should be apparent that entity a and, at least (in case a was transported to the future), entity b (the corpse) are the product of fission. To illustrate the problem let us use a three-dimensionalist's framework this time (ignoring for a moment that entity a is transported or shipped to the future and, therefore, not copresent with b):

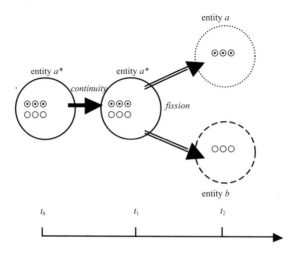

If this is a correct representation of a materialistically interpreted fission (which is different from the archaic idea that an immaterial soul leaves the body at the time of death), we might expect that the body at the time of fission shows, let's say, some significant increase of weight together with an almost simultaneously occurring weight loss which both lead to heavy signs of disintegration at t_2 if compared to a^* at t_1. But the death of human beings does not look like that. Anyone who looks at a corpse immediately after death will say—figuratively—that, somehow, the "spirit" and the personality, the mind and the soul are gone, while, physically, there is still quite a similarity between the premortem stage at t_1 and the postmortem stage at t_2. If we compare b to a^*, we can say: certain processes stopped and cannot be found in b anymore (processes that were once crucial for the life of a^*); a structure started falling apart which once provided the metaphysical integrity of a^*. But there are no material chunks that have been instantaneously added to the human body and that are, after the process of fission, missing in b. To get out of this problem one would have to assume that the simples we are talking about, when we describe the process of body-swelling and body-fission, aren't material atoms but *events* which might have a very unique nature—a nature that allows us to cut off the questions revolving around assumptions (i) and (ii). But even with this modification we still have the problem that some simples (whatever they are in detail may not bother us for now) are meant to be part of a while others are "condemned" to be part of b. What exactly makes one set of simples privileged over the other? Is it the brute fact that the simples that are meant to constitute a are the 'new' ones that have been miraculously produced during the process of body-swelling?[21] But wouldn't this be just another version of creating simulacra or replica (this time at the level of constituting simples) instead of offering a theory that preserves personal identity? Why would it do any good for personal identity to have micro replica instead of macrophysical replica in the first place if reduplication and replication isn't a mode of identity preservation at any rate?

But even if we say that these questions don't really threaten the consistency of the proposed model, there is still the leftover problem, coming from the reassembly theory which is also written between the lines of the fission model—a problem that will finally haunt us: how many simples are necessary to make a the rightfully closest continuer of a^*? If we try to identify the difference between a^* and a we will have to point to the situation of body-swelling: in a^* all the simples have been reduplicated in order to prepare fission. If we start counting the numbers, we will see that Corcoran's charts seem to have to play with a 50-percent standard.[22] But from a broader perspective this seems to be a rather arbitrary number, since nothing in our metaphysical rule book recommends this percentage over and above any other number we might want to come up with. What would happen if, by accident, only a certain number of simples had undergone reduplication? Is it important that all the simples constituting my body at the moment of death reduplicate? And is it necessary that all the duplicates jump in order to perform fission successfully? (Could there be a 'left behind' story of duplicate simples?) Of course, from a narrower perspective the 50-percent standard is the backside of the reduplication idea which is necessary to back up fission and to provide us with an answer why there is still a corpse left. Nevertheless, the broader perspective will remind us that identity-claims for the relation between a and a^* are based on a 50-percent preservation standard. And at this point the metaphysical puzzle still remains.

Of course, beyond the charts, Corcoran has another criterion to offer which, as a matter of fact, is much more important than any percentage we might want to figure out: it is van Inwagen's criterion of "wholeness": whichever simples may form a as a whole, it is clear that a can be the rightfully closest continuer of a^* if and only if a is a living being and is an instance of life (as was a^* an instance of life and a living being).[23] To be an instance of life is exactly what makes the difference between a and b at the end of the day: b is just a corpse; it does not have the life a^* used to have. Therefore, b cannot be regarded as the rightfully closest continuer of a^*. But, if this is the way it goes, why should we be bothered with the problem of "simple-parts" transmission and fission at all? Why shouldn't we build our case on what Corcoran and van Inwagen called "life" and "instance of life" in the first place? Per se, the notion of 'life' is open to a psychological criterion of personal identity and does not need the idea of 'material continuity' seen as the continuity of certain simples that were part of a^* once.

The discussion of the fission model of resurrection and of the atrocities of the reassembly theory adds two more dogmas which are the guiding rules for what I want to present on the following pages:

(1) Don't trust reassembly when it comes to identity questions.
(2) Don't put all your eggs in the basket of a mereological explanation of successive existence and continuity.

The tools I need to overcome some of the indicated problems are already available in van Inwagen's study *Material Beings* as well as in Corcoran's system of coordinates for his model of fission. I will offer a slight modification of the fission model. And I have to address a problem which is an implication of any kind of fission story the metaphysician is eager to come up with: Why should we tell the story of entities a^*, a, and b as a fission story? Why couldn't we tell it as a story of coinciding objects that share a certain spatiotemporal path for a good while before they part ways? Why shouldn't we use the category of 'multiple occupancy' to express what happened to a^*, a, and b? I will have to address the underlying problem later in this section. But for the moment, the strategy I will have to use might look like this: before the fission there are no discrete, full-blooded entities a and b in addition to a^*. The existence of a and b is the *result* of the fission. Therefore, it doesn't make sense to apply a 'multiple occupancy theory' of any kind (and let me add that some versions of constitutionalist theories[24] sound a bit too much like multiple occupancy for my taste) to the theological story of the resurrection of the dead. However, the pill I will force the benign reader to swallow is the idea that there is no identity relation between what I call my body during my life on the one side and the corpse in the tomb on the other side. But to get to this point, let me explain the slight modification of the fission theory.

It seems apparent that the simples in Corcoran's model are not meant to carry the burden of identity and sameness over time. For numerous reasons they simply can't lift the weight of identity claims; however, the most important reason was already seen by philosophers and theologians that had to work with the inconsistencies of a reassembly model of resurrection. Thomas Aquinas notes in his *Summa Contra Gentiles* that parts come and go during the earthly life of a human body: the human body changes all the time. Its stability is, paradoxically speaking, its instability. Matter and parts continually flow in and out; and for living organisms this is absolutely significant.[25] It is therefore fair to say that quite a number of simples get "dumped," while another number of simples are continuously integrated in the body. Thomas Aquinas reflected a comparable thought when he said that for the identity which is required the simples cannot be held responsible. What gives identity is the "species"— a *structuring* factor.[26] If it is the structure (and I am fully aware that this term is still pretty vague) which accounts for identity over time, then the sameness of the structure is what counts for the fission case, and for the determination of identity in a closest-continuer situation. In other words, entity a is the legitimately closest continuer of a^* because there is a sameness of structure as well as a structural[27] continuity that allows the application of the identity relation between a^* and a.[28]

The resulting chart that can help us to illustrate the fission situation might look like this:

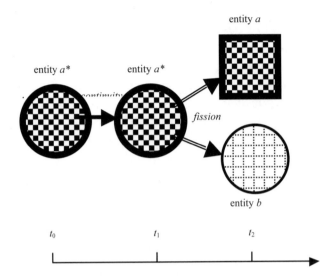

entity *a*

entity *a**   entity *a**

continuity

fission

entity *b*

t_0 t_1 t_2

If we allow structures to be ontologically thicker but still comparable to some sort of 'individualized' universals which can be, nevertheless, instantiated in different ways or through different periods of time, we might arrive at another model of resurrection, which looks like a case of fission only at first glance. We can call this model the "track-switch-model" of resurrection (to imagine it, just recall the countless movies in which the catastrophe of a train crash was avoided by a sudden track switch; and add to your imagination that one or the other car bumps into the barricade of a dead-end track while most of the train is saved thanks to the track switch). Entity *a* is a slightly different direction for the "train" called "my life," whereas entity *b* is a dead-end track for a decaying corpse which is a metaphysical "result" of my life as a human being. There is no evidence and no danger that my life could ever follow the dead-end track. Phenomenologically speaking, my life as a human person and the dead-end track are too different to be brought together as competitors in a closest-continuer situation. A closer look should reveal that *a* is the *ens successivum* of *a** because it is and has the same life, although the continuation of this life might look a little bit like a detour given the transformation that happened, a transformation that left us with *b* on another track. Again, what seems to be some kind of fission is, as soon as we look at it more carefully, a detour continuation.

But what, exactly, is the structure we are talking about? What makes it a structure, and what holds the elements of the structure together? And where is the place of the physical body in this picture? It might be insufficient to work eventually with the terms "form" and "whole" again. But this is exactly what structures do: they form a whole and integrate parts into a whole. Therefore, wholes are not just sums of parts. They are the result of structuring "powers" and forming forces. If we take a closer look at human beings, we will find that there are several layers of structures which themselves are tied together to form a structure we call "embodied" person. We can isolate certain aspects of these connected structures and talk about the human body or about the first-person perspective, which is the center of gravity for psychological continuity. The structures that *make* certain entities human persons include properties and events and allow for connections between macrophysical and microphysical properties and events. However, we have to ask what the primary properties and events that make the structure of human persons are in order to find the place of the physical body in this picture.

Now, this is the moment when the requested dosage of phenomenology should kick in. What we can learn from Maurice Merleau-Ponty, for example, is that "human embodiment" is—strictly *phenomenologically* speaking—a primary property which does not per se include the physicalist's or materialist's perspective (of course, it does not necessarily exclude it either): what we have as the object of our perception and our primary experiences is the body as a whole, which is, as one aspect of it, the person in her relations to other persons—relations that can be expressed and so be made visible in actions and different forms of communication.[29] Human embodiment is so basic that the true phenomenology of perception has to take it into account right from the start. When we talk about the focus or the horizon of our perception of experience, we do so based on embodiment. But it is noteworthy that such a way of talking is different from the usage of a purely physicalistic vocabulary. Merleau-Ponty offers an interesting example to make his point here:

> Bodily space can be distinguished from external space and envelop its parts instead of spreading them out, because it is the darkness needed in the theatre to show up the performance, the background

of somnolence or reserve of vague power against which the gesture
and its aim stand out, the zone of not being in front of which precise
beings, figures and points can come to light. In the last analysis, if
my body can be a 'form' and if there can be, in front of it, important
figures against indifferent backgrounds, this occurs in virtue of its
being polarized by its tasks, of its existence towards them, of its col-
lecting together of itself in its pursuit of its aims; the body schema
is finally a way of stating that my body is in-the-world. As far as
spatiality is concerned, and this alone interests us at the moment,
one's own body is the third term, always tacitly understood, in the
figure-background structure, and every figure stands out against
the double horizon of external and bodily space. One must therefore
reject as an abstraction any analysis of bodily space which takes account only of figures and points, since these can neither be conceived nor be without horizons. (Merleau-Ponty 2008: 115–16)

Although this quote is just a teaser which shows how phenomenology tries to describe embodiment in connection with as well as in
contrast to physical embodiment, the benign reader might be able to
conclude where the story goes: the resulting structure of primary
properties and events is not the physical body but the *experienced body*
(the German language offers a specific term for this distinction: *Leib*,
the experienced body, as opposed to *Körper*, physical body).[30] In the
line of Merleau-Ponty we might be able to say that the physical body
is just the result of an "abstraction," that is, the product of a certain
practice of looking at things. In Edmund Husserl's phenomenological philosophy (which, in its later years, admittedly started leaning
towards idealism) this specific way of looking at things is the way of
(natural) science.[31] But this way is, as Husserl points out, neither primary nor absolutely necessary. It is the way of a certain human practice which became indispensable because humans became disturbed
and bothered by certain problems (for example, medical problems,
which enforced the need to look at humans in another, scientific way).
But to say that this practice became indispensable does not include
that the theories which are the results of those practices can tell us
the ultimate "truth" about reality. Scientific ways of looking at things
don't tell us more truth about reality than primary experiences which

are related to primary properties. Embodiment is ultimately what shapes our perception and directs intentionality in various ways. From a phenomenological point of view, the following theorem is unproblematic: the primary properties and qualities we detect at the primary basis of sensing and perceiving something are relative to the primary properties we have as embodied persons.

But—on the basis of phenomenological analysis—we can take a step further: the notion of a "disembodied self" is (phenomenologically speaking) self-contradictory,[32] because to be a self includes being in relation to others (at least opened to the relation with others). And this is, as Paul Ricœur pointed out, the place of the body; to be precise, it is the place of the experienced body and of embodiment.[33] Ricœur tries to illustrate this by analyzing the phenomenon of *passivity* (and vulnerability). Passivity as the first, most basic reciprocal relation to otherness is the presupposition of any further, real, and "full-blooded" relation to others. And so, passivity is the primary property of embodiment:

On the first level, the body denotes resistance that gives way to effort. . . . The relational structure of the self itself is wholly contained here, effort and resistance forming an indivisible unity. The body receives here the indelible significance of being my body with its intimate diversity, its extension irreducible to any imagined or represented extension, its mass, and its gravity. This is the experience *princeps*, that of the 'active body' illustrated by the happiness and grace of the dancing body, submissive to the music alone. A second degree of passivity is represented by the coming and going of capricious humors—impressions of content or discontent . . . : passivity, here, becomes foreign and hostile. A third degree of passivity is marked by the resistance of external things; it is through active touch, in which our effort is extended, that things attest to their existence as indubitably as our own. Here, existing is resisting. It is therefore the same sense that gives the greatest certainty of one's own existence and the greatest certainty of external existence. With the variety of these degrees of passivity, one's own body is revealed to be the mediator between the intimacy of the self and the externality of the world. (Ricœur 1992: 321–22)

In the light of Ricœur's remarks, it makes sense to speak of embodiment as something which is necessarily enveloped in any (human) first-person perspective. As soon as I am aware of my self, I will be aware of my embodiment in its basic phenomenological meaning: directedness toward otherness, exteriority and passivity which allows resistance and tangibility, sensing and impression, effort and action.

What the experienced body is in contrast to a rather physical description of the body becomes clear once we compare the primary experience of embodiedness with the primary experience of a corpse from a third-person perspective: The living being in front of us is significantly different from the lifeless being we see. The one is the subject and addressee of significant actions and interactions, whereas the other is not, not anymore, and so on. It is therefore phenomenologically sound to say that the embodied person and the corpse are different entities and represent different kinds of entities. This is the reason why we cannot really claim that—to use the abbreviations of the previously introduced charts—entity b is the ontological successor (the rightfully closest continuer) of a^*. The weakness of any closest-continuer theory might be the threat coming from possible rivals, competitors in the candidacy of being the rightfully closest continuer. But in our case, phenomenology can help us to see that the corpse is no serious competitor in candidacy. The 'sortal' difference between embodied person and corpse excludes any possibility to apply an identity relation and a sameness relation. According to the proposed concept of fission, we can claim resurrection even though there is a corpse disintegrating in a tomb. It is conceivable that the person exists postmortem as a, which is an embodied person, because the passive first-person perspective remains intact and continues to open the self up to tangibility, receptivity, relationality, expressivity, and so on.[34]

I am not suggesting that the embodied self is somehow immaterial. My point is, however, that although the embodied self has to be "realized" in order to exist, it is not necessary (in the broadest sense of necessity) that it has to be *biologically* realized. The proposed fission-model presupposes some sort of *realization*: a cannot be the rightfully closest continuer of a^* if it is not realized. But since embodiedness (in its phenomenological meaning) does not analytically include biological realization, I don't feel obliged to propose the rather poor existence of an "anima separata" and can simply state that it is possible that *a* is the rightful closest continuer because of the continuance of an "inwardly" experienceable structure (based on primary properties and experiences) and its realization in—whatever God might have in stock for us.

And this point leads me to the final question revolving around the place of the physical body in the whole calculation. Well, I am inclined to regard the expression 'physical body' as a phase sortal we use under certain conditions in order to talk about compounds of material substances that are arranged 'physical-body-wise.'[35] The use of this kind of Merricksian[36] circumscription allows the suggestion that I don't think that physical bodies are real things (thick entities in the common use of the term 'thickness' in metaphysics). The Merricksian formulation suggests also that what we call physical body has no clear identity—which is, in my opinion, also correct. But in the light of Husserl's comments on the practice-relativity of metaphysical kind-membership, the core argument which supports the idea of 'physical bodies' being no real entities is based on the observation that what we describe as an instance of the 'physical body' is just an abstraction (which is correct in a certain language game). Of course, I don't deny that it is correct to say that human persons have physical bodies. But I would insist that the correctness of this statement depends crucially on the givenness of the mentioned context and the underlying practice. And I would befriend dualists in stressing that 'having a physical body' is not necessary in order to be a human person. From a phenomenologically supported perspective it is sound to say that being embodied is a necessary prerequisite of being human, while having a physical body is not.

Based on this, it might be clear why I am not at all bothered with and worried about the physical body, since the physical body as a 'thin' entity or, even, as a phase sortal cannot be what carries identity through time into the eschaton. The story of the physical body ends with death, while the story of the embodied person[37] continues if there is a possibility of realization in the afterlife. And—from the perspective of theology and metaphysics—there is no basis for excluding the possibility of such a realization. That the story of the new realization of the embodied person begins with the end of the ascribability of a certain phase-sortal (namely, 'having a physical/biological body') and the origin of another entity (the corpse) that looks like an ontological echo of the previous (biologically realized) entity is, admittedly, odd (and I will leave the oddness to further theological speculation as to why our lives include such oddness). However, this does not count against the consistency of a belief in resurrection.

3. Constitution, Realization, or What?

One might wonder why I don't straightforwardly move to a constitution view of persons in order to acquire the metaphysical tools I need to spell out the consistency of resurrection beliefs. Doesn't the constitution view offer a neat metaphysics which gets out of substance dualism[38] without throwing the baby out with the bathwater? My considerations entail three basic disagreements with the constitution view—disagreements which do not allow me to move further in that direction. The first disagreement concerns the criterion of personal identity; the second disagreement is related to the concept of 'body'; and the third disagreement has to do with the ontology of the physical body, which is the result of my phenomenological journey.

In her book *Persons and Bodies*, Lynne Baker argues that (1) it is impossible to find good criteria of personal identity over time, but that (2) the first-person perspective (FPP) could serve as a solid basis for identity claims, whereas psychological continuity does not.[39] At first glance, her point seems to be agreeable. Imagine a split-brain case of a rather drastic form: imagine that a physician informs me that my body cannot survive a terminal disease. But let's assume that the physician has cloned and nourished two new bodies using my (slightly improved) DNA material. To ensure the continuity of my personality, he has to transfer brain hemispheres to the new body. But to make sure that at least somebody will survive, he has prepared two bodies. In this scenario, we would have two equally good closest continuers for me. The question "Which one is I" seems to be unanswerable. One might turn away in a Parfitian mode and shrug one's shoulders. Yet Baker seems to offer a solution: whoever has *my* FPP is *I*. Since it is impossible that two individuals have the same FPP (this is a truism which should be put under a Wittgensteinian scrutiny), only one of the candidates in question will be I. Unfortunately, Baker cannot tell us which person is I; she cannot predict it before the procedure (which might be admissible), and she cannot help us after the procedure. Is there anything she could do to fight against a metaphysical story which tells us that I died on the surgeon's table and gave birth (in a nontraditional kind of way) to twin brothers that, accidentally, have my memories? Yet another example might illustrate that to count on the FPP is not sufficient when it comes to identity issues. Imagine, for instance, that I have a rare brain disease which, literally, erases all of my memories every two weeks by letting me fall into a coma for one day. Every time I awake, my mind is kind of blank. Let's assume that some basic skills are still present (speech, articulation, movement), but also that I have no memory of who I was or who I am, let alone what I did or intended to do. Although I have a FPP, I seem to have no clue about my identity. I have to rely on what others tell me about my past and my intended future. This example also shows that it might be unwise to make the FPP a competitor of the psychological-continuity criterion. The FPP singles out a unique individual and answers certain questions about the individuations of persons and personal attributes. It can account only for the individuation aspects of sameness questions, but it is forced to argue circularly if confronted with cases that are interested in the survival of the personality of a person.[40]

The second disagreement is related to the notion of 'body.' Baker presents a common definition of 'body' which says that body is a "spatially extended, solid entity, all of whose parts are contiguous" (Baker 2000: 112). In the light of phenomenology, I experience my body as extended (and therefore myself as extended) but also experience it as a whole; I don't experience it as an organism in a plainly biological sense of the word. Yet Baker has a second notion of 'body' which is interesting: "'x's body' = body some of whose parts x can normally move without moving anything else, simply by intending them to move" (Baker 2000: 112). Though this second notion comes closer to a phenomenological understanding of "being embodied," it still has certain weaknesses: although I experience some sort of privileged access to my body, I do not necessarily experience it as a composed entity. And, presumably, the privilege of immediate motion might not be the primary basis of bodily experiences. In addition to Baker, I would like to suggest that there is yet another notion of body that we should pay attention to: the body from the first-person perspective. Using Hector-Neri Castañeda's famous asterisk[41] to mark quasi-indexicals, we should state that there is a crucial difference between (1) "The editor of *Nous* felt that after a long flight his* body was left behind" and (2) "The editor of *Nous* felt that after a long flight the body of the editor of *Nous* was left behind." As one can see, sentences (1) and (2) don't have the same meaning; sentence (1) expresses the element of reflexivity indicated by the quasi-indexicalic use of 'his*.' In the light of this distinction Baker should differentiate between 'x's body' and 'my* body,' respectively, 'his*/her* body.' The definitions will be, along with the meanings of these various expressions, significantly different: 'x's body' can presumably be defined in the way Baker did it; but the definition of 'my* body' does not include composition or movement as a basic attribute. According to phenomenological reflections, we might focus on attributes like being placed and seated, being extended and a whole, being passive and tangible, having a perspective, being in a center of impressions and perceptions, being related to other beings, and so on.

The third disagreement is concerned with a basic metaphysical rule: if an entity *a* constitutes an entity *b* (and I am not discussing the further problems of the constitution view here),[42] it is a requirement that *a* represents a full-blooded entity. But what would happen if we came to the conclusion that entity *a* is not a full-blooded entity at all but just a bundle of phenomena picked out by a certain focus and brought under a (phase-)sortal for pragmatic (or scientific) reasons? In such a case, constitution cannot work properly. In other words, if the physical body cannot be considered to be a full-blooded entity, there is no case—neither for identity nor for constitution. No identity without entity. And also: no constitution without entity.

I admit that some esteemed readers might feel tricked, even mocked at the moment: "What happened to the physical body? When did I blink? What did I miss?" But if you are open enough to sign off on the phenomenological considerations at the very end of the last section, you might agree that 'being embodied' is significantly different from 'having a physical body' in a way that fosters the metaphysics of embodied persons but leaves physical bodies (apart and detached from embodiment and persons) quite homeless. The only homestead I have to offer for the physical body is the ontologically less concrete role as a phase-sortal under pragmatic guidance. There is also no reason for me to assume that, in addition to embodied persons, physical bodies exist as real substances.[43] Nonetheless, please note: in denying the substantiality of physical bodies I am not saying that persons don't have physical attributes.

So, if constitution is not the concept I want to use, which concept can be used instead? I am inclined to implement a notion of 'realization.' Departing from Shoemaker's excellent distinctions,[44] I would propose the idea that the relation between a mind-gifted person and her experienced body is a form of *realization$_1$* because the mental and phenomenological properties and qualities in question are thick properties that single out a very specific kind-membership (kind: human person and not just animal) and denote specific causal roles (behavioral patterns and agency, cognitive potentials, etc.). In addition, I would point out that the relation between the mind-gifted person and the physical body is a version of *realization$_2$*, because what we ascribe to the physical body are only thin properties. According to this distinction, human persons are not constituted, but *realized$_2$* by physical bodies or (to be precise, since 'physical body' is not a very clear expression with regard to metaphysical commitments) by physical properties and events.

Shoemaker describes the relevant difference in the following way (but please note that when he speaks of "body," he, of course, means the 'physical body'). Nonetheless, I might have to add some modifications in order to get to the difference I have introduced to back up my phenomenological idea of 'experienced body':

> On neo-Lockean accounts of personal identity persons are capable of changing bodies . . . , and so seem to be numerically different from, although coincident with, their bodies. Assuming that human animals have biological rather than psychological persistence conditions, such views also imply that persons are numerically different

from, although coincident with, human animals. Yet there seems a good sense in which, assuming physicalism, the physical properties of a person's body, and those of the coincident human animal, determine the mental properties I have.

Here is where we need the distinction . . . between thick and thin properties. The properties I share with my body will be thin properties. They are thin because their causal profiles do not limit their instantiation to things of a particular kind, things having particular persistence conditions. Thick properties are ones whose causal profiles do limit their instantiation to things of a particular kind. On a neo-Lockean view mental properties are thick, because their causal profiles limit their instantiation to things with psychological persistence conditions. Thick properties are not realized$_1$ by thin properties. That is why my body does not share my mental properties, despite sharing my thin physical properties. . . . But in some sense the thin properties of my body realize my mental properties. That is why we need realization$_2$. The definition I give of this will allow thin properties of a thing to be realizers$_2$ of thick properties of a different thing coincident with it. But its main purpose is achieved by its allowing thin properties of one thing to be realizers$_2$ of thick properties of a different thing co[i]ncident with that thing. (Shoemaker 2007: 29–30)

Unlike Shoemaker, I shy away from talking about *things*. I don't want to say that the *physical* body is a *thing* (a full-blooded entity). But this does not destroy the whole distinction between *realization$_1$* and *realization$_2$*, since the relevant relation is a relation that holds between properties. And unlike Shoemaker, I cannot talk blatantly about 'the mental,' as opposed to anything which is bodily, since a phenomenological determination of the human self ends up with the phenomenon of embodiment right from the start. The crucial difference is not a difference between mind and body, but a difference between persons on the one side and 'having a physical body' on the other side. Human persons are, as I pointed out already, *realized$_1$* as embodied persons because the relevant attributes are thick properties: they make human persons *human* and *persons*, and they have a very specific causal role. The physical properties attributed to human beings are thin properties because they cannot explain the specifics of being human (agency, responsibility, cognition, qualia, etc.) and they point to attributes humans might have in common with other kinds of beings (like animals or even plants). Therefore, the link between human persons and physical properties needs to be called *realization$_2$*. On the basis of this distinction, I am inclined to push the envelope a bit further (even at the risk of leaving Shoemaker behind me) in claiming that, on the basis of sortal dependency, *realization$_1$* for persons as embodied persons is strict, while *realization$_2$* is somewhat loose. In other words, human persons have to be realized as embodied persons, and they have to be realized in a second mode—however, the concrete forms of the second mode of realization are open. We know that in our actual world, and all worlds related to our world by the bond of nomological possibility, *realization$_2$* is presented as physical or biological realization—though this might not be the case for any possible world, whereas in *every* possible world the *realization$_1$* of human persons has to be a realization as embodied persons.

From a certain distance, the substance dualist might get the impression that I moved in a full circle: in getting away from something like a straightforward substance dualism, I presented another form of dualism. It is the dualism that makes the distinction between two kinds of "bodies" or, to say the least, two kinds of realization. In my proposal there is simply no space left for a substance called "physical body." The only substances that deserve this high-profile circumscription are embodied persons—substances for which it is essential to have their substantial attributes *realized$_1$* as attributes of the experienced body. Persons cannot be without an experienced body (and it doesn't take too much phenomenology to prove this statement)—and an experienced body, as soon as it is an *experienced* body, presupposes a person *necessarily*. It makes, therefore, no sense to talk about the possibility of disembodied persons along these lines.

4. The Dualistic Framework

The idea presented in this paper borrows heavily from dualism. On the other side it tries to avoid straightforward substance dualism—for a reason. One—eschatologically significant—reason was famously pointed out by Peter van Inwagen:

When one dies, one's body decays, and what one is, what one has been all along, an immaterial soul or mind or self, continues to exist. . . . Christians . . . will know that they are supposed to believe in something that doesn't fit this picture too well, something called the Resurrection of the Dead; if pressed, they will perhaps say that the burden of the doctrine of the Resurrection of the Dead is that eventually God will give everyone a body again—one of those mysterious and apparently pointless procedures for which God no doubt has some good reason that He has mercifully chosen not to bother us with. . . . (van Inwagen 1995: 475)

In following van Inwagen we can rephrase the problems implied by straightforward substance dualism as a dilemma: If the soul carries the burden of identity, then the bodily aspect of human existence is metaphysically irrelevant for personal identity. But if the body—in one way or another—contributes to personal identity or is involved in setting the criteria of personal identity, then the possibility of a disembodied soul after death threatens the claim of postmortem identity and survival.[45] In other words: if I could exist as a soul or a thinking substance after death (and if this mode of existence would suffice to identify me as myself), why would I need a body at all? The track-switch model of resurrection, instead, wants to take an entirely different route: phenomenologically speaking, it makes no sense to conceive of myself as a merely thinking substance or some sort of atomic entity, since whenever I experience myself I simultaneously experience myself tied to a bundle of properties which can be summed up as 'experienced body'—in a way Maurice Merleau-Ponty or Paul Ricœur might have described it. The core argument, thus, comes down to this:

(1) Whenever I experience myself, I experience a bundle of certain properties that are connected and related to each other.

(2) Whenever I experience myself, I experience myself as having an 'experienced' body (i.e., I am aware of myself as being seated and placed somehow, I have a grip on a now and here, I am aware of my relatedness, my sensitivity, my feelings, my reciprocity, etc.).

(3) Whenever I experience myself, I am aware that I am realized$_1$ as an embodied person.

(4) Whenever I am aware of myself as an embodied person, I am also aware of being realized$_2$. However, I am not aware of the means in which I am realized$_2$.

This argument is written down from a first-person perspective. Between (3) and (4) we can easily identify a certain shift. Again, phenomenologically speaking, from a first-person perspective we are aware of those primary properties that, as a bundle, form what is called 'experienced body.' But, nevertheless, the way in which realization$_2$ is actually set up requires a look at myself from a third-person perspective. To find out the details of this way, I have to look at myself as if I am somebody else. For example, within the dimensions of my self-consciousness I am aware of feelings and sensations I have; but, for instance, I am not aware of my liver functions or the metabolism in certain cells.

Introducing the notion of self-consciousness, we can say that the primary properties that form what I call 'experienced body' are, so to speak, 'transparent' properties which introduce transparent states of affairs. For example, to have a toothache or to feel a tickling in my nose is a transparent state of affairs, since I cannot be in such a state without being aware of it or without knowing it. In contrast, what happens in my liver right now or what goes on in my certain layers of my skin is not transparent to me, since I am not at all aware of it. I have to gain knowledge of these states of affairs as I have to gain knowledge about other, more distant states of affairs in the world. Coming from this distinction, we can soundly say that 'experienced body' is an abbreviation for a bundle of transparent properties that induce transparent states of affairs, whereas 'physical body' refers to variety of nontransparent states of affairs which are, nevertheless, related to me through what I have called realization$_2$. If it is true that I cannot be aware of myself without being (in one way or the other) aware of the so-called transparent states of affairs, then it is not conceivable that I am myself without being aware of these transparent states of affairs. Nevertheless, it is still possible that I am aware of all the transparent states of affairs in question while the nontransparent states of affairs (which serve as the ways in which I am realized$_2$) change dramatically. To say something like that, we just have to introduce one of a variety of thought experiments that force us to think what might happen if somebody would replace my biological brain and body parts with very sophisticated mechanical and electronic devices. There seems to be no logical contradiction in assuming that I could stay the same (and in my words: that I could be aware of the very same transparent states of affairs) although the physical parameters of my realization$_2$ might have been altered.

As one can see, I tried to avoid straightforward substance dualism. This move is based on two strategies. First of all, I wanted to introduce the idea that whenever I am aware of myself, I am not simply aware of an atomic substance called 'the Self' but am immediately aware of a bundle of properties which form a reality called 'experienced body.' Furthermore, there are some philosophical reasons to be very careful in interpreting the reference function of the word 'I' in terms of referring to an immaterial and atomic substance, since it is not at all clear whether 'I' is a referring expression or whether what the word 'I' refers to is indeed a *substance*. Even if one doesn't want to demote the dignity of the FPP pointed at with the use of the word 'I,' we aren't allowed to treat 'I' like an everyday referring expression, because, unlike proper names, the term 'I' has some unusual features: (A) There is no danger of misidentification or misrepresentation— meaning that 'I,' once used properly, always finds its referent with a 100 percent certainty. (B) The standard meaning of the word 'I' depends completely on its contextual meaning; that is, the meaning changes crucially with the change of the person that utters the phrase in question. (C) The word 'I' has a very basic indexical role— establishing a ground zero for the coordinates of other indexicals and indicating (pragmatically) a realm of consciousness (even self-consciousness) and communication.[46] As Hector-Neri Castañeda, one of the greatest analysts of the use of the phrase 'I,' has underlined: the referent of 'I' is an *I-guise*, a certain content of thought, which looks more like a very thin particular, since it is ephemeral and comes and goes at any instantaneous moment.[47] If Castañeda is right, we cannot simply conclude that there is a substance *behind* the I-guise; it could be (theoretically, however awkwardly) that a self comes and goes with every instantaneous existence of the I-guise.[48] We need further information and further criteria to find out how the instantaneously occurring I-guises are tied together and form a perduring unity that has some ontological gravity. Castañeda underlines that this is the point when we have to leave our thought experiments and look for applicable criteria of personal identity,[49] namely, psychological continuity and embodiedness (as a possible backup for the continuity we are looking for).

The second move had to do with the idea that whatever the physical body might be, it is not a full-blooded entity, since its identity conditions depend crucially on the person that is realized$_2$ by what we call 'physical body.' There are some reasons to stick to this— admittedly strange-looking—conclusion: If we took away the FPP and the person that, so to speak, owns the physical body, how could we single out the body among a variety of ecological and biological systems and subsystems? Why shouldn't we, instead, think of the body as a (somewhat arbitrary) sum of biological systems that join routes for a while and part ways after a certain amount of time? If we look at the body from a purely biological perspective, we cannot help calling it a sophisticated system tied to a variety of larger (ecological) systems and divided into subsystems. To draw the lines of identification at the level of movable individual systems remains arbitrary from a purely biological perspective—it is as arbitrary as talking about the grass in your front yard as a whole instead of counting every individual subsystem (the flowers and the plants). But, again phenomenologically speaking, we do not look at the physical body from a purely biological perspective. We look at it through the lenses of a reality described as 'experienced' body. In this view the physical and biological states of affairs are already immersed into a bundle of *transparent* states of affairs and tied to them by realization$_2$.

But still the strategy to avoid straightforward substance dualism does not avoid dualism at all. What is still left as a framework is some sort of property dualism—to be more precise: a dualism that rests on a difference between transparent and nontransparent properties and states of affairs as well as on the distinction between realization$_1$ and realization$_2$. Without such a requirement it is hard to see how we can spell out the idea of resurrection beyond the possible problems and shortcomings of materialistic accesses to this topic. But is such a dualistic framework itself justifiable? As one can see, the justification depends on some sort of conceivability argument. Let us state the cornerstone of this argument:

(1) Whenever I am aware of myself, I am aware of the primary (transparent) properties that form what is called 'experienced body' and am aware that my experienced body is realized$_2$ while I am not aware of *the ways in which* my experienced body is realized$_2$.

(2) It is conceivable that my experienced body is realized$_2$ by different kinds of properties (different from those I detect when looking at my body from a third-person perspective).

If conceivability arguments are sound, they might be transformed into arguments that deal with possibilities. In our case, sentence (2) might be written down differently:

(2*) In other possible worlds my experienced body is realized$_2$ by different kinds of properties (different from those I detect in the actual world when looking at my body from a third-person perspective).

If we can think of these other properties as nonbiological or even nonphysical properties, we can, at least, state that the experienced body does not have to be realized$_2$ in the ways it is realized at the moment. This opens the door for the track-switch model of resurrection. What carries the burden of identity statements is the self embodied in an 'experienced body.' The physical reality is still in sight; nevertheless it comes to a mode of realization$_2$ in the actual world.

NOTES

The figures in this chapter have been created by the author.

1. See Hudson 2001: 180–87. Compare also Hudson 2007: 230–32.

2. Elements of such a theory can be found in Hick 1994: 278–96.

3. Cf. Corcoran 2001b. The fission model was outlined as a materialistic alternative in Zimmerman 1999.

4. Cf. van Inwagen 1978.

5. Cf. Baker 2007.

6. Cf. Hudson 2007: 232–33; Hudson 2001: 180–87.

7. Merricks 2001.

8. Cf. Plantinga 2007.

9. Cf. Plantinga 2007: 100.

10. Cf. Schärtl 2002.

11. Cf. Cooper 2000.

12. Cf. Wenzel 2003.

13. I am fully aware that not everybody is willing to sign off on this dogma. Maybe there is no good justification for it. But a possible lack of justification doesn't make it untrue. Furthermore, this dogma seems to be a helpful tool to avoid what I would like to call the "original-copy confusion": if the above-mentioned dogma is true as it stands, then we can call the reappearance of a look-alike entity b the copy of an entity a unless we have solid grounds on which we are permitted to connect a to b based on agreeable criteria of identity. Now, for the time being, let's question the validity of the mentioned dogma: How could we ever determine whether entity b is a copy or not? And, if we sacrifice the criterion of continuity together with the metaphysical dogma we are discussing, how can we claim, on the other side, any form of identity relation that holds between a and b?

14. Cf. van Inwagen 1978.

15. Cf. Corcoran 2001b.

16. Cf. Baker 2007.

17. Cf. van Inwagen 1978: 120–21.

18. Cf. Augustine, *De Civitate Dei* 22.16.

19. Cf. Corcoran 2001b: 214.

20. I use this vague expression consciously and apologize for its vagueness. Corcoran himself uses the term "constitutes" and admits to being a constitutionalist. Cf. Corcoran 2006: 65–82. Although the constitutionalist perspective has some appealing features that might be beneficial for my own treatise on the matter, I am not sure if I should sign off on this theory for reasons that might become clear along the lines of this paper.

21. For comparable critique see also Hershenov 2002. Hershenov points to two problems of the Zimmerman-Corcoran model: (1) There is not much evidence (if any) in the corpse which shows that the corpse is the result of a fission which can be described in purely materialistic terms. (2) The heavenly body is the result of a pretty unnatural composition of simples (since it happens against the rules we see in place for biological assimilation of simple parts). Corcoran and Zimmerman could respond at this point that the fission which results in the heavenly body that survives death is the result of a divine miracle which replaces the usual causal ties between different stages of the earthly person and its earthly body. However, such a response could violate dogma (3) of my preliminary remarks, since an unnatural assimilation of simple parts could be seen as an impossibility. My very own solution, therefore, tries to move away from a purely materialistic concept of resurrection and the problem of assimilation of simple parts. For further discussions of the Zimmerman-Corcoran model see also Hasker 2011: 83-103.

22. Cf. Corcoran 2001b: 211–12.

23. Cf. Corcoran 2001b: 208–9; van Inwagen 1990: 81–97.

24. This seems to be a danger in some of Lynne Baker's remarks. Cf. Baker 2001: 160: "What makes a person a human person is that he or she is constituted by a human organism. But a person could start out as a human person and have organic parts replaced by synthetic parts until she was no longer a human person. With the persistence of the first-person perspective, she would still exist and still be a person, even with a synthetic body. If she ceased to have a human body but retained a first-person-perspective, she would still exist, but not as human. If she ceased to be a person (that is, ceased to have a first-person-perspective), however, she would cease to exist altogether."

25. Cf. Thomas Aquinas, *Summa Contra Gentiles*, bk. 4, ch. 81.

26. Cf. ibid.

27. For a recent study on the importance of form and structure and its place in a mereologically grounded ontology compare Koslicki 2008: 167–99.

28. I admit that this idea is still very close to Baker's constitution view, which allows the transfer of bodies, even the replacement of the physical body, although the identity of the person is preserved thanks to the integrity of the first-person perspective. Cf. Baker 2000: 141–46.

29. Cf. Merleau-Ponty 1962, repr. 2008: 77–232.

30. Cf. Husserl 1995: §§44 and 50; compare also Ricœur 1992: 322–23.

31. Cf. Husserl 1992: 113, 128, 134.

32. Husserl, of course, uses different concepts of "abstraction." There is the idea of abstraction as an integral part of the transcendental-phenomenological method—related to the bracketing of certain aspects. On the other side, we find the notion of abstraction related to a practice. The product of the latter can be called an "abstraction" because it is in some distance to the primary properties perceived at the richer level of basic experiences. The former can be called "abstraction" because it methodologically reduces the scope of primary experiences in order to find the most basic constituents. For Husserl, at this very basic level, the experienced body is a given. It is immediately related to any experience and awareness of the self *as* a self. Cf. Husserl 1995: §44. If this is true, then there cannot be a disembodied self with regard to the experienced body.

33. Cf. Ricœur 1992: 318–20.

34. For a more extensive and broader description of "being embodied" compare Waldenfels 2000: 30–44.

35. Let us be merciful with this expression, and let's treat it as a somewhat vague abbreviation for a 'package' of properties we use to describe a certain collection of matter in certain contexts relative to a certain practice.

36. Cf. Merricks 2003: 118–37.

37. Please note that I am using the phrase 'embodied person' in a manner that is strictly bound to the phenomenological explications I have outlined in previous paragraphs.

38. Cf. Baker 1995.

39. Cf. Baker 2000: 125–30, 132–41.

40. In another article I have argued that the referent of the FPP is just a thin slice of thought content which, if cornered, cannot be held responsible for diachronic identity. Cf. Schärtl 2008. For the circularity objection see Immanuel Kant, *Kritik der reinen Vernunft* A365–66.

41. Cf. Schärtl 2008: 87–89, 93.

42. For further discussion see, for instance, Zimmerman 2002, Noonan 1993.

43. For the notion of substances I am presupposing in this context compare Schnieder 2004: 295–362.

44. Cf. Shoemaker 2007: 10–31, 88–114.

45. Robert Pasnau pointed to a crucial problem in any Thomistic approach: If it is true that the soul is not the person (= that the soul is not identical with the person), since the human person is the composite of soul and body, then the disembodied soul, existing in a somewhat unnatural state in the afterlife, cannot be identical to the person as such. Therefore, anything that happens to the soul in the afterlife does not, actually, happen to me in the afterlife (since there is no relation of identity). This would have, along the lines of eschatological doctrines, the rather unfortunate consequence that any sort of "cleaning" or "purification" my soul might undergo in purgatory does not really affect *me*, and so on. Cf. Pasnau 2002: 380–93. In her response Eleonore Stump introduced the idea that there is no identity relation to be emphasized or questioned since the relation between the soul and the person is a relation of constitution. Cf. Stump 2006. Although this way out sounds elegant at first glance, it leaves us with other unfortunate consequences: (1) If constitution is not identity, we are still doomed, since we need an identity relation to connect the postmortem situation with the premortem situation. (2) If it is true—for the classic constitution view—that although *a* constitutes *b*, *b* can (theoretically) continue to exist although *a* ceases to exist, then we have a very uncomfortable situation with regard to the situation of "persons and their souls." At this very point a substance dualist might emphasize that "real" dualism is sovereign over any sort of Thomistic "dualism" (if such a category makes sense). And, indeed, the substance dualist claims nothing less than the identity between the person (or the self) and the soul. However, although this is a way to get out of the problem, it leaves us with the above-mentioned dilemma.

46. For a more detailed analysis cf. Schärtl 2008: 85–86, 106–8.

47. Cf. Castañeda 1999b: 187, 198.
48. Cf. Castañeda 1999c: 248.
49. Cf. Castañeda 1999c: 199–201.

REFERENCES

Baker, Lynne Rudder. 1995. "Need a Christian Be a Mind/Body Dualist?" *Faith and Philosophy* 12:489–504.

———. 2000. *Persons and Bodies: A Constitution View.* Cambridge: Cambridge University Press.

———. 2001. "Materialism with a Human Face." In Corcoran, *Soul, Body, and Survival,* 159–80.

———. 2007. "Persons and the Metaphysics of Resurrection." *Religious Studies* 43:333–48.

Castañeda, Hector-Neri. 1999a. *The Phenomeno-Logic of the I: Essays on Self-Consciousness,* edited by James G. Hart and Tomis Kapitan. Bloomington: Indiana University Press.

———. 1999b. "The Self and the I-Guises, Empirical and Transcendental." In *The Phenomeno-Logic of the I,* 180–203.

———. 1999c. "Persons, Egos, and I's." In *The Phenomeno-Logic of the I,* 228–50.

Cooper, John. 2000. *Body, Soul and Life Everlasting: Biblical Anthropology and the Monism-Dualism Debate.* Grand Rapids: Eerdmans.

Corcoran, Kevin, ed. 2001a. *Soul, Body, and Survival: Essays on the Metaphysics of Human Persons.* Ithaca and London: Cornell University Press.

———. 2001b. "Physical Persons and Postmortem Survival without Temporal Gaps." In *Soul, Body, and Survival,* 201–17.

———. 2006. *Rethinking Human Nature: A Christian Materialist Alternative to the Soul.* Grand Rapids: Baker Academic.

Hasker, William. 2011. "Materialism and The Resurrection: Are the Prospects Improving?" *European Journal for Philosophy of Religion* 3:83–103.

Hershenov, David B. 2002. "Van Inwagen, Zimmerman, and the Materialist Conception of Resurrection." *Religious Studies* 38:451–69.

Hick, John. 1994. *Death and Eternal Life.* Louisville: Westminster John Knox.

Hudson, Hud. 2001. *A Materialist Metaphysics of the Human Person.* Ithaca and London: Cornell University Press.

———. 2007. "I Am Not an Animal." In van Inwagen and Zimmerman, *Persons,* 216–34.

Husserl, Edmund. 1992. *Die Krisis der europäischen Wissenschaften und die transzendentale Phänomenologie.* Part 2. Hamburg: Meiner.

————. 1995. *Cartesianische Meditationen: Eine Einleitung in die Phänomenologie*, 3rd ed. Hamburg: Meiner-Verlag.

Kant, Immanuel. 1979. *Kritik der reinen Vernunft.* Leipzig: Reclam.

Kim, Jaegwon. 1998. *Philosophy of Mind.* Boulder, CO: Westview Press.

Koslicki, Kathrin. 2008. *The Structure of Objects.* Oxford: Oxford University Press.

Merleau-Ponty, Maurice. 1962. Reprint, 2008. *Phenomenology of Perception.* London and New York: Routledge.

Merricks, Trenton. 2001. "How to Live Forever without Saving Your Soul: Physicalism and Immortality." In Corcoran, *Soul, Body, and Survival,* 183–200.

————. 2003. *Objects and Persons.* Oxford: Clarendon.

Noonan, Harold W. 1993. "Constitution Is Identity." *Mind* 102:133–46.

Pasnau, Robert. 2002. *Thomas Aquinas on Human Nature: A Philosophical Study of "Summa theologiae" I a 75–89.* Cambridge: Cambridge University Press.

Plantinga, Alvin. 2007. "Materialism and Christian Belief." In van Inwagen and Zimmerman, *Persons,* 99–141.

Ricœur, Paul. 1992. *Oneself as Another.* Chicago: University of Chicago Press.

Schärtl, Thomas. 2000. *Jenseits von Innen und Außen: Ludwig Wittgensteins Beitrag zu einer nicht-dualistischen Philosophie des Geistes.* Münster: Lit-Verlag.

————. 2002. "Engel: Zwischen Popkultur und theologischer Reflexion." *Stimmen der Zeit* 220:811–22.

————. 2008. "Personsein—Indexikalität—Selbstbewusstsein." In *Was sind menschliche Personen? Ein akttheoretischer Zugang,* edited by Bruno Niederbacher and Edmund Runggaldier, 79–116. Frankfurt am Main: Ontos-Verlag.

————. 2009. "Mögliche Welten: Ein theologischer Aneignungsversuch." In *Parallelwelten: Christliche Religion und die Vervielfachung von Wirklichkeit,* edited by Johann E. Hafner and Joachim Valentin, 32–52. Stuttgart: Kohlhammer.

Schnieder, Benjamin. 2004. *Substanzen und (ihre) Eigenschaften: Eine Studie zur analytischen Ontologie.* Berlin and New York: de Gruyter.

Shoemaker, Sydney. 2007. *Physical Realization.* Oxford: Oxford University Press.

Stump, Eleonore. 2006. "Resurrection, Reassembly, and Reconstitution: Aquinas on the Soul." In *Die menschliche Seele: Brauchen wir den Dualismus?,* edited by Bruno Niederbacher and Edmund Runggaldier, 151–72. Frankfurt am Main and London: Ontos-Verlag.

Stump, Eleonore, and Norman Kretzmann. 1996. "An Objection to Swinburne's Argument for Dualism." *Faith and Philosophy* 13:405–12.

Swinburne, Richard. 1984. "Personal Identity: The Dualist Theory." In *Personal Identity*, by Sydney Shoemaker and Richard Swinburne. Oxford: Basil Blackwell.

―――. 1997. *The Evolution of the Soul*. Rev. ed. Oxford: Clarendon.

Van Inwagen, Peter. 1978. "The Possibility of Resurrection." *International Journal for the Philosophy of Religion* 9:114–21.

―――. 1990. *Material Beings*. Ithaca and New York: Cornell University Press.

―――. 1995. "Dualism and Materialism: Athens and Jerusalem." *Faith and Philosophy* 12:475–88.

Van Inwagen, Peter, and Dean Zimmerman, eds. 2007. *Persons: Human and Divine*. Oxford: Clarendon.

Waldenfels, Bernhard. 2000. *Das leibliche Selbst: Vorlesungen zur Phänomenologie der Leiblichkeit*. Frankfurt am Main: Suhrkamp.

Wenzel, Knut. 2003. *Sakramentales Selbst: Der Mensch als Zeichen des Heils*. Freiburg im Breisgau: Herder.

Zimmerman, Dean. 1999. "The Compatibility of Materialism and Survival: The 'Falling Elevator Model.'" *Faith and Philosophy* 16:194–211.

―――. 2002. "Persons and Bodies: Constitution without Mereology?" *Philosophy and Phenomenological Research* 64:599–606.

Contributors

John Foster was emeritus fellow of Brasenose College, Oxford. He has written six books: *The Case for Idealism* (Routledge, 1982), *Ayer* (Routledge, 1985), *The Immaterial Self* (Routledge, 1991), *The Nature of Perception* (Oxford University Press, 2000), *The Divine Lawmaker* (Oxford University Press, 2004), and *A World for Us* (Oxford University Press, 2008). He also is the author of the essay "Meaning and Truth Theory" in Evans and McDowell, eds., *Truth and Meaning* (Oxford University Press, 1976).

Benedikt Paul Göcke is a junior research fellow in philosophy at Blackfriars Hall, Oxford University. His recent publications include "Priest and Nagel on Being Someone: A Refutation of Physicalism" (*The Heythrop Journal*, 2008), "God, Soul, and Time in Priest and Swinburne" (*New Blackfriars*, 2008), "Physicalism Quaerens Intellectum" (*The Philosophical Forum*, 2008), and "What Is Physicalism?" (*Ratio*, 2009). He is also coeditor of *Idealismus und natürliche Theologie* (Verlag Karl Alber, 2011).

William Hasker is professor emeritus of philosophy, Huntington University, and editor emeritus of the journal *Faith and Philosophy*. Among the books he authored are *God, Time and Knowledge* (Cornell University Press, 1989), *Providence, Evil, and the Openness of God* (Routledge, 2004), and *The Triumph of God over Evil* (InterVarsity, 2008).

E. J. Lowe, Durham University, United Kingdom, authored, among other books, *Kinds of Being* (Blackwell, 1989), *Subjects of Experience* (Cambridge University Press, 1996), *The Possibility of Metaphysics* (Oxford University Press, 1998), *The Four-Category Ontology* (Oxford University Press, 2006), *Personal Agency* (Oxford University Press, 2008), and *More Kinds of Being* (Blackwell, 2009).

Uwe Meixner is professor of philosophy at the University of Augsburg, Germany. His books include *Ereignis und Substanz: Die Metaphysik von Realität und Realisation* (Schöningh, 1997), *Axiomatic Formal Ontology* (Kluwer, 1997), *Theorie der Kausalität: Ein Leitfaden zum Kausalbegriff in zwei Teilen* (Mentis, 2001), *The Two Sides of Being: A Reassessment of Psycho-Physical Dualism* (Mentis, 2004), *Einführung in die Ontologie* (Wissenschaftliche Buchgesellschaft, 2004), *David Lewis* (Mentis, 2006), *The Theory of Ontic Modalities* (Ontos, 2006), and *Modalität: Möglichkeit, Notwendigkeit, Essenzialismus* (Klostermann, 2008). He is coeditor of the journal *Metaphysica* and the yearbook *Logical Analysis and History of Philosophy*.

Alvin Plantinga is the William Harry Jellema Professor of Philosophy at Calvin College. His most important publications are *God and Other Minds* (Cornell University Press, 1967), *The Nature of Necessity* (Oxford University Press, 1974), *Warrant: The Current Debate* (Oxford University Press, 1993), *Warrant and Proper Function* (Oxford University Press, 1993), *Warranted Christian Belief* (Oxford University Press, 2000), and (with Michael Tooley) *Knowledge of God* (Blackwell, 2008). His most recent book is *Where the Conflict Really Lies: Science, Religion, and Naturalism* (Oxford University Press, 2011).

Stephen Priest is a member of the faculty of philosophy of the University of Oxford. He is senior research fellow of Blackfriars Hall, Oxford, and a member of Wolfson College, Oxford, and Hughes Hall, Cambridge. He is the author of *The British Empiricists* (Routledge, 2nd ed., 2007), *Theories of the Mind* (Mariner Books, 1992), *Merleau-Ponty* (Routledge, 2002), and *The Subject in Question* (Routledge, 2000). He is editor of *Hegel's Critique of Kant* (Gregg Revivals, 1993) and *Jean-Paul Sartre: Basic Writings* (Routledge, 2001) and coeditor (with Antony Flew) of *A Dictionary of Philosophy*. He has lectured widely in universities in Britain, the United States, Europe, and Japan, and his writing has been translated into Dutch, Spanish, Russian, Macedonian, Japanese, and Korean.

Howard Robinson is the author of *Matter and Sense* (Cambridge University Press, 1982) and *Perception* (Routledge, 1994, 2001, 2007) and the editor or coeditor of collections of articles on the philosophy of mind, Aristotle, and Berkeley. His main concerns have been with materialism, idealism, and the philosophy of perception.

Thomas Schärtl was assistant professor of systematic theology at the Catholic University of America in Washington, DC (2006–9) and is currently full professor of philosophical theology at the University of Augsburg, Germany. His areas of research are trinitarian theology, religious epistemology, theology and philosophy of language, foundational theology, eschatology, and metaphysics.

A. D. Smith, Warwick University, is the author of *The Problem of Perception* (Harvard University Press, 2002) and *Husserl and the Cartesian Meditations* (Routledge, 2003), as well as of numerous articles in philosophical journals, principally in the areas of perception, the philosophy of mind and action, metaphysics, and the history of philosophy.

Richard Swinburne is a fellow of the British Academy, and emeritus Nolloth Professor of the Philosophy of the Christian Religion, University of Oxford. He is the author of many books on the philosophy of religion and other areas of philosophy. In the philosophy of religion, he is best known for his trilogy on theism—*The Coherence of Theism* (Oxford University Press, 1993), *The Existence of God* (Oxford University Press, 2nd ed., 2004), and *Faith and Reason* (Oxford University Press, 2nd ed., 2005)—and his tetralogy on Christine doctrine. He has also written books on space and time, probability, and epistemology (*Epistemic Justification*, Oxford University Press, 2001). His book most relevant to the topic of this volume is *The Evolution of the Soul* (Oxford University Press, rev. ed., 1997).

Index